More Examples, Less Theory

In his new book, Michael Billig uses psychology's past to argue that nowadays, when we write about the mind, we should use more examples and less theory. He provides a series of historical studies, analysing how key psychological writers used examples. Billig offers new insights about famous analysts of the mind, such as Locke, James, Freud, Tajfel and Lewin. He also champions unfairly forgotten figures, like the Earl of Shaftesbury and the eccentric Abraham Tucker. There is a cautionary chapter on Lacan, warning what can happen when examples are ignored. Marie Jahoda is praised as the ultimate example: a psychologist from the twentieth century with a social and rhetorical imagination fit for the twenty-first. *More Examples, Less Theory* is an easy-to-read book that will inform and entertain academics and their students. It will particularly appeal to those who enjoy the details of examples rather than the simplifications of big theory.

Michael Billig is Emeritus Professor of Social Sciences at Loughborough University, UK. His previous books include *Arguing and Thinking* (Cambridge, 1987), *Freudian Repression* (Cambridge, 1999) and *Learn to Write Badly* (Cambridge, 2013). He received the Distinguished Contribution to Social Psychology Award from the British Psychological Society in 2010.

More Examples, Less Theory

Historical Studies of Writing Psychology

Michael Billig

Loughborough University

CAMBRIDGE
UNIVERSITY PRESS

CAMBRIDGE
UNIVERSITY PRESS

University Printing House, Cambridge CB2 8BS, United Kingdom

One Liberty Plaza, 20th Floor, New York, NY 10006, USA

477 Williamstown Road, Port Melbourne, VIC 3207, Australia

314–321, 3rd Floor, Plot 3, Splendor Forum, Jasola District Centre, New Delhi – 110025, India

79 Anson Road, #06–04/06, Singapore 079906

Cambridge University Press is part of the University of Cambridge.

It furthers the University's mission by disseminating knowledge in the pursuit of education, learning, and research at the highest international levels of excellence.

www.cambridge.org
Information on this title: www.cambridge.org/9781108498418
DOI: 10.1017/9781108696517

© Michael Billig 2019

First published 2019
Reprinted 2019

Printed in the United Kingdom by TJ International Ltd, Padstow Cornwall

A catalogue record for this publication is available from the British Library.

ISBN 978-1-108-49841-8 Hardback
ISBN 978-1-108-73602-2 Paperback

Contents

Preface

Having worked as an academic for many years, I have learnt that some books are more pleasurable to write than others. Fortunately, this has been one of the pleasurable ones. Perhaps this is because retirement has freed me from institutional demands, or perhaps it was the subject matter. Whatever the reason, I have enjoyed writing this book, and I hope that I am able convey my pleasure to readers.

I would like to mention colleagues and friends who have helped to make the task pleasurable: Charles Antaki, Jovan Byford, Susan Condor, David Kaposi, David Leary, Cristina Marinho, Yair Neuman, John Richardson, Tom Scheff, Steven Stanley, Cristian Tileagă and Bryan Williams. Many thanks to you all for suggestions and general comradeship; and special thanks to Cristina, who enthusiastically read all the chapters, including several drafts of some of them.

I am very conscious that my dear friend John Shotter is no longer here to offer his wise and learned insights. I miss him greatly, both personally and intellectually.

I would also like to thank Janka Romero and Emily Watton of Cambridge University Press for their help and support, which I have much appreciated. Janka even supported me when she received a review recommending not only that Cambridge should not publish this book but also that no publisher anywhere should ever publish it. Over the years, I have attracted a number of reviews like that. I'm not sure why.

As always, my biggest thanks are to my family. Special thanks and love, of course, to Sheila, the heart and soul of the family, and also to our children, Daniel, Becky, Rachel and Ben; and to thank them for giving us wonderful grandchildren, Ari, Monica, Hannah, Elsie, Arthur, Jacob, Felix, Juniper and Colette. We are so fortunate.

Acknowledgements

Parts of three chapters have used material which has been published previously.

Chapter 3

Billig, M. (2012). Abraham Tucker as an eighteenth century William James: Stream of consciousness, role of examples and the importance of writing. *Theory & Psychology*, 22, 114–29.

Chapter 5

Billig, M. (2006). Lacan's misuse of psychology: Evidence, rhetoric and the mirror stage. *Theory, Culture & Society*, 23, 1–26.

Chapter 7

Billig, M. (2014). Henri Tajfel, Peretz Bernstein and the history of 'Der Antisemitismus'. In C. Tileagă and J. Byford (eds), *Psychology and History: Interdisciplinary Explorations*. Cambridge: Cambridge University Press (pp. 223–41).

In each instance, the original publication has been re-written, re-structured and considerably expanded for the present book. The author is grateful to the original publishers for giving their permission to use the material here.

1 Introduction

This is a book about the ways that psychologists have used examples in their writing. Unusually for a psychological book, it contains little theory and less methodology; it brings no new sets of data, and it surveys no current populations. Instead, the book looks backwards, as I discuss some of my favourite writers of psychology from the past. My selection is unashamedly personal: with one exception, these are writers that I have enjoyed reading. Some are little known, while others are more obvious choices. Few would seriously question whether William James or Sigmund Freud deserve to be placed among the greatest writers of psychological issues. What is it about their writing that makes them so appealing? As I will be suggesting throughout the book, good psychological writers use well-chosen examples. Freud and James filled their works with superb descriptions; their books come alive because readers can grasp lives being lived, including the lives of the authors.

In a number of respects, this book complements my earlier work, *Learn to Write Badly: How to Succeed in the Social Sciences*. There, I criticised the way that social scientists tend to write these days: they often use lots of dry jargon and big theories, producing page upon page devoid of people. Throughout *Learn to Write Badly* I griped and I grumbled. Constant criticism can become tiresome, and some reviewers thought that I spent too much time saying what I disliked, without recommending positive steps. In effect, those critics were exclaiming in exasperation, 'Moan! Moan! Moan! Don't you like anything?'

So, here, with this present book, I come to praise, not to grump. However, I would advise any reader who is also a writer of psychology and who takes care with their writing not to rush to the index to check for their name. I will not be citing them in any list of honour, calling them to an imagined podium to receive an award – perhaps for 'Best Writer of an Article in Cognitive Psychology for 2018' or for 'Metaphor of the Year in Developmental Psychology'. There is a simple reason why no reader is about to be offered a fantasy award. In looking for examples of good psychological writers, I am going back in time. Rather than assessing living writers, I will be discussing in depth a few writers from the past, all of them deceased, some long deceased.

My mood might appear to have changed from the previous book, but the critical urge still remains. I will even be criticising some of my heroes: Freud, for example, does not emerge super-pure from the chapter that is devoted to him. Right in the middle of the book is a big, fat chapter of complaint. This chapter lets rip at a famous figure whose works I definitely have not enjoyed reading. The object of this criticism, the French psycho-analyst Jacques Lacan, is someone whose writings, in my view, contain far too much abstract jargon and far too few down-to-earth examples. He is included because he constitutes an extreme case of what can happen when analysts of the mind free themselves from the obligation to provide clear, detailed examples of what they are talking about.

Here, in this book, I am specifically concerned with the writing of psychology. As such, I am following in the wake of Kurt Danziger, the great historian of psychology, who showed in *Naming the Mind* (1997) how psychology's vocabulary has developed in the past 150 years. Rather than looking at individual concepts and their history, I will be looking at ways of arguing and, above all, ways of using examples. Like Danziger, I will be restricting my attention to psychology: I do not presume that my analyses will be applicable to academic writing about microbes, minerals or mediaeval plainsong.

In recent years, many books have aimed to help academics improve the quality of their writing – books with titles such as *The Quick Fix Guide to Academic Writing; Writing for Peer Reviewed Journals; Writing No Matter What: Advice for Academics*. The authors of these books do not tailor their messages to particular disciplines; rather, they offer advice to academics from across the university campus. Much of their advice is sensible: clarify what you want to say, write your article with a specific journal in mind, reserve a dedicated physical space for doing your writing and so on. The present book, by contrast, is not a general how-to-write-academically book. It is concerned only with writing psychology, and its examples are taken from the past.

Actually, I am not exclusively concerned with the past. I may be looking backwards much of the time, but my neck is not persistently turned away from the present. When discussing past psychologists, I will be raising psychological questions that are still current. Does the mind work like Locke said it did? How do we repress troubling thoughts? Why is it inappropriate to explain the Holocaust in terms of general theories of prejudice? How should we describe the lives of the poor? And, as a connecting theme, how should psychologists treat examples? These are not matters that are purely of historical interest, and, although the questions might have been raised through historical examples, attempted answers should involve more than history. This is why I see the book as being psychological as well as historical, with the history providing a background for the psychology.

Examples of Examples

Psychologists often consider that their discipline rests on two twin pillars: theory and methodology. Every student should be formally instructed about these, the discipline's Castor and Pollux. Psychological researchers need a theory from which to derive hypotheses, and then they need a method for testing those hypotheses. If their testing is sufficiently rigorous, they will be contributing to knowledge and thereby to the development of theory, from which more hypotheses can be derived and then tested. This is very much a self-sustaining business.

Psychology also requires a third element that tends to be overlooked and certainly is not treated as equivalent to the broad-backed twins: psychology needs to be written. If psychologists did not write down their hypotheses, theories, methods and findings, there would be no discipline, because every academic discipline needs its textbooks, journals and written records. Students of psychology are taught about theory and methodology, but they are expected to pick up, as they go along, the ways to write appropriately. They will acquire the disciplinary rhetoric through their reading of publications and through the critical marginalia that teachers might scribble on their essays and project reports.

As Charles Bazerman showed back in 1987, there are set rhetorical conventions for psychological writing (see also Billig, 2011, 2013). Writing experimental papers, for example, means presenting theory-derived hypotheses and summarising how previous experiments have not resolved the matters under question. Then, the author must describe the methods that they have used to test their hypotheses, using suitably impersonal rhetoric, typically achieved through passive-voiced verbs. They must also describe their results impersonally: '2 × 2 ANOVAs were conducted on the scores of the four experimental groups' and not 'I decided to search for significant results by running the scores through a load of programmes that I found on SPSS'. Lastly, researchers must write their interpretations of the significant statistical differences that they have found, and they should also interpret the statistical differences that they failed to find. If researchers encounter problems in writing their reports appropriately, and if they receive continual rejections from journal editors informing them of this, then they might well benefit from consulting one of the how-to-write-academically manuals.

Initially, the present book was conceived as a way of showing that there are more ways of writing psychology than the leading journals currently recognise. Basically, the standard experimental report is empty of humans. The authors discuss the effects of variables on other variables, for example the effects of 'priming' on the judgement of shapes. The researchers get groups of participants who have been 'primed' differently to judge shapes. Then, they combine the scores of participants in the different priming conditions and statistically compare aggregates of reactions. No actual participant is introduced to the reader; rather, the aggregate scores representing the tested variables are what seem to be real. In consequence, experimental reports can be example-free, human-free zones.

My early intention was to show that there is nothing natural or inevitable about this sort of writing. I hoped to show this by going back in time and presenting case studies of psychological writers who wrote in other ways; then I was going to show the advantages of these other ways to write psychology. This would be, I hoped, a means for demonstrating the importance of writing, because it would suggest that psychologists, especially if they know the history of their discipline, have choices in the ways they write. Accordingly, I would be able to suggest that writing should stand alongside theory and method and thus that psychology is supported by the more stable arrangement of resting on three pillars rather than two.

A confession about that early intention: I had hoped to produce a book on the cheap by putting together some articles that I had previously published. This would include pieces on John Locke, William James, Abraham Tucker, Henri Tajfel, Jacques Lacan and Freud, as well as a few others. However, I could not resist changing what I had already written. I then entirely re-wrote some of the pieces, such as the one on Freud, whose basic argument I now find unsatisfactory. Others were greatly changed and expanded, such as the chapter on Lacan, and I wrote some entirely new chapters, like those on Locke, Lewin and Jahoda. This was not, after all, to be a book compiled on the cheap. Fortunately, there was much, much more work to be done on all the chapters.

As I worked on these separate case studies, new themes began to emerge, particularly one theme which had initially been comparatively minor but which became increasingly major as I wrote and re-wrote. This was the theme that examples are crucial when writing about the mind. Example-free psychology was impoverished psychology, disconnected from the lives of those who were being studied. It became increasingly clear that the third pillar should not be 'writing' but rather 'examples'.

However, this brought a problem: what exactly was the role of examples in psychological writing? History could offer different examples of the ways that writers used examples. For instance, examples can be used to illustrate theory, and later I will be discussing how John Locke, as he analysed how the mind associates ideas, deployed examples to illustrate his theory. If examples are treated primarily as a means of illustrating theory, then they become subservient to theory rather than constituting an equal, self-standing pillar.

As I worked through my historical examples of psychological writers, I became persuaded that examples were often rhetorically in tension with theory. The more that theory was valued, the more examples were devalued or restricted. On the other hand, the more that examples were treasured, as in the writing of Abraham Tucker and William James, the more the role of theory qua theory was diminished. This tension between theory and example is clear in the work of the ultimate example of this book – Marie Jahoda. She was a great user of examples in her work, and she believed that psychologists constantly over-valued theory.

If there is tension between theory and examples, then it was always naïve to think that examples could simply be added as a third pillar supporting psychology. The metaphor of pillars is wrong, for it suggests that theory and examples offer each other mutual support. The difficulty of that assumption – that everything fits nicely together – is discussed in the chapter on the so-called father of social psychology, Kurt Lewin. There, it is argued that his motto, 'There is nothing as practical as a good theory', is more wishful thinking than a guide to what actually happens.

Championing the rhetorical role of examples in psychological writing means pushing against the dominance of theory. It means reassessing what Thomas Scheff, in his brilliant analyses of the social sciences, has called the relations between parts and wholes (e.g. Scheff, 1990, 2006, 2010). The parts may have privileged status in some areas of the social sciences, for instance in ethnography, conversation analysis and history, where analysts directly examine specific examples of life rather than trying to construct general, overall theories. In psychology, it is the wholes of theory that currently have the upper hand, squeezing examples to the margins. This creates a specific problem for anyone who wishes to re-balance the present rhetorical arrangements within the subject. How, in all consistency, can the case be argued?

Arguing through Examples

One might think, surely there should not be a problem. All one needs to do is clarify what constitutes a good psychological example and then argue why psychological research would benefit from good examples. We might base the case on what philosophers call 'epistemology' and argue that people generally acquire knowledge by acquiring particulars rather than abstract wholes, and that constitutionally, humans need to understand wholes in terms of particulars, and so on. What is the problem with doing this, apart from the fact that it would be nothing like the book that I was hoping to write?

The problem is simple: the means of making the argument would conflict with the content of the argument. I would be arguing theoretically against the role of theory and would not be basing my argument in favour of examples upon examples of examples. To be consistent, it is necessary to use examples rather than theory when arguing for the importance of examples in psychological writing.

And a word of warning: I will not be defining what I mean by the word *example* for reasons that I hope will become clearer later. I do not use the word in a single way, as a strict theoretician might try to do. Often I use *example* almost as a synonym for 'concrete, individual case'. In the context of psychology, both in the present and in the past, the word has been used in this way as a contrast to *representative sample, theory, abstraction* or *generalisation*. Sometimes I use *example* to indicate illustration and sometimes as a model to be followed.

To avoid the problem of privileging theory over examples (or over concrete individual cases) by proceeding theoretically, I stuck with my original intention of writing about particular psychological writers and their ways of writing psychology. I should concede that this is not the most efficient way of proceeding. If a reader were to turn at random to a later page, it is quite possible, maybe even probable, that they would find no mention of 'examples'. The page might be describing a writer's life, politics or intellectual approach. However, as will be suggested, this is characteristic of extended examples: they overspill the demands of theory.

As Lewin's teacher of philosophy, Ernst Cassirer, argued, scientific theories simplify. That is true of psychological theories, including those that Lewin formulated. When examples and case studies are described in detail, they go beyond the simplifications of theory. However, if we want to argue that point, then we should not rely on a simplified argument about the essence of examples. Instead, we should seek to express the point within the rhetoric of our own writing, that is, with examples of examples that will overspill any simplifications about the concept of an example.

In writing about past characters – whether Freud, James, the third Earl of Shaftesbury or the other historical figures featured in this book – I hope to overspill the narrow demands of any theoretical point about the usefulness of examples. Their usefulness is diminished when examples are only considered to be worthwhile because they serve a specific theory. I will consider it a success, not a failure, if the examples discussed in subsequent pages over-spill any attempt at a theory of examples. Theoretically superfluous details must be mentioned so as to convey a sense of particular lives, individual thoughts and the social worlds of those lives and thoughts.

There is something else about the book: it seems to be simultaneously looking backwards and forwards. The book is obviously historical by the choice of psychological thinkers to be discussed. The chapters on these figures can stand alone: to understand any of the individual chapters, a reader does not have to read the whole book. For instance, anyone interested in Kurt Lewin or Henri Tajfel could just turn to the relevant chapter, read what is written there and then put the book aside. Obviously, I hope that such readers will be tempted to read more, because there are inter-connecting themes between the chapters.

The double nature of the book is expressed in its title and subtitle. *More Examples, Less Theory* expresses the connecting theme of the individual chapters, and it is also a plea for the future of psychological writing. The subtitle conveys that the main work of the book looks backwards, for the work revolves around historical studies of psychological writing. These studies are the means by which the forwards-facing plea was formulated, and I hope they provide support for that plea. As such, the book is not properly a work of history: historians usually try not to be distracted by the future when they examine the past. As the subtitle suggests, the book is historical rather than a history. Yet, there may be a connection between title and subtitle, between looking forwards and looking backwards. Historians generally are more concerned with particular events and par-ticular people than with constructing general theories. Being historical, in this sense, means attending to the particular rather than the general.

How the present book should be categorised is not for me a major matter. My job has been to write the book, not to classify it. Personally, I prefer the term 'historical psychology' to 'history of psychology', as I am comfortable with the idea of doing psychology historically and this includes historically examining ways of writing psychology. Previously, I have referred to myself, not altogether seriously, as an 'antiquarian psychologist' (Billig, 1987). I also feel that the term 'historical psychology' gives a psychological writer more licence: there is not the obligation to produce a chronological account, for the writer of historical psychology, unlike the historian, can dive in and out of the past in the search for interesting examples that might help to understand the present in the hope of influencing the future.[1]

---

[1] At the start of Chapter 3, I will return to the topic of 'the history of psychology' and 'historical psychology'. In that chapter, I refer to the work of Kurt Danziger and Adrian Brock, who have considered in great depth and with considerable acumen the categories of 'history of psychology' and 'historical psychology'. I do so there, because that chapter does

Structure of the Book

There are seven chapters analysing thinkers, and they typically concentrate on particular pieces of writing which are set within the wider context of the thinker's life and work. Some of the chapters, such as those on Freud, Lewin and Lacan, deal with a single figure. Others deal with two thinkers, comparing specific pieces from each in order to highlight similarities or differences between the two. In the double-figured chapters, one of the figures is illustrious, while the other has been comparatively neglected in the histories of psychology. A sub-theme of this book is that academic fame is not necessarily a sign of intellectual quality nor is obscurity reserved for the second-rate.

The chapters are roughly arranged in chronological order, but strict chronology was neither achieved nor attempted. Chronology, as determined by birthdate, would have dictated that the final analytic chapter should have occupied the penultimate place. However, the final chapter has been held back so that its subject, Marie Jahoda, could be praised as the ultimate example, as the example who sets standards of writing and of intellectual humanity that psychologists today would do well to follow. Putting chronology aside is another sign that this book is not a straightforward history of psychology but an exercise in addressing some current issues historically.

The first analytic chapter, which of course is the second chapter of the book, goes back to a time before the word 'psychology' was part of the English language. It deals with John Locke, the founder of associationist psychology, and the third Earl of Salisbury, who described Locke as his foster father. I concentrate on Locke's chapter on the association of ideas which he added to the fourth edition of his *An Essay Concerning Human Understanding*. There we can see him presenting examples of the various types of association that he is carefully distinguishing. His examples are minimal, conveying little extra detail: they are shackled to the demands of his theoretical distinctions. In the work of the foster son, we find an altogether different view of the mind and Shaftesbury uses language in a very different way. His examples are extended, and he does not coerce them into a theoretical structure. In fact, Shaftesbury believed that theoretical systems prevent people from understanding themselves and their place in the world. In the contrast between Locke and Shaftesbury, we can see the beginning of debates about the mind that persist in the present.

something that some historians would consider unhistorical: I explore the similarities between two thinkers who lived in different times.

The following chapter deals with two figures who represent the extremes of eminence and obscurity: William James and Abraham Tucker. Despite their differences in fame and being separated by almost a hundred years, the two held strikingly similar views about the mind; and both were skilled experts of the telling example. Tucker anticipated James' view of consciousness as a stream and much more besides. He also recognised that theory and examples often stood in conflict one with the other. Both James and Tucker – the famous and the forgotten – take their places as heroes in this story of examples.

After the chapter on Tucker and James, comes one devoted to a single figure: Sigmund Freud. The chapter concentrates on his analyses of an episode in his own life. During a holiday he surprisingly forgot the name of the Italian artist Luca Signorelli. He wrote three slightly differing descriptions of the episode, the most famous being the first chapter of *The Psychopathology of Everyday Life*, a book filled with examples. By examining Freud's different accounts of this example and by comparing them with his insights about other people, we can see how Freud's analysis of the Signorelli incident both reveals and conceals. It is suggested that Freud, by analysing the episode and then immediately preparing his analysis for publication, may well have been trying to push something troubling from his mind.

The next chapter is slightly out of chronological sequence, but it continues with the psycho-analytic themes of the Freud chapter. This is the chapter whose tone does not match that of the other chapters. It looks at Jacques Lacan in a highly critical manner, and it offers no polite praise. The piece of Lacan's writing to be analysed is his account of the mirror stage – an idea that has been extremely influential in literary and cultural analyses. Ostensibly, Lacan bases the idea of a mirror stage on the work of psychologists, but when examined closely, his references to psychologists and to their work seem to evaporate. On the other hand, he avoids referencing a French psychologist who proposed very similar psychological ideas. The chapter is designed to counteract any tendency to say that, if psychology is based on writing, then all that matters is composing well-phrased, literary accounts and we need not bother gathering evidence and examples.

Kurt Lewin is the focus of attention in Chapter 6, which examines his general view of psychology as well as his famous study comparing the effects of different styles of leadership. In this study, Lewin showed how examples of real-life behaviour could be created experimentally. The focus here is upon his report of the study in a journal of social psychology, where Lewin seems to comply with the standard rhetoric of social psychological writing.

The chapter looks at the conflict between examples and theory in Lewin's own work – a conflict that is optimistically glossed over in his famous motto 'There is nothing as practical as a good theory'. Lewin claimed to have derived his idea of a good theory from his teacher, the philosopher Ernst Cassirer. However, he overlooked Cassirer's warnings that theories impoverish reality and that science needs good descriptions. Although the chapter criticises some of Lewin's specific ideas, he is praised for his wider vision, sense of humanity and optimistic character, all of which he expresses within his work.

The following chapter discusses another social psychologist, my teacher Henri Tajfel. I have not picked one of his famous papers, but I have chosen a short preface which he wrote for the re-publication of a neglected book on anti-Semitism, originally written in the 1920s by Fritz Bernstein, a German Jew living in the Netherlands. Bernstein had proposed a general theory of group relations to explain anti-Semitism. What Tajfel wrote about Bernstein's pre-war book is revealing, as are Bernstein's post-war reflections on his own book. The sort of language, which might have been appropriate for writing about anti-Semitism in the 1920s, had become wholly inappropriate after the Holocaust. The singularity of the Nazis' organised murder of millions would be misplaced if it were absorbed into a general theory of group relations. Significantly, Tajfel avoided using his own 'social identity theory' to explain Nazism. His praise of Bernstein expresses an understanding and depth of feeling that are beyond the simplifications of any theory.

The final analytic chapter presents the ultimate example, an example to be followed: Marie Jahoda. In so many respects, Jahoda embodied the virtues that are praised in the earlier chapters. She was the author of a classic report looking at the effects of mass unemployment on the lives of those living in an Austrian village in the early 1930s. Her report detailed the desperate conditions of the villagers and she made telling use of examples. Just as her examples overspill any theory of unemployment, so the reasons why Jahoda might herself be heralded as an example to follow overspill her abilities to use examples. She had a wider moral and political vision which she maintained throughout her life; she understood the tensions between theory and examples; she wrote directly with minimum jargon and maximum clarity; and she felt that the pressures to publish were corrupting academic values. In short, her use of examples and her suspicion of theory in psychology were just two aspects of a humane, courageous vision.

There is a final chapter, which does not offer an overarching theory of examples to cover all the psychological writers. On the other hand, I try to pull together some of the connecting themes from the previous chapters.

I also make some recommendations which are directed towards young academics. No strictly historical work, concerned with sorting out the past, is likely to end with such a list of recommendations. That is another reason why the previous chapters might better be described as historical psychology rather than the history of psychology, although they contain much history.

***

The writers whom I have chosen to write about do not represent a cross section of psychologists. They are not even a cross section of psychologists who are good writers. They are my personal choices. Someone else writing this book would have made a different selection. I cannot justify mine on theoretical grounds, and I am aware that my choices reveal more about me than about the nature of psychology. For example, the chosen twentieth-century psychologists are social psychologists rather than developmental, evolutionary or physiological psychologists.[2]

Most conspicuously, I have selected a disproportionate number of men; indeed, until Chapter 8, women are largely invisible. It might have been difficult to find women to celebrate as writers in the early years of psychology. In the twentieth century, there were far more women writers of psychology than there had been in the eighteenth and nineteenth centuries. No doubt, a woman writing this book would have chosen more women to celebrate than I have. Nevertheless, Marie Jahoda, the sole woman featured in this book, occupies a special place as the symbolic culmination of the previous examples. She is, above all others, the one for us to follow in the twenty-first century.[3]

---

[2] A cognitive psychologist, advocating the use of single examples, might have selected Wilhelm Wundt or one of his colleagues. Wundt's experiments did not use aggregated samples but examined the effects of experimental procedures on a single participant, who was often the experimenter. A learning theorist might have selected Skinner or Watson, who often presented the results of a study about conditioning a single person or animal. What neither Wundt nor the behaviourists did is to conduct experiments, as Lewin did, giving participants freedom to react more or less as they wished.

[3] I considered including a chapter on Hannah Arendt, focussing on her view of thinking as a conversation with oneself. In such a chapter, I would have paid tribute to the importance of Arendt's ideas generally and mentioned the influence that her writings have had on me personally. Reluctantly, I came to realise that including Arendt would have stretched the word 'psychology' too far. It is one thing to stretch the word back in time to the era of Locke before psychology existed as a discipline. It is another matter to stretch the word in the era of psychology so that it covers someone who did not see herself as a psychologist, and who, when discussing the nature of thinking, did not refer to the work of psychologists. I have, nevertheless, been able to include Arendt at various points. In the next chapter, for instance, I point out the similarity between her views on thinking and those of the third Earl of Shaftesbury. If their jointly shared position competes with that of Locke and other associationists, I hope that it is clear which of these two teams has my support.

My selection also contains imbalances of nationality and ethnicity. Among the first four figures to be discussed in the book, there are three Englishmen together with the only American-born psychologist in the whole selection. I expect that an American would have included more American-born psychologists, and perhaps fewer British ones, whether native-born British or migrants to Britain. If Lacan is excluded on the grounds that he is hardly an object of admiration here, then the final five figures are all European Jews. The last gentile to be selected is William James, whose psychology belongs to the nineteenth century. But what descriptions, what examples he left us!

It is inevitable that my selection should say more about myself than I might have intended.[4] But, no matter, the choices have been made. Now, the parade of examples should start.

---

[4] I should add that, in choosing work by authors of psychology whom I have learned from and enjoyed reading, I am not selecting the books that have most influenced me. There were three books which I read as a young man and knew, as I was reading them, that they were irrevocably changing my outlook on the world. None of them was written by a psychologist. The first was Wittgenstein's *Philosophical Investigations* (1968), which I read as an undergraduate and which ruined my chances of becoming a 'proper' psychologist. Hannah Arendt's *Eichmann in Jerusalem* (1965/1977), for all its faults and provocative asides, shook me deeply. Then, there was C. L. R. James' *Beyond a Boundary* (1964). I can still remember the excitement of reading that book and never wanting it to end. Is it, I ask myself, significant that none of these three books which so changed me was written by a psychologist or even by a professional academic?

2 Locke and Shaftesbury
Foster Father and Foster Son

John Locke and the third Earl of Shaftesbury come from a time when the study of psychology as we know it today did not exist. In the second half of the seventeenth century and in the early years of the eighteenth, the word 'psychology' had not yet edged its way into the English language, although for about a hundred years the Latin term *psychologia* had been used to indicate the study of the soul. Philosophers who wished to write about the way the mind works did not have an established format to follow. In consequence, writers such as Locke and Shaftesbury were free to create their own formats. As will be seen, they chose very different styles. We can see in Locke's writing the beginnings of the way that psychologists would come to write about the mind in years to come. With Shaftesbury we see a very dissimilar style, as he took a rhetorical path which mainstream, scientifically minded psychologists would avoid.

For them both, literary style was more than just a personal choice about how to wrap up their ideas for the benefit of the public. Should they choose plain, dazzling or technical words? Their styles, it will be suggested, were very part much of their general ideas. Locke and Shaftesbury could not have swapped their ways of writing and still have produced the analyses of the mind that they did. By comparing their great works – Locke's *Essay Concerning Human Understanding* and Shaftesbury's *Characteristicks of Men, Manners, Opinions, Times* – we can see the inter-relations between content and literary form more clearly than if we had considered either one on its own. Also, we can compare first editions with later ones. The revisions that the authors made to their books reveal their contrasting views about language and the mind, and show how Locke's changes prefigured later psychological writing in ways that Shaftesbury's revisions did not. Against this background, it becomes easier to understand why their respective handling of examples should have differed so greatly.

Locke and Shaftesbury: the 'Foster' Father and Son

One might ask why, out of all the possible exemplars of psychological writing, Locke and Shaftesbury have been selected, and what exactly they might exemplify. The quick answer is that they illustrate very different views on the way that the mind works, and they expressed their views in very different ways. As such, they show that right at the start of psychological thinking in Britain, psychology was more than theory and methodology, but, because it had to be written, it was a deeply rhetorical enterprise. In this and later chapters, it will be argued that examples overspill what they are intended to exemplify. Accordingly, Locke and Shaftesbury exemplify more than the specific point that a psychological thinker's view of the mind may be closely connected with his or her style of writing. Their lives, as well as their writings, can be used to exemplify a variety of other matters.

To begin with, Locke and Shaftesbury exemplify something that is sadly all too rare in the history of philosophy and psychology. We are used to hearing about those who advocate contrary theories becoming bitter rivals. Even small differences can lead to petty quarrels and incurable jealousies; and the lack of differences, not even small ones, can lead to furious battles about priority. Locke and Shaftesbury were divided by large differences of philosophy. Whatever Locke, the older of the two, proposed, the younger man rejected. Locke developed an integrated, systematic view of the mind. Shaftesbury did not propound an alternative system to confute Locke, but he went even further and rejected the very idea of a system. Locke was very much a scientifically minded writer, and that is one of the reasons why many later psychologists have taken him to be a founder of their discipline. Shaftesbury was most certainly not scientifically minded, and the overwhelming majority of psychologists have never heard of him.

Locke and Shaftesbury exemplify something much scarcer and more precious than intellectual rivalry or academic jealousy. Whatever their philosophical differences, their lives were entwined and they maintained close mutual affection and respect. When Locke died, Shaftesbury in a warm tribute referred to Locke as his 'friend and foster father' (Shaftesbury, 1900, p. 332). It was only after Locke's death that Shaftesbury compiled his writings into his only book, *Characteristicks* (1711). Shaftesbury had not wished to embarrass his foster father by publishing his book when Locke was alive.

Shaftesbury's grandfather, the first earl, had been one of the most powerful and feared political figures in the land. During the English Civil War, Shaftesbury (or rather Anthony Cooper, as he was known before his ennoblement and, indeed, as the third earl would be known before he inherited the title) had been a parliamentarian, supporting the victorious Oliver Cromwell. When Cromwell's rule started to crumble, Shaftesbury switched sides, helping to restore the monarchy and assisting

Charles II, who rewarded him with high political positions and an earldom. It was during this time that chance brought him into contact with Locke, who was teaching at Oxford University and also working as a medical doctor. Shaftesbury, a chronic sufferer of ill health, had travelled to Oxford to see his regular doctor.

However, his doctor was unavailable, and Shaftesbury was recommended to consult John Locke instead. Shaftesbury was impressed by the young substitute medic, who had similar views to himself. Locke had grown up in a protestant family that had supported the parliamentarians. Like Shaftesbury, he feared extreme Protestants, while being deeply suspicious of Tories, Catholics and kings. So impressed was Shaftesbury that he hired Locke as his personal assistant. In that capacity Locke participated in the politics of the day, but Shaftesbury also encouraged him to pursue his intellectual interests. That led to Locke writing his *Essay*, while still employed by Shaftesbury. Locke wrote much of the *Essay* in exile in the Netherlands, where he had fled with Shaftesbury after the earl had been suspected, quite correctly, of plotting against the King. Locke returned after King James was dethroned in the so-called Glorious Revolution of 1688, and the *Essay* was published two years later, without the author's name appearing on its title page.

The old politician had entrusted Locke with a difficult and delicate task: Shaftesbury asked Locke to find a suitably well-born wife for his unprepossessing son and the great philosopher fulfilled the task with his customary lack of fuss. When the selected wife became pregnant, Shaftesbury assigned Locke to oversee the pregnancy and the birth. The baby boy was safely delivered, and Locke was then charged with supervising the education of the earl's only grandson and ultimate heir. So successfully did Locke fulfil his educational duties, applying the principles that he had outlined in *On Education*, that the young boy grew up with a love for scholarship, especially classical studies (for details, see Billig, 2008a, chapter 5; Voitle, 1984). In many respects the unmarried Locke acted in the paternal role for which the boy's own father was so palpably unsuited.

Locke might have succeeded in passing on a love of philosophical inquiry to his young charge, but he failed to transmit his own philosophical outlook. Intellectually, the teacher was the modernist who followed the latest scientific discoveries, while the pupil was the traditionalist, steeped in the literature of ancient Athens and Rome. Their philosophical differences, nevertheless, did not indicate political differences. The foster son, a Whig like his teacher, strongly opposed monarchical authoritarianism and supported a politics of liberty – at least liberty for English gentlemen like Locke and for English noblemen like himself.

Locke's *Essay* in the Histories of Psychology

Out of all Locke's many writings, I will be focussing on his *Essay*, which was one of the first extended analyses of the mind written in English. Locke's analysis was much more detailed than Hobbes' *Human Nature*, which had been written fifty years earlier. Three revised editions of the *Essay* were published in Locke's lifetime, and a fourth revision was published posthumously as the book's fifth edition in 1706. The second and fourth editions contained the most significant changes; the publishers of both editions, and also the publishers of the posthumous fifth edition, declared on the title page that the new edition contained 'large additions'. Each edition, including the first edition, contained a prefatory 'Epistle to the Reader', in which Locke commented on his book and how it came to be written. In the Epistles for the second and fourth editions Locke remarked upon the changes that he was making for the new edition, also saying that his publishers had wished him to draw attention to the new additions. As someone who had held the government post of Secretary for the Board of Trade, Locke would have understood the commercial considerations behind this request from his publishers.

Locke did not present his *Essay* as if he were a specialist writing for the benefit of fellow specialists. From the second edition, which appeared four years after the first edition, its author was identified on the title page as 'John Locke, Gent'. It was as if one gentleman was writing for the benefit of other gentlemen – an impression that Locke conveyed in the prefatory Epistle of the first edition. He was not writing for the geniuses of his day, or for 'the men of large thoughts and quick apprehensions', but he was addressing himself to 'men of my own size' (in early editions, the pages of the Epistle are not numbered).

Nor was he writing for the benefit of philosophers, the majority of whom in England were Platonist metaphysicians. Locke attacked the language of these specialist philosophers who produced little but 'artificial ignorance and learned gibberish' (*Essay*, III, x, 9).[1] He particularly criticised their use of Latin terminology. He wrote that it would be better if Latin terms like *inhærentia* and *substantia* were put into the appropriate 'plain English ones', and then their meaning would become clearer (II, xiii, 12; see also II, xxiii, 2). In his Epistle he wrote that he

---

[1] It is customary, when quoting from Locke's *Essay*, to list three numbers: the first stands for the book, the second for the chapter within the book and the third for the subsection within the chapter. The *Essay* comprised four books, which were not physical books but were the major divisions of the work. Unless otherwise stated, quotations are here taken from the text of the 1824 edition of the collected works of Locke reproduced by Liberty Fund (1824/2002). The advantage of using this text is that the spelling and capitalisation have been modernised.

had no desire to build a great metaphysical system; he was just 'an under-labourer, clearing the ground a little, and removing some of the rubbish that lies in the way of knowledge'. In such comments Locke was using plain language to introduce a work that he hoped would clearly examine how the mind understands the world.

Despite Locke's characteristically modest portrayal of his own work, historians of psychology have recognised the *Essay* as more than a bit of rubbish removal but as a highly original, groundbreaking investigation of the mind. Kurt Danziger described Locke as signalling a new era in 'the conceptualization of the human person' (1997, p. 46). According to Ludy Benjamin, the *Essay* is 'one of the most important books in the history of psychology' (2007, p. 14). The philosopher George Santayana went so far as to call Locke 'the father of modern psychology' (1933, p. 1).

Textbooks on the history of psychology often emphasise Locke's importance. One textbook claims that Locke produced 'psychological works' and 'launched a serious inquiry into an empirical theory of knowledge' (King and Woody, 2016, p. 128). According to Pickren and Rutherford (2010), Locke's 'greatest contribution' was his emphasis on experience, and this had 'the greatest import' in political and psychological realms (p. 8). Another textbook describes the *Essay* as a 'major work of importance to psychology' (Schultz and Schultz, 2016, p. 35). Those textbooks, which encourage students to read original texts by including extracts from key works, frequently include lengthy extracts from the *Essay* (e.g. Munger, 2003; Gentile and Miller, 2009; Schultz and Schultz, 2016).

The textbooks will inform students why Locke is an ancestor worth remembering. Some textbooks (Hothersall, 2004; Kardus, 2014; King and Woody, 2016) describe Locke as an empiricist (a good thing), even claiming him to be the founder of empiricism (an even better thing). And some (Goodwin, 2015; Kardus, 2014; Leahey, 2017) stress that Locke bequeathed to psychology the important concept of 'association' (a very good thing indeed). Some American textbooks (Hothersall, 2004; Kardus, 2014) tell their student readers that Locke helped to write the Constitution of Carolina (another very good thing); more than this, they say that Locke's ideas were to inspire the writers of the US Constitution (the best of all good things).

Because I will be comparing Locke's style of writing with that of Shaftesbury, it might be opportune to say a brief word about Shaftesbury's appearance in the history of psychology textbooks. Quite literally two words will suffice: no Shaftesbury. The overwhelming majority of the textbooks do not mention the third earl. One of the most subtle and nuanced of current textbooks is an exception, as it mentions

Shaftesbury's rejection of Locke's ideas (Walsh, Teo and Baydala, 2014, pp. 115–16). This textbook is entitled *A Critical History and Philosophy of Psychology*, and the word 'critical' is revealing. The authors criticise the standard histories of psychology, and they are critical of the sort of mainstream psychology that can count Locke as an unproblematic ancestor. The authors align themselves with the type of psychology that seeks alternative theories and methodologies to mainstream psychology and is now known as 'critical psychology'. Some of today's critical psychologists, who position themselves against the sort of orthodox psychology that can be traced back to Locke, often unwittingly express ideas that bear echoes of Shaftesbury's view on the mind (Billig, 2008a).

Shaftesbury's *Characteristicks* might seem a minor, little-read work today, especially when compared with the continuing fame of Locke's *Essay*. In the eighteenth century, however, *Characteristicks* was considered to be a work of major significance with the book being reprinted many times in Britain. Shaftesbury's ideas, especially those relating to his views on common sense, influenced the philosophers of the Scottish Enlightenment, including Thomas Reid, Francis Hutcheson and Adam Smith (Yaffe, 2002). Nowadays some Scottish philosophers prefer to emphasise the indigenous character of the Scottish Enlightenment and tend to downplay the influence of the English aristocrat (Ahnert and Manning, 2011). Arguably Shaftesbury had an even greater impact in Germany than in his native land. He was much admired by Leibniz and Kant (Kleist, 2000; but see also Cook, 1998). *Characteristicks* had a profound effect on German romantic theorists such as Herder and Mendelssohn. In his *Philosophy of the Enlightenment*, Ernst Cassirer, another admirer of Shaftesbury, wrote that the third earl's work gave 'expression to the fundamental forces which shaped the philosophy of nature of Herder and the young Goethe' (1932/1951, p. 85).

Shaftesbury's influence spread to France, where the radical Denis Diderot, whose first book was a translation of Shaftesbury's essay on morality, was a great enthusiast. In his *Encyclopédie* Diderot compared the talents of Locke and Shaftesbury; the balance of his admiration noticeably tipped towards the virtuosity of the latter and away from the steady seriousness of the former. Diderot wrote, 'There are very few errors in Locke and too few truths in Milord Shaftesbury: the former is only a man of vast intellect, penetrating and exact, while the latter is a genius of the first order'.[2]

---

[2] The quotation and its translation are taken from Stephen Darwall's book on *The British Moralists* (1995, p. 181; see also Pons, 2014).

An Atomist Theory of Mind: Locke

Locke's and Shaftesbury's very different views of human thinking rested on wider philosophical differences, with Shaftesbury acting as the negative to Locke's positive, or the antithesis of his teacher's thesis. To summarise this difference crudely, we could say that Locke was the atomist, the scientifically minded thinker who wanted to find the basic matter of the human mind in ways that corresponded to the scientific atomists of his day who were seeking to discover the basic indivisible properties of matter. Shaftesbury, by contrast, was the holist who believed that understanding did not come from taking things apart to find their basic elements, but from connecting everything in the world together. In this, Shaftesbury resembled the metaphysical Platonists, such as Ralph Cudworth, whose abstract approach to understanding the universe Locke was dismissing as gibberish (see Cassirer, 1932/1953; Balibar, 2014). In other respects, particularly in his chosen style of writing, Shaftesbury was as distant from the Platonist schoolmen as they were from the dramatic literary style of Plato.

Within the realm of psychological understanding, the basic difference between atomists and holists can be summarised in terms of two principles, one methodological and one theoretical. Atomists believe that, if you want to study psychological phenomena, whether mental or behavioural, then you should break them down into their essential, non-divisible components. That basically is a methodological principle guiding the way that atomists should analyse the mind or behaviour. They also have a theoretical principle. According to atomists, humans are able to think and behave in complex ways because they are capable of combining psychological atoms, whether they are atoms of thought or of behaviour.

By contrast, holists argue that humans should be studied as parts of greater wholes. For instance, they insist that individuals should be understood in relation to their networks of social relations and to the environments in which they live. Holists also argue that humans do not build complex thoughts or behavioural patterns from basic psychological elements. Instead, the mind naturally sees whole patterns rather than constructing them mentally step by step from their components. In these respects, Gestalt psychologists were the holists of the twentieth century while behaviourists were the atomists. More than 200 years earlier, Locke had been the atomist and Shaftesbury the holist.

The underlying purpose of Locke's *Essay* was to construct an account of the mind to support his belief that objective empirical knowledge was possible. Key to Locke's account is his rejection of innate ideas in the first book of the *Essay*. If the human mind is empty at birth, then our ideas must come from outside and that means through perception. As an atomist, Locke thought that the basic units of ideas were simple perceptual ideas. According to Locke, we passively receive the outside world through our senses:

In the reception of simple ideas, the understanding is for the most part passive. In this part, the understanding is merely passive ... For the objects of our senses do ... obtrude their particular ideas upon our minds whether we will or no. (II, i, 25)

This is what Locke called 'bare naked perception', where 'the mind is, for the most part, only passive' (II, ix, 1; see Lähteenmäki, 2014). It should be noted that modern psychologists generally do not side with Locke on these matters. As the noted ecological psychologist J. J. Gibson argued, we actively seek out the world and certainly do not construct our complex perceptions from simple ones (Gibson, 1986; see also Wagemans et al., 2012).

The notion that the perception of simple elements is essentially passive enables Locke to say that when we perceive basic elements, we generally do so accurately: our perceptions of simple elements are not distorted by our own mental processes. Thus, our simple ideas, or what Locke famously called 'clear and distinct ideas', are generally perceptions that represent the world as it is (Connolly, 2017). Our minds then reflect upon these basic, simple perceptions, and for Locke, such reflection is a secondary process that occurs after perception. Through reflection we are able to join simple ideas together to form more complex ones. These complex ideas can be impressions of complex objects, such as faces in which the simple elements are amalgamated. Our reflections can also produce abstract ideas and complex concepts.

If we put together our simple perceptual ideas with care, then we will construct complex knowledge that is based on accurate views of the world. In this way, Locke's theory of perception as a passive process enables him to construct a theory of mind that allows for the possibility of accurate, scientific knowledge. Errors are not generally based on perceptual mistakes but on the ways we reflect upon simple perceptions. If we combine simple ideas carelessly, or reflect inaccurately on our perceptions, then we will construct erroneous views of the world. Much of Locke's *Essay* was concerned with analysing how we can accurately or inaccurately build complex beliefs from simple clear and distinct ideas. For example, general concepts that are not based on particulars sharing a common quality (or 'nominal essence') are likely to be sources of error. Concepts that can be broken down into clear and distinct ideas are likely to represent the world accurately.

Locke's psychological theory is both atomist and empirical, at least 'empirical' in the sense that the word was used in the late seventeenth century. To think clearly it is necessary to bring our complex ideas and concepts into line with our perceptions. Correcting errors means clearing away mental rubble and tidying up the courtyard of the mind. It is a fitting theory for a man described by Diderot as having a mind that was penetrating and exact but not given to leaps of imagination.

A Holist Theory of Mind: Shaftesbury

Shaftesbury did not take issue with specific elements of Locke's theory, as a modern cognitive scientist might, for instance, argue against Locke's passive theory of perception or against his notion that reflection is a separate process following perception. Nor did Shaftesbury take issue with the specific terminology that Locke used. Hume in his *Treatise of Human Nature* was to criticise Locke for using the word 'ideas' to represent all the conscious contents of the mind. According to Hume, it would be less misleading to reserve 'ideas' for their normal sense of thoughts and to distinguish them from perceptual 'impressions'.

Shaftesbury was not interested in drawing up precise, analytic distinctions. His objection to Locke's approach was much more basic: it was a trivial waste of time. Regarding Locke's account of how we construct our knowledge from perception, Shaftesbury was unimpressed. He dismissed 'philosophical speculations' about the 'formation of ideas, their compositions, comparisons, agreement and disagreement' (1714/2001, p. 134).[3] It did not matter how ideas were compounded but whether they were morally just.

Shaftesbury imagines an exchange between a Descartes-type rationalist and a Lockean-style empiricist. Both are searching for a point of certainty. The Cartesian says he can be certain of himself; the Lockean claims to possess 'clear ideas'. Shaftesbury responds to these two imaginary philosophers: "'And what", say I, "if in the whole matter there is no certainty at all?"' (1714/2001, p. 135). If Shaftesbury is criticising the views of Locke,

---

[3] Unless otherwise stated, quotations from *Characteristicks* are taken from Lawrence Klein's version of the second edition. Klein modernises Shaftesbury's English, especially its spelling, without changing the wording or sense. Klein also modernises the spelling of the book's title, but here the old-fashioned spelling – '*Characteristicks*' – is retained, as it often is in academic works, for it seems to convey Shaftesbury's backward-looking outlook. I have followed the custom of modernising the spelling of the title of Locke's book. In the editions published during Locke's lifetime the book was entitled *An Essay Concerning Humane Understanding*, not *Human Understanding*. Today, *human* and *humane* have different meanings, and we can say without contradiction 'many a human is not humane'. On the other hand, *characteristicks* is to modern eyes merely a spelling mistake.

mocking the language that he used and dismissing the problems that he addressed, then it must be stressed that Shaftesbury does not mention Locke by name. That would have been unjust – not to say, ungentlemanly.

Shaftesbury was not attempting to construct an alternative, more rigorous theory of the mind, as Hume was to. He was following the stoic philosophers of the ancient world in believing that philosophy should aim at practical self-improvement. Looking in detail at the way that the mind forms concepts by combining ideas was not a stoic aim. However, as Shaftesbury presented ways to improve thinking in practice, almost as a by-product he outlined a theory of thinking that seems to be an alternative to Locke's painstaking atomism.

At one point in *Characteristicks*, Shaftesbury advised an unnamed author how to think. His advice was not that authors should tidy their minds and organise their thoughts systematically before putting their pen to paper. Drawing inspiration from the ancient Delphic oracle, he wrote that we should 'divide ourselves into two parties' (1714/2001, p. 77). We should then set the two parties to debate with each other, for this would be the way to try to clarify our thoughts. He did not imagine that one of the two debating selves would then win the imagined debate, forcing the other into silent submission. As in Socratic debates, there would always more to say, more to argue about, and thus more to think about.

In this way, Shaftesbury was putting at the core of thinking an activity that Locke had dismissed. In his *Essay*, Locke had mocked those 'all-knowing doctors' whose learning was 'estimated by their skills in disputing' and who produced 'artificial ignorance, and learned gibberish' (III, x, 9). Disputation was nothing but 'a very useless skill' which was 'the direct opposite to the ways of knowledge' (III, x, 8). For Shaftesbury, as it had been for Socrates, discussion lay at the heart of thinking. If we do not have suitable others with whom we can debate, then we should learn how to debate with ourselves, engaging in what Shaftesbury called the practice of 'self-converse' (1714/2001, p. 75). In this regard, Shaftesbury did not envision thinking as a matter of internal cognitive processing but as a dialogical activity that was essentially social, even when practised in isolation (Billig, 1987, 2008a).

Locke's and Shaftesbury's opposed views on the nature of thinking reflected differing views on the basic function of language. For Locke, language was, or at least should be, the means by which one mind communicates to other minds the thoughts that it had already formulated; and these thoughts should be expressed with concepts, which even if they are complex concepts, can ultimately be unwrapped and related to clear and distinct simple ideas. For Shaftesbury, on the other hand, language was not the means of communicating thoughts that had already been formulated, but it was the means by which we think, whether we are engaged in an actual dialogue with others or in a dialogue with ourselves. We think because we can speak, rather than speaking because we have already thought.

In Shaftesbury's view, thinking joins us to others. We think by talking to others, who in their turn have others to talk to. Thus, to think is to participate in widening circles of relations. It is little surprise that Shaftesbury did not believe that we are born with empty minds. We are born with various senses that may take time to develop. Above all, we have a 'common sense' or a sense for forming social bonds with others. We also have, Shaftesbury suggested, an innate moral sense, and perhaps most surprisingly, we are born with the potentiality for exercising an aesthetic sense. The aesthetic sense, he suggested, is linked to the moral sense, for we think immoral conduct to be ugly. All these senses – the social sense, the moral sense and the aesthetic sense – are, according to Shaftesbury, important aspects of human nature. They testify that we do not naturally live apart from others, as if we are isolated individuals with nothing but our perceptions to reflect upon.

Thus, Shaftesbury's vision of thinking in particular, and of human nature in general, is very different from Locke's. The *Essay* depicts the problems of the mind as being essentially individual: how does the individual mind construct its beliefs about the world from its perceptions? Later psychologists have taken up the problem, examining how the mind processes information. Such cognitive psychologists can see Locke as a distant ancestor. If they knew about Shaftesbury they would view him as a thoroughly alien figure.

In recent years, a number of modern social psychologists have reacted against the Lockean assumptions of cognitive psychology and have expressed the view that the human mind is essentially dialogical or argumentative (e.g. Billig, 1987, 1991; Edwards and Potter, 1992; Harré and Gillett, 1994; Hermans, 2018; Hermans and Hermans-Konopka, 2010; Marková, 2016; Mercier and Sperber, 2011). Mostly, such dialogical psychologists do not see Shaftesbury as an ancestor. For example, none of the contributors to the *Handbook of Dialogical Self Theory* mentions him (Hermans and Gieser, 2014). They are far more likely to attribute the dialogical view of the mind to the Russian linguist Mikhail Bakhtin, without realising how much Bakhtin seems to have drawn from Shaftesbury, albeit without acknowledgement and indirectly via the German philosopher Ernst Cassirer (Billig, 2008a; Cassirer, 1932/1951; Poole, 2002).

Shaftesbury also anticipates Hannah Arendt, who linked intense self-dialogue to proper thinking, as opposed to the sort of thinking that she dismissed as mere cognition. In *The Life of the Mind* (1978) she gave examples from her own life to show how thinking was based on internal argument. In presenting her view of thinking, Arendt did not mention Shaftesbury, and there is no reason to suppose that she knew his work. Arendt drew directly from classical sources, as Shaftesbury had done. She began *Life of the Mind* by saying that she had ended her earlier book *The Human Condition* (1958/1998) by quoting Cato's saying that a man is never less alone than when he is by himself (1978, pp. 7–8; 1958/1998, p. 325). Shaftesbury had included the same quotation from Cato to illustrate the integral connection between internal dialogue and thinking (1714/2001, p. 77).

Neither Arendt nor Shaftesbury was claiming that her or his thoughts on thinking were original, and both were keen to credit the ancients with discovering and practising the dialogical nature of thinking. In this matter, Shaftesbury and Arendt saw themselves as merely re-discovering old wisdom that had been pushed aside, unlike the modernist Locke, who wanted to push aside the veneration of ancient texts.

Two Contrasting Book Structures

Locke and Shaftesbury did more than express different views about thinking; they expressed these views in very different styles. This is evident in the contrasting structures of the *Essay* and *Characteristicks*. As Diderot's comparison implied, Locke wrote and structured his writing as an organised, coherent analysis, while his 'foster son' aimed to write with the insight and playfulness of a poet.

Although Locke apologised in his Epistle that his work was overlong and that it rambled at times, he gave his *Essay* an organised structure that emphasised its internal coherence. He divided the work into four 'books' with numbered chapters, each book representing the major sections of the work. The first two books, which are comparatively short, discuss the origins of human knowledge. In the first he dismisses the notion of innate ideas, while in the second he argues that, if knowledge is not innate, then it must come from our senses. In the final two books, Locke examines how we can create true and false complex ideas. Each chapter contains numbered sections, which bear subtitles. The numbering conveys the impression that Locke is building his argument in an orderly way, proceeding from basic principles to applications, from simple ideas to complex ones.

There is one feature of the *Essay* that would scarcely need mentioning except in the context of Shaftesbury's *Characteristick*s. From the first sentence of I, i, 1 to the final sentence of IV, xxi, 5, Locke's style remains the same. He attempts to write in plain language throughout, avoiding the pompous gibberish and artificial technical terms that he criticised in the works of the scholastics. Rhetorically, it was as if Locke's writing were an application of his theory of understanding. At all points, he was attempting to produce clear statements that matched the facts of the matter. This was an English gentleman writing in plain English for others of his class.

Shaftesbury demonstrated that there were other ways for the English to write philosophy. Rhetorically and structurally, *Characteristicks* is the very antithesis of the *Essay*. Shaftesbury does not use a comprehensive system of numbering to suggest that the sections are part of a coherent whole. It has been suggested that Shaftesbury even devised the title, with its portmanteau of topics, to convey that he is not presenting his ideas within an overarching system (Prince, 2004). At one point he declares that 'the most ingenious way of becoming foolish is by a system' (1714/2001, p. 130).

The first two volumes of the first edition *Characteristicks* (1711) comprise five chapters, each of which Shaftesbury had already published anonymously and privately as a separate essay. Shaftesbury uses a variety of literary genres: the chapters come in the form of a letter to a named friend; a letter to an unnamed friend; a dialogue in which Shaftesbury takes on the persona of an ancient Greek debating with his friends; advice which is being sent to an unnamed author; and, almost as a novelty in this context, a philosophical essay on virtue and morality that is conventional in its philosophical style. This essay, entitled 'An Inquiry Concerning Virtue or Merit', has numbered sections, sub-sections and even sub-sub-sections, so that its format conveys a tightly argued, internally consistent thesis. Apart from this philosophical essay, the other chapters of the first two volumes are dialogical, in that the author presents himself as addressing another person or, in the case of his dialogue, or what he calls a 'philosophical rhapsody', engaging in an imagined conversation.

The third volume is perhaps the most remarkable of all in terms of its literary form. Shaftesbury presents five miscellanies, or seemingly light-hearted essays. These miscellanies could not be further from the style of 'proper', ordered philosophical writing. Without numbered parts and sub-parts or other rhetorical devices conveying a strict internal ordering, Shaftesbury's miscellanies, in sharp contrast with the doggedly serious tone of Locke's *Essay*, combine debate with amusement. In the first miscellany Shaftesbury writes in praise of this type of writing: 'since this happy method was established, the harvest of wit has been made more plentiful' (1714/2001, p. 339). He writes that his aim is to serve 'as critic and interpreter' of a new 'British author' (p. 342). The national identity of this new writer, who of course is himself, is important: because our tragedy 'is so much deeper and bloodier than that of the French' (Shaftesbury is referring to the English Civil War), then we, the British, have more need than the French of 'the elegant way of drollery and burlesque wit' (p. 341).

We should not be deceived by the way that Shaftesbury presents his drollery and burlesque. In finishing his only book with these light-hearted miscellanies, Shaftesbury has a serious purpose. Each of the five miscellanies reflects upon and mocks one of the five preceding chapters. Shaftesbury may have adopted the conceit that he is a different author from the one who had written the previous chapters, but he does not expect his readers to be fooled. In his short preface to the whole work, he declares that 'the author of these united tracts' is no 'friend to prefaces'. So, in the very first sentence of the whole book, in its first edition of 1711, the author announces himself to be the author of all the 'united' chapters that follow. By implication, he is not presenting the miscellanies as add-on fripperies.

In his miscellanies, Shaftesbury is publicly enacting his dialogical theory of thinking. He has divided himself, being both the author of the five main essays and the author of the five miscellanies that criticise those essays. In so doing, he can be seen to be debating with himself, although there is an extra, concealed level of debate. To write the individual chapters and their attendant miscellanies, Shaftesbury would have followed his own advice and debated with himself. He did not believe that his internal, pre-publication debates should be presented to the public (Sellars, 2016).

The sharpest of the miscellanies is the one which addresses his only conventional piece of philosophical writing. Shaftesbury had written this chapter before he had developed his more literary style. In the miscellany for this chapter the mature Shaftesbury mocks his younger self, calling him: 'a real dogmatist' (1714/2001, p. 395); 'a man of method', who calls to mind 'the figure of some precise and strait-laced professor in a university' (p. 396); 'a system-writer, a dogmatist and expounder' (p. 418).

Shaftesbury is doing more than amusing his readers, adding wit to serious philosophy or mature cynicism to youthful earnestness. The miscellanies give *Characteristicks* an appropriately Socratic form. In most of the Platonic dialogues, Socrates does not silence his fellow conversationalists by overwhelming them with a winning argument that demolishes all their stances. The conversations typically end in *aporia*, or argumentative deadlock, with the speakers agreeing to continue their debate the next time they meet. Likewise, Shaftsbury's book has no final conclusion. There is no summing up, asserting that the rubble of other philosophies has been conclusively swept away and that a tidy intellectual universe awaits us. By his chosen literary form Shaftesbury was demonstrating his point that there might be no certainty, no final end to debate.

Johann Gottfried Herder was to see the philosophical importance of Shaftesbury's way of writing. Like Shaftesbury, Herder rejected the idea of philosophical certainty and his 'negative philosophy' consciously broke with traditional metaphysics. As Leventhal (1990) has pointed out, literary style was integral to Herder's philosophy, especially to his view that thinking involved using language (Herder, 1765/2008). Herder realised that his negative philosophy needed to be expressed appropriately, in non-systematic, even internally contradictory, ways. Herder knowingly followed the example of Shaftesbury and wrote essays and miscellanies, rather than organised, long tomes. Both he and Shaftesbury saw their literary style as integral to their thinking about the nature of thinking.

Specialist Terminology, Plain Language and Linguistic Atomism

In contrast to the literary games and conceits of *Characteristicks*, Locke attempted to write his *Essay* in a plain, seemingly straightforward style. He may have mocked the metaphysicians for their airy style of writing, claiming that they used abstract concepts that had no grounding in simple ideas, but this does not mean that his own plain English was altogether plain. In it, we can see traces of the technical writing that would come to characterise modern academic psychology, not that Locke wrote like a modern psychologist.

Locke did not entirely eschew the terminological habits of scholastic metaphysicians such as Ralph Cudworth (1731/1996), amongst whose many terminological inventions was the phrase 'cognoscitive powers'. This phrase, which Cudworth employed to denote the innate cognitive powers of humans for knowledge and which Locke certainly did not use, sounds as if it could come from a modern work of cognitive science. Cudworth, however, also devised the word 'consciousness' and Locke did not object to that term although he objected to the way that the metaphysicians were using it. He claimed that when metaphysicians talked about 'consciousness', they often implied that it was possible for people to think without being aware of their own thinking. For Locke, but not for modern cognitive scientists, that was an absurdity. Locke tried to define Cudworth's new word to preclude the possibility of thinking without conscious awareness. He wrote that 'consciousness is the perception of what passes in a man's own mind' (II, i, 19).

Locke used the word 'consciousness' in the important section on personal identity that he added to the second edition of the *Essay* (1694). As has been pointed out, Locke was not entirely clear in his use of 'consciousness' because he did not stick to his own definition of the word (Balibar, 2014). He was doing something similar to what many modern psychologists and social scientists do. They will often define their technical concepts with great care; but when they come to use these concepts, they will employ them in ways that burst through the restrictions of their own formal definitions (Billig, 2013).

Two pressures, one negative and the other positive, were pushing Locke towards forming new technical concepts rather than using plain English. The negative pressure was that he was keen to identify common, widely held prejudices and then replace them with empirically based views. Some of these prejudices, he thought, were encouraged by the words and phrases of ordinary speech. In his chapter 'Of Power', Locke argued that common language leads us to think of passive processes as if they were active. He was thinking particularly of the common phrases that we use to describe how we perceive objects, for, according to Locke, we often use verbs that grammarians call active. For instance, we are likely to say 'I see the moon, or a star, or I feel the heat of the sun'. In these instances, plain English leads us to describe essentially passive processes as if they were active. Because I am passive when I receive the image of the moon or receive the rays from the sun, ordinary language misleads when it conveys that we actively engage in perception (II, xxi, 72).

Locke's argument about perception being passive, while its description in language is active, was leading towards an argument for reforming ordinary language so as to keep it in line with his theory of perception. Interestingly, Locke wrote his chapter on power for the second edition of the *Essay* with the help and encouragement of Damaris Cudworth, Ralph Cudworth's daughter and one of the few published women philosophers of her time (Broad, 2006). Damaris Cudworth greatly respected her father's philosophical work while at the same time she maintained a close friendship with Locke. At one point, she entertained hopes that her good friend John might move towards a closer relationship; but, despite sending her some flirtatious letters, he remained the same reserved, secretive bachelor that he ever was.

The positive pressure on Locke to formulate technical concepts was that, as he developed his own inquiry into the nature of thinking, he was making distinctions that others had not previously made. Natural scientists were doing much the same and knowledge was advancing because scientists, using powerful new microscopes, were able to distinguish between things that had previously been assumed to be similar. For example, Harvey had been able to distinguish the structure and functions of veins that brought blood to the heart from those that took it from the heart; and he needed separate words to distinguish between the two. In a brief section on wit in the *Essay*, Locke contrasted serious judgement, which distinguishes between things that seem similar but are actually different, with the sort of playful wit that pretends, for the sake of humour, that things which are different are the same (IV, xiv).

If serious judgement involves distinguishing between things that are actually different then new terminology is required so that they would no longer be confused with each other: hence the need to distinguish 'arteries' from 'veins'. In the *Essay*, Locke distinguished between different types of complex ideas. In doing this, he was noticing previously unnoticed differences and sometimes he provided new terms for these newly distinguished entities. For example, Lock discussed complex ideas that were formed by identical simple ideas, and he cited numbers as an example. To identify this sub-type of complex idea, Locke introduced the concept of 'complex ideas of simple modes' (II, xiii).

The concept of 'complex ideas of simple modes' is certainly not plain English. In the late seventeenth century, few gentlemen or ladies would have thanked Locke for now being able to talk informally over the dining table about complex ideas of simple modes. Locke, in devising a new phrase to describe his new, specialised distinction, was doing what modern psychologists and other academics regularly do today. His term 'complex ideas of simple modes' does not quite have the linguistic structure of modern academic terminology in which nouns predominate in noun phrases that are easily rendered into acronyms. A modern academic, formulating a term like Locke's, might propose 'Complexity Ideas of Mode Simplicity (CIMS)' (Billig, 2013; Biber and Conrad, 2009; Biber and Gray, 2010).

Locke's new phrase, although lacking nouns as adjectival modifiers, represents a foretaste of things to come, and it also fits his view of language. He believed that every clear and distinct idea should ideally have its own name and conversely that every name should represent a single distinct idea with a clear 'nominal essence'. In practice, Locke recognised that 'there are not words enough in any language, to answer all the variety of ideas that enter into men's discourses and reasonings' (Epistle). Nowadays, as academics are quick to name their conceptual 'discoveries', the invention of technical terms has become very much a growth industry in psychology and other sciences and social sciences (Billig, 2013; Gigerenzer, 2010). The result is that academics pack their articles with noun phrases that non-specialists struggle to understand.

Locke applied his views about clear terminology to his own use of language. He sought to track down the elements of the mind to their basic, indivisible elements. As he subdivided the cognitive elements, or what he rather misleading called 'ideas', to smaller and smaller units, so he needed terms to describe the basic units. In this way, Locke's psychological atomism necessitated a parallel linguistic innovation. He came up with the famous phrase 'clear and distinct ideas' to describe the psychological atoms of the human mind. However, towards the end of his life, as the *Essay* was proving a great commercial success, Locke was becoming dissatisfied with his basic category.

The Clear and Distinct Innovation of the *Essay*'s Fourth Edition (1700)

Historians of psychology, who are interested in the development of psychology's technical language, often look at changes of language over a long period of time. As Kurt Danziger (1997) has shown, psychology's current ways of 'naming the mind' took many years to develop (see also Danziger, 1994a; Richards, 1992, 2002; Rose, 1985). Those of us who are more concerned with examining present psychological questions historically rather than writing full and proper histories of psychology have more liberty to contract the time periods that we examine. The revisions that writers make to the various editions of their books can be revealing. It is possible to focus upon such micro-changes to see whether these small changes prefigure, or do not prefigure, the bigger changes that occur over a much longer timescale. Instead of examining how Locke (and Shaftesbury) changed the psychological thinking of those that came after them, we can see how they might have sought to improve or clarify their own thinking. In the case of Locke we can see in magnified close-up the pressures that led him to make some small differences and that would eventually lead to much bigger changes over time. The changes that Shaftesbury made to the second edition of *Characteristicks* show how much he was out of step with the main psychological trends that were to follow.

As has already been mentioned, when Locke prepared the fourth edition of the *Essay*, he criticised some ordinary ways of speaking about the world. He also made two further changes, one of which had little impact even on Locke's followers. The other was a terminological innovation that would prove to be enormously influential on future psychological writing, although Locke did not present his linguistic innovation as if it were important in itself.

'Clear and distinct ideas' is one of Locke's most famous philosophical phrases, but towards the end of his life he was becoming bothered by the term, for the phrase itself no longer seemed to be sufficiently clear and distinct. So, Locke suggested that 'clear' and 'distinct' be replaced by 'determined' and 'determinate'. Here he was straying from plain English into the sort of specialist terminology that scholastic philosophers, including his good friend's father, could not resist. Locke felt that his new pair of terms would offer a 'way of speaking less liable to mistake' (Epistle, fourth edition, 1700). The words 'determinate or determined, instead of clear and distinct', would be more likely 'to direct men's thoughts to my meaning in this matter'. If perception were passive, then it would generally be based on an objective image of an object in the world. So, a simple idea such as the perception of a circle would be determined by an actual circle, and therefore this perception, which Locke loosely called an idea, could be called 'determined'. A complex idea would be formed by a 'determinate number of certain simple or less complex ideas' (Epistle, fourth edition). Thus, the perception of a dog would be both determined and determinate – determined by an actual dog and by a determinate number of simple parts of the dog, such as ears, paws or tail.

The issue here is not to determine whether Locke was correct in judging his revision to be a clear and distinct improvement. There is a much simpler point: Locke was again struggling against ordinary language. He was wanting to make distinctions that ordinary words were not usually employed to make. To make his distinctions clear, he thought it better to introduce special terminology. To this day, in the work of psychologists, there is a continuing tension between specialist and ordinary language. Psychologists today want to investigate psychological phenomena scientifically and they will use special terminology to do so. Nevertheless, they also use ordinary terms, particularly to describe their broad topics of inquiry. For example, today's cognitive scientists, just like Locke many years earlier, will claim to be studying 'memory', 'beliefs', 'ideas', etc., thereby using plain words to describe the subject matter of their investigations (Jacobson, 2007). However, in the course of studying such ordinarily named phenomena, psychologists will find themselves wanting to make distinctions for which there are no ready terms in everyday use. Then, they will devise specialist terms, distinguishing between different types of memory, beliefs or ideas – just as Locke had done more than three centuries ago.

Locke was showing how analysts of the mind can have an uneasy relationship with plain language. Those who claim to have discovered new aspects of the world, including new aspects of the human mind, may need to be linguistic innovators if they want their discoveries to be accepted as discoveries. Locke might have mocked the airy and pompous language of scholastic philosophers, but in his own small way he was prefiguring modern psychology's own forms of scholastic language.

Association of Ideas: an Influential Afterthought

Locke's major linguistic contribution to the study of the mind was almost an afterthought. For the fourth edition of the *Essay*, he wrote a new chapter to end the second book, entitling it 'Of the association of ideas' (II, xxxiii). 'Association' had not been used in this way before, and it was to become a central concept in psychology. In the nineteenth century, British psychology was often known as 'associationism'. The French psychologist Théodule Ribot (1870) wrote that English psychologists considered association to be the fundamental process of mental life. William James, in his chapter on association in *Principles of Psychology*, quoted Ribot at great length (1890, Vol. 1, pp. 597–8), and, like Ribot, he acknowledged Locke as the progenitor of associationist psychology. So did Edwin Boring (1929) in his classic history of psychology.

Locke did not pack his new chapter with the phrase 'association of ideas', like modern academic authors might when promoting their own newly minted phrases. In fact, Locke only used the word 'association' once in the new chapter's text. Discussing antipathies and hatreds, Locke wrote 'that there are such associations of them made by custom in the minds of most men I think nobody will question' (II, xxxiii, 7). He used 'association' one more time in the chapter, this time as the title of a section: 'Further instances of the effect of the association of ideas' (II, xxxiii, 14). He did not use the word in the text of that section.

In his new chapter Locke used a variety of other words to suggest how ideas become associated with each other. In section 11 he wrote about how a man, who ruminates on an injury caused by another, 'cements those two ideas together'; in section 15, he described how children, who suffer pain at school, impute the pain to their books and so 'join those ideas together'. In section 5 Locke discussed the difference between ideas that have a 'natural connection' and those whose 'connection' is established by 'chance' or 'custom'. In the case of two ideas with a natural connection, it is the task of our reason 'to hold them together in . . . union and correspondence'. In the case of chance connections, these ideas 'always keep in company', so that if one comes into a person's mind, 'its associate appears with it'. In the following section, Locke describes a musician hearing the start of a familiar tune: then ideas of the next notes 'will follow one another orderly in his understanding' (II, xxxiii, 6). Locke presents all these examples of 'association' without using verb 'associate' or the noun 'association'.

Instead of 'association', Locke uses a series of synonyms. In section 15, for example, he uses 'connection'; in section 5 'correspondence' and 'combination'; in section 6 'the tying together of ideas'. In section 7, he uses the word 'associations' in the first sentence, but not afterwards. So, although Locke uses 'association' in the title of the chapter and in the title of one of the sections, he only uses the word once when discussing the chapter's topic.

Locke might not have given his term 'association' any special treatment, but the word was to become increasingly prominent in the writings of eighteenth-century British analysts of the mind. It did not happen immediately. The fourth section of the first book in Hume's *Treatise of Human Nature* (1739/1964) was entitled 'On the connection or association of ideas'. It was as if either term would suffice without Hume giving 'association' preferential treatment over its plainer cousin. However, David Hartley in his *Observations on Man* (1749/1834) firmly gave his linguistic favours to 'association'. Hartley's aim, as expressed on the first page of his opening chapter, was to combine Locke's analysis of the mind with a theoretical neuro-physiological model inspired by Newton's *Opticks*. On that opening page, Hartley proposed uniting the doctrine of 'vibrations', which were supposedly transmitted to and from the brain through the nerves and which operated on Newtonian principles, with Locke's 'doctrine' of association. Hartley wrote, 'One may expect that *vibrations* should infer *association* as their effect, and *association* point to *vibrations* as its cause' (1749/1834, p. 4, italics in original).

Robert M. Young (1973), the historian of psychology, credited Hartley with being the real founder of modern empiricist psychology because he linked an analysis of the mind with hypothesised physiological processes. Other historians have followed Young and credited Hartley with being one of the first 'proper', scientific psychologists.[4] In praising Hartley for anticipating neuropsychology and 'the reflex arc', such historians tend to overlook, perhaps in embarrassment, the religious, even mystical, aspects of *Observations* (on Hartley's theology, see Allen, 1999; Ulmer, 2006). There is a linguistic aspect; by choosing a technical term to denote the basic mental process, rather than using familiar nouns such as 'connection' or 'combination', not to mention a verbal phrase such as 'join together', Hartley was writing as a modern psychologist might.

Two other aspects of 'association' are noteworthy. First, the word is longer than its closest linguistic competitors, with five syllables as against

---

[4] Historians of psychology who have drawn attention to Hartley's significance in the development of modern psychology include Glassman and Buckingham (2007), Goodwin (2015), Hergenhahn (2001), Wade (2005) and Wertheimer (1987).

the four or fewer syllables of 'combination' or 'connection', let alone the single syllable of the verb 'join'. The world of modern academic terminology differs from most other areas of language because it seems to encourage the linguistic survival of the longest. In ordinary talk, much used, long words get shortened: refrigerators becoming 'fridges' and bicycles becoming 'bikes'. In academic circles, the opposite seems to occur as words sprout extra syllables. Suffixes such as '-ology', '-isation' and '-ification' attract attention rather like the tail feathers of the male peacock. During the twentieth century, academics in the social sciences, including psychology, have come to describe the methods that they use in their research as their 'methodology' (Billig, 2013).

Secondly, it is not mere length that gave the word 'association' its edge. According to the linguist Michael Halliday (2006), scientists in Locke's day needed to be grammatical revolutionaries. They were not just naming new 'things', as Locke did when naming different types of ideas and when Harvey linguistically separated 'veins' from 'arteries'. They were inventing names for processes that occur over time. Previously processes would have been described by verbal clauses. For example, Newton in his *Opticks* begins by describing how glass refracts light, but soon he transforms this verbal clause ('glass refracts light') into a single noun 'refraction'. The replacement of verbal clauses by a noun or noun phrase was, in Halliday's view, essential for the development of science for it enables scientists to formulate theories of processes – theories of refraction, vibration and association. The process becomes, as it were, a thing or an object to be investigated and theorised.

There is a good linguistic reason why in the human sciences formulating nouns or noun phrases to describe actions does not necessarily lead to greater precision. Verbal clauses contain more information than a noun that has been formed from a verb. If writers use a verb in the active voice to describe an action then they have to specify the subject who performs that action. When Locke describes the act of joining ideas together, he specifies who or what is doing the joining. In section 5, Locke describes natural connections that 'the office and excellency of our reason ... hold together'; in the following section Locke describes 'the combination of ideas' that 'the mind makes in itself either voluntarily or by chance'; in section 11, Locke talks hypothetically that a man, who has received something from another man, 'cements those two ideas together'; and in section 14, he describes how one image 'brought back' another image.

In these examples, Locke is indicating different subjects who join ideas together: 'our reason', 'the mind', 'a man' and 'an image'. Is there a difference when a person or a mind links ideas together? Is it a conscious or unconscious process? If the analyst merely says that there has been an association of ideas, then such tricky questions can be avoided. In modern psychological writing, authors commonly describe processes being caused or causing other processes without specifying any human agents of these processes. Hartley provided an early foretaste with his principle that vibrations will cause associations and associations will be the effect of vibrations. He expressed his principle in a person-free statement.

An originator of a new term cannot control how others will use his or her linguistic innovation. In the standard histories of psychology, Locke is credited for inventing 'association' as a psychological term because others, such as Hartley, Mill, Bain and James, picked up the concept and passed it on to twentieth-century psychologists. These thinkers, whether notables or under-labourers, are likely to use the term for their own purposes and in different ways. In consequence, the term will gather new meanings, just like a small snowball pushed down a hill will increase in size. There are no linguistic police to enforce that subsequent users will abide by the originator's usage or definition. This is the problem when terminology becomes successful. As Locke grew older and his *Essay* was proving to be a success, he worried that the clear and distinct ideas of his younger self were in danger of becoming distinctly cloudy.

Polishing Philosophical Prose

In all this discussion of Locke and his revisions, Shaftesbury seems to have been forgotten. Locke's pursuit of conceptual clarity was not for Shaftesbury. Unlike Locke, Shaftesbury did not find himself having to create labels for the entities that he had created through finer and finer distinctions. His holism paralleled linguistically the ways by which categories can accumulate more and varied meanings when they are widely used. Shaftesbury, philosophically and in his own practices of writing, did not seek to avoid this gathering of meanings around commonly used words. In fact, he wanted his writings to echo, rather than reform, such meanings.

We can see the different priorities of Locke and Shaftesbury as they revised their books in the knowledge that they only had limited time left to them. Locke in his later years lived as a permanent house guest in the home of Damaris Cudworth, who by now was Damaris Masham, having married the good-natured country gentleman Sir Francis Masham. We can imagine Locke at his desk, searching for ever clearer distinctions and in the process increasing the length of his already overlong *Essay*. Shaftesbury revised *Characteristicks* for its second and final revised edition when he was still a comparatively young man. His weak lungs were becoming ever weaker, and he divided his time between his estates in

Dorset and the sun of Italy. With his revisions he did not seek conceptual clarity of key terms such as 'common sense' but to put some beauty into his prose.

If humans have a natural sense of beauty, then in Shaftesbury's view philosophers have a duty to strive to make their writing elegant. In the first and second editions of *Characteristicks*, Shaftesbury complained about the current standard of philosophical writing, which, he said, was full of 'gouty joints', of 'whereuntos', 'wherebys' and 'thereofs'. Philosophers were producing sentences that were 'curiously hooked on, one to another' and demonstrating no concern for 'the cadency of words' (1714/2001, p. 450). They were using words, he wrote, like the hammers of a paper mill (p. 451). Loyalty and good manners kept him from citing the writings of his 'foster father' or, indeed, naming any philosophical writer guilty of such faults.

When Shaftesbury made changes for his posthumously published second edition, he concentrated on reconstructing sentences, balancing paragraphs and generally improving the rhythm of his words. He also added an extra essay on Hercules to the final volume of the book. Unlike Locke he did not add new sub-sections, new chapters or new terminology in order to clarify or qualify his arguments. Shaftesbury's revisions were what he termed, following the Roman poet Horace, *limae labor* or the work of polishing. He criticised English philosophical writers for not polishing their prose. They seemed to fear, he wrote, that if they tried to write eloquently, then their learning would be called into question (1711, Vol. III, p. 258; 1714/2001, p. 448).

Shaftesbury might have been thinking of the passage in the *Essay* when Locke voiced his suspicion of flowery, figurative language: 'If we would speak of things as they are, we must allow that all the art of rhetoric, besides order and clearness, all the artificial and figurative application of words eloquence hath invented, are for nothing else but to insinuate wrong ideas, move the passions and thereby mislead the judgment; and so indeed are perfect cheats' (III, xi, 34). In his lectures delivered to students at Glasgow University, Adam Smith used similar arguments against Shaftesbury's style, which he said had sacrificed 'precision and propriety' for 'a grand and pompous diction' (1983, p. 146); using a metaphor to complain about the use of metaphors, Smith complained that Shaftesbury was lost in 'a dungeon of metaphorical obscurity' (p. 13).

Shaftesbury used his final months to continue polishing his words. In this, of course, he was not behaving like a modern analyst of the mind. Today, cognitive scientists, along with other academic psychologists and social scientists, are under extreme pressure to keep publishing again and

again in so-called high-ranking, small-circulation journals. The editors of
such journals prefer technical terminology rather than words that have
been selected for their cadence and then have been polished laboriously.
In this regard the editors of psychology journals and their authors are
much more Locke than Shaftesbury.

Shaftesbury's philosophy of language was very different to Locke's.
Whereas Locke, in his linguistic atomism, was seeking to link conceptual
categories to distinct ideas and to link distinct ideas to single categories,
Shaftesbury's philosophy was travelling in the opposite direction. He did
not wish to reduce the different meanings of key terms so as to establish
a semantic landscape with clearly bordered fields. His landscape was
more rugged, more overgrown.

Shaftesbury played with the different meanings of a term such as
'common sense', letting his own use of the word echo its various common
meanings. Being a classicist, Shaftesbury let the English phrase 'common
sense' also echo with the meanings of *sensus communis*, especially as used
by Juvenal. In the second chapter of *Characteristicks*, entitled '*Sensus
communis*, an essay on the freedom of wit and humour in a letter to
a friend', Shaftesbury used 'common sense' and its Latin equivalent to
indicate amongst other things: a sense of social responsibility; a sense of
social identity; common or ordinary beliefs, as opposed to the beliefs of
philosophers; good sense; the good sense that philosophers lack; the
instinct or sense to have social feelings.

Shaftesbury wrote as if there were inner connections between these
different meanings and as if these inner connections contained their own
meanings. In this way, he was not trying to undo the social and intellectual
processes by which widely used words gather meanings. Just as poets do
not seek to tidy up the echoes of language, so Shaftesbury sought understanding through these patterns of accumulated meaning. This was the
rhetorical and poetic practice of his linguistic holism. Significantly,
Shaftesbury praised the language of Plato's dialogues which he said
showed 'real characters and manners' and 'were in themselves a kind of
poetry' (1714/2001, p. 87).

The history of psychology's language has been on the side of Locke, not
Shaftesbury. However, there have been proponents of the tendency to
gather meanings within single terms, rather than to seek conceptual
tidiness. Thomas Reid, the eighteenth-century Scottish philosopher
who claimed that his work followed the principles of common sense,
sought to demolish Locke's analysis of the mind, which he believed had
paved the way to Hume's anti-religious scepticism. As a highly religious
man, Reid did not openly associate himself with Shaftesbury because he
feared that the earl's reputation for questioning Christianity would cast

a shadow over his own work. Nevertheless, Reid followed Shaftesbury in playing with the meanings of 'common sense'. He argued that it was generally 'common sense' (good sense) to side with 'common sense' (ordinary belief) against the ideas of those philosophers like Locke, who showed little common sense when they ignored the common sense of ordinary people. Reid has attracted some, but not many, followers in modern psychology, the most important being J. J. Gibson, who in the mid twentieth century devised the ecological approach to studying perception. Gibson (1983) certainly sided with Reid's commonsensical approach to the mind over Locke's theory of ideas.

There have been other modern analysts who have thought it important to examine the human mind by playing with the combined meanings of key concepts. Kenneth Burke, who was both a poet and a theorist of rhetoric, strongly opposed, as Shaftesbury did, systems of thinking. The nature of human communication was, according to Burke, inherently ambiguous; this ambiguity would be lost in any classificatory scheme that aimed to clarify everything. Accordingly, Burke pursued a rhetorical approach that mischievously aimed to be unsystematic. In his *Philosophy of Literary Form*, Burke wrote in praise of gaining insight by adopting a strategy of incongruity, which involved taking a word out of its usual usage 'so as to see round the corner of everyday usage' (Burke, 1974, p. 400; see Simons, 2007). Burke's method of incongruity expanded rather than contracted the meanings of key concepts; his dialogical and playful writing style, like that of Shaftesbury, was essential to his philosophy (Henderson, 2017).

Hannah Arendt was another philosopher who valued a poetic approach to meaning. She particularly admired Walter Benjamin whom she called a philosopher with the mind of a poet (Arendt, 1973). In her writings, she liked words to echo with different meanings, shifting, like Shaftesbury, from one meaning to another without confusing readers. After she moved to America from Germany, she feared that she would be unable to write like this in English. However, she soon learnt to, but found, as English became her first language for writing, that she had lost her ability to write German poetically (Knott, 2015). In *Life of the Mind*, Arendt stressed the links between philosophy and poetry. She wrote that language's greatest gift to thinking, and hence to philosophy, was metaphor, which 'itself is poetic rather than philosophical in origin' (Arendt, 1978, p. 105).[5] The

---

[5] Arendt often traced familiar words back to their etymological roots to show how they gathered, changed and lost meanings over time: see, for example, her discussion of the word 'philosophy' as a prelude to the section in which she explores the nature of thinking in *Life of the Mind* (1978). Janover (2011) gives the example of the word 'world' and the

organised definitions of a Locke were not for her. As we have seen, her conception of thinking, like Shaftesbury's, was dialogical.

Within psychology, the rejection of clear and distinct concepts can be seen in John Shotter's 'poetics'; in his view it was not sufficient to resist experimentalism theoretically and methodologically but it needed also to be resisted rhetorically by creating a new poetics (Shotter, 2005a, 2005b). When I claimed thinking to be argumentative, I played with two main meanings of 'argument' (as a quarrel and as a piece of extended, reasoned discourse). I assumed that the connection between the two meanings was significant and that to exclude one in favour of the other would be to miss the point (Billig, 1987). The present book does the same with the word 'example'. I do not define 'example'; nor do I try to choose between 'example' as an instance of a category and 'example' as a model to follow, as if the word should only bear one meaning. My strategy is to examine historically how various psychological writers have used examples, and I do this in the hope of finding writers who can be presented as examples to follow.

Examples of Examples

Both Locke and Shaftesbury used examples in their analyses of the mind, but they did so in different ways. Locke, fitting Diderot's characterisation of him as an organiser and not an imaginative thinker, backed up his theoretical distinctions with examples. Shaftesbury was much more expansive in his examples, matching them not to theoretical categories but to real-life dilemmas of thinking. Here we see a possible pattern with a much wider significance. Regarding the mind, there is a tension between theory and examples – a tension between emphasising general psychological features and examining specific cases.

Of the two, Locke is the theorist, who is systematising the various processes of the mind. His examples are often hypothetical instances, which he presents with minimum details, and they are designed to illustrate the mental categories that he is distinguishing. In the chapter on association in the sub-section about 'antipathies', Locke offers the instance of a person who has felt sick because he has eaten too much honey, then associates the idea of honey with feeling sick: 'A grown person surfeiting with honey, no sooner hears the name of it, but his fancy immediately carries sickness and qualms to his stomach, and he cannot bear the very idea of it' (II, xxxiii, vii). It is the sort of sequence that

concept of 'worldliness' as an illustration of how Arendt used the various meanings of a word to explore new ideas.

many years later Pavlov would describe as a form of negative conditioning: the unconditioned response of being sick after over-eating honey becomes associated with, or conditioned to, the word 'honey' as a conditioned response (Pavlov, 1955).

In Locke's example, there are no details except those that are strictly necessary for the example to be an example. It is the outline of a plot rather than a proper story. Locke does not tell us how the surfeiting of honey occurred or the sequence of feelings that the surfeiter feels after hearing someone uttering the word 'honey'. Nor does Locke say how a habitual drinker can be sick without developing an antipathy to alcohol. The central character of the honey example is not an actual person who has a life outside of the honey incident. He only exists as a type in order to support Locke's theoretical distinctions. Locke has offered what the anthropologist Clifford Geertz would call a 'thin description' (Geertz, 1973).

Some of Shaftesbury's examples are much more descriptive, as he provides the reader with the sort of surplus details that Locke excludes. As would be expected of an admirer of Plato, when Shaftesbury uses lengthy examples to make his points, he introduces his readers to characters and their lives. One example comes in the first section of his chapter on giving advice to an author. Like Locke, he uses his story to support a philosophical point – in this instance, that humans can be 'two persons in one individual self' (1714/2001, p. 83). In practically all other respects, Shaftesbury's example differs from Locke's example of the honey-surfeiter.

There is the obvious difference in length. Locke's example occupies only a couple or so lines and the details are minimal. Shaftesbury takes his example from a story told by Xenophon. In the first edition of *Characteristicks*, the story takes up ten pages (1711, pp. 175–85) and it is filled with details that are superfluous to Shaftesbury's main point. The story has three central characters: 'a virtuous young prince of a heroic soul', a beautiful princess and a nobleman (1714/2001, p. 80). None of the characters is identified by a name, nor is the country in which the story occurs. To modern sensibilities, it sounds more like a fairy tale than an actual piece of history, as if it could start 'Once upon a time, in a far-away land, there lived a good prince ...'. However, given Xenophon's reputation as a historian, Shaftesbury offers it as a story that might actually have happened.

In the story the honourable prince successfully wages war on a tyrant and he takes a beautiful princess captive. He then appoints a young nobleman to take care of the princess. The young nobleman constantly urges the prince to visit the princess, for she is in his eyes the most beautiful woman in the world and, thus, a fitting match for the prince. However, the prince resists the temptation of seeing her. The young nobleman falls in love with the captive but she spurns him. Rejected, he threatens to take her by violence. He begins to fall into melancholy and fails to fulfil his duties to the prince. Finally, the prince summons the nobleman but does not punish him for his failures. Instead the prince urges the nobleman to tear himself away from the princess but questions whether he will be able to do so. The young nobleman answers that he can now do what he could not do before because he has learnt that 'I have ... within me two distinct separate souls'. He adds, 'this lesson of philosophy I have learned from that villainous sophister, Love' (1714/2001, p. 83).

Locke's *Essay* does not contain any such storytelling about love or any other villainous sophister.

Self-Discourse and Self-Analysis

Shaftesbury's story about the prince, the nobleman and the beautiful princess is not just an example to show that we can possess more than one self – a theory of mind that would be developed by William James, whose work is discussed in the next chapter. Nor is it just an example to show that our desires can conflict with our duties in ways that Freud would recognise. There is something else in the story that is close to the heart of Shaftesbury's philosophical (or psychological) practice. Xenophon's story touches on themes basic to the stoic philosophy that Shaftesbury tried to practice in his own life. This is a story about the way that a young man comes to understand his own desires and thereby his own self. Moreover, this self-knowledge is not just theoretical but it has the practical benefit of the young man being able to free himself from his obsession with the princess and to exert control over his desires. Stoic philosophers, such as Epictetus and Marcus Aurelius, would have approved of the moral. Many years later, Freud would not disagree that knowledge about oneself, and especially about one's less than virtuous desires, should be practical, rather than theoretical, knowledge.

The example of the nobleman coming to self-awareness illustrates a paradox in the history of psychology. Locke, as was suggested earlier, has been hailed as the founder of empirical psychology. However, his *Essay* does not provide a plan for further research into the mind. As the supposed founder of a methodologically minded science, Locke was offering no method to show how we can increase our knowledge of the mind in general or how to make psychological discoveries in specific cases. It is the classicist foster son, and not the scientific foster father, who provided a method for discovering psychological knowledge.

This method can be found in the exercise of what Shaftesbury called 'self-converse' (1714/2001, p. 75) or 'self-discoursing practice' (p. 74). If we divide ourselves into two and then conduct an internal dialogue questioning our own motives about specific matters, then we can gain knowledge about ourselves. This was important because Shaftesbury upheld that all knowledge rested on self-knowledge. As he wrote, 'wisdom as well as charity may be honestly said "to begin at home"' (p. 85).

To illustrate how we ought to probe ourselves, Shaftesbury imagines a self-dialogue in which someone is questioning, defending and finally exposing his own motives. How would you react, the character asks of himself (and in Shaftesbury's examples, it is always a male who is self-conversing), if someone else acted in this way? The character counters with a justification: 'And for what reason has the greatest rogue in nature for not doing thus?' But that is the point, the answer comes. Back and forth it goes, until the character seems to persuade himself of his wrong-doing by asking why 'I belie my own interest and, by keeping myself half-knave, approve myself a thorough fool?' (1714/2001, pp. 78–9). This self-questioning, Shaftesbury is saying, is the way to knowledge about the way our mind works.

This sort of self-knowledge, however, is not easily attained. The problem is that it involves using 'a language we can by no means endure to hold with ourselves, whatever raillery we may use with others' (1714/2001, p. 79). We would normally cut ourselves short before reaching a point of disturbing self-insight. We can direct the self-conversation to exclude troubling turns of questioning, or we can end the conversation, claiming that we have fully answered the questions that we have been directing against ourselves. We might do this because we are motivated to avoid knowing about ourselves: 'to appear fools, madmen or varlets to ourselves and prove it to our own faces that we are really' that is something that we find 'insupportable' (p. 79).

What the young nobleman in Xenophon's story discovers in himself is something troubling: he is 'passionate for virtue and vice, desirous of contraries' (p. 83). As Freud would later argue, our sense of morality (and of reason) conflicts with our basic desires, which we repress or hide from ourselves. Moreover, according to Freud, we resist uncomfortable knowledge which, in the words of Shaftesbury, we cannot endure with ourselves. Here is not an equal division between two selves but something altogether more unbalanced.

To use Shaftesbury's, but not Freud's, terms, there is a conflict between our appetites and our reasons, but, as Freud would also suggest, Shaftesbury declares that the victory in this uneven conflict typically goes to our appetites, the stronger of the two. Shaftesbury employs a metaphor: 'Appetite, which is the elder brother to Reason, being the lad of stronger growth, is sure, on every contest, to take the advantage of drawing all to his own side' (p. 84). So, we hide our baser motives from ourselves: a man can 'scarce dare tell himself his wishes' (p. 78). To use the language of Freud, we show resistance to any attempt to reveal our repressed desires.

Therefore, in our internal dialogues, we face the temptation not to expose the older, stronger sibling and to keep our desires hidden from ourselves. Yet the desires whose existence is denied continue to tempt. Shaftesbury suggests that our appetites 'are strangely subtle and insinuating', possessing the ability 'to speak by nods and winks' and thereby they 'conceal half their meaning'. It is the goal of self-discourse to force these insinuating and hidden appetites into the open, 'to declare themselves' (pp. 84–5). That is why the practice of self-dialogue is both so necessary and so difficult.

Something analogous occupied a crucial place in the history of psychoanalysis. As we will see in Chapter 4, it was not by conversing with his neurotic patients that Freud came to the conclusion that all humans, and not just neurotics, have hidden, repressed desires which are derived from childhood. Only when Freud conducted his self-analysis – a particular and peculiar type of self-dialogue – did Freud come to the conclusion that everyone has shameful desires, insinuating themselves by half-hidden nods and winks, but kept from clear, distinct conscious awareness. Freud identified those desires as sexual and aggressive, whereas Shaftesbury wrote more decorously about unidentified appetites.

There is a further parallel between Freud and Shaftesbury and their respective techniques of self-analysis and self-dialogue. Neither writer published accounts with examples to show exactly how they engaged in such conversations with themselves. Freud must have divided himself between an imagined analyst and a patient. Interestingly, when Shaftesbury wrote about self-questioning, he said that we become our own patient, and he referred to the ancient belief that 'we had each of us a patient in ourself' and were properly 'our own subject of practice' (1714/2001, p. 77). Freud, to be sure, published some of the results of his self-analysis but not the process itself. We will see that his published self-revelations can also be self-concealments. In *Characteristicks* Shaftesbury presents the imaginary self-dialogues of other people or recounts stories like that of the prince and the nobleman, but he does not reveal his own internal debates.

Stoic Rhetoric

Shaftesbury's private notes contain more details about his inner conversations. The philosopher Benjamin Rand collected and published these notes in 1900, along with some of Shaftesbury's previously unpublished correspondence. Rand entitled Shaftesbury's notes about his self-dialogue his 'Regimen' – a disciplined exercise that Shaftesbury regularly practised and that he called his 'exercises' (Shaftesbury, 1900). Even then, Shaftesbury's notes only cover half of the self-dialogue. He presents his questions, but not his answers. He does not take the risk of committing his personal secrets to paper.

The Regimen reveals Shaftesbury questioning himself about everyday decisions. At one point he poses the question whether he should go out on a social visit. 'Learn to be with self, to talk with self. Commune with thy own heart' (1900, p. 144). Ask yourself what sort of company you would be keeping, what you will gain from seeking out others; is it genuine friendship or just a desire for 'talk and story'? 'Is this what prompts thee in the case? Is this the affection that draws thee to the sociable acts and commerce with mankind?' (p. 144). And if his motive is not genuine friendship, then he should remain at home. Here Shaftesbury is only presenting the questioning voice of his two-voiced internal dialogue. Moreover, he does not pose his questions in relation to a particular visit to an actual acquaintance. Similarly, Freud was to leave no specific case notes of his own self-analysis.

There is no evidence that Shaftesbury ever intended to publish his Regimen. The prose is not polished like the text of *Characteristicks*, but he is careful not to divulge too much about himself. Most of the questions that he asks are general. Readers of Rand's edition can adapt these questions to ask them of themselves, just as Shaftesbury adapted some of his questions from his hero Marcus Aurelius, the stoic philosopher who also held the position of Roman emperor. Marcus Aurelius' *Meditations*, too, were addressed to himself and were not intended for publication. In fact, they were not published until the sixteenth century.

It has been suggested that the stoics practised a definite rhetorical style which comprises two major features (Stroud, 2012; see also Hadot, 1995). The first feature is that stoic authors posed many rhetorical questions, which, in the cases of Shaftesbury and Marcus Aurelius, are addressed to themselves. The other feature is that stoic writers tended to use vivid examples as they tried to persuade themselves and their pupils to imagine situations in which they are facing difficult moral choices. By exploring vivid examples one can gain knowledge about oneself. Thus, Shaftesbury's detailed examples are not just literary adornments, but they are part of his philosophical practice.

According to the stoic, the imagining of examples can lead to the sort of self-knowledge that is the basis of all knowledge. We can see clearly the difference between Shaftesbury's (and also Marcus Aurelius') use of examples and that of Locke. For Shaftesbury, examples are means of exploration in the pursuit of self-knowledge; for Locke, they illustrate theoretical distinctions and need not be explored further. We might also note what Arendt wrote in relation to examples. She suggested that if we want to understand the nature of thinking, then we need an example, not a generalised theory. When professional philosophers ask about the nature of thinking, we only get answers that 'are too general and vague to have much sense for everyday living' (1978, p. 166). Instead of proceeding abstractly through professional philosophy, we need 'a model, an example of a thinker who was not a professional' (p. 167). Her example, unsurprisingly, was Socrates. He would have also been Shaftesbury's choice.[6]

There may be similarities between Freud's self-analysis and Shaftesbury's self-converse, or between Shaftesbury and Arendt, but care should be taken in assessing what, if any, historical significance such similarities have. These are the sort of similarities that historians tend to avoid drawing attention to, especially if there is no direct historical connection, or a chain of historical associations. We can say that Locke, and especially his chapter on the association of ideas, prefigured cognitive psychology and even prefigured behaviourism; we can say this because there are historically substantiated links with intervening psychologists. However the same can hardly be said about Shaftesbury and Arendt, except that they both read and admired the same classical texts. In the case of Shaftesbury and psycho-analysis the historical links are even weaker. While Freud was engaged in his most intense period of his self-analysis, Shaftesbury's notes remained unpublished deep in the London Records Office. When Rand published them, neither Freud nor his followers seemed to notice or to connect them with the practices of psycho-analysis.

Historians who have traced the development of psychology's experimental methods have also ignored Shaftesbury's methods. If experimentalists had known of his methods, most would have dismissed them as non-scientific, just as most of them dismissed Freud's methods as inappropriate for 'proper', scientific psychology.

---

[6] Arendt's comment that we need an 'example' is itself an example of her using a word to convey at least two principal senses that are related but different. She is saying that we need an instance – possibly even a typical instance – of a thinker because abstract categories will not convey what a thinker is like and how thinking takes place in life. By her choice of an instance and by the high value that she places upon thinking, she is simultaneously treating her example of Socrates as an example to be followed. She is, in effect, also saying that Socrates sets an example to us all because he exemplifies the practical virtues of thinking. Unlike the professional philosophers, whom she disparages in this passage and elsewhere, she is not trying to distinguish different meanings, but she is seeking insight through using them simultaneously.

Experimentalists tend to claim that they seek general discoveries, to be applied to humans as a whole, rather than discoveries that are particular to an individual case. However, as will be argued later, it is too simple to dismiss Freud as only being concerned with the particular case of a particular patient.

The analysis of particulars can be a means of gaining general insights, and this is why Marie Jahoda described Freud as being scientific (see Chapter 8). It is also why Kurt Lewin argued that experiments that should be designed and analysed as particular case studies (see Chapter 6). It is also why Arendt used Socrates as her model for thinking and why Shaftesbury claimed that the Platonic dialogues enabled us to know others and also that 'they taught us to know ourselves' (1714/2001, p. 87). In the same vein, Shaftesbury's self-discoursing exercises might have brought him insights about himself, but he never saw those insights as being confined to the particular case of himself. Like other stoic philosophers, he believed that self-knowledge was the route to wider wisdom. As he wrote in *Characteristicks*, 'he who deals in characters must of necessity know his own or he will know nothing' (1714/2001, p. 85).

After more than 300 years, the contrast between Locke's and Shaftesbury's visions of the mind remains sharp. The textbooks of psychology give the plaudits to Locke: the empiricist, the founder of 'associationism', the early modern psychologist and so on. Shaftesbury's influence on psychology has at best been indistinct and indirect. Yet, his views on the dialogical nature of thinking still persist. The fact that the debate about the nature of thinking continues itself points in favour of Shaftesbury. History has not cleared up the rubble that Locke was hoping to sweep aside. There is always more to say and more to think about – and the piles of rubble increase.

There are other lessons to be gained from remembering the contrast between 'foster father' and 'foster son'. Locke and Shaftesbury demonstrated how to differ respectfully, even affectionately. They also showed that analysts, who have opposing ways of understanding the mind, may do more than use different theoretical concepts, follow different procedures, use different sorts of example and strike different balances between theory and examples. They may also have different ways of writing and what analysts do with their words can be very much part of their ideas about the mind. There are many ways that we can treat words. We can take a knife to them, chopping their meanings into bits and then attaching new labels to those bits; we can stick words together in awkward gluey lumps; and we can treat them like precious jewels, endlessly polishing and re-polishing them, on the off chance they might reflect back a little more light.

3   Tucker and James
In the Same Stream of Thought

By comparing Locke with Shaftesbury, I was putting side by side two thinkers with contrasting views of the mind and very different styles of writing. Their intellectually opposing positions, formulated before psychology existed as an academic discipline, were pointing towards distinctly different ways of doing psychology. The twist was that the two men knew each other well and were bound by close personal ties. Another type of comparison forms the basis for the present chapter. Two thinkers, living in different ages, with the one enjoying great, continuing fame and the other on the receiving end of widespread neglect, formulated very similar views of the mind and wrote in comparable ways. Both were great exponents of finding, and then describing, apt examples on which to build their highly original views of the mind.

Their contrasting fortunes of fame would be understandable had it been the earlier thinker who was the feted figure. But it is the other way round. Abraham Tucker, whose whole life was lived in the eighteenth century, died more than seventy years before the birth of William James. There will be no suggestion that James cheated to gain his fame by appropriating ideas from Tucker and then presenting them as if they had been his own – no suggestion of that at all. Neither of the two would have behaved so dishonourably.

Abraham Tucker (1705–74) produced one major work, *The Light of Nature Pursued* (1768–77), whose multiple volumes developed Locke's theory of mind in an interesting and highly original manner. I know of no history of psychology – whether the early histories by Baldwin (1913) and Boring (1929) or more recent works such as Richards (2002), Alexander and Shelton (2014) and Walsh, Teo and Baydala (2014) – that discusses Tucker's ideas. I only know of one, Greenwood's *Conceptual History of Psychology* (2015), which mentions Tucker, and then only with a passing reference in one-half of a sentence on a single page (p. 123). Martin and Barresi (2000) do discuss Tucker, but their book, *Naturalization of the Soul*, is not a general history of psychology but a specialised work that examines a specific issue in eighteenth-century theories of mind, namely the turn from religious to material explanations. Their discussion of

Tucker concentrates on a different aspect of his work than does the present discussion. It is safe to assume that virtually no students of psychology's history, and very few of their teachers, have ever heard of Abraham Tucker, let alone read him.

William James did not mention Tucker in his great work of psychology, *The Principles of Psychology* (1890), which took him twelve years to write. In contrast to Tucker and his *Light of Nature*, neither James nor his *Principles* has been neglected. David Leary, in his excellent *Guidebook to James's 'Principles of Psychology'* (2018), points out that the *Principles* seems never to have been out of print since it was first published more than 125 years ago. To this day it rightly commands attention, admiration and, above all, affection. James has been appreciated by such diverse psychologists as Edwin Boring, Lev Vygotsky and John Watson, as well as by other historically important thinkers, including George Herbert Mead, Jorge Luis Borges and Ludwig Wittgenstein (Leary, 1990, 2018). The praise continues. One historian of psychology has claimed that James' *Principles* contains the richest descriptions of human experience in non-fictional writing (Wozniak, 1999). The psychologist and neuroscientist Antonio Damasio (2006) has written that only Shakespeare and Freud equal James' understanding of human behaviour (p. 129). If the histories of psychology ignore Tucker, then all of them give honourable mention to James. A history of psychology without William James would be like a history of the United States without Abraham Lincoln.

During his lifetime James was hailed as an important, original theorist of the mind. His admirers tended to select two aspects of his psychological work for special mention. The philosopher F. C. S. Schiller claimed that James made 'a great discovery when he described consciousness as a stream' (1930/1996, p. 149). James Angell, who worked as James' research assistant at Harvard and later became professor of psychology at the University of Chicago, pointed to the concept of habit as 'the most important interpretative principle' running through James' work (1911/ 1996, p. 135). Both these ideas – the mind as a stream and the importance of habit – can be found in Tucker's book.

In addition, James has been praised as a great writer who discussed human experience with wit and humanity. Leary refers to 'the magic of James's writing' (2018, p. 16), calling him 'one of the great prose stylists of his generation' (p. 21). Angell described *The Principles of Psychology* as 'perhaps the only thoroughly entertaining account of reasoning that we have in the English language' (p. 136). Leslie Stephen, the English writer and historian, who today is better known for being the father of Virginia Woolf and Vanessa Bell, wrote in his *History of English Thought in the*

Eighteenth Century, 'He was an example of that rarest of all intellectual compounds, the metaphysical humourist' (1876, Vol. II, p. 110). He could have been writing about James, but he wasn't. In fact, James had not yet begun writing *Principles* when Stephen wrote those words. The quotation comes from Stephen's section on Tucker. Angell's statement about James' uniqueness as an author writing entertainingly on the mind could only have come from someone who had not read Tucker.

In this chapter, I have four principal aims, three of which are analytic. The first is to show the similarities between Tucker and James as analysts of the mind and as writers, despite the historical gap between them. This is something that, as far as I am aware, others have not yet attempted. Second, I want to show that as writers about the mind both Tucker and James showed flair in using examples. The third aim is to suggest why the use of examples is so important for understanding psychological phenomena; and why the sort of talent for examples that James and Tucker possessed should not be considered as the poor relation of talents for theoretical thinking, for when exercised well, this talent cuts into the province of theory.

The fourth and final aim is less analytic: it is to introduce the work of Tucker to readers for whom Tucker remains a pleasure to be discovered. 'I have always held the opinion', wrote William James, 'that one of the first duties of a good reader is to summon other readers to the enjoyment of any unknown author of rare quality whom he may discover in his explorations' (1911, p. 371). When James wrote those words, he was recommending a neglected writer from his own times. It is also possible to stumble across a neglected writer of rare quality from the distant past. Reading is an individual activity, but, when without warning we find ourselves smiling with sudden pleasure, then, like James, we want to leap from our solitary seat to share our delight with others. Any scholarly analysis in this chapter is, I suspect, an excuse to act like James' good reader. As well as summoning others to the pleasures of Tucker, I hope to be sharing my enjoyment of James.

History and Analysing Historically

I will be suggesting that Tucker is an early Jamesian, at least with respect to his views on the mind and the way he expressed those views. Making this suggestion must involve some small awareness of psychology's history; but, to a far greater degree, it requires a readiness to disrupt that history by jumping over time to connect Tucker with a figure from a very different historical period. These days, historians of ideas often fear being accused of 'presentism', or interpreting the past in terms of the present rather than understanding the past on its own terms. If historians analyse particular thinkers from the past, they will, quite understandably, seek to place those thinkers in their historical context. However, that is no guarantee that they are avoiding the supposed sin of presentism, especially if they try to understand past figures in the light of present debates. Roger Smith, a notable historian of psychology, has argued that all history must show some elements of 'presentism' because the historian is telling stories about the past to a present audience (Smith, 1988, 2010).[1]

My aim is unashamedly 'presentist' in the sense of taking a historical approach to problems, which I see as persisting in present psychology. My primary concern is to explore the problem of examples rather than write a chronological history of those problems. This can involve comparing different ways of writing about psychological issues. In the previous chapter, Locke and Shaftesbury were compared. They might have belonged to different generations, but their lives overlapped. Yet, they wrote in very different ways that matched their different views of the mind. Because there is no chronological overlap between Tucker and James, any comparisons between the two, and especially the search for similarities, would be limited if the primary purpose were to examine each in relation to their own historical context.

It would, for instance, be possible to place Tucker firmly within an eighteenth-century British context, by pointing to similarities and differences with his contemporaries such as David Hartley, David Hume or Thomas Reid. The historian might properly emphasise that Tucker, Reid and Hartley showed a desire to combine Protestantism with the rational study of the mind, while Hume wished to expel religion from such study. The flow of Protestant intellectual history could be drawn backwards to

---

[1] Kurt Danziger and Adrian Brock have considered closely the similarities and differences between what can be called 'history of psychology' and 'historical psychology' (e.g. Brock, 2006a, 2006b, 2006c, 2016a, 2016b; Danziger, 1994b, 2002, 2003). At its simplest, the history of psychology involves trying to understand how the discipline of psychology emerged and how it has changed over time. Essentially, this means examining the past in its own terms. Danziger and Brock have recommended using the term 'historical psychology' to describe investigations of the ways that psychological states and emotional feelings might have changed over time. According to this conception, historical psychology resembles a historical counterpart of cross-cultural psychology. The present work fits neither category neatly. It is not concerned with the past for its own sake, as it aims to address current psychological issues by looking at figures from the past. Nor does it examine how experiences have changed over time. Nevertheless, Danziger and Brock also recognise that in practice the distinction between history of psychology and historical psychology is not so simple. Histories of psychology need not focus on the past exclusively but they can often celebrate or criticise the present state of psychology, whether explicitly or by implication (Danziger, 1994b; Brock, 2016b). Danziger makes no secret that his histories express his critical views on orthodox psychology, whose emergence from the past he does not celebrate.

Locke, and then it could just about be stretched forwards to William James, as if the latter represents the final bookend on the tradition's substantial shelf of works about the mind.

The dominance of 'historical context' would flatten out some of the peculiarities of the figures to be discussed. Of course, 'context' links Hartley and Tucker; and much could be written about their theological aims. Yet, at a literary and imaginative level, something unites Tucker with James and divides him from Hartley. In terms of published pages, this 'something' may represent a small proportion of what either James or Hartley wrote in total. However, the present chapter aims to do more than just compare two writers. It celebrates them and does this in front of a present audience. Such a celebration is not wholly naïve. By picking examples from the past, or from different pasts, such a tribute can, by implication, criticise the present. Between the lines, a voice is quietly nagging: 'Why can't we write a bit more like James or Tucker? Why can't we polish our words like Shaftesbury?'

For critics of the present state of psychology, this is not just a matter of retreating from the world of today to find solace in figures from the past; I hope it is also to learn from the past. As Tucker's contemporary Edmund Burke said, those who do not know history are destined to repeat it. Therefore, there is a case for picking out past figures and then bringing their ideas and ways of writing to life again, rather than bedding them down with their long departed contemporaries. A poet or storyteller from the past can break through their historical context to stride across time and to whisper in our ears with immediacy. Also a psychological writer, such as William James, can do this; and so too might Abraham Tucker, at least if we permit him the opportunity.

In his 'Theses on the Philosophy of History', Walter Benjamin, another time-strider, wrote that historians should seek to do more than create empathy with past times. Benjamin believed that moments from the past had to be rescued in order to liberate the present. For this to happen, according to Benjamin, we need to dissociate ourselves from the standard ways of writing history. To quote Benjamin's wonderful words, we should try 'to brush history against the grain' (Benjamin, 1970, p. 259). The present chapter, like other parts of this book, involves a modicum of counter-grain brushing, although at a far less significant and much more mundane level than Benjamin was envisaging. Here, the steady flow of calendrical time is being interrupted by placing side by side two writers from different ages who thought similarly about the steady flow of human consciousness.

The Life of Tucker

Abraham Tucker led an uneventful life. He did not move in the intellectual circles of his age, and unlike most other notable British thinkers of the time, he does not crop up in Boswell's records of the period. Nor did Tucker correspond with philosophical contemporaries in Continental Europe. For the most part, he lived quietly in Surrey on a large country estate near Dorking. Most of the information about his life comes from a brief biography which his grandson, St John Mildmay, wrote as a preface for a re-publication of Tucker's *The Light of Nature Pursued* (Mildmay, 1831; see also Young, 2004). Tucker's father, a wealthy merchant, died when Tucker was still a child. Having inherited the family fortune, Tucker never needed to work for a living. Unlike his contemporaries, such as Hume, Hartley and Reid, who figure much more prominently in today's histories of psychology, Tucker did not seek a university post or clerical position; nor, like Hume, did he have to rely on the sales of his books for an income. Unwilling to engage in public controversy, and being reluctant to push himself forwards, Tucker could financially afford to retreat to his country home. There he remained, pursuing his intellectual interests and attending to the education of his two daughters, Judith and Dorothea.

Tucker published nothing under his own name. He published a minor tract in 1755 and another in 1773. The first, an anonymous, light-hearted piece, was supposedly written by a country gentleman advising his son to avoid politics; in fact, Tucker had no son. The second booklet, published under the pseudonym of Edward Search, suggested how English spelling could be reformed to match phonetically the spoken word. Apart from these two booklets, Tucker's literary efforts were devoted to *Light of Nature*, which he started in 1756, two years after the death of his much loved, much missed wife, Dorothy. He published a lengthy, preliminary chapter on free will as a separate booklet in 1763, under the pseudonym of Edward Search. This booklet, *Freewill, Foreknowledge and Fate* also contained a preface by Tucker's other pseudonymous self, 'Cuthbert Comment', who described himself as Edward's cousin and a member of 'an under branch of the Searches' (Tucker, 1763, p. xxv). Mr Comment also added several footnotes to Edward Search's main text, thereby living up to his invented name.

In this way, Tucker was fulfilling Shaftesbury's idea that authors should divide themselves. In creating the personae of Search and Comment, the gentle, non-disputative Tucker was creating selves who supported each other, not who set upon each other's arguments. In his preface to *Freewill*, Comment says of his cousin that the two of them were 'cut out for one another' for he 'pleases me by furnishing me with matter to spend my thoughts upon and I please him with a fondness I know for his speculations' (1763, p. xxvi).

Following a review of *Freewill* in the magazine *Monthly Review*, Mr Comment made a spirited but good-humoured defence of his cousin in a separate booklet, *Man in Quest of Himself*. More than seventy years later, this booklet was re-published by Samuel Parr under Tucker's real name in a collection of short works by eighteenth-century English philosophers (Parr, 1837). In his reply to the *Monthly Review* Mr Comment claimed to have discovered another family member. He noted that the reviewer had mainly objected to some footnotes in *Freewill* but 'he has kindly spared the main work' (1763/1837 p. 176). Because the reviewer had treated him and his cousin in so kindly a fashion, Mr Comment concluded that he must have been a member of their family. So, in the *Monthly Review*, Cuthbert Comment referred to its reviewer as 'our good cousin Mr Monthly Comment' (p. 209).

Tucker went further than Shaftesbury in the conceit of dividing himself into different personae. He gave names and a family background to his personae. He even gave addresses. Cuthbert Comment signed off his preface for *Freewill* 'from my apartment in Search Hall, 4th October, 1762' (Tucker, 1763, p. xxxi). In chapter 10 of his *Principles of Psychology* James wrote that all of us have many different social selves; but always in his writings, William James was just plain 'William James'.

The first two volumes of *Light of Nature*, which comprised five separately printed parts, were published in 1768, under the name of Edward Search. They contained no editorial interventions from Cuthbert Comment. Tucker continued working on his great opus, finishing it shortly before his death in 1774. The last years had been difficult. He had gone totally blind as a result of cataracts, but his older daughter, Judith, helped him complete the work, transcribing her father's words and reading drafts back to him. She read aloud those books that he needed to consult and she even taught herself ancient Greek to assist with the task.

In 1777 Judith oversaw the posthumous publication of the final third volume, which consisted of four parts. She abandoned her father's literary conceit of being Search or Comment, and she ensured that the final four parts were published under his own name, each bearing the sub-title *The Posthumous Work of Abraham Tucker*. According to today's standards and sensitivities, she would deserve to be credited for her work, maybe even as the second author of that final volume, and certainly as its editor. Following the conventions of her day, she put forwards her father as the sole author, without her name appearing as a collaborator or editor. She wrote no preface drawing attention to her great labour of love.

In Judith Tucker's edition of the third volume, there was nothing to indicate that she had omitted one of the chapters, chapter XXIII, 'Word or Logos'. She feared that the chapter contained controversial remarks that would incite Anglican readers to accuse her father of being a Unitarian. At that time, Unitarians were suspected of being non-Christian because some of them considered Jesus to have been human rather than divine. When Judith's nephew, Dorothea's son St John Mildmay, re-published *Light of Nature*, he restored the missing chapter, since the fierce theological controversy over Unitarianism had by then died down. In the present work, when I quote from this missing and then restored chapter, I am taking the quotations from Mildmay's 1848 edition; otherwise I am quoting from the original first editions of the various volumes of *Light of Nature*.

Publication of the *Light of Nature* in its entirety was not sufficient to make Judith's late father famous. A couple of illustrations will show just how unknown Tucker was. The first is somewhat personal. I am fortunate to have in my possession several volumes of *Light on Nature* from the first edition of 1768. One of them was owned by Samuel Parr, who in 1837 would re-publish Tucker's *Man in Quest of Himself*. Parr, a man of great scholarship and cantankerous eccentricity, was known in his lifetime as the Whig Doctor Johnson (Derry, 1966). Unlike Tucker, Parr was well connected with the intellectual world of England. He had the habit of scribbling notes in his books. On one of the blank preliminary pages of my book, Parr had written in his characteristic scrawl that the 'author of this book was a Mr Tucker who lived in Bettesworth [*sic*] castle near Dorking' and that he 'married a daughter of Sarah Parker'. Significantly, Parr was not writing about the book's contents but he was seeking to remind himself of the social position of an author about whom he knew just a few details. For the author to be merely 'a Mr Tucker' (and certainly not 'the Mr Tucker') shows just how far he and his Dorking home were from London's literary life.

On his death Tucker was mourned by family and close friends, but his passing hardly bothered the outside world. Every year *The Annual Register* recorded the notable political and literary happenings of the previous year. The 1769 edition did not include Tucker's work when it reviewed the noteworthy books which had been published during 1768; and it failed to mention Tucker in its chronologically arranged list of prominent deaths for 1774. It recorded the death of the town clerk for the City of London, who died a few days before Tucker; and then it listed the death of a co-heiress to a Lincolnshire landowner, who died a week later (*Annual Register*, 1775, pp. 198–9). In between these two listings, there is nothing to record the passing of the author of *Light of Nature*.

Tucker's Project

Even Tucker's most dedicated admirers have to admit that *Light of Nature* is not a tightly structured work. It digresses, as Tucker allows his imagination to wander down some quirky byways. This is particularly pronounced in the last volume, which was written when the author could no longer read his own drafts and may have forgotten what was in his early volumes. Nevertheless, his basic project is clear: he wished to present a case for rational Christianity, opposing both materialist atheism and the bigotry of unreasoning faith. There was nothing unusual in the project itself. Rational Christianity for Tucker meant faith rooted in a rational understanding of nature. God had established 'the laws of nature' and so any Christian philosophy 'proceeds by the study of nature', including human nature (Tucker, 1848, p. 462). The first volume of *Light of Nature* was subtitled 'Human Nature', whilst the second volume was 'Theology': the posthumously published volume bore the subtitle *Lights of Nature and Gospel Blended*.

For his volume on the study of human nature, Tucker drew inspiration from Locke's *Essay*, modestly presenting his own efforts as merely elaborating upon Locke's great insights. In his introduction, Tucker wrote that 'whatever I may be able to do I stand in indebted to Mr Locke'. It was Locke who had increased our knowledge 'by pointing out the sources and channels from whence it must be derived'. Despite his great respect for Mr Locke, Tucker wrote that he nevertheless found himself at liberty 'to dissent from him in some few instances', adding that 'this happens very seldom' (1768, I, ii, pp. xviii–xix). Tucker did not feel that he deviated from Locke on great ethical, political or theological matters. However, in downplaying his divergences from Locke, Tucker may have been doing himself less than justice. As will be suggested, his view of the way that the mind works, and just as importantly how these workings should be described, leads Tucker away from Locke and points towards James.

The idea of producing a rational Christianity, combining Locke's analysis of the mind with theology, was something that Tucker's contemporary David Hartley also attempted. As a broad project, Tucker's *Light of Nature* resembles Hartley's *Observations on Man*, which was published twenty years earlier. Both books contain two parts, of which the first part is an analysis of human psychology and the second is a theological analysis supposedly based on the first part (the *Light of Nature* also had its third, posthumously published part). As was discussed in the previous chapter, some historians of psychology have detected a modern feel to Hartley's work, because he combined Locke's notion of association with a theoretical physiology loosely derived from Newton.

The historians who see Hartley as an early, if not the first, proper empirical psychologist tend to avert their gaze from his diverse discussions, which include a justification for vegetarianism and an argument that Jews should return to Palestine.

Unlike Hartley, Tucker was not particularly attracted to specialised, technical concepts such as 'association' and 'vibration'. In fact, one of those rare matters on which Tucker outwardly dissented from Locke concerned the use of Locke's term 'association'. Locke used the term as a catch-all concept to describe the general joining together of ideas. Tucker's chapter on the issue was entitled 'The combination of ideas' (1768, I, ix). He wrote that there were two ways of combining ideas: 'by composition' when two ideas are merged together 'to form one single complex idea'. Composition differs from 'association' when ideas 'appear in couples strongly adhering to each other but not blended into the same mass' (1768, I, ix, 1, p. 221). For Tucker 'association' is a sub-division of 'combination', whereas Locke had treated the two as synonymous.

Also, Tucker dissented from Locke's tendency to reform ordinary language when its concepts failed to be sufficiently clear and distinct from one another. In his chapter on the combination of ideas, Tucker notes how words tend to become associated with a variety of meanings, which do not compound together into an overall single meaning. He gives the example of the word 'man'. It has 'various significations', such as the human species, a male, a fully grown male, a chess piece or a statue. Yet, despite these different possibilities, we never 'mistake the meaning' because the context makes clear how the word is being used (I, ix, p. 241). This is because single words do not carry the whole meaning; the structuring of a phrase and the ordering of words are also important. The management of words, adds Tucker, constitutes 'a great part of the arts of rhetoric and poetry'; according to Locke, the former was a perfect cheat, while the latter held no interest for him. Here, Tucker was siding with Shaftesbury's view of language rather Locke's – not that Tucker associated himself with the heretical earl. He certainly had no wish to blend his views with those of such a theologically dubious thinker.

Tucker distrusted Hartley's theory of vibrations as being fundamentally materialist. In Tucker's view, Hartley was reducing human action to the laws of physiology and thereby denying free will (1768, I, iv, pp. 66ff.). According to Tucker, Hartley had reduced the mind to being inactive and the will to being 'a spectator only not an agent of all we perform': Tucker saw Hartley as depicting the mind as if it were a fly on a chariot wheel, who imagines that it has created the cloud of dust but who has, in fact, done nothing to create it (I, iii, p. 50). On the other hand, Tucker believed that human experience required a body. Without eyes, ears and nervous connections to the brain, we would be unable to see or hear: 'For what is sight but an impression of things visible on our eyes and by them conveyed to the mind'. Like Locke, Tucker depicted perception as being essentially passive. It is the objects that are 'the agents' and the mind that is passive; 'it can neither see blue in a rose nor hear the sound of a trumpet from a drum' (I, i, p. 6).

Tucker was aware that, by assuming a body to be necessary for sensation and conscious awareness, he might be wandering into theologically perilous territory. If there can be no experience without a body, then this would mean that there could be no conscious life after death, when supposedly the soul has departed from the body. In the theological part of *Light of Nature* Tucker produced a mystical hypothesis to get around this difficulty. He proposed that on death the soul departs from the earthly body in a tiny body, or vehicle, that is too small to be seen by the naked human eye but which contains all the organs and internal connections of a normal body but reproduced in miniature. The soul continues to exist in this vehicular state until it ultimately progresses to the 'mundane state', when it loses its individuality and becomes at one with all previous souls.

Tucker took mystical themes seriously, but without abandoning good sense and playful humour, just as James would do many years later, especially in *Will to Believe* (1908a; see also Gitre, 2006). Tucker illustrated his idea of the tiny vehicle by describing an elaborate vision that he has died and entered into the vehicular state. In this condition he meets the equally vehicular John Locke. He imagines the dead philosopher in his tiny body greeting him warmly: 'Welcome, Ned Search, into the vehicular state ... I have observed a faint resemblance in your way of thinking with mine' (1768, II, ii, p. 127). Tucker (or Search) then has an enjoyable chat with Locke about matters philosophical and vehicular. Locke explains how he can still speak, despite lacking a mouth between his vehicular nose and disproportionally large chin. Tucker might never have actually met Locke, but he would be familiar with Locke's angular face from the engraving next to the title page in most good eighteenth-century editions of *Essay Concerning Human Understanding*.

I will not be discussing these aspects of Tucker's work (but see Martin and Barresi, 2000, for an excellent discussion of Tucker's ideas about the unity of the person). Nor will I deal with the theme that brought Tucker a little bit of posthumous fame, which, perhaps in the company of the vehicular Locke, he might have been able to observe with enjoyment. In the late eighteenth century and early part of the nineteenth, the reverend William Paley became the most important ethical philosopher in England, although he commanded neither a university post nor a bishopric. He advocated a form of Christian utilitarianism and recognised in Tucker a fellow spirit and perhaps a fellow outsider. Tucker had argued that humans do not solely pursue their own individual pleasure or happiness, as Locke seemed to have implied, but they also pursue, or rather they should also pursue, the common happiness of all (Tucker, 1777, III, i).

In the preface to his *Principles of Moral and Political Philosophy* (1791), Paley declared that Tucker's *Light of Nature* was the one work 'to which I owe so much, that it would be ungrateful not to confess the obligation' (p. xxv). Interestingly, Paley informed his readers who Tucker was and how the *Light of Nature* came to be published, as if he expected that many would not to recognise the author's name or be familiar with his book. That did not deter Paley from lavishing higher praise upon Tucker than he gave to thinkers of supposedly greater repute: 'I have found in this writer more original thinking and observation upon the several subjects that he has taken in hand than in any other, not to say, than in all others put together' (p. xxv).

A Great Exemplar: Tucker

In addition, Paley wrote that he found Tucker to be a more acute observer of human nature than other philosophers. This was because Tucker possessed a particular skill: he could use an example to go to the heart of a matter. According to Paley, 'his talent for illustration is unrivalled' (Paley, 1791, pp. xxv–xxvi). Tucker may not have had admirers in their masses, but there were some other notable individuals, besides Paley, who recognised the quality of his thinking and his writing. The poet Coleridge was an admirer. He felt, as did Paley, that the unyielding bulk of *Light of Nature*, not to mention its author's tendency to ramble down too many byways, was restricting the scope of Tucker's readership. To remedy this, Coleridge sought to encourage his friend the young William Hazlitt, who would become known as one of England's finest essayists, to produce an abridged version of *Light of Nature*. Coleridge agreed to write a preface and to help Hazlitt find a publisher (Grayling, 2000).

Coleridge and Hazlitt had talked about the possibility of an abbreviated edition in 1803, but nothing directly resulted from their conversation. However, a few years later, Hazlitt returned to the idea but this time without Coleridge's help. In 1807 he produced an abridgement, which was actually more than a simple shortening, for, to quote one of Hazlitt's biographers, his edition involved 'a vigorous rephrasing of Tucker's work, not without some rethinking' (Bromwich, 1999, p. 415). In his preface to the abridgement, Hazlitt echoed Paley's praise, writing that Tucker possessed the power of illustration 'in the highest degree' and it was 'only necessary to look into almost any page of his writings' in order to witness that power (1807, p. viii). As will be suggested later, we can see Tucker, and also James, as wonderful practitioners of the literary art of using examples and also as advocates of that art.

In his preface to *Freewill, Foreknowledge*, Tucker (as Search) discussed his approach, aims and literary style. He said that he neither expected nor sought applause for his writing: 'the Searches were never remarkable for a fondness for fame' (1763, p. xiv). Although he worked in isolation, nevertheless he took great care with his writing: 'I am sure it has cost me infinite pains to save pains to my Reader' (p. xviii). Because his topics were 'generally unentertaining and dry', he endeavoured 'to embellish them with a diversity of style in order to relieve the Reader and keep his attention awake' (p. xiii). He treated his Reader as a friend, 'as if we were sitting together over a bottle' (p. xiv). Thus, we can see Tucker, like Shaftesbury before him, as a polisher of words, as well as a writer who favoured a light miscellaneous style over a heavy, po-faced one.

Freewill, Foreknowledge had another preface, in which Tucker's other literary persona had his say. In the 'Preface of the Annotator', Cuthbert Comment wrote of his cousin that 'few since Plato have attempted to intersperse humour and gaiety among close arguments, metaphysical refinements and dissertations on the most serious subjects' (p. xxvii). His mixing of humour and religion, Comment continued, might offend some. Although both topics were 'agreeable in themselves', he conceded that others might think that 'by their commixture, as tea and snuff laid in the same drawer spoil one another's flavour' (p. xxvii). Such a remark would have been unlikely to have appeased pious readers, who might have frowned upon Search's mixing of religion and humour but would certainly not have appreciated Comment comparing religion with tea or snuff. They probably would have objected to the vision of a tiny John Locke warmly greeting Ned Search. How could the grave matter of an after-life be treated in such a flippant, fictitious fashion?

William James would also add humour to serious argument, treating his readers with kindness and not worrying about offending the sanctimonious. Hugo Münsterberg, who worked with James at Harvard, wrote that James' lectures had 'the intimate warmth of a friend' and 'the charm of a perfect artist'; and that his textbooks had 'a vividness and freshness' and students read them as if reading a novel (Münsterberg, 1907/1996, p. 109). The comparison with a novel was appropriate. It was often said that William wrote psychology like a novelist, while his brother Henry wrote novels like a psychologist.[2] William, who understood the serious

---

[2] The saying seems to have originated with Rebecca West (1916, p. 11). Psychologists and literary critics have continued to repeat it, almost as if it were a common-place (e.g. Gregory, 1994, p. 179; Crawford, Kern and Needleman, 2007, p. 211).

side of humour but who would not have wished his work to be considered as fiction, might well have taken a similar line to Tucker when the latter cautioned his Reader against treating his writing as if it were a novel 'where one has little else to do than drive on post haste to see how it ends' (1763, p. xxi).

There is a reason why some of James' readers might have read his books as if they were novels, and why Tucker might have worried lest his readers did likewise. For intellectual analysts of the mind, both took unusual pains with their words. James claimed that he wrote every page of *Principles* four or five times over (Leary, 2018, p. 23). Quite apart from their respective literary skills – and the efforts they took to acquire such skills – both James and Tucker placed great emphasis on examples. Like novelists, they respected the particular, rather than treating particulars as the mere servants of theory. James' biographer has commented that what brings *Varieties of Religious Experience* to life is its 'parade of examples' (Richardson, 2007, p. 414; see also Taylor, 2002). James' examples in that book resemble mini-stories, encapsulating moments of life and drama.

Tucker outlined his general strategy in the preface of *Freewill, Foreknowledge*. He sought understanding through 'experience and observation of ourselves' (1763, p. vii), and he would do this by examining the workings of the mind 'in the common occurrencies of life' (p. viii). In giving the reader examples of the way that the mind worked, both Tucker and James gave examples of events and actions from their own lives. Neither told stories of their philosophical ego triumphing over ignorance or implausibly doubting its own existence, but they reflected on themselves with humanity and homeliness. As Tucker wrote, 'our business lies with the common actions of life, familiar to every one's and every day's experience' (1763, p. 2).

Tucker gave examples of how he relaxed from his studies. Criticising Locke's claim that a good student only leaves his studies to satisfy an appetite such as hunger, Tucker wrote that after a serious morning's work on his book, he would find himself in need of a break:

I then throw aside my papers sometime before dinner; the veriest trifle suits my purpose best: the philosopher can loll out at window like Miss Gawky, to see the wheelbarrow trundle, or the butcher's dog carry the tray, and is perfectly contented with his situation. (1768, 1, i, p. 140)

The dinner bell sounds. The philosopher-cum-Gawky immediately stops his gawping out the window and runs down to the parlour. The events do not follow Locke's schematic description of how they ought to unfold, with philosophers only leaving their desk when the pains of hunger compel them. We can note the unnecessary details in Tucker's account: the wheelbarrow, the butcher's dog, the tray, the running downstairs. They may be unnecessary to the theory, but 'the veriest trifle' brings the scene alive, thereby giving it psychological authenticity. It is because the details overspill the theoretical outline that we can understand Tucker's point; and we can understand why Locke's abstracted version needs to be amended. Tucker's unnecessary details are so necessary both rhetorically and conceptually.

We might note that Tucker's example runs in both directions: we see the philosopher as Miss Gawky, and in reverse, we see Miss Gawky as a philosopher. When she leans out of the window, Tucker writes, her mind is by no means vacant. If it were, she would be unable to understand what she sees. She is using her faculty for understanding 'all the time' to interpret what she sees (I, i, p. 24). Later, Tucker gives the detailed example of servant girl who rests after having worked hard; she relaxes by looking out of the window and then her attention is drawn to noises in street and she uses imagination, curiosity and understanding to discover what is happening (I, xii, 341–2). In other words, she, like Tucker observing his own behaviour, is using observation as a means of discovery.

Many of Tucker's disagreements with Locke came when he examined particular examples in detail. Locke, of course, used examples, but his examples are often perfunctory categories of action lacking vivacious details. The person who develops an aversion to honey, which was discussed in the previous chapter, was one such perfunctory example. When Tucker examined examples of motive in chapter VI of *Light of Nature*, it becomes clear that Locke's treatment of his examples was unsatisfactorily superficial. Locke in his *Essay* had produced a rather sketchy account of human motivation, based on the search for pleasure and the avoidance of pain (e.g. II, xx–xxii). Locke had suggested that pains can create uneasiness, and that we are motivated to remove this uneasiness; hence we engage in motivated actions. Tucker saw great merit in Locke's account, but he felt it was limited. To be sure, there were moments when uneasiness would lead us to satisfy desires, but, if we look closely at particular incidents, it becomes clear that not all our actions stem from uneasiness.

Locke had tended to concentrate on important actions in life rather than common occurrences. Tucker saw that we are continually filling our time by performing small actions without deliberation or inner uneasiness, such as the moments 'in our idle hours or vacant spaces of time [when] we turn our eyes to look at a butterfly, or put down our hands to remove the flap of our waistcoat that had gotten between us and the chair' (1768, 1, i, p. 101). Tucker cites examples from his own experience: 'I speak only for myself: when I sit down to dinner I feel no uneasiness in being hungry, rather rejoice in having a good appetite' (pp. 126–7). Frequently, the expectation of pleasure itself can produce further pleasures, not uneasiness. When we are thirsty on a hot day, we may derive pleasure in seeing the wine sparkle as it is poured from a bottle and in hearing 'the little glug glugs' (p. 127).

In Locke's *Essay*, there are no disquisitions on the psychological effects of glug glugs. But, as will be suggested, the expectation of future pleasure (or pain) reflected something fundamental about human experience that Tucker stressed. Tucker, however, denied that he differed from Locke substantially. They merely differed in their 'manner of handling' the issues of action: 'Though I do not pretend to a clearer, perhaps I may to a more microscopic eye: I consider action more minutely, endeavouring to analyse it into its primary parts' (1768, 1, i, p. 119). It is as if there is only a minor difference separating him from Locke – a matter to which we will return towards the end of this chapter.

On a number of occasions, Tucker used the metaphor of a microscope to describe his mode of analysis. 'We Searches', he wrote, 'although many of us are not clever at handling the telescope, are observed to be in general very fond of the microscope' (1848, p. 455). In essence, Tucker was defending the sort of method that a James or a Goffman would use: looking in detail at what people do and feel, rather than constructing a grand scheme and then searching for examples, or inventing hypothetical ones, to support their theory. Characteristically, Tucker mocked his chosen metaphorical method. The microscope is not always useful: 'if you walk in the street with a pair of microscopes tied to your eyes, you will perpetually be running against people' (1848, p. 459).

Tucker advised his readers not to expect him to be 'unveiling a secret unknown to them before' but that he was merely 'pointing out an observation they cannot fail of making themselves upon such notice' (1768, 1, vi, p. 76). In his introduction, Tucker made the same point. No reader should expect new discoveries: 'I shall present him with nothing but what he may have had within his view before; I pretend only to remind him of things that may have slipped his memory or point out to him objects that may have escaped his notice' (1768, p. xvi).

Tucker may have written in a characteristically modest, even apologetic, manner about drawing attention to what is generally unnoticed, as if he were working at a less serious level than an organiser of theoretical concepts like Locke. However, it takes a special talent to notice the unnoticed, and in the twentieth century, some of the most gifted observers of language and life, such as Wittgenstein, Goffman and Arendt, did precisely this. They were not offering grand theories or discovering hidden forces. Geertz (1973), in his praise of thick descriptions, suggested that when we read accounts of other cultures, we can often then become aware of our own unnoticed assumptions, customs and everyday rituals. Drawing attention to what had been so taken for granted that it had passed unnoticed can have deep effects. Having noticed the unnoticed, then it can become hard, and sometimes impossible, to travel back in time and fail to notice as before.

Another Great Exemplar: James

You do not have to read *Principles* for long before realising that you are in the company of another great user of examples. A classic Jamesian example comes at the start of the second chapter. James is introducing the subject matter of his chapter: the functions of the brain. He illustrates the striking difference between an organism that is equipped with a brain and a nervous system and one that is not. As always James addresses his readers directly. His chapter starts, 'If I begin chopping the foot of a tree, its branches are unmoved by my act and its leaves murmur as peacefully as ever in the wind'. But if I chop at the foot of a 'fellow-man', then 'the rest of his body instantly responds to the aggression by movements of alarm and defence' (I, p. 12). The difference between the two reactions is not that the tree is more long suffering than the human. It is that the human can feel the assault because it possesses a brain and nervous system, while the tree, being unable to feel, carries on in exactly the same way.

James' example explains his point perfectly. But note: James does not write 'trees are different from humans because they can't feel pain'. He guides us to imagine the idyllic scene at the top of the tree, with the leaves murmuring peacefully (yes, peacefully!) in the wind, while down below there is mayhem. Humans do not behave like the tree. If someone aggressively chops at another's legs, the victim does not continue peacefully as if nothing has happened: there might be cries of pain, a rush to escape, counter-aggression, screams, swearing, writhing, blood – anything but calm. James has done more than pick an apt example. He has described its elements with care, inviting his readers to picture the two scenes that he has tellingly described without a wasted word.

This is not a simple talent. It would be incorrect to react 'Oh, James, what a writer!' as if James were displaying a talent that can be admired but that is essentially supernumerary to all those talents that psychologists *really* require for doing psychology. James did not just produce examples in order to ease the pain of his readers by illustrating his arguments clearly, but examples are integral to his psychology. As Tucker appreciated, examples must be closely observed and analysed if we are to understand why we act as we do. Theories cannot relieve us of this labour.

Like Tucker before him, James was producing a psychology in which all human life can find its place. As we have seen, Tucker includes fiddling with the flap of his waistcoat or staring out the window. James took many such habitual acts as his subject matter. No act was too humble for his psychology, not even how we dress ourselves or adjust our clothing. In the opening pages of *Principles*, James outlined the scope of psychology: it included habitual actions such as 'standing, walking, buttoning and unbuttoning' (1890, Vol. I, p. 5). He had much to say about such actions. James noticed something odd about putting on clothes: 'Few men can tell off-hand which sock, shoe or trouser-leg they put on first'. To remember, they must mentally rehearse the act and 'even that is often insufficient – the act must be *performed*' (I, p. 115, emphasis in original). Another mundane example: while talking with others we might become aware of some dust on our sleeve or notice a pin on the floor. Then, without interrupting our conversation, we might brush the dust off or bend down to pick up the pin (II, p. 522). Or a man says to himself 'I must change my shirt' and immediately he has taken off his jacket and 'his fingers are at work in their accustomed manner on his waistcoat buttons' (II, p. 519). These are actions which are frequently performed but infrequently noticed.

There is seldom any conscious decision-making behind such actions. Far from being rare anomalies, these acts are very much part of our ordinary, everyday lives. In one of the most famous passages of *Principles*, James confessed that he found it difficult to get out of bed on a freezing cold morning. He expected others to have similar experiences but he cites his own. 'If I may generalize from my own experience', he writes, we remain in bed, conscious of the warmth there and of the cold in the room. But we know that we have to rise. There is not usually a distinct moment in which we make the conscious decision to leave the warmth of the bed and face the cold. Suddenly we find ourselves having got up without actually having made a decision to do so at that very moment. As James puts it, 'a fortunate lapse of consciousness occurs' (II, p. 524).

In this instance, James is using a familiar example from his own experience to give substance to the concept of 'ideo-motor action', a vaguely defined technical concept that the nineteenth-century physiologist William Carpenter, celebrated for his studies of the mind, originally formulated (1879, pp. 279ff.). An ideo-motor action, according to James, occurs when there is nothing intervening between the conception and the action (II, p. 522). Without the example of getting out of bed and the other examples that James gives in the same section, the concept, despite its impressive title and official definition, would remain vague. The example, rather than the definition, gives the phrase its meaning and conveys its psychological importance. If James had not assumed that his readers also knew the attractions of a warm bed on a cold day, then his chosen example would have fallen flat. So would have the trouser-leg example, had James belonged to a rare group of people suffering from a specific cognitive deficit of being unable to recall which leg they first slotted into trousers. In these cases, James was using an example as a means of discovery, not just as an illustration of an abstraction.

William James was, according to the psychologist Ernest Hilgard, 'the pre-eminent psychologiser' (1987, p. 50). To 'psychologise' was, in Hilgard's view, 'to reflect on ordinary observations' and then to offer such a plausible interpretation that 'detailed proof would seem irrelevant – or at least too tedious to be worth the effort'. Hilgard realised that it is no mean skill to show people something about themselves that they regularly do not notice. We can smile with self-recognition when reading *Principles*, for James had produced 'a full-bodied, warm-hearted psychology' (1987, p. 50). James was engaging in a looser form of self-examination than the formal psychology of German introspectionism, which was often conducted in laboratories stocked with machinery for delivering controlled stimuli (Myers, 1997). Just as some readers had found Tucker – another warm-hearted psychologiser – far too rambling, so in James' day, there were psychologists, notably James Mark Baldwin and G. Stanley Hall, who criticised *Principles* for being too personal and too unsystematic (Henley, 2007; Richardson, 2007, pp. 301ff.).[3]

Of course, there is a big historical difference between the times of Tucker and James. Tucker was writing before the days of systematic empirical research into the human mind: he had to rely upon his observations of others and his insights into himself. James was living at a time when specialised journals were being established to publish the latest psychological research. He had a 'literature' to survey, hundreds of experimental studies that he had to read and to mention. The vast majority of those studies have long outlived their usefulness and but still *Principles* continues to attract new readers. It cannot be the literature

---

[3] Stroud (2012) draws attention to the influence of ancient stoic philosophers, especially Marcus Aurelius, on James' use of examples. Stroud argues that the stoics used vivid examples in their writings and teachings, imagining hypothetical situations in great detail in order to pose questions about what would be the moral reaction in those circumstances. Stroud notes that James read Marcus Aurelius' *Meditations* as a young man and that the book seems to have had a great effect on him both personally and intellectually. According to Stroud, James' use of stoic rhetoric was particularly noticeable when he gave public lectures. These lectures did not proceed by means of detailed arguments but were packed with vivid examples, quotations from poets and personal anecdotes.

reviews that draw them in, but, at a distance of well over a hundred years, readers are still able to recognise themselves in James' examples. It can be hard to get out of bed on a winter's morning, even in the age of central heating.

Stream of Thought

The parallels between Tucker and James would be interesting, but not necessarily crucial, if they were primarily based on their writing styles. Yes, it is true that both could be amusing writers; yes, it is true that both looked at unimportant actions. Yes, they both observed closely their own unconscious movements, but that is not enough to claim Tucker as an early Jamesian. There have to be important similarities of substance: when they looked at their own mental lives, did they both notice something that others had overlooked? James' most famous 'discovery', for which the histories of psychology have given him great credit, was that consciousness is a stream, not a series of separate mental states. Boring (1929) claimed that the stream of consciousness was the major reason for James' importance. George Mandler (2007), another distinguished psychologist, stated that nothing produced a greater departure from the old tradition of assuming experience to be composed of 'elementaristic particles' than did James' idea of consciousness as a stream (p. 110). More recently, it has recently been claimed that James was 'revolutionary' in his thinking because he overturned 'the traditional Lockean notion of consciousness as a series of discrete states or static ideas' (Evans, 2015, p. 5).

To be sure, James was a creative and highly original thinker, but even his great revolutionary idea was prefigured in Tucker's analysis of the mind. Tucker differed from Locke, and also from later associationists, in an important regard. He did not use his metaphorical microscope to isolate particular states of mind which supposedly exist self-contained at any given instant. Tucker saw actions and thoughts occurring over time, and in consequence, he believed that the mind had to be analysed in relation to sequential patterns of life. This is apparent in Tucker's descriptions of pleasure and uneasiness. The common 'occurrences' that he described are actions taking place across time: we are hot and thirsty, sit down and wait for the drink to be poured, etc. He is envisaging a sequence of feelings and actions, rather than isolated, psychological moments succeeding one after another, as if it might be possible to stop the action and then with fine surgical tools remove the experience of that specific moment and place it under the microscope for closer examination. That would not be possible, however fine the tools, because, in Tucker's view, experiences are always running into each other, rather than existing at a precise instant.

When discussing the anticipation of pleasure, Tucker wrote that the present moment does not really exist as such, for we are always looking forwards. Although philosophers might talk of the present and claim that our will affects the present moment, 'this present time is in reality the next succeeding instant' (1768, 1, i, p. 108). This can be seen in the way we perceive things. Our perceptions 'flow in upon us without intermission and we generally have a foresight of them before they come' (p. 109). As such, the future is mixed with the present. This was also something that James emphasised, adding the past to the mixture of present and future. James wrote in *Principles* that the present only exists in an abstract sense and that we have no consciousness of it. Where is the present? James asks. He answers: 'It has melted in our grasp, fled ere we could touch it, gone in the instant of becoming' (1890, Vol. I, p. 608). The perception of any object is complexly bound up in time and 'part of the complexity is the echo of the objects just past, and, in a less degree, perhaps, the foretaste of those just to arrive' (p. 606).

For James, the notion of perception mixing past and future follows from his famous conception of consciousness as a stream, which he described as 'the primal fact' of the science of psychology (1899, p. 15). James wrote that consciousness is unbroken and feels unbroken, although it can be interrupted when we sleep; otherwise 'consciousness remains sensibly continuous and one' (1890, Vol. I, p. 238). James could equally have repeated Tucker's description that perceptions flow in without intermission. James went on to stress that consciousness was not chopped up into bits or constructed from putting those bits together: 'A "river" or a "stream" are the metaphors by which it is most naturally described'. He declared that henceforth we should refer to '*the stream of thought, of consciousness, or of subjective life*' (p. 239, emphasis in original).

Tucker used the same metaphor of a river. He argued that the mind is both active and passive. We cannot completely control our thoughts, even if we are deliberating upon an issue intently, rather than staring out of the window. The thinker is like a hound sniffing a trail: we might decide to follow the trail but we have not laid it down, so that we do not know where it might lead. The mind only begins a train of thinking 'but the thoughts introduce one another successively' (1768, 1, i, p. 11). As such, Tucker says we can compare the thinker to a 'man who has a river running through his grounds' (p. 12). The river might break into several channels; if the landowner tries to dam up one of the channels, the river still flows through others. The flow of the river is unstoppable, and so it is with our thoughts which 'are perpetually working so long as we are awake' (p. 13). We may divert our thoughts but we 'can never totally prevent them from moving' (p. 13).

The river of consciousness for James meant that thoughts and feelings never repeat themselves in exactly the same way: there is always movement and change. Tucker emphasised another point, from which James would surely not have dissented. However much we try to control our thoughts – and both James and Tucker agreed we should try to – we can seldom, if ever, succeed in fully retaining control. Our conscious life happens to us, as much, if not more, than we direct it to happen. The rational, dominant ego (or 'will') is a myth. We are not the masters and mistresses of our own minds. As Tucker wrote, 'we cannot constantly keep a watchful eye on our thoughts' but notions will start up 'in the fancy' (1768, 1, i, p. 370). According to Tucker, the mind 'cannot lie a moment inactive' for 'she works incessantly ... and if her weightier motives suspend their action ever so little, some lighter will slip in to keep her in play' (1768, 1, i, p. 91). Some ideas are like lightning, they 'flash, strike and vanish; they pass so swiftly we cannot get a look at them nor remember their existence' (p. 92).

Tucker was again departing from Locke, for he was denying that thinking or mental activity can be equated with consciousness. Tucker wrote that the mind can continue working even when we are asleep. On waking, we can find that our ideas 'have ranged themselves anew' and this shows that 'our organs do not stand idle the moment that we cease to employ them but continue the actions that we put them into after they have gone out of our sight' (1768, 1, i, p. 249). This is one of the few passages of *Light of Nature* to be quoted by a nineteenth-century psychologist. William Carpenter quoted this passage to support his notion of 'unconscious cerebration' or brain activity giving rise to thinking without conscious experience (Carpenter, 1879, p. 531). By the time James was writing, it was becoming acknowledged that unconscious thinking not only existed but that its study was central to the new discipline of psychology: we don't have to be aware that we are fiddling with our buttons and waistcoat flaps or brushing the dust from our sleeves. One American textbook, published five years after *Principles*, claimed that the largest class of mental activities that psychologists studied were unconscious ones (Krohn, 1895, p. 18). James gave great attention to our habits, fidgets and the 'fringes of experience' of which we are largely unaware. So also in his way did Tucker.

The Importance of Habits

One historian of psychology has claimed that James' chapter on habits is the most widely quoted chapter of *Principles* (Hothersall, 2004). James argued that much of our behaviour and experience is habitual, and he may have had personal reasons of his own for according habit such importance (Leary, 2013). We develop habits of language, habits of mind, bodily habits and so on, often through the processes of association. James stressed that some of our habits are 'known' by the body, not by the conscious mind. The habitual behaviour creates physiological connections, and 'habits diminish the conscious attention with which our acts are performed' (1890, Vol. 1, p. 112). This can free up our mind to concentrate on heavier matters. Sometimes the fiddling with sleeves, pens or buttons, far from distracting our attention, can help us to keep concentrating.

There are also habits of mind, as well as body. It is through the development of perceptual habits that we come to understand the world. In a famous phrase, James described the infant as being assailed by all its senses at once and perceiving the world as just 'one great blooming buzzing confusion' (1890, Vol. 1, p. 488). Gradually, the infant learns to make sense of this confusion, selecting some elements and ignoring others. This selectivity becomes habitual, as the mind, without conscious awareness, learns to focus on some things and weed out others.

Conscious thinking can also be guided by habits. Although James described thinking as a stream, he wrote that thoughts pass before us 'in a train or a chain' (1890, Vol. 1, p. 240). In this respect thought is jointed, as we pass from one train of thought to another.[4] Because our brains are continually building up connections between nerves, so our minds build up habitual trains of thought; as we start thinking of one thing, so we move habitually to another. These conceptual habits ensure that we do not have to start from scratch each time we think. It can also mean that sometimes we are trapped by our mental habits into thinking in rigidly repetitive ways. Thus, habits are conceptual, perceptual and behavioural. The individual could have no meaningful life without habits and habits provide the routines that are vital for social life. In yet another striking phrase, James described habit as 'the enormous fly-wheel of society' (1890, Vol. 1, p. 121).

All these ideas, with the exception of the physiological speculations about the nervous system building up well-used connections, can be found in Tucker, who likewise saw habits as being individually and socially vital. He, too, envisaged the world of the infant as overloaded by confusing sensations. Nature presents her objects to the newborn babe, he wrote, 'in a chaos, or confused multitude, wherein there is nothing distinct, nothing connected'; instead, sights, sounds, smells,

---

[4] See Bailey (1999) for a discussion of the issue whether the idea of separate or jointed chains of thought conflicts with James' basic notion of the continuity of thinking.

tastes and feelings 'rush in all the five avenues of sensation, and accost the mind in one act of perception' (1768, 1, i, p. 223). The mind learns to select, to pay attention to some things not others: there is a 'culling of particular objects from the whole number exhibited to view' (p. 225). Thus, we begin to associate some objects with feelings, memories and so on.

It is the same with thinking. The similarity between James and Tucker is semantic as well as conceptual, as they both used the word 'train'. Tucker paid great attention to the nature and operation of trains of thinking. He saw it as part of our nature to form and use trains: 'Though the mind by her notice begins the formation of a train, there is something in our internal mechanism that strengthens and completes the concatenation' (1768, 1, i, p. 248). Once we have formed trains of thought, then, 'whatever suggests the first link, the rest follow readily of their own accord' (p. 249). So, too, we might have behavioural habits; and Tucker discussed such small gestures of re-arranging the flap of a waistcoat when it becomes caught in a chair. Possessing chains of thought and habits were vital for life. Our first attempts at so many actions are awkward and slow, 'while we are forced to dig up everything by dint of application'; but when we have formed 'proper trains, that will spring up of their own accord', then we find 'we can go on expeditiously, readily and perfectly' (p. 254).

In Tucker's view, the importance of habit eclipses that of conscious judgement for the conduct of everyday life. He suggested: 'The tenor of our lives, and success of our endeavours, depends more upon habit than judgement' (1768, 1, ii, pp. 93–4). Moreover, he claimed that 'our habits both of thinking and acting' depend on the same cause, namely 'the spontaneous or mechanical rising of ideas in thought' (1777, 3, iv, p. 175). Habit does not triumph by force, 'but steals upon you imperceptibly, or teases or tires you into a compliance' (1768, 1, ii, p. 93). Because habits include our perceptions of objects, management of limbs, trains of thought and 'common forms and modes of behaviour', then 'there is no living in the world without falling into habits' (1777, 3, iv, p. 183).

Tucker may not have used the metaphor of the flywheel (although, as we have seen, he did imagine a fly on a wheel), but his meaning was similar to James. He had an additional argument that distinguished rules from habits. Rules, habits and customs share an affinity for 'for they all tend to produce a uniformity of conduct' (1777, 3, iv, p. 246). We need rules for social life, but rules are often so irksome and restrictive that people can react against them. However, habitual customs are far more efficacious than consciously followed rules. When rules become familiar, they cease to be consciously followed or resisted. Instead, they become 'habits or ways of acting fallen currently into without care or reflection' (p. 246). Some customs and habits can have ill consequences, such as the habits of prejudice or 'habits of misapprehension and misjudging' that are common 'among all degrees of men' (1777, 3, iv, p. 188).

James pointed out that habit, the great social fly-wheel, was society's 'most precious conservative agent' because it is only habit 'that keeps us all within the bounds of ordinance and saves the children of fortune from the envious uprisings of the poor' (1890, Vol. 1, p. 121). On the other hand, habits need not be entirely conservative in their effects. They can free the mind for creative, even revolutionary, thinking: 'The more of the details of our daily life we can hand over to the effortless custody of automatism, the more our higher powers of mind will be set free for their own proper work' (Vol. 1, p. 122). If James were thinking of himself, then he would not have dreamt of saying so. It would have sounded so boastful, so superior. Tucker appreciated, as did James, that the conservatism of habit had its dangers, as well as its benefits. It was much the same with microscopes. We can put them on and see so much detail; but if we were to strap them to our eyes, they would render us virtually blind.

Almost a Connection

One can ask how significant are these parallels between James and Tucker, beyond suggesting that admirers of James might take a look at Tucker. Any answer needs to be considered alongside an obvious question: why has Tucker been forgotten? It is insufficient to follow Paley and say that the reason lies in the rambling nature of Tucker's great book. Some thinkers have made and sustained considerable reputations on the basis of long, unreadable works. Although Hazlitt knocked the work into a single, well-ordered volume, this fared little better than the much longer original. Hazlitt's abbreviation did not enjoy the success of James' compact version of *Principles* which was published under the title *Psychology: Briefer Course* (James, 1892). There is a difference between the two abbreviations. James was writing for an identifiable market of undergraduates who wanted accessible textbooks to help them through their courses. Tucker never had such a captive readership: his publishers were still vainly searching for hordes of general readers.

Perhaps Tucker suffered because his ideas did not match the intellectual mood of his times. He was qualifying the notion that we can achieve a perfectly rational view of the world. In effect, rather than by intention, Tucker was showing the psychological limitations of Locke's project to base thinking on empirical knowledge because we are not in control of our minds. This was not a specific cognitive failure capable of being fixed but a part of human nature. By the mid to late nineteenth century, this idea was becoming acceptable, especially as new advocates, such as Carpenter, could produce physiological evidence in support. By the second half of the nineteenth century, psychological analysts like Alexander Bain and Herbert Spencer were directing their attention to the little, non-intellectual, and even non-conscious, things that we do. They were preparing the way for James and his magnificent fourth chapter on habits. Much more historical investigation would be required to relate Tucker's lack of success to the wider movements of intellectual change. He very much looks like a thinker with ideas ahead of his time, but who, when his time finally arrived, was overtaken by a rush of exciting new thinkers, including James.

Forgotten figures can, nevertheless, have intellectually important effects. One of the themes of my book *Hidden Roots of Critical Psychology* was that the psychological ideas of comparatively neglected eighteenth-century figures, such as the third Earl of Shaftesbury and Thomas Reid, are now returning to prominence after circuitous historical journeys (Billig, 2008a). Some of Shaftesbury's indirect influences of psychological thinking were mentioned in the previous chapter. It is common for historically minded psychologists, who champion the cause of a neglected or forgotten figure, to claim that the individual in question really did have a major, but sometimes concealed, impact despite outward appearances of complete neglect. In this spirit, I mentioned in *Hidden Roots of Critical Psychology* that Shaftesbury had a roundabout effect on Bakhtin through Cassirer, and then, through Bakhtin, had an impact on today's critical psychology. When Marie Jahoda is discussed in Chapter 8, I will mention that she was influenced by Karl Bühler, who is all but forgotten today but who in his day influenced some premier-league philosophers and psychologists (Wettersten, 1988; Brock, 1994). Tucker is far more obscure than Shaftesbury, Reid or Bühler, and there is no evidence that he directly influenced any scholar in the league of Bühler's most eminent admirers. Certainly, Paley is no longer a major figure, although, of course, Coleridge's poetry is still celebrated as are Hazlitt's radical essays. Nevertheless, one would struggle to find intervening links to show that Tucker indirectly affected the development of psychology, whether through Coleridge or Hazlitt. Should anyone wish to find a good example of an original but overlooked psychological thinker, they would do well to consider the case of Tucker.

A minor and not very mysterious mystery would be why James did not know of his forebear. There is, however, an almost-linkage between the two, through the self-taught English philosopher Shadworth Hodgson. James and Hodgson first met in 1880 and shortly afterwards became corresponding friends. Hodgson's philosophy was based on analysing the mind and its operations, and James quoted his work extensively in *Principles*. In his approach to the mind, Hodgson was much more theoretical than James, and he certainly lacked the gift of illustration. His works are ponderous, to say the least, and today attract more dust than readers. In one letter to Hodgson, James complained that a piece of his friend's writing 'hangs in the air of speculation and touches not the earth of life' (30 December 1885; H. James, 1926, p. 244).

James seems to have been influenced by Hodgson's ideas about consciousness, and he certainly found Hodgson's work useful when writing *Principles*. James included a lengthy quotation from Hodgson's *Philosophy of Reflection* (1878) to support his own notion that perception involves past and future and that this gives consciousness its continuity 'without which it could not be called a stream' (1890, Vol. 1, p. 607). Hodgson too was suggesting that in consciousness, there is strictly no present, and that experience is continuous. Hodgson did not actually describe consciousness as a stream in *Philosophy of Reflection*, nor in *Theory of Practice* (1870), which James also cited in *Principles*. However, he did so in his first book, when he defined the purpose of metaphysics as tracing 'the stream of consciousness and of existence to its source or sources' (Hodgson, 1865, p. 74). By the time Hodgson came to write *Metaphysic of Experience* (1898), several years after James' *Principles*, he was regularly using the metaphor.

More work would be needed to trace the influence of Hodgson on James, and vice versa. There is some evidence that James, in thinking of consciousness as a stream, may have been influenced by Ralph Waldo Emerson (Leary, 2007). What is of interest here is another possibility. There is no evidence that James read Tucker, but he certainly read Hodgson's *Theory of Practice* and, particularly, the sections on emotion (James, 1890, Vol. 1, p. 130). In *Theory and Practice*, Hodgson lengthily criticised Tucker's approach to the emotions, especially the idea that emotions could be causes of other emotions (Hodgson, 1870, pp. 108ff.). Hodgson might have been familiar with Tucker's work, but he did not cite him when discussing the continuity of consciousness or the absence of a pure experience of the present.

Although it is not possible to tie down any possible influence Tucker might have had on Hodgson, and then through Hodgson on James, one thing can be said. Had Hodgson referred to Tucker when he was in agreement with him, rather than citing him when he disagreed, he might have alerted James to the earlier writer. In academic life, some scholars boost their claims to originality by selectively citing previous writers. Imagine that someone has already written what you are now proposing: you can cite them, giving credit to their priority. Or you can do something else to boost your own appearance of originality: you can criticise the earlier writer on other matters, while ignoring what they wrote about the issue on which you hope to appear original. To be effective, the strategy of selective citation, of which another example will be discussed in Chapter 5, does not need to be consciously and cunningly pursued. The strategy can become an academic habit, the scholarly equivalent of adjusting the waistcoat flap.

We can say that if Hodgson had cited Tucker unselectively, mentioning his views on the continuity of consciousness, then James, on reading Hodgson, would have become aware that he and his friend Shadworth were not alone in seeing the mind as a stream. We might speculate a bit further. The seriously dry Hodgson would not have appreciated the glug glug, Miss Gawky side of Tucker. James, on the other hand, would have enjoyed it. Such conjectures, however, must remain, to use the words of Tucker when describing his vision of the vehicular Locke, 'hypotheses ... concerning things unknown' (1768, 2, ii, p. 5).

Concrete Examples and the Dangers of Abstraction

Tucker and James both viewed concrete examples as more than stylistic adornments to amuse their readers. They were also a means for discovering how the mind operates. With Tucker particularly, we can also see the glimmer of a philosophy of the example. He often contrasted abstract philosophising with examining concrete examples, and his sympathies were clearly not on the side of abstraction. In the Introduction to *Light of Nature*, Tucker wrote that he was not going 'to hunt after abstract notions' but, instead, he was going to examine humans in terms of their actions and thoughts: we may discover our own nature 'by diligently observing what we do, how we come to act in such or such manner, together with the consequences or effects of our actions' (1768, I, pp. xxvi–xxvii).

It was by considering examples in detail that Tucker believed that we can understand ourselves and others, because 'the abstract is seen clearest in the concrete', especially when we seek to understand the meaning of actions (I, i, p. 149). It was, Tucker wrote, the way of science that the ' abstract must be learned from the concrete' (I, p. xxviii). Therefore it is from concrete examples that 'we must fetch our materials' but when we have gathered a 'competent store' of them, then 'I am so far from being an enemy to abstract reasonings that I shall pursue them as far as can be desired' (pp. xxviii–xxix). But note Tucker's escape route: 'as far as can be desired' which, in the example of Tucker and his writing, was not that far. He was always coming back to concrete examples.

A similar trend is detectable in James' *Principles*. He works from the particular to the general, from the concrete outwards. If you examine a specific experience in detail, understanding how its elements combine together, then you have the basis for a wider understanding. The example of getting out of bed is a case in point. It comes in his section 'Ideo-motor action' in his chapter on Will. Having presented the example in some detail – recounting the ideas flashing across his mind in bed and describing when inhibitory ideas ceased – James comments: 'This case seems to me to contain in miniature form the data for an entire psychology of volition' (II, p. 525). James claims the example shows how wider insights come from examining the particular case: 'It was in fact through meditating on the phenomenon in my own person that I first became convinced of the doctrine which these pages present, and which I need here illustrate by no farther examples' (p. 525).

Nor was James an enemy of what Tucker called 'abstract reasonings', although like Tucker, he wanted them based upon actual examples. As he outlined in his chapter on reasoning, there is a difference between two sorts of thinking. There is the thinking which does not get much beyond associating 'empirical concretes', one with another; according to James, this type of thinking can be rational but it could 'hardly be called reasoning in the strict sense of the term'. Then there is the sort of productive and creative thinking, which is 'reasoning proper', or 'reasoning distinctively so called', and which goes beyond empirical givens (1890, II, pp. 325–6).

When we pick out essential qualities, rather than just link two things together, then we are, according to James, engaging in 'reasoning distinctively so called' as contrasted with reverie or association (1890, II, p. 329). The movement of genuine reasoning was from the particular to the abstract. As he put it, the reasoner is not helpless when confronted with a fact but 'through analysis and abstraction', the reasoner isolates 'the essential attribute' (p. 530). To reason in the full sense of the word, then, we must be able to 'extract characters – not *any* character, but the right characters for our conclusion' (p. 343, emphasis in original). James could have been describing his own aspirations as a psychological thinker. He wants to progress from the concrete facts – such as being unable to get out of bed – to finding the essential attributes of the situation. Then, when he has found them, he can reduce complex situations to their basic components.

However, there is a problem. According to James, when we conceive of a concrete fact in terms of its essential attributes, 'we neglect all the other attributes' and, in so doing, we 'mutilate the fullness of . . . [its] reality' (II, p. 332). In this sense, science and abstraction represent a mutilation of reality. Hazlitt, in the preface to his abridged version of *Light of Nature*, expressed something similar: 'Abstraction is a trick to supply the defect of comprehension . . . The most perfect abstraction is nothing more than the art of making use of only half of the understanding, and never seeing one half of a subject' (1807, p. x). Hazlitt went on to describe someone who seeks to arrive 'at the highest point of philosophy' by disdaining common sense and by 'denaturalizing his understanding' as a person 'who should deprive himself of the use of his eye-sight, in order that he might be able to grope his way better in the dark' (pp. x–xi).

We will encounter more of this notion – namely that abstraction and general theory mutilate or oversimplify the reality of concrete examples – when, in later chapters, we discuss the ideas of Ernst Cassirer, who was to influence the social psychologist Kurt Lewin. For now, we can note something curious. James appears to be advocating that genuine thinking, especially in relation to analysing the mind, involves abstracting from complexity to simplicity, from particularity to the general law. However, we should be careful not to imagine that James here is wandering too far from the direction in which Tucker also walked. When James describes examples he does not generally mutilate the fullness of their complexity. For instance, his analysis of getting out of bed does not progress to abstraction but his whole section on 'ideo-motor action' still hums with the particularity – and the implicit visual image – of James tucked up between his sheets. James does not translate the language which he uses to describe the scene into the language of abstractions beyond the phrase 'ideo-motor action'.

It is characteristic of James' writing that he does not surrender his well-worked examples to theory. David Leary expresses the point well: 'What is perhaps most striking about James' psychology is that it stays so close to the descriptive, empirical level, without ascending, except tentatively and provisionally, into the realm of formal theories' (2018, p. 28). This should not be seen as a failure of James, as if he should have ascended further from the concrete and moved from description to theoretical writing. In Chapter 6, we will encounter Cassirer's view that descriptions are not mere descriptions but they involve theoretical understandings, just as Miss Gawky, staring at the street below her window, is not just staring – she is also understanding.

There is also a clue in Tucker why describing our actions might not represent a failure of understanding, as if all successful thought and successful analysis should ultimately end in abstraction, otherwise it is not successfully analytical. In his address 'To the Reader' at the start of *Freewill, Foreknowledge*, Tucker declares that he would wish the reader to 'dwell as little as possible upon mere abstractions but to judge of the abstract in the concrete' (1763, pp. xxi–xxii). We should note here

Tucker's phrase 'mere abstractions', for later we will encounter the contrasting phrase of modern psychologists: 'mere descriptions'. If Tucker
himself has formed some abstractions – and, as we have seen, he declares
himself no enemy of abstracts – then his readers should bring any hea-
venly abstractions down to earthly life. Abstractions are not the end of
thinking, but they must be judged in concrete terms: do they help us to
understand this or that particular situation?

Tucker did not stand back and admire Locke's abstractions about
needs and emotions. Instead, he applied Locke's views to examples
from life and he found his hero wanting. If there is movement from the
concrete to the abstract, then there should be a further movement back to
the concrete: back to the waistcoat flap, to the glug glugs and to
Miss Gawky at the window. James' own literary practice conveyed the
same return to the concrete and, like Tucker, he did not bow down in
reverence before abstracted theory. The means of discovery is not the
abstraction but the examination of something specific, an example, even if
we do not quite know what the example exemplifies when we begin our
examination.

James warned about the danger of psychologists having fixed, abstract
ideas. In *Principles*, he wrote about the 'psychologist's fallacy'. This 'great
snare of the psychologist' occurs when psychologists confuse their 'own
standpoint with the mental fact' that they are reporting (1890, Vol. 1,
p. 196). For years the associationists were trapped within their own
version of the fallacy. Generations of psychologists had believed in the
theory that there were discrete, moment-by-moment mental states. This
was, in James' view, a fallacy brought on by psychologists permitting
theory to distort their examination of experience. We might say that one
of the great virtues of Tucker and James was not that they independently
formulated a better theory of experience. It was that they could empty
their minds of pre-held theories and look directly at their own experiences, at what happens when they pour a glass of wine or struggle to leave
their bed. This explains how they could both see something similar
despite living so many years apart. They had been able to escape from
'the great snare' of the same theory of mind.

James commended his general approach when he wrote that 'pragmatism unstiffens all our theories, limbers them up and sets each one at
work' (James, 1908b, p. 53). The way to unstiffen theories about the
mind is to keep finding examples to test them against. Examining a new
example might show that this time other factors are at work than in the
previous example. Not all 'ideo-motor actions' might be equal: getting
out of the shower might not have quite the same dynamic as getting out of
bed. We have to return to concrete examples if we want to prevent

a theoretical category, such as 'ideo-motor action', from stiffening up, mutilating reality and becoming a trick. If analysts of the mind should possess the ability to abstract, then equally, if not more importantly, they should also possess the ability to return abstractions to concrete details; and they should resist the temptation to believe that their main work has been completed when they have come up with theoretical abstractions.

We might say that there should be an unending dialect between abstracting from and returning to concrete details. But if we said that this is a 'dialectic', we would be trapping the concrete movements back and forth within a single abstract concept; and with our own choice of words we would thereby be favouring the abstract over the concrete. As Tucker recommended, it is better to understand abstractions in concrete terms. The concept of 'dialectic', for all its being a philosophically posh word, or probably because it is so philosophically posh, in this context does not really contribute anything clear or concrete. It is another word to impress the impressionable.

So, we should look for a more homely way of expressing the thought. The routines of modern life are filled with endless sequences of contrasting small actions, just as James and Tucker recognised in their times. There is standing, sitting; going to bed, rising from bed; talking, not talking; taking the smartphone from the pocket, putting the smartphone back into the pocket; logging on and logging off, and so on. Whenever we button, there will be unbuttoning to come, and then more buttoning – and so it should be with our thinking: abstracting from examples and unstiffening our abstractions back into examples; conceptually buttoning the example within a theoretical pocket and then unbuttoning the pocket to look again at the example. A dialectic? Perhaps. Buttoning examples, unbuttoning them? Definitely.

However we choose to call this movement between the abstraction of theories and the concreteness of examples, there is a point that I hope this chapter has made clear – that the ideas of Tucker and James are linked across time. Both of them produced theories of mind that envisaged a person having different moments of experience within the same, continuous stream of consciousness extending over time. Perhaps the same can be said for the ideas of different people across a stream of historical time. The apt metaphor of a stream can be stretched. Tucker and James represent different moments of consciousness on the uplands close to the source of the same stream of psychological thinking.

4   Freud
Writing to Reveal and to Conceal Himself

Now it is the turn of Sigmund Freud, one of the most famous writers in psychology's history and himself a serious collector of examples. In his writings, Freud offers countless examples designed to illustrate the various ways in which unconscious motives affect what people do. Most notably, there are stories taken from the case histories of his patients but he also amassed major collections of dreams, jokes and slips of the tongue. Freud, who trained as a neuropathologist, was well aware that, when he presented lengthy, detailed examples, he might appear to be writing in a manner that conflicted with the conventional way of writing science. In his first book, *Studies on Hysteria*, published in 1895 and written in collaboration with his older colleague Josef Breuer, Freud wrote, 'It still strikes me as strange that the case histories I write should read like short stories and that, as one might say, they lack the serious stamp of science' (Freud and Breuer, 1895/1991, p. 231).

As with William James, Freud's style of writing has attracted many admirers, who have praised his literary skills, comparing them with those of the best novelists (e.g. Mahony, 1987; Grayling, 2002; Spence, 1994). The quality of his writing is evident not just in the stories he tells from his case histories, but in the way that he constructs arguments, formulates striking metaphors and uses examples to convince his readers. Harold Bloom, the well-known American literary critic, wrote an article for the *New York Times* with the unambiguous title 'Freud the Greatest Modern Writer'. Bloom compared Freud with Montaigne and Shakespeare, claiming that such were Freud's persuasive skills that he is a difficult writer to resist, particularly when one reads him deeply.

Here, in this chapter, I will not be dwelling on Freud's greatness as a writer, for I will be taking his literary talents for granted. Nevertheless, I will be doing what Bloom said was difficult – namely trying to resist what he says, especially what he says about himself and his own motives. This is not because I want to discredit him personally or bring his reputation as an analyst of the mind into disrepute. Many others have done that in the past, are doing it in the present, and will continue their work of demolition well into the future. The reason for questioning Freud's analysis of the examples from his own life relates to the fact that the founder of psycho-analysis taught his readers and his followers to look suspiciously upon what people say about themselves.

As we will see, he did not exclude himself from this suspicion. However much some of his followers might have venerated him, Freud certainly did not present himself as if he were the only human who was able to conquer the all-too-human failings of self-deception. Quite the reverse, he mentioned some of his failings, and he argued that he came to many of his ideas by looking at his own hidden motives and by suspecting his own self-justifications. As a result, when it comes to examining what Freud says about himself, we are faced with a paradox: to follow Freud, and to accept his word at face value, is not to follow Freud.

This chapter will be using the example of Freud to explore the possibility that the link between an example and what the example is being used to exemplify is not necessarily straightforward. Freud's use of examples can be much more complex than either Tucker's or James'. In his case histories Freud offers so much detail, bringing complex characters to life, that he seems to be inviting subsequent readers to re-interpret his interpretations – to use his case histories as a means for further discovery. When followers re-interpret Freud's cases, then an example may become an example of something different than that which Freud had originally intended. This is especially so when Freud himself is the central character in the story.

If we want to show that Freud's interpretations of his own actions might not be straightforward, then we need to select an example from the many examples that he presents in his writings. The chosen example here comes from his collection of slips of the tongue and temporary losses of memory that forms the basis of his classic work *The Psychopathology of Everyday Life*, which was first published in 1901. I will be examining the first example of that book. In this example Freud tells the story when he came unexpectedly to forget the name of the Italian painter, Luca Signorelli, and then explained why at that moment he forgot this name that he knew so well.

The title of *Psychopathology of Everyday Life* is instructive. Freud was not presenting the dramatic case histories of patients who could not cope with the demands of everyday life, as he and Breuer had done in *Studies on Hysteria*. Like James and Tucker, Freud was now exploring the psychology of everyday life (or *Alltagslebens* in the original title). Like James and Tucker, Freud's subject matter covered seemingly trivial matters such as the readjustment of a waistcoat flap, buttoning and unbuttoning or what Freud described as 'fiddling with one's clothing in all kinds of ways' (1901/1975, p. 250).

Unlike James and Tucker, Freud says that these small acts contain hidden significance: 'Every change in the clothing usually worn, every small sign of carelessness – such as an unfastened button – every trace of exposure, is intended to express something that the wearer does not want to say straight out and which for the most part he is unaware of' (pp. 250–51). If the forgetting of names or the failure to button an article of clothing are 'psychopathologies', then we all, whatever our general psychological health, will show such psychopathologies. To prove the point, Freud had collected his own everyday failures, and he publicly presented them as examples.

Here it gets trickier. Freud, as we will see, offered accounts about the unconscious motives that supposedly produced his temporary failures. It was as if William James had confessed to a rather personal, but not entirely shameful, reason why he did not want to leave his bed in the morning. Would we not suspect that he might be holding something back about himself and his bed? Or perhaps he was unwittingly deceiving himself about why he wanted to remain in bed, in his night-wear alone with his stream of thoughts. The problem is all the more pronounced in the case of Freud, who Paul Ricoeur (1970) famously called 'the master of suspicion' (p. 64).

But how should we proceed? We are necessarily dealing with Freud's own self-analysis. This must have been somewhat similar to what, almost 200 years earlier, Shaftesbury had called his 'self-discoursing practice', in which he divided himself into two persons to question his own motives and to seek out any self-deception (see Chapter 2). Freud's self-discoursing practice saw him treating himself as if he were his own patient. As will be suggested, by comparing how Freud treated his patients' accounts of their motives with the way he presented his own motives, we can start to assess whether or not we should suspect that he is holding things back in his own self-discoursing practice.

To go further, it will be necessary to try to understand how people might repress troublesome thoughts and what they have to do to drive them from conscious awareness. Freud was to write that the concept of repression was 'the corner-stone' of the psycho-analytic understanding of neurosis and became 'the centre' of psycho-analytic theory, for without repression, there could be no unconscious (Freud, 1925/1993, pp. 213–14). Although repression is such a key concept in both Freud's theory of mind and in psycho-analytic practice, Freud was often curiously vague about what people actually needed to do in order to repress thoughts that might have been conscious at one time but which become unconscious as a result of repression (see Billig, 1999, 2006a; Boag, 2010, 2012).

Freud offered some suggestions in *Studies of Hysteria*, especially when he wrote about the case of Elisabeth von R. Taking elements from the Tucker/James account of the mind, as well as certain aspects from the case of Elisabeth, we can begin to understand the processes of repression in terms of re-directing the stream of consciousness in ways that habitually and non-consciously divert attention from troubling matters. Above all, we should be prepared to admit that an investigator, who is probing the secrets of the mind, as Freud did, might actually be using their investigations to avoid making embarrassing admissions about themselves to themselves.

For academics, the activities of analysing, arguing, writing and so on are everyday actions. As we sit at our desks being, at least in our own minds, fearless investigators of the truth, we might be escaping truths about ourselves. Was Freud, by analysing the example of his forgetting the name of the Italian painter, actually pushing something else from his mind, so that the more he analysed the unconscious features of the episode, the more this something else was being driven from his conscious attention?

To address this possibility, which Freud's ideas about memory lapses invite us to entertain, we will have to examine events in Freud's life at the time of incident. We will also have to take into account how keen he was to write up the incident. This will mean raising something scandalous: Freud had just shared two nights in a hotel room with his sister-in-law. He had something that he could not reveal publicly to the world at large or privately to his family. It will be suggested that as he reveals, so he conceals. The two activities are not polar opposites, as Freud himself well appreciated. As was mentioned, to follow Freud is not to follow him.

Freud's Self-Analysis

As an individual, Freud seems to have been discrete and guarded – something that friends and followers often remarked upon. The man who probed the hidden secrets of humans was, according to his pupil Theodor Reik, 'reserved and reticent about himself' (1956, p. 30). His official biographer and friend Ernest Jones described Freud as being personally secretive, seeking to control 'how much of his personality he would reveal to others and how much not' (1964, p. 466).[1] It is in Freud's

---

[1] Paul Roazen (1979) interviewed many of Freud's surviving followers, pupils and patients. They said he rarely let his guard down with them. Roazen quotes Hans Sachs as saying that at his last meeting just before Freud's death, his teacher remained as remote as he had been when he had first met him thirty years earlier.

writings, however, that the simultaneous connections between revelation and concealment become apparent, and they do so for a very good reason.

Freud, after training as a doctor, specialising in neuropathology, and also after conducting original physiological research, started his medical practice as a 'nerve-doctor' treating those who suffered from psychological disorders, particularly neuroses. Breuer, who had similar psychological and medical interests, helped Freud in a number of ways, including sending patients to his young colleague.[2] Initially Freud attempted to use hypnosis, but he turned to encouraging his patients to relax and speak about themselves. Both Freud and Breuer became convinced that many of their patients were concealing memories from themselves. In *Studies on Hysteria*, he and Breuer argued that neuroses were based on the repressing, or motivated forgetting, of a troubling memory.

Freud began to suspect that the motivated forgetting, which he and Breuer had observed in neurotics, was something that we all do. If that were the case, then Freud, just like anyone, would have repressed memories. In that spirit, Freud began to investigate the workings of his own mind. His period of intensive self-analysis, between autumn 1897 and autumn 1898, was vital for the development of psycho-analysis, and later followers would see it as a decisive, courageous step. Ernest Jones wrote that Freud's analysis of his own unconscious was a momentous achievement and 'the uniqueness of the feat remains' (1964, p. 276). A later biographer Peter Gay writes that Freud's self-analysis 'has become the cherished centrepiece of psycho-analytic mythology' (1989, p. 96). According to Laplanche and Pontalis (1983), Freud's self-analysis was unique because it did not 'involve the application of prior knowledge' (p. 413).

We do not really know how Freud went about conducting his own self-analysis. Much of what we know comes from his correspondence with his close friend Wilhelm Fliess, who was also a medical doctor, specialising in treating patients with nervous complaints and given to bold psychological and neurological theorising some of which was highly eccentric. At the time of Freud's self-analysis their relationship was close and they corresponded regularly, although later their friendship would collapse on account of their respective intellectual insecurities and mutual jealousies (Breger, 2000, pp. 149ff.).[3] From time to time, Freud would inform

---

[2] See Breger (2000, 2009) for details of the ways that Breuer assisted Freud in the early days and how they engaged in a fruitful collaboration.

[3] Freud's friendship and collaboration with Josef Breuer also collapsed, as Breger (2009) has detailed. The subtitle of Breger's book succinctly summarises his overall thesis: *How Freud Betrayed His Mentor and Invented Psycho-analysis*. There may be a pattern in Freud's relations with some, but not all, close male colleagues. Roazen (1979) discusses Freud's

Fliess how his self-analysis was proceeding, although typically his remarks were brief and he withheld details.

In a letter which he sent to Fliess on November 1897, Freud wrote that his self-analysis had suddenly started when he returned from holiday that summer and that 'the most important patient for me was myself' (Freud, 1985, p. 279). In that letter he gives a tantalising hint of how he conducted the analysis of himself. 'True self-analysis' was impossible, he wrote, but he had realised that 'I can analyse myself only with the help of knowledge obtained objectively (like an outsider)' (p. 281). It was as if he had to divide himself, treating himself as if he were his own patient. In this regard, Freud's self-analysis is a version of Shaftesbury's self-discourse and interestingly, as was mentioned in Chapter 2, Shaftesbury referred to himself as becoming his own patient. Shaftesbury suspected that as people analyse their own conduct, they often fail to apply the same exacting standards as they do when assessing the conduct of others.

If we combine Shaftesbury's remarks about his own self-discourse with Freud's brief comments to his friend about his self-analysis, we can see a way of assessing Freud's claims about himself. We can ask about any of the examples of his self-analysis, including his self-analysed dreams and slips of memory, whether he is judging himself as he would have judged another person, and most particularly, a patient. That, as we shall see, is a crucial question to be asked about his analysis of the reasons why he forgot the name of Signorelli – and, along with this, there is the question whether he treats his feelings for his sister-in-law as he treated Elisabeth von R's feelings for her brother-in-law.

The theoretical results of Freud's self-analysis would decisively affect the theory and practice of psycho-analysis in two principal ways. First, the self-analysis reinforced Freud's conviction that 'normal' people, and not just neurotics, had secrets that they concealed from conscious awareness and that these secrets would intrude on mental life in curious, uncontrolled ways. The insight would affect the training of psycho-analysts. All those wishing to train as psycho-analysts would first have to be psycho-analysed themselves so that they could become aware of their own hidden secrets and would avoid supposing that it was only their patients who had hidden, repressed psychological lives. As Shaftesbury had said, anyone dealing with characters must first know their own character.

The second major influence of Freud's self-analysis on the development of psycho-analytic thinking was the belief that the major secrets that people keep from themselves were derived from childhood traumas and

___

quarrels with other former collaborators and followers, such as Carl Jung, Alfred Adler and Wilhelm Steckler.

that these repressed traumas principally, but not exclusively, related to infantile sexuality. Freud was to write that his self-analysis, which he conducted 'with the help of a series of my own dreams', led him back 'through all the events of my childhood' (1914/1993, p. 78). Henceforth Freud's treatment of patients, whether neurotic or ostensibly 'healthy', would involve him leading them back to their childhood, and then he would seek to connect the hidden feelings of childhood to their adult desires. This was different from the results of the 'talking cure' that Freud and Breuer presented in *Studies on Hysteria*, which was published before Freud had begun his self-analysis. Principally, Freud and Breuer were connecting adult neuroses to adult experiences.

The case of Elisabeth von R. (Ilona Weiss) is an example. She was the youngest of three daughters in a prosperous family. She suffered from sudden pains and loss of mobility in her limbs as well as from other painful symptoms. Freud, after a careful examination, concluded that her symptoms had a psychological rather than physical cause, and he traced her neurotic symptoms to repressed memories. Principally, these were adult memories and feelings that she was trying to push from her mind, especially her erotic feelings for her brother-in-law. As such, the pre-self-analytic Freud was able to 'solve' the case of Elisabeth without linking present problems to childhood traumas – something that the post-self-analytic Freud would not do. Nearly thirty years later, he was to write that 'the decisive repressions all take place in early childhood' (1926/1993, p. 304).

The Effects of Social Demands

The immediate literary consequence of Freud's self-analysis was three major psychological books, exploring the operation of the human mind. First came *The Interpretation of Dreams* (1900) and then *Psychopathology of Everyday Life* (1901); then these two were followed by his great work on humour, *Jokes and Their Relation to the Unconscious* (1905). In these works, Freud developed the highly original and controversial idea that the 'waste-products' of the mind, such as dreams, temporary lapses of memory and many, but not all, jokes, were governed by unconscious, repressed desires.

Faced with understanding the meaning of dreams or why someone might forget a familiar name or word, or laugh at an improper joke, Freud was advocating that analysts should search for unadmitted motives. In these books, Freud included a wealth of examples. In *Dreams* Freud analysed more than 140 dreams. No one before *Jokes* had previously written a serious book on humour with as many jokes as Freud did. In fact, both Locke and Shaftesbury had been able to write on wit and mockery respectively without including a single joke. *Psychopathology* contained even more examples than *Dreams* had – 276 examples of what Freud called *Fehlleistungen*, literally failed performances, but translated into English for the Standard Edition as 'parapraxes'. These included temporary losses of memory, uttering wrong words, bungled actions and so on.

Many of the examples that Freud used in these books, especially in *Dreams* and *Psychopathology*, came from his life and their analysis was part of his self-analysis. In *Jokes* he used examples of the sort of humour that he enjoyed. Freud acknowledged that his tactic of using examples from his own life created particular difficulties. In the preface to *Dreams*, Freud explained why he needed to use his personal material. The only dreams that he could analyse in depth were either those that his patients had told him or his own dreams. The dreams of his patients were complicated by the presence of 'neurotic features' because most of his patients at that time had come to him because of their neuroses.

In addition, Freud felt a duty to protect the privacy of his patients. Therefore, he could not use as many of their dreams as he would have wished. Freud felt that he could only circumvent these problems by using his own dreams. However, this brought other problems, as it became apparent that this reticent man would have to reveal 'more of the intimacies of my mental life than I liked'. This was a 'painful but unavoidable necessity'. Freud admitted that he had been 'unable to resist the temptation of taking the edge off some of my indiscretions by omissions and substitutions' (1900/1991, p. 45). Thus the revelation of his inner self simultaneously involved careful and deliberate self-censorship.

In *Psychopathology* Freud used many examples of failed performances or parapraxes from his own life. Again he alluded to the problem of writing publicly about personal material. This time he could reflect on his previous experience of writing about himself and he mentioned how his dream book contained errors of a personal nature. Of course, he was well aware of these when he had been deliberately 'taking the edge' off some of his revelations about his dreams. There were, however, other 'falsifications which I was astonished to discover after the book was published' (1901/1975, p. 276). Some of these falsifications in *Dreams* became the sort of examples that he examined in *Psychopathology*. Freud claimed that these errors were often the result of failures of memory which in their turn were 'derivatives of repressed thoughts' (p. 278). These were principally linked, so Freud claimed, to memories of his dead father. Such unconscious falsifications were, in his view, psychologically more deep-rooted than the conscious, careful falsifications that merely rounded off the edges.

Freud wrote that the discovery of the unconscious errors in his dream book put him in an awkward position. If he were to correct those errors, then the original concealments would become obvious with the consequence that he would end up publicly revealing even more about himself. So, his self-analysis had an unforeseen literary result: some of the unconscious errors in *Dreams* had become conscious errors. Freud added that he expected his present book, *Psychopathology*, which contained many personal examples, would also have unconscious errors that were derived from repressed thoughts. Like the errors of *Dreams* he would only discover these new errors when it would be too late to do much about them. In this way, Freud was advising his readers to be cautious of what he was writing about himself. If he could not entirely trust what he had written about himself, then neither should his readers.

However, by no means all – and perhaps not even the majority – of Freud's own examples in *Psychopathology* would necessarily contain unconscious errors. There is a good theoretical reason for saying this. In the case of dreams, Freud was dealing with highly individual phenomena. He argued that people's deeply hidden and highly personal desires surfaced as the conscious mind slept. After his self-analysis, Freud believed that the content of dreams would reflect the decisive repressions of childhood. In the case of everyday parapraxes or psychopathologies, and even more so in the case of jokes, Freud was dealing with phenomena that are intrinsically social in the way that dreams are not. Such phenomena, unlike the dreams of the solitary sleeper, largely occur in social situations. For instance, in *Psychopathology*, Freud described an incident when the president of the Lower House of the Austrian Parliament opened proceedings by declaring, 'Gentlemen, I take notice that a full quorum of members is present and herewith declare the sitting *closed*' (1901/1975, p. 101, emphasis in original). Freud's explanation for the error was that the president was tired of the proceedings and secretly wished to close the parliament that he was being required to open.

The president's error was greeted with general merriment, and Freud's explanation resembled those that he was to apply to motivated, or tendentious, jokes. Social life makes demands upon us, and under normal circumstances we have to conform to those demands, however irksome we find them. We must be polite and restrained, respecting the social proprieties of everyday life. The president of the Parliament had to act in a formal way that took no account of his personal preferences. As Freud suggested in *Jokes*, we can rebel against the demands of everyday life by making jokes. Because a joke is not a serious rebellion, we can get away with the infraction; moreover, the receivers of the joke can share the pleasures of rebellion with their laughter. Nothing, however, is seriously threatened and the joke can be dismissed as just a joke, although psycho-logically it is much more than a joke (Billig, 2005). Similarly, we can make a mistake, like the parliamentary president saying the opposite of what he should have said. The consequence, like the consequence of a good joke, was shared enjoyment, as others momentarily escaped from the serious constraints of the occasion. When the laughter died down, the proceed-ings of parliament began: nothing had changed.

There was no need for Freud to invoke the hidden repressions of childhood to explain the parliamentary president's slip or the pleasure that the deputies took in the slip. Individually, the deputies might have had very different childhood traumas, but these differences were not relevant to the shared pleasures of the moment. Freud's theory of ten-dentious joking suggests that the laughing deputies might well have denied that they were enjoying the moment because they were aggres-sively laughing at the expense of the authority of the president. Even if there was denial and momentary aggression, it was socially shared and, consequently, not to be explained by each deputy's distant, individually experienced childhood trauma.

It was the same with many of the examples that Freud gave of his own slips and errors in *Psychopathology*. In fact, many examples in *Psychopathology* show the links between everyday errors and humour. Freud writes of one particular error that he constantly made and that he found 'irritating and laughable' (1901/1975, p. 158). Whenever he was on holiday walking down the streets of a strange town, he found himself mistakenly reading shop signs as if they were advertising the sale of 'Antiquities'. This eagerness, he wrote, reflected the spirit of the collector. The Freud Museum in London now houses many of Freud's antiquities, and its catalogue, *20 Maresfield Gardens* (Freud Museum, 1998), contains a very interesting chapter on Freud's eclectic collection of antiquities and his constant desire for accumulating further objects. The catalogue records that Freud enjoyed, rather than analysed, his passion for collect-ing antiquities.

Antiquities and self-mockery made another appearance in *Psychopathology* when Freud discussed the topic of 'Bungled actions'. He recounted that he kept some of his collection of antiquities on his desk. In front of his antiquities, he had placed an inkpot with a marble cover. Freud was perplexed one day when he found that, as he worked at the desk, he had accidentally swept the inkpot's cover to the floor, break-ing it. Perhaps the accident had been not quite so accidental and 'the explanation was not hard to find' (1901/1975, p. 221). Earlier in the day, his sister had come into his study and admired his antiquities. She said that the collection was being spoiled by the inkpot cover and that he should replace it with a more attractive one. Freud surmised that he wanted to buy a new cover but felt guilty about the unnecessary expenditure; perhaps he hoped that his sister would buy him a new cover on the next festive occasion. Freud suspected that his 'accident' was unconsciously deliberate as the sweep of his arm created the need for a newer, more attractive inkpot cover.

As in the case of the parliamentary president, Freud's destruction of the inkpot cover could be explained in terms of the demands of the present (and future), not those of the distant past. It was what his sister had said that very day, his hopes for a future purchase and his own nonconsciously deliberate action that had condemned the old inkpot cover. In *Psychopathology*, as in *Jokes*, Freud rarely explains his examples in terms of childhood repression. This is the case with his forgetting the name of Signorelli. In the versions that he published, he hinted that an intentionally suppressed theme was associated with repressed thoughts, which might well have related to his childhood but without explicitly saying that his memory loss was actually caused by the repression of childhood memories.

Freud did, however, include a very short chapter on childhood memories in the first edition of *Psychopathology* and he expanded this chapter in a later edition of the book. Here Freud argued that our surviving memories of childhood typically are 'screen memories' which function to screen off the important memories of childhood. He suggested that screen memories operate in similar ways to the temporary forgetting of names for both are screening out experiences. In discussing screen memories, Freud stressed that he was only pointing out the similarity between the 'formation of screen memories' and the adult forgetting proper names and that he was also aware of their substantial differences, not least because the former are permanent while the latter are temporary (1901/1975, p. 84). He was not suggesting – and this must be emphasised – that the adult's temporary lapses of memory must be explained in terms of what the screen memories of childhood might be screening.

Freud's self-analysis has a double-edged consequence. If we want to understand the whole person, then we must relate their present to their childhood, with the analysis of dreams providing a royal route to the forgotten, or screened off, past. On the other hand, if we want to understand why a particular everyday failure had occurred, it is often unnecessary to trace the failure back to childhood – although if we want to understand the particular failure in terms of the whole personality, it might be useful to do so. The adult parapraxis, unlike a dream, generally occurs within a social context and, in consequence, it can often be seen as an unconscious reaction to the demands of that situation. The distinction is important when we come to discuss Freud's forgetting the name of Signorelli. He partly explains his lapse of memory in terms of the demands of the social situation in which he found himself rather than in terms of childhood repressions. I will be suggesting that Freud omitted crucial aspects of the wider and still recent context that he may have been trying to screen from conscious awareness.

Forgetting 'Signorelli': Different Accounts of the Episode

Freud's memory lapse occurred in the summer of 1898 when he was holidaying on the Adriatic coast. He had travelled on 31 August to Ragusa (now Dubrovnik) with his wife, Martha, who then fell ill and remained in Ragusa, while Freud continued on his own to Cattaro in Bosnia (Simmons, 2006, p. 33). It was on the journey to Cattaro that he experienced his famous loss of memory. The whole holiday took place during Freud's famous period of self-analysis.

Freud left three versions of the episode – one private and two public. There are small differences in the way that he described the incident and, as will be seen, these minor differences can be linked to major self-concealments:

1 The private letter to Fliess. On 22 September, three days after returning to Vienna from his holiday, Freud wrote to Fliess telling him of his surprising lapse of memory and informing him that he had already solved the mystery why the lapse occurred (Freud, 1985, pp. 326–7).
2 The Scientific Article. Five days later, Freud again wrote to Fliess, this time telling him that he had 'turned Signorelli into a little essay' which he had sent to the editor of *Monatsschrift für Psychiatrie und Neurologie* (Freud, 1985, p. 328). The article was published later that year under the title of '*Zum psychischen Mechanismus der Vergesslichkeit*' ('The Psychical Mechanism of Forgetting') (Freud, 1898/1948).
3 The Popular Chapter. Freud next wrote about the episode when he turned it into the opening chapter of *Psychopathology*. Freud wrote this chapter between late 1900 and February 1901 (Freud, 1985, pp. 467–8). Of the three versions this is the one that has become the most widely known and quoted.

The basic features of the episode remain the same in all three versions. The lapse of memory occurred as Freud was travelling from Ragusa by carriage in the company of another man. The two were talking and Freud found that he could not remember the name of the artist who painted *The Last Judgement*, which Freud had viewed in Orvieto the previous year. All he could think of were the names 'Botticelli' and 'Boltraffio', but he knew that neither of them was the artist whose name he was unsuccessfully trying to recall. That much is the same in all three versions, but the descriptions of the travelling companion, the conversation that they shared and the timing of the incident vary.

The Travelling Companion and the Fairy Story

In his letter to Fliess, Freud described and named the travelling companion: 'a lawyer from Berlin (Freyhau)'. Freud mentioned that they 'got talking about pictures' and that 'in the conversation which aroused memories that evidently caused the repression, we talked about death and sexuality' (1985, p. 327). That is all Freud has to say in the letter about the conversation with Freyhau and some commentators have suggested that Freud and Freyhau might have already been acquainted before the carriage ride (Simmons 2006; Weber, 2017). Freud tells Fliess that the name 'Boltraffio' is 'no doubt an echo of Trafoi, which I saw on the first trip'. He then asks, 'How can I make this credible to anyone?' (p. 326).

The 1898 *Monatsschrift* version does not contain the information about the travelling companion that Freud had given Fliess in his letter. In the article he is merely my 'companion' (*Begleiter*) or 'travelling companion' (*Reisegefährte*), anonymous and without occupation (Freud, 1898/1948 p. 520; 1898/1960, p. 479). When he made his account public, Freud would have been aware of the need to preserve his companion's anonymity.

In the *Monatsschrift* article Freud describes the conversation in greater detail than he had in his letter to Fliess. He recounts that he talked about the Turks of Bosnia and that he repeated a story that he had heard from a medical colleague who had lived in Bosnia. The story was about a dying Bosnian patient, and it illustrated the respect that Bosnians have for doctors. Freud adds that 'another recollection lay in my memory close to this story' (1898/1960, p. 480). The doctor had told him that Bosnians attached great importance to sexual pleasure, and he had told Freud a story that illustrated this. Freud describes remembering this second story on the drive, but he stopped himself from telling it. It was after this that the conversation with his travelling companion turned to art. Freud spoke about the frescoes he had seen in the cathedral of Orvieto. At this point the name of the artist who had painted those frescoes escaped him.

The account in the first chapter of *Psychopathology* follows the *Monatsschrift* article with regard to the conversation, but it contains some further elaborations of the unspoken story. Freud, having recounted his telling the story about the Bosnians' respect for doctors, then continues: 'I recall in fact wanting to tell a second anecdote which lay close to the first in my memory' (1901/1975, p. 39). Freud then specifies why he resisted telling the story – something he had not done in the *Monatsschrift* piece: 'I did not wish to allude to the topic in a conversation with a stranger [*mit einem Fremden*]' (1901/1975, p. 39; 1901/1948, p. 8). In *Psychopathology*, but not in the letter or the scientific article, Freud specifically calls his travelling companion a 'stranger'. He uses the term when describing his trip: 'I was driving in the company of a stranger [*Ich machte mit einem Fremden eine Wagenfahrt*] from Ragusa in Dalmatia to a place in Herzegovina' (1901/1975, p. 39; 1901/1948, p. 7).

The three accounts present a sequence in the way that the companion is described. In the private letter to Fliess, he is identified by name, city and profession. In the second, he is an anonymous travelling companion. By the third, he has become a stranger. One might think that Freud is merely assuring the anonymity of his companion in the published versions, whereas in his private letter to Fliess he felt free to identify some personal details. However, that does not explain the difference between the two published versions.

The changing description of the fellow conversationalist can be linked to the way that Freud describes their conversation. In his letter to Fliess, Freud not only implies that he might have been acquainted with his companion, but he states that the two speak of death and sexuality. Here there is no suggestion that he needed to suppress a topic from the conversation because it was unsuitable for a conversation with a stranger. In the *Monatsschrift* article, sexuality has become a topic that Freud suppresses from the conversation. *Psychopathology* emphasises this point: it is *because* the other is a stranger that Freud claims to have felt the need to suppress his second story.

This version of the episode – or, to be more precise, this part of this version – contains a significant absence in its story within a story. Freud's account is that he held back from telling his second story out of social propriety. He does not suggest that he might have had personal reasons for not bringing sex into the conversation. In this way, the description of the other conversationalist as a stranger is rhetorically necessary for the reason that Freud gives for not telling his tale about Bosnians and sex. To sustain this, he cannot then describe the actual conversation as covering sex as well as death, as he did in his letter to Fliess.

Each of these small changes is insignificant in itself, but when combined they show how Freud's descriptions of the incident fit his interpretations. He subtly changed the wording of his story, so that in his final version Freud was describing the incident in a way that supports a socially respectable explanation, rather than a deeply personal one. In *Psychopathology*, he was implying that preventing oneself from saying something socially inappropriate may disrupt the mechanisms of individual memory. Nevertheless, unspecified repression hovers around the account. 'Repressed thoughts' are at the base of the diagram that Freud used in both publications to illustrate the incident.

The examples show that Freud's descriptions of the incident are not rhetorically neutral, but that they match his interpretations of what happened. At this point, it should be stressed that I am not implying that Freud was cheating in his descriptions. I will be returning to Freud's descriptions later in this chapter; and in later chapters I will be discussing the general point that good descriptions typically contain interpretations. Here we have an example of the way that a description of an event need not be 'neutral' or 'interpretation-free'. As we describe an event, our descriptions, whether implicitly or explicitly, will be carrying interpretations. Freud was artfully providing an example of this.

There is something interesting about the way that Freud began his description of the event in the *Monatsschrift* article as compared with *Psychopathology*. When describing the incident in *Monatsschrift*, Freud did not write in the impersonal tone that editors of scientific journals now expect (Biber and Conrad, 2009; Billig, 2013; Hyland, 2009). He begins his description with the sort of storyteller's tone that he had employed so successfully in the case histories of *Studies on Hysteria*: 'During my summer holidays I once went for a carriage drive from the lovely city of Ragusa to a town nearby in Herzegovina' (1898/1960, p. 290; 1898/1948, p. 520). The word 'lovely' (*schönen*) seems to add a purely literary flourish, which is irrelevant to Freud's scientific argument. Yet, Freud is a clever writer. He knows that the description of an episode needs to exceed the barest of theoretical necessities, but, especially in a serious scientific journal, it should not be overblown. 'Lovely' reinforces economically why he is in the area: he is there seeing the sites.[4]

There is another word in the same sentence of the *Monatsschrift* article that Freud does not use in his description of the incident in *Psychopathology*: 'once' (*einmal*). It is the sort of small word that is easy to overlook. Freud wrote in *Studies on Hysteria* that his case histories seemed not to carry the serious stamp of science. Certainly 'once' appears

---

[4] Freud does not use 'lovely' when mentioning Ragusa in *Psychopathology*. He merely says that the incident occurred when he was travelling 'from Ragusa in Dalmatia to a place in Herzegovina' (1901/1975, p. 39). In *Psychopathology*, he does not begin the account of the incident with the carriage journey. He began it earlier with the artist who painted 'the magnificent frescoes' in Orvieto cathedral (p. 38). Again, he is using an adjective with rhetorical effect and literary economy. The adjective 'magnificent' lets the reader know that Freud has personally seen and been impressed by these paintings. In consequence, the artist's name should not be one that slips from his memory. Again, with a single, seemingly irrelevant adjective, he accomplishes much rhetorically.

to be an example of non-serious, unscientific rhetoric. It conveys vagueness about when the episode might have occurred. Moreover, it is a word often used at the start of a folk tale or fairy story: Once upon a time (*es war einmal*) I went for a carriage ride from the beautiful city of . . .

Why should the scientific article use a word that echoes the language of fairy tales, while the popular account does not? I will suggest an explanation later. For now, I will drop a hint. The *Monatsschrift* piece implies that the event may have taken place a while ago. However, to judge from Freud's letters to Fliess, the earliest date when the event could have occurred is 1 September and the latest date for Freud completing his article is less than a month later, on 27 September. Freud's description in *Monatsschrift* offers no clue that he writing about something that had occurred so recently. This is not an innocent description.

Freud's Explanation for His Memory Lapse

In his *Monatsschrift* article and in *Psychopathology*, Freud used the incident to illustrate his general thesis that hidden, unconscious motives can produce surprising mental accidents. As he wrote in *Psychopathology*, 'nothing in the mind is arbitrary or undetermined' (1901/1975, p. 303). Lapses of memory, including the temporary forgetting of proper names, are not random events, however much they might seem to be at the time. Behind them, argued Freud, can lie repressed motives. As he wrote in his *Introductory Lectures*, people are unlikely to forget a proper name which has 'no special meaning' to them; instead they are only likely to 'withhold from strangers a name which seems to them reserved for intimate connections' (1915/1991, p. 104).

When Freud involuntarily withheld the name of Signorelli from his travelling companion, then, according to his own theory, the word 'Signorelli' must have been linked to intimate personal factors. Merely wishing to observe social proprieties could not explain why it was Signorelli's name, rather than any other, that he forgot. Nor could social proprieties explain fully why 'Signorelli' was mentally replaced by the incorrect names of 'Botticelli' and 'Boltraffio'. Something extra was required to explain this mental accident.

Freud offered some clues, using the same diagram in *Monatsschrift* and in *Psychopathology*. Essentially the diagram traced the associations between the names of the three painters – that is, between 'Signorelli' and the two substitute names. The three names were arranged along the top of the diagram with 'Signorelli' on the left side. The associations attached to 'Signorelli' were listed downwards, finally arriving at 'Repressed thoughts' at the bottom of the diagram. Then, there were two arrows pointing upwards from 'Repressed thoughts' on the right side passing through 'Trafoi' on the way to the substitute name 'Boltraffio'; a chain of associations from 'Signorelli' reaches upwards to both 'Boltraffio' and 'Botticelli' (1901/1975, p. 41; 1901/1948, p. 524).

First, it should be stressed that Freud does not arrive at a single explanation. As he had argued in *Interpretation of Dreams*, mental events can have multiple causes; to use his own term, they can be overdetermined. In his dream book Freud wrote that when a dream is exhaustively analysed, it can be demonstrated that its 'content is overdetermined' (1900/1976, p. 399). In the *Monatsschrift* piece, he wrote that 'experience has taught me to require that every psychical product shall be fully elucidated and even overdetermined' (1898/1960, p. 481). As Freud writes of forgetting 'Signorelli', it was 'not enough that I suppressed it once in conversation' but the topic itself was 'also intimately bound up with trains of thought which were in a state of repression with me' (p. 481). Most commentators have assumed that the repressed thoughts on sex and death were associated in Freud's mind with his father who had died in 1896 (e.g. Breger, 2000).

There is no need to go through all the details of Freud's explanation, linking the three names to each other. He divides the name 'Signorelli' into two parts – 'signor' (Italian for 'mister') and 'elli'. Freud declares that 'elli' is not relevant to the forgetting since it appears in one of the substitute names (Botticelli), and so this part of the forgotten name cannot have been a target for motives to forget. Freud links the *signor* part of Signorelli's name to the German word *Herr*, which then has two further links. The first is to Bosnia and Herzegovina, with the first part of 'Bosnia' ('Bo') being uplinked to the first syllable to the two substitute names (Bo-tticelli and Bo-ltraffio). The second link is to the polite patient who habitually called his doctor 'Herr' and who told him the story about the Turks of Bosnia valuing sexual pleasure above life itself.

Thus, death and sexuality become associated with 'Signor'. This linkage is reinforced by the distressing news that Freud said he received in Trafoi: he was told about the suicide of a patient who was suffering from an incurable sexual disorder. Again Freud is referring back to recent events, not distant ones. 'Trafoi', now also associated with death and sexuality, points upwards in the diagram to 'Boltraffio', and, thus, the themes of sexuality and violence are unwittingly expressed in one of the substitute names. The connection between death and sexuality also points downwards towards Freud's own repressed thoughts. Of these, Freud writes in *Monatsschrift* that he had 'plenty of evidence', which was derived from his own 'self-investigation', of the powerful linkage of these two themes whose elements were being kept from consciousness. Freud states that the evidence for these hidden themes was something that 'he need not bring up here' (1898/1960, p. 481).

Nor did Freud reveal his personal secrets in *Psychopathology*. Here he used an active verb rather than the phrase 'state of repression'. He wrote that he had not wanted to think about the thoughts associated with the news that he received in Trafoi: 'I wanted therefore to forget something; I had *repressed* something' (1901/1975, p. 40, emphasis in original). What he wanted to forget was not the artist's name but something associated with it, and in consequence, 'I forgot *the one thing against my will*, while I wanted to forget *the other thing intentionally*' (p. 40, emphasis in original). Again, he is using active verbs, as if repressing is an action to be performed intentionally, but he does not say how one goes about performing this action. In his description, he is concentrating on the effects of the action, not the action itself.

Difficulties with Freud's Account of His Motives

Some critics have claimed that Freud's arguments about the connections between the forgotten name and the substituted names are flimsy and unscientific (e.g. Timpanaro, 1976; Erwin, 1996; Grünbaum, 1984). Swales (2003), a dogged critic of Freud, has said that there was a simpler association between the three artists: Freud had seen their works displayed together in Bergamo, and this could have provided the basis for his substituting those particular two names for 'Signorelli'. Swales also doubted other aspects of Freud's story and has claimed that Freud had his own secrets to hide. Other commentators have sought to take Freud's analysis further by adding themes such as religion, the content of the artists' work and Freud's own Jewish identity (e.g. Anzieu, 1986; Billig, 2000; Lippman, 2008; Owens, 2004; Simmons, 2006; Weber, 2017).

Freud's analysis of his memory lapse was part of his self-analysis, but his accounts do not tell us how he went about the business of analysing himself in general or this incident in particular. Even the defenders of Freud do not attempt to fill this gap. Didier Anzieu's magisterial book *Freud's Self-Analysis* (1986) is generally recognised to be the classic work on the subject. By relating factors in Freud's life to the accounts of his dreams and of his childish memories, Anzieu develops some of Freud's explanations, but he does not discuss how Freud might have actually engaged in the process of self-analysis. Instead, he concentrates on the results of the self-analysis rather than on the process itself.[5]

---

[5] One historian has written about Freud's self-analysis, contrasting it with 'introspective hypnosis' (Mayer, 2001–2). A hypnotist like Charcot expected his patients to submit

We can imagine Freud, rather like Shaftesbury many years earlier, dividing himself into two selves. Shaftesbury had noted that when we are our own inquisitor, we can sometimes avoid asking ourselves difficult questions. So, we can ask: When Freud examined himself was he being gentler with himself than he would have been with a patient? This question should lead us beyond the question of Freud's self-analysis to the question how people can repress guilty thoughts from their minds. As we will see, Freud had a guilty secret at the time of the conversation in the carriage and, afterwards, when he was analysing that incident.

First, there is the problem that Freud seems to uncover his repressed thoughts without great difficulty. He writes that the name 'Signorelli' was connected with trains of thought which 'were in a state of repression with me' (1898/1960, p. 481). If thoughts are in a state of repression, then they should not be available for conscious inspection by the thinker. By implication, Freud was saying that, since the episode, he had been able to bring these repressed thoughts into conscious awareness; otherwise, he would not have been aware of their existence. In neither *Monatsschrift* nor *Psychopathology* does he indicate how he did this; nor, most crucially, how long it took him to do so.

Here Freud's vagueness about when the episode took place is relevant. In *Monatsschrift*, by using the word 'once', as in 'I once went for a carriage drive', he can avoid saying that within the last three weeks, I have experienced the incident, been able to analyse it, understand how my repressed thoughts caused me to forget a name that I knew well, and also write up the whole matter for a scientific publication. Most importantly, he avoids saying or implying that, at the centre of all this activity, within the same three weeks I have been able to make my repressed thoughts conscious.

There was no reason to use 'once' *Psychopathology*. The actual event was no longer recent and Freud had already conveyed this to his readers. The chapter and, thus, his whole book, opens with the words: 'In the 1898 volume of the *Monatsschrift für Psychiatrie und Neurologie* I published under the title of "The Psychical Mechanism of Forgetfulness" a short paper the substance of which I shall recapitulate here' (1901/1975, p. 37). Not only is Freud stating that the episode occurred a while ago, but also, by naming the journal in full and giving the article's technical title, he is at

themselves to his will. Freud, by contrast, expected his patients to argue with him and to resist his suggestions. Thus, Freud's self-analysis, Mayer suggests, cannot have been a form of introspective hypnosis. This line of thinking can be taken further. If Freud, when he analysed himself, had divided himself into two selves – that of doctor and that of patient – then we might expect the resulting internal conversation to resemble his conversations with his patients and these often involved the exchange of conflicting views and, most crucially, resistance on the part of the patient.

the outset giving the serious stamp of science to his book. Surely, a scientific journal can be trusted to print scientific material. The use of 'once' in the first sentence that describes the incident is now unnecessary.

Had Freud let slip how short the time period between the incident and its analysis had been, he would have would have been implying that it can be a simple, speedy matter to translate thoughts that are in a state of repression into consciously acknowledged ones. That, of course, runs counter to the psycho-analytic practice and theory that Freud was developing. He was claiming that patients generally resist acknowledging their repressed thoughts. They will deny the suggestions that their analyst might make. They will do this, even if they believe in psycho-analytic theory. In *Introductory Lectures* Freud discussed what he called 'intellectual resistance': someone can accept psycho-analysis in theory 'on condition that analysis spares him personally' (1915/1991, p. 331). Was Freud sparing himself?

When Freud forgot 'Signorelli', he had already published the case history of Elisabeth von R. in *Studies on Hysteria*. He had begun treating her in the autumn of 1892. Elisabeth was the youngest of three sisters and Freud suspected her of being unconsciously in love with the middle sister's husband. This observation did not require specialist techniques for Elisabeth's mother later told Freud that she had 'long ago guessed Elisabeth's fondness for the young man' (Freud and Breuer, 1895/1991, p. 229). When Freud put the suggestion to Elisabeth, she displayed strong resistance. She cried out that she was incapable of such wickedness; she accused Freud of making it all up; and then her painful neurotic symptoms returned with such force that she and Freud had to put an end to their conversation (Freud and Breuer, 1895/1991, p. 227). Freud suspected that Elisabeth was using her neurotic symptoms to resist his suggestion and, thus, to resist self-insight.

Elisabeth's reactions contrast markedly with those of another patient, Lucy R., whose case also appears in *Studies on Hysteria*. Freud suspected that Lucy might have been in love with her employer and he put the suggestion to her. She replied: 'Yes, I think that's true' (Freud and Breuer, 1895/1991, p. 181). Freud commented that she was willing to discuss his suggestion and therefore her feelings showed no sign of being repressed. Had Elisabeth willingly accepted Freud's suggestion, as Lucy R. did, then she would not have been displaying the signs that her love was repressed, because repression without some resistance and denial is not really repression.

If Freud were showing signs of intellectually resisting uncomfortable reasons for forgetting 'Signorelli', then he should be making the sort of implausible, outright denial that those with repressed thoughts make.

There are two statements of denial that seem to close off his exploration of obvious connections. First, Freud denies that the examples from his own life, which he examines in *Psychopathology*, are related to sexual desire. In the book's final chapter he wrote that 'sexual currents' usually play 'no small part' in the failed performances of everyday life. However, they rarely appear in the examples, which he was taking from his own life, because the selection of his own examples was 'partial from the first and aimed at excluding sexual matters' (1901/1975, p. 341). Readers might suppose that the key illustrative example, which so prominently formed the basis of the book's first chapter, might be one of the examples that he selected because it excluded sexual matters.

The second denial concerns his chain of associations from 'Signorelli'. In his analysis, *signor* is associated only with 'Herr', and all subsequent associations are connected with 'Herr'. Thus the Italian word *signor* plays no other part in the analysis, except to lead to 'Herr'. As Freud wrote, the reason why name Signorelli was lost 'is not to be found in anything special about the name itself or in any psychological characteristic of the context in which it was introduced' (p. 38). He offers no reason for this categorical statement. As we shall see, there are some obvious reasons to doubt the assertion, in relation both to the Italian word *signor* and also to the wider context in which the slip occurred. This wider context relates to Freud's relationship with his wife's sister, Minna Bernays.

Minna Bernays and Sigmund

The Signorelli episode occurred during the series of holidays that Freud took in the summer of 1898. In mid-August he holidayed with Minna, travelling together in the Tyrol and Switzerland. Then, almost immediately after this trip, he began the holiday with his wife Martha, heading towards the Adriatic coast. However, as has been mentioned, Martha fell ill and Sigmund left her in Ragusa to undertake the famous carriage journey on his own. The background to the episode, therefore, was his trip with Minna, followed by the broken trip with Martha. Freud does not mention any of this in his published versions.

During Freud's lifetime, there was gossip that he had an affair with Minna. Jung, one source for the gossip, claimed that Minna told him of their affair, when he first met her on a visit to Freud's house in 1907. Admirers of Freud have not been slow to point out that Jung had much to gain from discrediting Freud within the world of psycho-analysis (e.g. Gay, 1989, 1990). There even seem to have been rumours of an affair circulating among some more distant members of the Freud family (Gale, 2016). Paul Roazen (1997), who was generally sympathetic to Freud, wrote that he was sceptical about 'the legend' of an affair. In an effort to counteract the gossip, Ernest Jones (1964) emphasised in his biography that Freud was 'peculiarly monogamous' (p. 474). He wrote that Martha was 'the only woman in Freud's love life' and claimed that the passionate side of Freud's marriage 'subsided with him earlier than it does with many men' (p. 453).

Critics of Freud have given credence to Jung's story of an affair. Some have interpreted Freud's dreams to suggest that Freud was drawn to Minna sexually (e.g. O'Brien, 1991). The most persistent and persuasive of the critics has been Peter Swales, who claimed Freud's story in the second chapter of *Psychopathology* to be evidence of an affair (Swales, 1982). There, Freud told of meeting a young man who spoke of forgetting the Latin word *aliquis*. Freud interpreted this lapse in terms of the young man having an affair and his lover becoming pregnant. Swales claimed that the young man was Freud himself and the lover was Minna. Critics of psycho-analysis have tended to support Swales on this matter (e.g. Crews, 1995; Webster, 1996), while sympathisers have stressed the weaknesses of Swales' interpretation (e.g. Breger, 2000; Gay, 1989). One commentator has written that Swales seems unaware that his complex interpretation sounded for all the world like a parody of Freud (Hux, 2017). There is, however, no longer a neat division between critics and supporters of Freud regarding their stance on Swales and his claims of an affair. Barry Gale (2016) carefully reviewed the evidence in his book *Love in Vienna* and concluded that Minna and Sigmund probably did have an affair, but he criticised Swales' arguments for being based upon far too much conjecture.

Putting aside for the moment the question whether Sigmund and Minna actually had an affair, there is the issue whether Sigmund may have been consciously or unconsciously in love with Minna, rather as he supposed that Elisabeth had been in love with her brother-in-law without actually engaging in an affair. There is evidence that Sigmund had a strong affection for Minna and that he was able to talk to Minna in ways he could not with Martha. It is clear that Martha did not show much interest in Sigmund's work. She once remarked that 'if I did not realize how seriously my husband takes his treatments, I should think that psycho-analysis is a form of pornography!' (Breger, 2000, p. 92). Anna Freud was to say that 'my mother believed in my father, not in psycho-analysis' (quoted by Young-Bruehl, 1988, p. 30). In contrast to Martha, Minna was greatly interested in Freud's ideas from the earliest days. In a letter to Fliess, dated 31 May 1894, Freud described Minna as 'my closest confidante' (p. 73). Towards the end of his life, Freud told his good friend Marie Bonaparte that Minna Bernays and Wilhelm Fliess were the only two people who really understood his ideas (Carter, 2011, p. 35).

It is clear that there was great warmth between Sigmund and Minna. When he began courting Martha in the spring of 1882, Sigmund wrote Minna a number of affectionate letters. In one, he called Minna 'My Treasure' (quoted in Gay, 1989, p. 76). Leonore Davidoff, in her study of nineteenth-century siblings, describes Freud's letters to Minna as 'frequent and even passionate' (2011, p. 197). There is little doubt that had Elisabeth von R. written similarly to her future brother-in-law, Freud would have considered such letters to be much more than innocent missives of friendship.[6]

There is a further parallel between the case of Elisabeth and her brother-in-law and that of Sigmund and his sister-in-law. In both cases, there was tragedy. Elisabeth's sister suffered from hereditary heart disease, and she died suddenly at a young age. According to Freud, when Elisabeth saw her sister lying dead in her bed, an immediate and shocking thought ran through her mind like a flash of lightning: 'Now he is free again and I can be his wife' (Freud and Breuer, 1895/1991, p. 226). She needed to dismiss the thought from her conscious mind and then keep it firmly in a state of repression. This is why, according to Freud, Elisabeth resisted so strongly when Freud brought up the idea.

Minna, too, suffered a tragedy. She became engaged to Ignaz Schönberg during the period when Sigmund was writing his 'My Treasure' letters. Freud's friendship with Schönberg dated back to their student days (Anzieu, 1986, p. 17). Unfortunately, Schönberg suffered from ill health, and he developed tuberculosis. In June 1885, conscious of his illness and its certain outcome, he broke off the engagement with Minna, and he was to die early the following year. Sigmund had not yet married Martha. Did he have an analogous, sudden thought: 'Now she is free again and she can be my wife'? But, of course, Sigmund was not free. He and Martha had been engaged for three and a half years, and they were to marry in the September of that year.

In the days following Ignaz's death, Sigmund wrote Minna a letter. It was a strange letter of consolation, as Sigmund did not observe the propriety of refraining to speak ill of the dead. He alluded to Ignaz breaking off the engagement to spare Minna the pain of losing him. Then Sigmund added that it was less Ignaz's 'high-minded intention

---

[6] Appignanesi and Forrester (1993), writing before the revelation about Sigmund and Minna sharing a hotel room, suggest that we cannot know whether or not there was an affair between the two. However, according to Appignanesi and Forrester, there is something that we can be more confident about: Minna represented the sort of woman to whom Freud was attracted (p. 52).

than the moral weakness of his last years that prompted him to do so' (Freud, 1960, p. 204). He did not comfort Minna by advising her to think back to happier times with Ignaz. Quite the reverse, he advised her not to look back: 'You have suffered a lot, you have had little joy and a lot of worry, and in the end a great deal of pain from this relationship'. Sigmund advised her to cut off contact with Ignaz's family and 'to burn your letters while it is still winter' (p. 205).

What Sigmund does not write is just as revealing as what does write. To modern readers, there is a huge, significant absence in his letter. Having advised her not to look back and even to burn her letters from Ignaz, one might expect Sigmund to offer comforting words saying that Minna should look forwards with hope: one day she will possibly meet someone who will give her real love and happiness, and so on. He does not write that, but Sigmund does not ignore all thoughts of Minna's future. He advises her to give her emotions 'a long rest' and to 'live quietly with the two of us who are closest to you now'; she should think 'what a long life we have ahead of us and what wonderful and extraordinary things may still happen to our little circle' (p. 205).

In this way, Sigmund was drawing Minna towards him, as he and Martha offered the isolated young woman a psychological home. After their marriage they also offered her a physical home: in late 1896 Minna came to live with them. Sigmund's letter of consolation may have been an act of kindness, but as Freud knew, acts can be overdetermined. Just because his words to Minna were motivated by kindness, this does not mean that at the same time they could not also be motivated by hidden, or even not-so-hidden, feelings of love.

For many years the gossip about an affair between Sigmund and Minna remained just gossip. Most of the letters, which the two wrote to each other between 1893 and 1910 and which might have clinched the matter one way or another, have been lost. However, in 2007, Franz Maciejewski, a Polish sociologist with a long-standing, sympathetic interest in psycho-analysis, published an article that shocked the psycho-analytic establishment. As he explained in an interview with Alma Bond from *Medscape*, he had long suspected that Sigmund and Minna did have an affair (Bond and Maciejewski, 2007). He did something so simple that it seems extraordinary that no-one had done it previously, but discoveries in the social sciences often depend on ideas that afterward, but not beforehand, seem obvious. Maciejewski visited the hotels in which Sigmund and Minna had stayed and which still remained in business. He asked if they had kept their old registers. The Hotel Schweizerhaus in the Swiss resort of Maloja still had its register for 1898. Freud had signed it on Saturday, 13 August, in his own hand: *Dr Sigm. Freud u[nd] Frau/*

Wien (Dr Sigm. Freud a[nd] wife/Vienna). They were staying in room number 11, checking out on the morning of Monday, 15 August, after two nights together in the same room.

Here surely was the proof for the affair that had long been suspected. Certainly Maciejewski thought so. He also speculated on the psycho-analytic significance of Sigmund calling Minna his 'wife' in the register (Maciejewski, 2007, 2008). Of course, it is likely that the hotel would have refused them the room if he had written in the register 'sister-in-law', rather than 'wife'. Within the psycho-analytic world there were accusers and defenders in what Silverstein (2007) called the 'Minna wars'. The accusers followed Maciejewski in taking the hotel register as decisive evidence of an affair. Freud's defenders pointed out that Maciejewski's discovery did not prove that Sigmund and Minna actually had sex (Hirschmüller, 2007; Lothane, 2007, 2009). Perhaps the two had been forced to share a room because the hotel was busy and all other rooms had been taken. Barry Gale (2016) suggests that, although the Schweizerhaus' register does not definitely prove that Sigmund and Minna had an affair, it makes the possibility all the more believable.

Of course, we do not know what went on in that hotel bedroom during those two August nights. For present purposes, we do not need to know what actually happened. Possibly Sigmund and Minna enjoyed passionate sex and might have repeated the pleasures on other occasions; or perhaps they had tried to have sex but found it unsatisfactory, embarrassing and never to be repeated. Or maybe each had kept to their own side of the bed, awkwardly and chastely avoiding physical contact, spending two prim, largely sleepless nights until it was time to rise for the morning. Even if they had remained chaste, Sigmund could hardly have been unaware of the close physical presence of his 'treasure' in her nightwear.

But what if it had been someone else, and not Freud himself? What would he have made of the incident? Certainly if Elisabeth von R. had admitted to her nerve doctor that she once shared a bed, or maybe just a room, with her brother-in-law for two nights, but that nothing untoward had happened, can one imagine that Freud would have taken her explanation at face value? Even if she had been pure in body, would he have accepted that she had been pure in thought and desire, either consciously or unconsciously? And what thoughts, conscious or unconscious, led to the sequence of events that ended with her sharing a room with her brother-in-law?

Any conjectures about what exactly occurred during Sigmund and Minna's stay at the Hotel Schweizerhaus must remain, to use Abraham Tucker's phrase once again, as hypotheses concerning things unknown. However, after the shared room in Maloja, there is something beyond mere conjecture. He could not tell his wife everything about his trip with Minna. The evasion had started early. While at the Maloja hotel, he had sent Martha a postcard saying that they were staying at a 'modest Swiss house', but, as Gale (2016, p. 27) comments, the hotel was anything but modest. Clearly, Freud returned home from his holiday with a secret that he could not share. The secret does not relate to the distant desires of childhood but to a very recent event that had breached accepted protocols of propriety, especially the proprieties of family life.

Maloja and Signor Signorelli

As far as I am concerned, the question is not what exactly happened in the Maloja hotel but whether Freud's analysis of his Signorelli incident might have been affected by Maloja. To offer an answer, it is necessary to demonstrate that there are links which Freud failed to make in his analysis – and that such links are so obvious that if Freud fails to make them, then, according to his own theory, some sort of denial must be suspected. There is a further matter: without indicating how thoughts might be pushed from the conscious mind, we have no way of linking Freud's speedy publication of the Signorelli incident with his nights in Maloja.

First the obvious gap: why specifically should Freud's temporary loss of memory concern the name 'Signorelli'? As Freud wrote, a central aspect of his theory is that the names which are forgotten are intimately linked with the motives to forget. Although Freud denied the importance of the Italian painter's name, there are easily made connections. Didier Anzieu points out that Sig-mund and Sig-norelli shared a similar first syllable and he speculated that Freud may have identified with Signorelli (1986, pp. 360–61). That is suggestive, but, for present purposes, we need to go further, for some sort of link must be established between the shared nights with Minna and the lapse of memory a few weeks later. Therefore, we need to ask if there is a specifically Italian association with the stay in Maloja that might be associated with 'Signorelli'. This is surprisingly easy to make, without even speculating on Freud's inner state of mind at the time.

Maloja is a small resort in the Swiss Alps, famous for its views that overlook Italy. The writer Stefan Zweig, who would become a close friend of Freud, wrote about the Italian views from Maloja in his posthumously published novel *The Post Office Girl*. The impoverished young woman who is the central character of the story is taken by a distinguished older man to Maloja. As they look out over the mountains, he points out to her that Italy is down below:

'Italy' says Christine wonderingly, 'is it really so close?' Her astonishment expressed such longing that Elkins asks immediately, 'You've never been there?' 'No, never'. (Zweig, 2009, p. 74; for Zweig's admiration of Freud's work, see Zweig, 2012)

We do not have to rely on Zweig's fiction to link Maloja, Italy and pleasure: Freud himself did so. A month before he wrote to Fliess about forgetting the name of Signorelli, and a week after the shared bedroom in Maloja, Freud wrote to his friend about his recent holiday in Switzerland. The letter, dated 20 August 1898, describes 'the pleasures of our trip' without mentioning Minna by name. 'It really was glorious', he wrote. He specifically picks out the visit to Maloja and its connection with Italy: 'Maloja, with Italy beyond, with an Italian air about it (probably merely imposed on it by our expectations)' (Freud, 1985, p. 322). So, he and Minna were enjoying themselves in Maloja, associating an Italian atmosphere with the place.

The significant absence in the explanatory diagram in *Monatsschrift* and *Psychopathology* becomes clearer. '*Signor*', the first part of Signorelli's name, in the diagram loses its Italian character as Freud translates it at the first step into '*Herr*', which he then associates with Herzegovina and with a patient who addresses the doctor as '*Herr*'. Not only is the Italian connection lost but so is the direct connection with any feelings of manliness – of Freud in Maloja being *il signor* with his *signora* or registered wife; and also the association of Sig-mund and Sig-norelli. The translation of '*signor*' into '*Herr*' permits a geographical translation from Italy to Bosnia and Herzegovina. The translation supports Freud's denial that *signor* has any significance; and this denial removes the possibility that the association with sexuality might concern Freud's sexuality, especially his recent sexuality. In this way, Freud's interpretation is directing attention away from his secret – that for two nights Sig-mund was his sister-in-law's *sig-nor*.

The question is not, How do these connections contribute to Freud's temporary loss of memory? It is, Why did Freud fail to make such obvious connections in his analysis? Something must have been stopping him. And then, there is a further question: What would Freud have thought if one of his patients had denied that there were such associations with the forgotten Italian name? Freud's own ideas about resistance and repression would have alerted him to suspect that something was being concealed.

Writing to Repress

Then there is the other question: Why should Freud have returned from his holiday determined to analyse immediately and then to write about an incident that prima facie seems to bear witness to an event that he would wish to keep secret? It seems a strange decision. Was it a tactic to divert attention from his secret? Nicholas Weber (2017), who briefly draws attention to the surprising exclusion of *signor* from Freud's analysis of the episode, called Freud's interpretation, which blamed the memory loss on what happened in Trafoi, a 'subterfuge' and 'cover up' for what happened in Maloja (p. 294). That might be too strong because it implies a deliberate, conscious strategy of deceit. We might be seeing something more interesting than subterfuge: we might be seeing an example of the early stages of someone repressing a troubling memory.

In his *Monatsschrift* article, Freud mentioned his unconscious thoughts which were in a state of repression. If thoughts are said to be in a state of repression then they must have already been repressed. But what does an adult have to do, in order to push troublesome thoughts out of their mind, and then to keep them pushed away? I have argued elsewhere that Freud does not really address the question, at least in his later works. He tended to write about 'repression' as if it were a mechanical process that occurs without conscious intervention (Billig, 1999, 2006a).

In *Studies on Hysteria*, written before his self-analysis and his emphasis on childhood repression, Freud offer some clues about the ways adult patients, like Elisabeth von R., might prevent themselves from thinking troubling thoughts. The very first time that Freud used the notion of repression in print was as an active verb, rather than the noun 'repression' (*Verdrängung*). In the opening section of the book, Freud and Breuer wrote about the memories underlying neuroses: 'It was a question of things which the person wished to forget, and therefore intentionally repressed from his conscious thought' (1895/1991, p. 61). Repressing is something that one has to do consciously, at least initially. The idea of intentionally repressing a troubling thought appears in Freud's chapter on Lucy R., when he wrote that a troubling idea 'must be *intentionally repressed from consciousness* and excluded from associative modification' (1895/1991, p. 181, emphasis in English translation but not in original German text: 1895/1952, p. 174).

Immediately after that sentence, Freud also used the noun 'repression', employing a rhetoric that bears the serious stamp of science. He wrote that 'the intentional repression', in his view, was the basis of 'the conversion' of the 'sum of excitation'; and this sum of excitation, 'being cut off from psychical association, finds its way all the more easily along the wrong path to a somatic innervation' (1895/1991, p. 181). Thus, Freud linguistically moves from active language – where repressing is something that a person does intentionally – to the language of technical nouns (conversion, psychical association, sum of excitation, somatic innervation, etc.), where these technical things seem to perform actions. For all the appearance of technicality and the serious stamp of science, the language of these technical nouns and noun phrases is less clear and conveys less information than the active language describing someone like Lucy R. intentionally repressing a troubling thought (for more details, see Billig, 2008b, 2008c, 2013; see also Schafer, 1976).

According to what Freud wrote in *Studies on Hysteria*, the act of repressing involved transforming a known idea into an idea that ceases to be consciously known, at least in a straightforward way. Elisabeth was, Freud wrote, 'in the peculiar situation of knowing and at the same time not knowing' her feelings for her brother-in-law (Freud and Breuer, 1895/1991, p. 236). She used her neurotic symptoms to distract herself whenever the conversation with Freud seemed to be turning towards her feelings for her brother-in-law, or worse still, towards her wish for her sister to die so that she could possess her husband. By distracting herself she could avoid becoming aware of what she knew and did not know. When Freud returned from holiday, he would know that he had spent two nights with Minna. How could he also begin not to know this? How could he distract himself?

Two aspects from the James/Tucker view of the mind illustrate how Elisabeth and Sigmund might have pushed their troubling thoughts from conscious awareness. First, if the mind is a continuous stream, then one cannot simply dismiss a memory or guilty desire from awareness, as if it could be removed from the conscious part of the mind and then be relocated in the unconscious area. Memories and desires are not physical objects that can be packaged up and then delivered to a different part of the mind. Nor can there be gaps in consciousness – empty spaces, as it were. If one wishes to push a thought from awareness, then what is required is a process of distracting oneself with other, safer things to think about. For this, there must be another train of thought ready to occupy the attention and it must be summoned quickly and automatically every time the dangerous thought threatens to appear. Thus, Freud would need to return from his holiday with something else to occupy his attention, not just for a moment but for a protracted period of time.

Second, it is not enough just to divert one's thoughts once. Habits of diversion need to be established, so that the new train of thoughts can regularly replace the old troubling train. Freud could not merely return from holiday with an intellectual problem to preoccupy him. To be effective, the problem must become *the* problem of the holiday so that, in future, if he starts to think of the holiday, he will think of the Signorelli episode – and if he thinks of Signorelli then he will think of his Bosnian and Herzegovinian solution for his memory loss. In this way Freud will divert his mental train eastwards from Maloja. At first the diversion might be conscious, but after a while it will become habitual – an association that is unconsciously made when the topic of the holiday is raised or seems about to be raised. To take the example of a trained pianist that Locke used in his discussion of associations (II, xxxiii, 6), Freud would be like a musician who plays, or hears being played, the opening notes of 'Holiday 1898' and then his fingers automatically go on to supply the notes for the tune 'Forgetting Signorelli' rather than the delightful melody 'Two Nights in Maloja'. In this way, Sigmund will still know at the back of his mind that he spent two nights with Minna, but he now habitually knows how not to think consciously of what he knows. In effect, he knows and he does not know.

Publishing his account of the episode, with its denials and its transformation of '*signor*' into Bosnia and Herzegovina, was important for objectifying the association between the holiday and the example. Freud does not just add the episode to his growing collection of memory lapses. The incident does not sneak its way into *Psychopathology*, joining other brief examples of parapraxes, such as his breaking the inkstand cover or misreading shop signs. These events attract no special attention among the numerous collected examples of the book. The Signorelli episode is different. Freud gives it pride of place and he presents it in detail, despite (or, possibly, because of) his implausible dismissal of sexual associations with *signor*. *Psychopathology* does not have an introductory chapter in which Freud outlines his general approach to everyday failures. It begins with the example of forgetting Signorelli. Publicly the episode has become the famous account of Freud's summer holiday of 1898.

To know and not to know means that the forgotten memories can in theory be re-remembered at any moment. Routines need to be established to keep the memories at bay. Sigmund would continue as the devoted *pater familias*; and Minna becomes the equally devoted aunt and the constant helpmate of her beloved sister. Sigmund and Minna would continue to holiday together, especially travelling to Italy (Simmons, 2006). Some observers have taken these regular Italian holidays as evidence for a continuing affair. There is another possibility which would be in keeping with the character of Freud and with his theories. Perhaps the later holidays were an attempt to demonstrate to Sigmund and Minna, not to mention the world at large, that their relationship was, and had always been, innocent. Perhaps it is no coincidence that they often travelled to Italy. Each subsequent holiday would be providing further evidence that they had remembered to forget the Maloja moments.

There is some evidence to support such speculation. Lothane (2009) quotes another discovery of a hotel register. In September 1913, Sigmund and Minna checked into separate rooms in a hotel in Rome. 'What a relief!' comments Lothane, acknowledging that Maciejewski's discovery of the Hotel Schweizerhaus' register had caused him much disquiet (2009, p. 19). 'What a relief!' Sigmund and Minna might have thought as they holidayed together but roomed separately. When they took these trips together, who could have doubted their propriety, especially as Sigmund became greyer and Minna stouter by the year?

The Example of Freud: Revealing and Concealing

In *Psychopathology*, as in his dream and joke books, Freud was advancing a highly original theory of mind but he did not allow theory to dominate his examples. Rhetorically, he presents his theory through his accumulated examples. It is fitting that the opening chapter of *Psychopathology* is not a theoretical statement to guide the reader through the subsequent examples. The book starts with the Signorelli example and Freud presents the book's only diagram, in which he schematically outlines the processes of the particular example. The many examples in the following chapters are not leading to a final diagram that illustrates a general model of motivated forgetting. Freud, as a serious collector of examples, is demonstrating by the structure of *Psychopathology* that his theoretical understanding is based on examples rather than vice versa. In practice, Freud's analysis of his examples and the development of his theory of mind went hand in hand, as he used the particular to understand the general and the general to illuminate the particular.

The present re-analysis of Freud's example of forgetting Signorelli suggests that there is not a simple relation between an example and what it might exemplify. I have used the example of forgetting Signorelli very differently from the way that Freud did. I have not even been concerned with the same problem as Freud was: why he might have forgotten the artist's name. Accordingly, I have not offered an alternative explanation to account for his momentary lapse. I have used the example to exemplify how Freud explains his own loss of memory and how he might have repressed an actual memory by the intellectual work of his analysis. Just as Freud suggested that everyday failings may have multiple causes, so examples can exemplify multiple phenomena.

Also the example illustrates just how difficult self-analysis might be. Shaftesbury had appreciated that it is not easy to judge ourselves as we judge others, for there are too many temptations to go more gently on ourselves. As Wittgenstein was to write, 'nothing is so difficult as not deceiving oneself' (1980, p. 34). Freud, as he showed in his remarks in *Psychopathology* about his errors in *Dreams*, was well aware of the temptations to take the edge off uncomfortable matters. The example of Freud also shows that dividing oneself into two is a metaphor and like all metaphors it can be misleading. We are divided anyway, as Freud stressed, but when we consciously divide ourselves – into analyst and patient – it is still this divided person who is doing the dividing. It is still Sigmund with all his complexities who is analysing himself as if he were his own patient.

Sigmund, like everyone else, has matters to avoid thinking about. Even his self-analysis, rightly praised for its innovation and bravery, can become a means for diverting attention. 'Look over here', the self tells itself; and in looking over here, it is not looking over there. The example of Signorelli can be interpreted in this way. By examining some thoughts in detail we might be creating significant absences elsewhere, for in looking over here we divert ourselves from looking over there. In his self-analysis, Freud drew attention to his childhood desires which he had repressed but which, all the same, resurface in coded ways – or, as Shaftesbury would have said, with nods and winks. However, *Psychopathology* is filled with examples of recent events. Freud does not need to cite his childish love for his mother or his aggressive jealousy towards his father in order to produce a convincing explanation why he might have been motivated to knock the inkpot cover from his desk.

Sometimes it might be easier to talk about distant desires than more recent ones. We might speculate that Elisabeth von R. would not have terminated the session had Freud guided her to talk about her childhood desires rather than more recent ones. She need not have felt as guilty about those desires as she would about a desire for her adult sister to die. In *Studies on Hysteria*, Freud suggests that sometimes his patients found it easier to talk about the past than the present, and then he would try to divert their attention from the past to the present. In two footnotes, Freud mentions a patient who suffered from neuroses and panic attacks; he commented that 'like so many such patients', she had a 'disinclination to admitting that she had acquired these troubles in her married life and would have liked to have pushed them back into her early youth' (p. 176n). On this matter, Freud commented, 'I remained firm' (1895/ 1991, p. 192n).[7]

---

[7] Freud commented that she was 'unwilling to admit that her illness arose from her married life'; instead, she claimed that her anxiety attacks stemmed from seeing and hearing her parents having sex when she was still a young girl (p. 192n). Was this a case of something that Appignanesi and Forrester (1993) discuss in detail: that Freud's female patients often suggested ideas that would be become central to psycho-analysis? When Freud was analysing his anonymous, footnoted patient, he was resisting her attempts to interpret her neuroses and their sexual elements in terms of what would become an orthodox part of

Perhaps Sigmund might not have felt as much guilt, or embarrassment, about his childish desires, for which his present self would not be responsible, as he would about the nights in Maloja. So, it might have been easier for him to be delving back into his distant past. Yet he could not avoid living in the present: Maloja occurred, and he had to live with that knowledge. By concentrating his attention on the memory lapse, he could divert his own attention. By publishing his account, he could also divert the attention of his friends, his colleagues and, more distantly, his readers.

All these matters might seem to lead to dramatic conclusions about Freud and his memory loss. Yet there is something that is easily overlooked amidst the drama and the scandal – something more relevant to the understanding of examples in general, if not to the specific example. The entry into reinterpreting Freud's interpretation of his memory lapse came through the different versions of the event that he provided. Earlier in the chapter, we noted some of the small differences in Freud's descriptions: how he was vague about when the event occurred, how he differed in the way that he described his travelling companion and so on. These might seem insignificant compared with the stories of Sigmund and Minna. It would be easy to dismiss these details as this chapter's bland hors d'oeuvre before the extra spicy main dish.

Yet these little differences in description are themselves exemplars of something else. Because of Freud's literary skills, his examples can be reinterpreted, and of course, they have often been. From this, it might be thought that describing an example is separate from interpreting it, as if first we tell a story and then we interpret it.[8] If we want to re-interpret the story, then we have to go back to the original description and start interpreting differently. But which description? Freud, by the minor changes in his descriptions of the episode, shows that description and interpretation are not entirely separate. How he describes his travelling companion is related to the way that he interprets his own action.

In Chapter 6 I will be returning to the possibility that descriptions are not just descriptions, but they are also interpretations. This possibility has already been raised when discussing the examples used by Tucker and James. It might be supposed, especially by empirically minded psychologists, that the possibility of interpretation and description being bound together shows the weaknesses of using examples – that, for example, Freud failed to describe his examples 'objectively'; and that, conversely, if

psycho-analysis: that adult neuroses can be based on the child witnessing 'the primal scene' (see e.g. the case of the 'Wolf Man'; Freud, 1911/1991).

[8] Mayer (2001–2) quotes Freud as saying that he would first write down a dream and then analyse the written report to construct the motives and associations behind the dream. The procedures suggests a distinction between describing the dream and interpreting it.

we cannot have 'objectively' described examples, then, to be properly scientific, we should dispense with examples. Yet, the example of Ernst Cassirer will, I hope, show this to be a naïve reaction. Cassirer did not take his ideas about describing examples from the founder of psycho-analysis but from the founder of thermodynamics.

In addition, Cassirer, as we will see, cited the scientifically minded poet Goethe to support the idea that describing and understanding are interrelated. Freud, too, was a great admirer of Goethe. In 1930, to his great surprise and even greater joy, the city of Frankfurt awarded him the Goethe Prize. Freud felt his health to be too fragile to collect the award in person. Instead, he prepared an address for his daughter Anna to read out at the ceremony, which was being held in Goethe's old house. In this acceptance speech, Freud thanked the city of Frankfurt and speculated that had the great poet lived in a later era, he might well have been sympathetic towards psycho-analysis. At the end of his address, Freud hinted at a literary link between himself and Goethe when he praised the poet for not only being 'a great self-revealer' but also 'a careful concealer' (1930/1990, p. 472).

Freud could have been talking of himself. When he uses himself as an example, he simultaneously reveals and he conceals. He shows that the two are not opposites: in revealing ourselves, we are concealing ourselves; and in concealing ourselves, we are also revealing ourselves. That is why examples in general and Freud's own examples in particular are so important. Through respecting the richness of examples, we can hope to avoid mutilating reality, as William James claimed, theories do. At the same time, through his own example, Freud is giving us a warning: we should not imagine that our examples will reveal reality simply and clearly.

5 Lacan
An Ego in Pursuit of the Ego

The tone and purpose of this chapter are different from those that have come before and those that will come after. Up until now, I have been discussing writers whose works have given me pleasure. I have derived great enjoyment, as well as enlightenment, from reading Shaftesbury, Tucker, Freud, James and Locke. Even when I have disagreed with their arguments, I have learned much from them. Being suspicious of what Freud said about himself was itself a tribute to the power of his arguments and the grace of his writing. I would thoroughly recommend others to read him closely. I have always found that just at the moment when Freud's arguments appear to be becoming a bit silly, then he will suddenly hit the reader with a piece of profound wisdom. The procession of the admired will be resumed after this chapter. Later I will be writing about my teacher, Henri Tajfel, to whom I owe so much. I will be building up to a finale with Marie Jahoda, whose writing, politics and views on the academic world I wish to hold up as an example.

This chapter is different: it is not part of the procession. It is more like a tax that has to be paid for all the pleasures that have been gained elsewhere. Others have found considerable pleasure in the writings of Jacques Lacan, but personally I have not. My good friend, the late John Shotter, a deeply intellectual scholar of the mind, used to call those whom he was drawn to read regularly his 'textual friends' (Shotter, 2003, p. 232). He would carry around with him, in his head and stored on an electronic device, quotations from his textual friends, particularly Wittgenstein and Bakhtin, so that he was never separated from their words. Lacan was never Shotter's textual friend, nor has he been mine.

Actually the term 'textual friend' is not one I would use to describe my habits of reading. The word 'friend' implies an equality that I cannot pretend to feel, because, when I read James or Freud, there is no give-and-take. I do all the taking, again and again. The authors from whom I take have no control over what I do with the stuff that I have grabbed. Freud would have been angry with what I did with his words in the previous chapter. I do not fool myself that either Locke or Shaftesbury, if they could read what I have written, would embrace me warmly as a friend. Yet

I am grateful for the unreciprocated pleasures such writers have given me, and in this book, I want to convey some of that gratitude – but not in this chapter.

Academics, especially in the human and social sciences, often forget the aesthetic aspects of doing scholarly work. Liking or disliking a piece of academic writing can sometimes be similar to liking or disliking a song, a picture or a shirt. There is more than cold logic at work, for spending time reading an author, as Shotter knew well, is like being in a relationship. In being drawn to the writings of some thinkers – towards a Freud or a James or towards an obscure scholar – we might not be aware of the extent that we are being attracted by the style of their words which convey the unique persona of the writer.

We can also be drawn by the way that a writer is treating us. Some authors are considerate to us, their readers. They keep us amused, they tolerate our shortcomings and they answer our questions before we have formulated them. Freud was an old charmer, and, I must admit, I have enjoyed being charmed by him. There are other writers who bully us, hector us with their self-importance and leave us feeling inadequate because we cannot grasp their meaning. I would rather be charmed – whether in life or on the page – than bullied. I cannot help it, but I am not drawn to Lacan's writings. When I read him, there seems to be something wrong. It is as if my body is bristling against his words. The only way that I can try to explain why this happens is to write the present chapter.

That, however, is not sufficient reason for me to interrupt the parade of the prized. A question must be asked: is it just spite and personal inadequacy that make me introduce a false note at this midpoint in my own book? There is, however, a scholarly justification behind the present chapter. I have been arguing that the way psychologists write about the mind is important, but I do not want to be misunderstood on this point. It might be easy to assume that I am seeking to turn psychology into what is essentially a literary activity where the turn of phrase is more important than the turn of evidence. That is not my intention: hence the need to stress that writers about the mind should offer evidence, especially in the form of examples, to justify their ideas.

It might then be useful to examine what can happen if a notable writer about the mind seems to dismiss the importance of providing evidence and examples, and then acts as if his own psychological theories need neither. In the age of Locke and Shaftesbury, writers about the mind did not need to cite psychological research for there was little or none to cite. By the time of William James, that was no longer the case. Nowadays, those who wish to write about the mind should take into account the findings and theories of others. There are standard academic ways of doing this, including codes for referencing and citing evidence. What happens if writers wilfully refuse to comply with such academic codes? What if they write as if their ideas are too important to be bound by commonplace standards of evidence? Does it matter? These are the questions – or rather the worries – behind the present chapter.

To make this chapter consistent with the arguments of the other chapters, such questions should not be treated as if they could be answered purely in the abstract. Any answer needs the substance of an actual, extended example. Therefore: Chapter 5, enter Jacques Lacan.

Lacan: the Influential Return to Freud

The French psycho-analyst Lacan is much more than a typical scholarly writer whose books are principally of interest to a narrow range of fellow specialists. Just as Freud became an icon in his own lifetime and has remained one since, then so did Lacan and so he remains a cultural phenomenon today. He was like a magnet drawing the major intellectuals of his age to his presence, establishing Paris as the new Vienna – the new centre of the psycho-analytic world. Like Freud before him, Lacan divided opinion. Some have treated him as if he were an intellectual god whose every word carried truths; for others Lacan was a *poseur*, whose words were little more than inflated nonsense designed to impress.

Lacan died in 1981 at the age of eighty, and, since then, his fame has continued to grow both within the small world of psycho-analysis and in the larger world of intellectual life. In 1999, the French newspaper *Le Monde* organised a survey to reveal the hundred most important books of the twentieth century. The newspaper asked potential respondents to indicate which books published in the previous hundred years had stuck in their memory. Lacan's book *Écrits* was at number seventy-six. Freud, the vast majority of whose books were published in the twentieth century, also had a book in the top hundred, at a higher position than *Écrits*. No other psychiatrists or psychologists were up there with those two. Lacan's admirers view him as much more than just a psycho-analyst: he is seen as an all-round sage. Eugene O'Brien (2017) speaks for many when he describes Lacan as 'a polymathic intellectual presence across a number of fields of human inquiry'. Élisabeth Roudinesco, the French historian of psycho-analysis, writes in her final assessment of Lacan: 'The twentieth century was Freudian; the twenty-first is already Lacanian' (2014, p. 7).

For twenty-seven years, from 1953 until 1980, Lacan held a regular public seminar in Paris. This seminar, which until 1969 was held at the École normale supérieure, attracted faithful followers and Parisian intellectual celebrities. It was always a grand performance. Jean-Michel

Rabaté (2003a), who began attending the seminars in the late sixties, describes how Lacan would be driven to the entrance of the École and would emerge from the car with a beautiful woman on his arm. He would make his way to the office of Louis Althusser, the famous Marxist theorist and then the École's administrative secretary. From there Lacan, dressed like a cabaret performer, would walk to the seminar room, where his words would be received in silence by an enrapt audience. Those words would be recorded for posterity by a line of microphones.

Cult figure that he was, Lacan would often say that he was seeking 'a return to Freud'. The ambition sounds modest, as if Lacan were merely hoping to return psycho-analytic thinking to the words of its founder. Certainly Lacan believed that psycho-analysis had taken a wrong turning since Freud's death. Ego psychologists were concentrating on the defences by which the ego protects the self rather than exploring the nature of the unconscious and the irrationality of the ego. Therefore, according to Lacan, it was necessary to take 'the antithesis' to the 'psycho-analytic movement since the death of Freud', and that entailed 'showing what psycho-analysis is not' (Lacan, 1977, p. 116).

Lacan's opposition to ego psychologists like Anna Freud did not amount to an unequivocal return to the theories of her father. Lacan was seeking to return to Freud in order to take possession of psycho-analysis and to direct what was in effect a reinterpretation of Freud's theories. This reinterpretation would not re-instate Freudian theory as it had been but would supposedly re-discover Freudian theory in the alto-gether new ideas that Lacan was proposing in the name of Freud. This was very much a new sort of 'return to'. Rabaté took his own personal notes of the seminars that he attended and he records Lacan as saying that 'no individual alive today has contributed more than I to the idea of the "return to", particularly in the context of Freud' (Rabaté, 2003a, p. 8). There is no false modesty in these words – indeed no modesty at all.

As Roudinesco (1990, 1997), in her appreciative yet critical biographies, makes clear, Lacan's ambitions were neither narrow in their range nor faintly pursued. His psycho-analytic theory was very different from Freud's in a number of crucial ways. First and most obviously, there is a whole array of puzzling concepts, not to mention apparent mathematical formulae, which have no equivalent in Freud's works. Then, there is the difference in the key childhood event that supposedly splits the child's self and that determines later psychological unhappiness. For Freud, the decisive event was the Oedipus complex, which occurs between the age of three and five, although Freud was not always specific about when the complex might occur or the extent to which the analogous complex of girls might resemble that of boys. By contrast, Lacan was of the opinion that the psychologically decisive event took place earlier and did not rely on repressing feelings of rivalry, even hatred, towards the same sex parent and erotic love for the parent of the opposite sex. The pivotal Lacanian moment occurs when children recognise their image in a mirror.

Theoretically there is an even greater difference between Freud and Lacan. To put it simply – and probably too simply – they take a different view of the relationship between the ego and the unconscious. In essence, Freud claims that the ego creates the unconscious. When the child realises that its oedipal desires are shamefully unacceptable, it represses them or drives them away from conscious awareness. The act of repression, which is performed by the ego, creates the unconscious, since only what has been repressed is, in the true sense of the word, unconscious. For Lacan, it is the other way round. The ego does not create the unconscious; rather, the unconscious creates the ego. The mirror stage results in the creation of an ego, but not the potentially strong ego envisaged by Freud – rather, it is a weak, fractured and misrecognising ego that emerges from unconscious life. To adapt the language of railway travel, the 'return to' is very much a 'departure from'. If you travel on this return ticket, you will not end up in the same station that you started from.

Lacan succeeded in becoming the leader of the French psycho-analytic movement. If he was the monarch of the movement, then, in the words of Roudinesco, he was supported by an army of barons who 'spoke like Lacan, taught like Lacan, smoked Lacan's cigars' (1990, p. 113). Lacan's followers would speak of the man, whom they were copying, as the master, *le maître*. Rabaté claimed that for many years after Lacan's death he could spot fellow French Lacanians by their grammatically odd, distinctive turns of phrase that mirrored those of their leader. It appears that however large a following Lacan attracted in his lifetime, it was never sufficient to satisfy him. In the previous chapter, Paul Ricoeur's book on Freud was mentioned. Roudinesco recounts that, when Ricoeur's book appeared, it put the master in a fury because Lacan thought that Ricoeur had paid insufficient attention to his work.

There is no doubting that Lacan's ideas have become extraordinarily influential within sections of the international academic world. Apart from his influence on psycho-analysts and psychiatrists, Lacan's greatest influence has been in the humanities. One of the most well-known and influential of contemporary social philosophers, Slavoj Žižek, is very much a Lacanian (e.g. Žižek, 2001). Lacan's impact on literary studies has been apparent for many years. More than thirty years ago, Juliet MacCannell (1986) examined the influence of Lacan's ideas in her book *Figuring Lacan*. She suggested that his concepts had 'touched nearly all the leading areas of literary criticism' and that 'Lacan's words, his terminology, have found a ready response in the literary criticism of our time' (p. 2). Feminist critics like MacCannell might find some of Lacan's notions problematic because of their phallocentrism, but nevertheless, she believed that the feminist critique of Lacan was extremely productive because Lacan had formulated many of the concepts necessary for such a critique.

Probably the area of literary analysis that has been most deeply influenced by Lacanian theory has been film studies. Lacan's idea of a mirror stage gives the visual image a prominence which it never had in classic Freudianism. Laura Mulvey's (1975) article in *Screen* was one of the first to apply Lacanian ideas to the study of films. This paper, which argued that Hollywood films appeal to the psychic structures of male audiences, has been identified as the most important and widely cited article in film theory (MacKinnon, 2001). Analysts of film still continue to use Lacanian terminology in general and his concept of the mirror stage in particular (e.g. Nolan, 2009; Rösing, 2016; Sheehan, 2012).

Rabaté, a professor of literature, writes that Lacan's ideas have demonstrated 'a literary and humanities drift' in terms of their influence (2003b, p. xiii). Another Lacanian scholar has commented that since 1980s the ideas of Lacan 'have stealthily yet steadily penetrated the social sciences, the arts and the humanities' (Nobus, 2017a, p. v). In his bibliographic study of Lacan, Eugene O'Brien (2017) claims that Lacanian ideas have been particularly influential in psychiatry, psycho-analysis, philosophy, literary and critical theory and film studies.

There is a significant absence in these listings of Lacan's spheres of influence: psychology. No one is saying that Lacan has touched nearly all areas of psychological inquiry. There are critical psychologists who have championed Lacan's ideas, particularly in parts of Latin America. However, when put against the massive size of psychology as a multi-faceted, worldwide discipline, the Lacanians today very much remain a tiny minority, confined for the most part to the embattled fringes.[1] Indeed, the Lacanian minority is often divided between assimilationists, who argue that Lacanian psychological ideas can be integrated with other psychological ideas, and rejectionists, who claim that Lacan's whole oeuvre is so radical that it supersedes all other psychologies.

The notion of a mirror stage is a psychological idea and not just a means for interpreting literary texts and film. The idea suggests that children will

---

[1] For examples of critical psychologists who have championed the work of Lacan in Britain, see most notably Frosh (2002, 2006), Hook (2012), Parker (2003, 2005, 2011) and Walkerdine (1988).

display certain mental and physical reactions at a particular stage of their development. Psychological ideas are different from interpretive concepts, especially when they suggest that certain psychological events will regularly occur in specific ways. The mirror stage is not credible as a psychological idea because analysts can use the concept to throw light on Hollywood films. To be convincing, the idea of a mirror stage should be supported by evidence – not of adult films or of interesting pieces of literary criticism – but of children's reactions in front of a mirror. Therefore, to assess the mirror stage as a psychological idea, it is necessary to examine how Lacan justified his key concept and what sort of evidence he cited in its favour.

Difficulty in Understanding Lacan

Before that, a few words should be said about the special qualities of Lacan's writing. He might have advocated a return to Freud, but in one matter he certainly did not return. Lacan's style of writing could hardly be more different from Freud's. In his small book on Lacan, Malcolm Bowie wrote, 'Among the many notable differences between the two writers as writers none is more extraordinary than this: that where Freud cultivates clarity in the presentation of his ideas, Lacan cultivates obscurity' (1991, p. 12). Bowie chose the word 'cultivates' carefully. He was implying that obscurity was not a failure on Lacan's part but something that he deliberately pursued, just as Freud deliberately pursued the ideal of writing clear, graceful prose.

Lacan used to deny that he was deliberately writing or speaking obscurely. In an interview given to an Italian magazine when he was more than seventy years old, Lacan was asked about his difficult writing (Granzotto, 1974). He replied that he did not find his own writing in the least bit difficult to understand, but he had 'never made the least effort to cater to my readers' tastes, no matter who they are'. He merely had things to say and 'I said them'. Then Lacan added mischievously that in about ten years everyone would find his writing 'entirely transparent, like a good glass of beer'. Then they will say 'This Lacan, he's so banal!'

Even after more than forty years, this has not happened, and Lacan's style of writing continues to divide opinion sharply. His supporters claim that his style is a necessary part of his message. If the ego – the so-called seat of rationality – has emerged from the unconscious, then the irrational nature of the ego's rationality will be obscured if its workings are described in transparent, rational prose. Clear writing would encourage readers to misrecognise the irrational nature of their own so-called rationality. Instead, the irrational nature of the ego must be allowed to speak for itself, freed from the constraints of clarity. In consequence, Lacanian discourse must achieve its ends by disrupting accepted ways of analysing, describing and justifying.

To opponents of Lacan, this is dangerous nonsense, because it reduces Lacanian thinking to a cult where the more obscure the master is, the more his followers will treat his every cloudy word with exaggerated respect. Roudinesco (1990) interviewed Lacan's long-standing friend, the great anthropologist Claude Lévi-Strauss, also the author of a *Le Monde* top hundred hit. Lévi-Strauss attended some of his friend's seminars and said that he did not understand what Lacan was saying but found himself 'in the middle of an audience that seemed to understand'. Lévi-Strauss was impressed by Lacan's personal magnetism. It was as if some sort of radiance was emanating from his presence: 'I have seen quite a few shamans functioning in exotic societies, and I rediscovered there [in Lacan's seminars] a kind of equivalent of the shaman's power' (p. 362). Significantly, Lévi-Strauss virtually never cited Lacan in his own writings (Scubla, 2011).

The philosopher Maurice Merleau-Ponty, another friend of Lacan, also said that he failed to understand Lacan. Merleau-Ponty thought that Lacan's seminars might have been of value, but he personally did not have enough time to find out whether they were (Roudinesco, 1997, p. 209). Forgive me if I add a personal note. I have found Lacan's writing difficult to understand – actually impossible in places – and I was much heartened to discover that I might be in the company of Lévi-Strauss and Merleau-Ponty. It is easy for readers to blame themselves when they are baffled by much praised books. Clearly many in Lacan's audiences took it for granted that the strange utterances coming from the star speaker must contain important, hidden meanings.[2]

The problem of Lacan's written meaning is compounded for a technical reason. The majority of his published work has been directly based on oral presentations, whether from his seminars or from talks that he delivered at conferences. He would speak from notes but would not stick to his script and improvised at will. He would record his own words or have typists take down what he was saying. Editors then would derive printed versions from a mixture of notes, transcripts and recordings. We have the reminiscences of one of his typists describing her years of work taking down Lacan's words. Marie Pierrakos (2006) writes of Lacan's ways of bullying his audience, bestowing and withdrawing his favours and

---

[2] One can share the feelings of Lévi-Strauss and Merleau-Ponty without necessarily going as far as Chomsky, who has been quoted as saying that he had met Lacan a number of times and he thought that he was an affable fellow but 'a total charlatan' (Wolters, 2013).

completely ignoring humble, female 'key-board bashers' like herself (at least until she became a psycho-analyst). She describes Lacan at his seminars assuming 'the place of the god' and acting as the 'Oracle and High Priest who both states and resolves the enigma' (p. 26).

Most academics use their oral presentations of papers as preparatory trials for their final written version. The spoken version might contain references to the audience, as the speaker utters polite words of greeting and expresses gratitude for their invitation, but these will be removed when the speaker turns into author. The published version will be addressed to what Chaim Perelman (1979) called 'the universal audience' which extends beyond any physical gathering of listeners. In working up the final version the writer will add a complex scholarly apparatus that includes references to other studies, citations in the text, carefully hedged qualifications, lengthy quotations, a bibliography and other rhetorical matters that are often, perhaps usually, omitted in spoken versions.

Lacan characteristically did not follow the standard pattern of academics. He seems to have accorded the spoken event priority over the written version. Lacan's publication *Television* followed his appearance on television in 1974 and was one of his most conceptually abstruse writings. At the conference of École freudienne de Paris Lacan apparently urged his audience to watch him on television rather than read his text. Nobus (2016), commenting on this, wrote that Lacan was putting the 'sensory qualities of the spoken word' above the written text (p. 38).

Most of Lacan's publications are records of spoken performances, and they retain the deictic cues that refer to the time, context and audience of the original performance. The printed second person pronoun – 'you', *vous* – often does not address the imagined, universal audience of readers, but it addresses the actual audience that attended the original talk. Most of the seminars printed in *Écrits* and *The Four Fundamental Concepts of Psycho-analysis* start with a short address that excludes us, the later readers, and draws our attention to the fact that the printed words we are reading represent spoken ones that were delivered to others. My personal favourite introduction is 'Because I am beginning on time today, I will start by reading a poem which, in actual fact, has no relation to what I am about to say' (Lacan, 1991, p. 17).

In his 'Overture' to the first edition of *Écrits*, Lacan mentioned how his style related to his two different audiences: 'With this style, which the audience to whom they were addressed required, I want to lead the reader to a consequence in which he must pay the price in elbow grease' (2007, p. 5). The phrasing is, as always, somewhat awkward, but the implication seems apparent. Lacan was claiming that his style was suited to the listening audience, and the reading audience would have to work hard to understand the meaning. By inference, he was suggesting that the listening audience did not need 'elbow grease' as they sat in silence watching the speaker deliver his words.

The priority given to the attending audience may demand elbow grease from the reader, but it also spares the author some elbow grease. Anyone who transforms the notes for a talk into an academic publication typically has to expend elbow grease to add the scholarly apparatus for the published version. This extra effort is not required when written texts are presented as records of spoken talks. Then, authors, relying on others to transcribe their spoken words, can relieve themselves of the trouble of collecting, checking and inserting the scholarly details. Their words will be left unpolished, as vestiges of that magic moment when they were uttered in front of an audience.

The Mirror Stage: Its Origins and Importance

Lacan's famous mirror stage paper has occupied an important place in his oeuvre. According to one commentator, the paper 'remains one of the most frequently anthologised and referenced of Lacan's texts' (Homer, 2005, p. 25). Another commentator has written that the mirror stage paper is one of the cornerstones for the popularisation of literary and cultural theory (O'Brien, 2017). Like most of Lacan's publications, it began its life as a talk. As Roudinesco (2003) shows, the paper has a complex history.

Lacan introduced the idea of a mirror stage in a talk that he delivered to the fourteenth congress of the International Psycho-analytic Association, held at Marienbad in 1936. Freud was too ill to attend, and the location had been chosen in case Freud's condition suddenly deteriorated and his daughter Anna Freud had to rush back to Vienna. After the war, Lacan delivered a much revised version of the paper at the sixteenth congress at Zurich in 1949. In the words of Nobus (2017b), Lacan's revised paper was like a pearl that he had carefully cultured for several years. Later that same year, the paper was published in *Revue Française de Psychanalyse* under the title of 'Le stade du miroir comme formateur de la fonction du Je telle qu'elle nous est révélée dans l'expérience psychanalytique' (The mirror stage as formative of the *I* function, as revealed to us in psycho-analytic experience). The paper was included in both the full and abbreviated versions of Lacan's *Écrits*, a compilation of his major talks/papers (1966, 1977, 2002).

The mirror stage was a key concept in Lacan's reworking of Freudian ideas about the ego, for, according to Lacan, the way that the child comes to recognise its own reflected image in the mirror was 'the turning-point in development' (1988, p. 146). He wrote that the mirror stage is 'not simply a moment in development' but it constitutes 'the primary identification' (Lacan, 1993, p. 39) and represents 'the Urbild [prototype] of the ego' (1988, p. 74). According to Nobus (2017b), Lacan viewed his article as a 'solid piece of theorising, a paradigm retaining its value to explain human self-consciousness, aggressivity, rivalry, narcissism, jealousy and fascination with images in general' (p. 104). The phrase 'solid piece of theorising' is revealing: the paper is not seen by its author and its admirers as a solid piece of evidence for the theorising that is claimed to explain so much.

There is a story attached to Lacan's first version of the paper – the one that he gave at the Congress in 1936 (see Roudinesco, 1997, 2003). Apparently the speakers were all informed that they should speak for only ten minutes. Ernest Jones was chairing Lacan's session and, in accordance with the congress' rules, he interrupted Lacan after ten minutes to bring his talk to an end. Lacan was incensed: he still had much of importance to say. As Lacan recalled in a talk delivered twenty-two years later, he left the congress the next day and made his way to Berlin to watch the Nazi Olympics (1966, p. 600).[3] It was as if in that moment of high tension and injured feeling, Lacan, who was much given to making puns, was caught within his own living pun: he had swapped '*le stade du miroir*' (the mirror stage) for '*le stade olympique*' (the Olympic stadium).

In a three-part talk, 'Propos sur la causalité psychique' (Presentation on psychical causality), which he delivered at Bonneval in September 1946, Lacan referred to his Marienbad presentation. After ten years and a whole world war, his sense of grievance was still strong. In the Bonneval talk, which was reprinted in *Écrits* (1966), Lacan mentioned his concept of the mirror stage. Then, he could not resist making a thematic diversion to recall what had happened at Marienbad. He said that he had been talking about the mirror stage

at least until exactly coinciding with the fourth strike of the tenth minute, when Jones interrupted me. He was presiding over the congress as President of the Psycho-analytic Society of London, a position for which he was no doubt qualified by the fact that I was never able to meet one of his English colleagues unless he shared with me some unpleasant feature of his character. Nevertheless the

---

[3] At that time, in 1936, many foreign tourists and travellers were still enjoying trips to Germany, especially to view the Olympics; there were also many writers visiting Nazi Germany, regardless of whether they sympathised with the regime (Boyd, 2017). However, Jewish psycho-analysts had already left Germany and, according Elisabeth Young-Bruehl (1988), 'by 1934, German psycho-analysis was an "Aryan" business' (p. 199).

members of the Viennese group, gathered there like birds before an imminent migration, gave my talk a sufficiently warm welcome.

du moins jusqu'en ce point coïncidant exactement au quatrième top de la dixième minute, où m'interrompît Jones qui présidait le congrès en tant que président de la Société psychanalytique de Londres, position pour laquelle le qualifiait sans doute le fait que je n'ai jamais pu rencontrer un de ses collègues anglais qu'il n'ait eu à me faire part de quelque trait désagréable de son caractère. Néanmoins les membres du groupe viennois réunis là comme des oiseaux avant la migration imminente, firent à mon exposé un assez chaleureux accueil. (1966, p. 185)

What Lacan leaves out of his account is as revealing as what he includes. He depicts the event in personal terms so that Jones' unpleasant character appears to be the reason for the unwarranted interruption. There is no mention that speakers had been given a ten minute slot or that by interrupting precisely after ten minutes, Jones might have been fulfilling his duties of chairing the session. In fact, Lacan does not mention any other speakers: they are irrelevant to what he wants to say. Nor does he mention exactly what he was prevented from saying: it is the interruption that concerns him most. He remarks that the Viennese liked what they heard, thereby implying that he was not interrupted because his talk lacked quality. Another interesting absence: Lacan does not tell his post-war audience where he went next or why. Everything is secondary to what is construed as a personal affront by a chairman with a flawed personality. By selecting his details, the man who was seeking to uncover the irrational secrets of the ego was unintentionally revealing the sensitivities of his own.

The Mirror Paper and Its References to the 'Facts'

For a paper that has been hailed as a major contribution to psychoanalytic theory, Lacan's *Stade du miroir* is surprisingly short. When published in *Revue Française de Psychanalyse*, it amounted to no more than six pages. Lacan's argument is densely presented. The technical terminology that he used is not what is of prime importance here, although I will be commenting on some of his big words. To understand how Lacan justifies his ideas and mentions the ideas of others, it will be necessary to look at some of his small, rhetorically unobtrusive words. These words can seem so insignificant that his English translators occasionally omit or change them. Yet, the little words repay closer inspection for they can reveal as much, if not more, than the big words and the famous phrases.

Lacan began his *Revue Française de Psychanalyse* paper with a claim of priority. His opening sentence, delivered at the Zurich congress in 1949, states that the conception of the mirror stage, which he introduced thirteen years ago at the last congress (*la conception du stage du miroir que j'ai introduite à notre dernier congrès*), has since then been more or less adopted by the French group (Lacan, 1949, p. 449; see also Lacan, 2002, p. 4). He is the introducer – the conceiver – of the conception of the mirror stage. Lacan then says that it is appropriate to bring the idea to the audience's attention, especially today, because of the light it sheds on the '*I* function' in the 'experience psycho-analysis provides us of it'. In his final sentence of the first paragraph, Lacan declares that his conception puts 'us' in radical opposition to any philosophy derived from the *cogito*. The opening paragraph of the written paper retains Lacan's typical deictic markers referring to the context in which the talk was given (i.e. 'today', 'your attention', 'our last congress thirteen years ago', etc.).

Those in the audience, who were unfamiliar with Lacan's talks, may have been somewhat surprised by some of the talk's contents, or, to be more precise, by some of the absences in the contents. The title and opening sentence refer to the 'psycho-analytic experience', but the talk/paper contained no references to psycho-analytic case histories. Lacan does not refer to any psycho-analytic patient, whether his, Freud's or anyone else's. In short, Lacan discusses his themes without evidential examples from the psycho-analytic experience.

The paper may have become one of the first and most important of Lacan's return to Freud, but it contains no quotations from any of Freud's works. That in itself is not unusual. As John Forrester (1997) noted, Lacan rarely includes quotes from Freud: his return to Freud was not a return 'to the letter' of Freud because the letter of Freud was 'largely absent from Lacan's work' (p. 110). Of course, talks which are based on notes and which contain many improvised sequences are unlikely to contain many quotations, especially lengthy ones. What perhaps is surprising is that Lacan did not add quotations when he was afforded the opportunity to prepare versions for publication. What is doubly surprising is that the mirror stage paper does not even mention Freud. The only Freud to be mentioned is Anna (twice), whom Lacan was seeking to supplant as the inheritor of the original master's legacy.

The third surprise is that Lacan, rather than citing psycho-analytic examples, mentions conventional psychological research. Although some Lacanian psychologists today tend to dismiss conventional psychological research (Parker, 2003, 2005), Lacan based his mirror stage paper on so-called psychological and biological 'facts'. Three times in the paper, he refers to *les faits* (the facts). The first time comes after he has mentioned, but not referenced, a biological experiment which found that the maturation of a female pigeon's gonad depended on seeing another member of its species regardless of that pigeon's sex. A mirror image of the female pigeon herself can serve equally well. Lacan comments that such 'facts' are inscribed 'in an order of homeomorphic identification' (1949, p. 451).

The second mention of facts comes in the next sentence when Lacan refers to the 'facts of mimetism' (*les faits de mimétisme*). The final reference comes when he mentions the psychological research of Charlotte Bühler who, according to Lacan, has demonstrated 'the facts of child *transitivism*' (*les faits de transitivisme enfantin*; p. 454, emphasis in original). In such references, and others to be mentioned below, there is no indication that Lacan is rejecting conventional psychological research *tout court*. Instead, he incorporates it to show the psychological importance and reality of the mirror image.

All three instances share a common linguistic feature. In citing the 'facts' Lacan uses technical phrases which add little in the context except perhaps to convey the impression of his own familiarity with the relevant technical matters. He does not explain what he means by 'homeomorphic identification' or why he has borrowed the concept 'homeomorphic' from algebra, rather than using a more conventional biological or psychological concept. The term does not clarify Lacan's description of the unnamed pigeon experiment and he does not use it so that the reader/listener can understand better the experiment's procedural details or its findings. Lacan does not repeat the term as he switches in the next sentence to the facts of 'mimetism', another abstract term that adds little to the context. The last reference to the facts is a reference to 'transitivism', which also is unexplained at that point and which could have been paraphrased in simpler language. Lacan does not illustrate what he means by 'transitivism' with a brief example to help those readers/listeners who are unfamiliar with the research and its so-called facts. Instead, the big words stand as daunting monuments.

As so often is the case in psychological writing, an addiction to the pleasures of technical terminology is not necessarily a sign of precise thinking (Billig, 2013). Nor is an addiction to inventing new words. It has been calculated that Lacan devised 789 neologisms (Bénabou et al., 2002). Using so many words of one's own making, instead of making do with shared vocabulary, is not usually a means of improving clear communication with others. Élisabeth Roudinesco, discussing Lacan's mania for neologisms, comments: '"neologistic" excess is an abuse of language that turns thought into a pile of words, into delirium' (2014, p. 113).

Lacan's paper contains only a single reference to a specified publication. He mentions the concept of 'symbolic efficacity' and in a footnote he directs the reader to Lévi-Strauss' publication of the same name, giving the full bibliographic detail of journal, date, volume and page numbers.

As we will see, Lacan also mentions three psychologists by name but he does not cite any of their publications. In this respect, the written version lacks the conventional scholarly apparatus whereby statements, especially those about 'facts', are supported by references to published evidence which readers can check for themselves.

The Mirror Paper and Its References to 'My'/'Our' Findings

In his mirror stage paper, Lacan also refers to his own findings. In the version of the paper published in *Revue Française de Psychanalyse*, Lacan writes, 'We ourselves have shown in the social dialectic which structures human understanding as paranoiac the reason that renders it more autonomous than that of the animal from the field forces of desire' (1949, p. 452; 1966, p. 96). The original article contains no bibliographic detail to guide the reader to find out what the findings actually were. When the article was re-published in *Écrits*, there is an added footnote after this passage.

The added footnote guides readers to two further pages of *Écrits* (pp. 111 and 180). The first page is part of *L'agressivité de psychanalyse* (Aggressiveness in psycho-analysis), originally published in *Revue Française de Psychanalyse* the year before the mirror stage paper. The second page reference comes in *Propos sur la causalité psychique*, which, as we have seen, was based on a talk that Lacan originally gave in 1946. Academic readers would find this sort of footnote familiar. When it is positioned after an author's claim to have shown something, they would expect to find the evidence for the claim on the footnoted pages. That is not the case for this footnote.

A small point is worth noting before following the trail of the footnote. Lacan's claim begins with the words 'we ourselves have found': *nous avons nous-mêmes montré*. In his translation of the article, Bruce Fink has replaced the first person plural of the French with the first person singular, rendering it as 'I myself have shown' (2002, p. 5).[4] For the moment, it

---

[4] At several further points in this chapter, I will be comparing Bruce Fink's translation of *Écrits* with Alan Sheridan's earlier translation. I will not be commenting on which might be the better translation overall, as opposed to which is the more literal translation of specific phrases. All does not seem to be well in the world of Lacanian translators. A few years ago on the Amazon website, Fink gave the lowest one-star rating to Sheridan's translation of *Écrits*. He criticised Sheridan's grasp of French and complained of his 'non-existent' knowledge of Lacan's seminars. He wrote that Sheridan's old translation should no longer be reprinted and that readers 'seeking to study the Écrits [*sic*] should consult the 2002 translation by myself'.

might be worthwhile to keep the distinction between the first person plural and singular.

The original French first person plural echoes the sorts of claims that scientists, including psychologists, typically make when referring to results found by their research groups. It conveys an element of personal modesty as speakers, who may lead research teams, distribute the credit for their findings to the team as a whole, rather than taking all the credit for themselves. The addition of the unnecessary, and in this context unusual *nous-mêmes* (ourselves), rhetorically undermines the modesty, especially as, in this case, there is no research team to share the credit.

In academic papers, the claim that 'we have shown' something is typically accompanied by a statement about how we showed what we did, or by a reference to a paper that will tell interested readers about the findings and how they were obtained. In a talk, delivered before the age of PowerPoints, it might have been sufficient for a speaker merely to say 'we have shown' without interrupting the flow of their delivery with bibliographic references. When speakers prepare their talks for publication both now and then, this would be the sort of thing that they will be expected to add.

The first reference guides the reader to the section of *L'agressivité de psychanalyse* where Lacan discussed how paranoiacs explain their discordance from the living world and show aggressive reactions that form a continuous series. There, Lacan comments that 'I have shown' (*j'ai montré*) that in each case the series keeps to an original organisation of the forms of the 'me' (*tenait dans chaque cas à une organisation originale des formes du moi*; 1948, p. 376; 1966, p. 111). This claim to have shown something (this time expressed in the first person singular not plural) was not supported by a further footnote or reference in *L'agressivité de psychanalyse*. Hence, the first added reference in the *Écrits* mirror stage paper does not lead the reader to the supporting evidence for the claim he is making. Instead it leads to a further and different claim to have found something. This claim is also unsupported and, consequently, has to be taken on trust. There the trail stops.

The second footnoted reference, like the first, leads to a further claim rather than to supporting evidence. On the specified page in *Propos sur la causalité psychique* Lacan discussed paranoia and stated that in relation to the genetic psychology of the ego any postulate of functional integration should be dropped. He then asserts: 'I myself have given proof of this by my study of the characteristic phenomena that I have called the *fecund moments* of ecstasy' (*J'en ai moi-même donné la preuve par mon étude des phénomènes caractéristiques de ce que j'ai appelé les moments féconds du délire*) (Lacan, 1966, p. 180, emphasis in original). Lacan is using the first person singular again, this time with the added emphasis of 'myself' (*moi-même*).

Here Lacan is providing slightly more information about how he supposedly proved the lack of integration in the paranoid's ego. He wrote/said that he did so by using the phenomenological method (*la méthode phénoménologique*) that he was advocating in his current talk/article. Again he provides no example or other type of evidence to support his claim to have proved the phenomenon. Instead, he says that his conception of the ego (*ma conception du Moi*) has been followed by those who have been able to listen to the talks and lessons that he has given over the years (*qui ont pu suivre les auditeurs des conférences et leçons que j'ai faites au cours des années*) but which, despite remaining unpublished, have nonetheless promoted the term destined to be striking: paranoid knowledge (*qui, pour être restées de mon fait inédites, n'en ont pas moins promu le terme, destiné à frapper, de connaissance paranoïaque*) (1966, p. 180). It is as if formulating the striking term takes precedence over providing the evidence to justify the new term.

Consequently, those who read the mirror stage article in *Écrits* and follow the second reference in the added footnote will come to another claim – this time a claim, first made in 1946, to have provided evidence. Again, that is as far as the reader can go because, as Lacan said then, the evidence remained unpublished. Lacan implies that those who have attended his talks and seminars over the years will have heard his proofs and have accepted them. Readers, by contrast, will have to take those claims of proof on trust.

The shaman's secrets are entrusted to those who gather in front of him. His audience is privileged to hear his proofs. Outsiders cannot witness the demonstrations that he reveals to his followers. There is a basis of unwavering trust and secrecy, which is quite unlike academic inquiry whose conventional procedures, at least at their best, encourage scepticism and openness. By 1966, when Lacan re-published his mirror stage article with the added footnote, there were increasing numbers of readers and listeners willing, even enthusiastic, to accept without question the master's word.

Referring to Psychologists: Wolfgang Köhler

Not only do Lacan's claims about what he has proved have to be taken on trust, but listeners and readers are invited to take on trust what he says about the works of others. We have already seen how in the mirror stage paper/talk he refers to 'facts' of biology and psychology without providing bibliographic references. In addition to Charlotte Bühler, Lacan refers to two other psychologists in his mirror stage paper: Wolfgang Köhler and James Mark Baldwin. All three are major figures in the history of experimental psychology, and none can be considered to have been particularly sympathetic to Freudianism. Bühler, if anything, was more sympathetic to Alfred Adler rather than to Freud. In his paper, Lacan does not cite any French psychologists; the significance of this absence will be considered later.

Lacan used the work of his three psychologists to establish the mirror phenomenon: he presents the psychologists as demonstrating the 'fact' that children at a young age are captivated by their images in mirrors, especially as they suddenly see the reflected image of their whole bodes. The majority of Lacan's audience, who heard his mirror stage talks in either 1936 or 1949, would not have been psychologists. Given the literary drift of his popularity, the majority of his readers today will not have backgrounds in psychology. In fact, for many followers, Lacan's ideas will be the main sort of psychology with which they are familiar. Such readers will not be in a position to judge the accuracy or otherwise of Lacan's references to psychological work and, thus, to judge for themselves the basis of the mirror phenomenon. Examining how Lacan referred to the three psychologists in his mirror stage paper will, once again, involve looking at the small words that he used to display his knowledge. I will take the psychologists in the order in which Lacan mentioned them in his paper.

The first was Wolfgang Köhler (1887–1967), whom Lacan refers to in the second paragraph of the paper (1966, p. 93). Köhler was one of the leaders of the Gestalt movement in psychology that emerged in Germany during the late nineteenth and early twentieth centuries (Ash, 1998; see also the following chapter). According to the Gestaltists, perception involves the immediate apprehension of shapes, patterns and objects (Köhler, 1929). As such, we directly perceive the world in terms of *Gestalts* (or sensory shapes) rather than combining small elements of perception to form shapes and objects, as associationist psychologists from Locke onwards had assumed.

Köhler is also famous for his study about the insightful behaviour of apes and chimpanzees (Köhler, 1925/1973). Köhler used Gestalt principles in his analysis of primates and their insights, for he argued that apes and chimpanzees, in common with humans, were able to grasp the total form of a problem as a step towards solving that problem. In his famous book *The Mentality of Apes*, Köhler described how he observed one ape working out how to use a stick to hook a banana into its cage before actually using the stick.

Köhler showed political courage as well as intellectual originality. After the Nazis came to power in Germany, Köhler was one of the last writers to publish a newspaper article critical of the new regime. He fled Germany and settled in the United States. American psychologists, at least before the cognitive revolution of the 1980s, tended to see Köhler's work as conflicting with the prevailing behaviourist mood, for Köhler and other Gestalists wrote about the operations of the mind. The behaviourists often saw as Köhler being overly theoretical, despite the fact that he insisted on the importance of conducting laboratory experiments and making empirical observations.

Lacan's second paragraph begins with him wondering whether there are some among his audience who remember that 'the aspect of behaviour from which we start' is illuminated 'by a fact of comparative psychology' (1966, p. 93). The phrases convey a somewhat sympathetic stance towards psychology. Lacan is using the terminology of empirical psychology including the term *comportement* which was the word that French behaviourists were using for 'behaviour'. The fact to which Lacan alludes is a particular difference between human and animal behaviour. He states that the young human for a time is outstripped by the chimpanzee in terms of 'instrumental intelligence', but nevertheless, the human child already recognises its own image in a mirror as an image.

This recognition is signalled by the 'illuminative mimicry of the *Aha-Erlebnis*' (the aha-experience), which 'for Köhler expresses situational apperception, an essential moment in the act of intelligence' (p. 93). Actually the term *Aha-Erlebnis* was formulated by Karl Bühler, not by Köhler (Zwart, 2014). Lacan does not give the source of the 'fact' that there is a distinction in behaviour between that of the human infant and the chimpanzee in response to the mirror image. However, the name of Köhler rhetorically conveys authority, especially since his book on apes had been translated into French.

In the following paragraph, Lacan goes on to say how the infant's act of regarding itself in the mirror is superior to that of the monkey. Both can recognise their own images in the mirror, but the human child, unlike the monkey, remains preoccupied by its image. The act of the monkey looking at itself is extinguished once it acquires control of the inanity of the image (*dans le contrôle une fois acquis de l'inanité de l'image*). The human child's response is different: there is a series of gestures as the child playfully tests the relation between the movements assumed in the image and with its reflected environment (*chez l'enfant en une série de gestes où il éprouve ludiquement la relation des mouvements assumés de l'image à son environnement reflété*: 1966, p. 93). This is only part of the single sentence that comprises the whole third paragraph. The sentence is more than six lines long and like many of Lacan's sentences its meaning is hard to grasp and to render clearly. This is despite it being an apparently factual description of the behaviour that the child is said to perform in front of the mirror. Köhler's descriptions, it must be said, are much clearer than Lacan's descriptions of Köhler's descriptions.[5]

At this point, Köhler is the only authority that Lacan has cited for describing the differences between the child's and the chimpanzee's reaction to the mirror. He implies that Köhler warrants the claim that the child shows an immediate understanding of its image but Lacan does not reference or quote a specific work. Later in the article when Lacan discusses the image seen in the mirror, he uses the German term *Gestalt*. Köhler wrote that Gestalt theorists use the word 'Gestalt' to mean 'any segregated whole', especially one that is perceived as a whole (1929, p. 192). Thus, according to Lacan, the child sees the total form of its body as a Gestalt in an immediate 'aha' moment (1966, p. 94). Lacan claims that this perceived Gestalt prefigures the child's alienating destiny (p. 95). In this way, Lacan can be seen to be using concepts and ideas from Gestalt psychology to describe the event in front of the mirror that is supposedly crucial in the history of the individual and that is so central to Lacan's psycho-analytic theory.

The 'fact' of comparative psychology is also important for Lacan in another way. If there is no difference between human children and members of other species in the way that they recognise themselves in the mirror, then there is no reason for supposing that only the human child uses this experience to develop a complex, unintegrated, pre-linguistic sense of self. Chimpanzees might be thought to have a similar psychic formations if they react similarly to mirror images. That is not what Lacan wishes to imply. In consequence, he uses the authority of Köhler to suggest that there is a difference between monkeys and human children: the monkey's interest in the mirror image soon extinguishes itself because it is not instrumentally useful, while children remain captivated by their own reflection.

Lacan's oblique style of description makes it difficult for his readers to check his statements, and he does not help them by providing bibliographic details. The original audience, attending one or other of the mirror stage talks, would have had no immediate way to check the master's assertions about psychological findings. By using German technical terms (e.g. *Gestalt, Aha-Erlebnis*) Lacan conveys that he is familiar with the relevant evidence. His rhetoric assures his readers and his listening audience that they can trust what he asserts about 'the facts'.

---

[5] Both Fink and Sheridan, as translators, have a tendency to 'de-convolute' Lacan's convoluted sentences, making them easier for English readers. That is why I sometimes here provide my own more literal translations of Lacan's original phrasing, especially when his descriptions, claims and general sense are by no means clear.

There are, however, good reasons for questioning whether Lacan's 'facts' of comparative psychology are straightforwardly factual. Recent evidence confirms Köhler's finding, which Lacan accepts, that apes and chimpanzees are able to recognise themselves in a mirror. When their faces are marked and they are presented with their mirror image, they will move their hands to their own face as if to remove the mark (see e.g. Gallup et al., 1995; Povinelli et al., 1997; de Veer et al., 2003). However, not all primates can do this: there is no corresponding evidence that rhesus monkeys or gorillas can pass 'the mark test' (Gallup and Suarez, 1991; Shillito, Gallup and Beck, 1999). Increasingly more species have been identified as being able to recognise themselves in the mirror: land-living mammals such as elephants (Plotnik, de Waal and Reiss, 2006); birds like magpies (Prior, Schwarz. and Güntürkün, 2008); and also bottlenose dolphins and killer whales (Marten and Psarakos, 1995; Reiss and Marino, 2001; Morrison and Reiss, 2018; Delfour and Marten, 2001). In terms of recognising their own mirror images, humans are by no means unique.

Although it would be unfair to criticise Lacan for making statements in 1949 that conflict with recent evidence, it not unfair to expect that his followers today should take note of the relevant evidence rather than accepting what Lacan wrote more than sixty years ago as if it expressed an unchanging truth. One recent example should be sufficient to illustrate this attitude: Gillian Alban in her book *The Medusa Gaze in Contemporary Women's Fiction* (2017). When discussing Lacan's notion of the mirror stage, Alban asserts, overstepping Lacan's interpretation of Köhler, that self-recognition is 'an entirely human reaction'. She claims that animals are 'puzzled by the strange cold image presented to them, attempting to sniff the flat surface, and walking round it in order to find the absent depth of the perceived image', whereas humans 'respond warmly to such reflected images'. She uses this alleged difference between humans and 'animals' to explain human social behaviour: we humans thrive amongst others in society, while 'animals quickly manage to survive alone, and are early thrust out from the nest' (Alban, 2017, pp. 18–19). None of these statements about animals is warranted by the evidence. Nor is the assumption that any animals likely to recognise or be puzzled by a mirror image will naturally walk, rather than swim or fly. This represents an extreme example of the literary drift, whereby literary theory and literary imagination take priority over biological and psychological evidence.

However, it would be wrong to create to sharp a distinction between Lacan and his followers, as if it were only the latter who have not bothered with the relevant evidence. Some of Lacan's statements were highly questionable at the time when he was writing/speaking. His descriptions of Köhler's work were at variance with Köhler's own account of how chimpanzees behaved in front of the mirror (1925/1973, pp. 317ff.). Köhler wrote that chimpanzees became extremely interested in their reflected images when presented with hand mirrors. This interest was not extinguished, as Lacan implies, when the image was seen to have little instrumental value. Instead, Köhler's chimpanzees continued to be absorbed by their reflection.

Köhler recounted that the floor of the chimpanzees' sleeping dens often collected drops of urine. The chimps could be observed catching sight of their reflections in these drops, moving their heads backwards and forwards. Köhler commented that chimpanzees differed from other animals because other animals 'soon lose interest in the reflections when non-optical control proves their "unreality"'. By contrast, the chimps seemed to be 'permanently attracted by the contemplation of such phenomena, which can bring them no tangible or "practical" benefit' (Köhler, 1925/1973, p. 319). Significantly Lacan uses the word 'control', as did Köhler, in describing chimpanzees' reactions. However, Lacan asserts that monkeys lose interest once they gain control of the inanity of the image or realise its uselessness. Köhler had, in fact, described the opposite.

Referring to Baldwin

James Mark Baldwin (1861–1934) was the second psychologist whom Lacan mentioned in the mirror stage paper. He was a curious figure to be cited by Lacan. He was one of the founders of psychology as an empirical discipline in the United States, helping to establish the American Psychological Association, of which he was an early president. He also founded the journal *Psychological Review*, which remains to this day the most prestigious journal of experimental psychology. It is not the sort of journal that would have ever welcomed a submission from Lacan. Baldwin was committed to experimental and observational methods. In an autobiographical sketch, Baldwin claimed that, while working at Toronto University, he was the first person to establish a laboratory of experimental psychology on British soil (Baldwin, 1930). On the other hand, Baldwin also had a deep interest in philosophy and its history

Baldwin wrote on a number of psychological topics, but his most original books were probably those on developmental psychology. In *Mental Development in the Individual and the Race* (1895) Baldwin attempted to integrate the observation of children's behaviour with ideas of biological and evolutionary development. His *Social and Ethical Interpretations in Mental Development: a Study in Social Psychology* (1897) was the first book to have the term 'social psychology' as part of its title. Baldwin left the United States in 1908 after a scandal in which he was linked with an African American prostitute (Horley, 2001). He settled in France, lecturing at several provincial universities before being appointed in 1919 professor at the École des hautes études sociales in Paris.

Lacan makes his reference to Baldwin at the start of the fourth paragraph of his mirror stage piece. This is the paragraph where he switches from Köhler and the comparison with monkeys to describing what happens when the child recognises its reflection in the mirror. He says that this event can occur from the age of six months 'as one has known since Baldwin'. This is his sole reference to Baldwin in the article or, indeed, in *Écrits*. He then asserts that the repetition of the spectacle of the human infant in front of the mirror has often made us think (or, literally, has often stopped our meditation). In a phrase that has been much quoted, Lacan describes the infant producing before the mirror what the English translator has rendered as 'a flutter of jubilant activity' (*un affairement jubilatoire*: 1966, p. 9; 2002, p. 4). Significantly Lacan does not offer an example of an actual child displaying such joy, whether from his observations, those of other psychologists or from the expert whose name he has just cited.

Lacan at this point is still describing outward, observable behaviour rather than interpreting the psycho-analytic significance of such behaviour. He does not mention any specific book or article that Baldwin wrote. The reference is curious both in terms of Lacan selecting Baldwin as someone to cite at this point and in the way that Lacan makes the citation. Baldwin probably deserves credit for being the first psychologist to use the term 'stage' to describe necessary sequences in the development of the child. Lacan uses the general idea of a developmental stage in his article, but without attributing that idea to Baldwin or, indeed, to anyone else.

Lacan is appearing to attribute to Baldwin the idea that children can recognise themselves in the mirror from the age of six months. He does not quite say this. His exact wording is *on le sait depuis Baldwin*: one has known it since Baldwin. Lacan's English translators take on an impossible task. Should they preserve the oddities of his phrasing or should they make things easier for their readers by using more conventional English? Regarding this specific phrase, which in terms of Lacan's whole theoretical oeuvre, might seem trivial, Alan Sheridan stuck close to the original: 'as we have known since Baldwin' (Lacan, 1977, p. 2). Bruce Fink, in his more recent translation, makes the phrase more conventionally academic: 'as we know from Baldwin's work' (Lacan, 2002, p. 3). The wording *depuis Baldwin* (since Baldwin) is somewhat imprecise: because Baldwin had a long and varied academic career, the phrase hardly pinpoints how long one has known the so-called fact. Nor does it actually say that we derived the knowledge from Baldwin, although it gives that impression. Certainly Fink, when he translated the phrase, assumed that Lacan was meaning that we have known the fact from Baldwin's publications. In his original text, however, Lacan only mentions Baldwin and not his work.

By normalising the phrase, Fink seems to be accepting that Lacan had in mind some specific work by Baldwin, but that assumption is questionable. Lacan might have wished to appear to have a specific work in mind, as if he were familiar with Baldwin's books, although, as Émile Jalley (1998) has shown, Lacan had a habit of citing works that he had not read. The phrasing adopted by Lacan might be used by someone who wanted to avoid being tied down to specifics. In the context the tactic makes sense. Baldwin certainly discussed the way that the child develops a sense of self in *Mental Development* and in *Social and Ethical Interpretations*, but in neither of these two books did Baldwin discuss research about mirror recognition. The credit for showing that infants are able to recognise their own mirror image from about six months onwards should properly go to others, not to Baldwin.

Darwin (1877) reported his close observations of his oldest son, William. He recorded that William could recognise himself in a mirror at just over six months, unlike one of Darwin's daughters, who took much longer. Darwin also noted that apes reacted very differently than his children did, for the apes seemed to take no pleasure from the mirror images and quickly ceased to look at them. Many early developmental psychologists relied upon the observational studies of Wilhelm Preyer, who wrote detailed accounts of his own children in *The Mind of the Child* (1889). Preyer put the start of mirror recognition at around six months, although his descriptions certainly do not suggest an immediate 'aha' understanding (pp. 194–5). Sully, in *Studies of Childhood* (1895), quoted Preyer's work when offering the date for mirror recognition at around six months. By the time Lacan gave his address to the Psycho-analytical Congress, there were more authorities that could be cited regarding the age of mirror recognition. Kurt Koffka, the Gestalt psychologist, citing Preyer, gave a somewhat later date in *Growth of the Mind* (1928), as did Guillaume (1926/1971) and Wallon (1934/1949). Guillaume (1926/1971, pp. 150–51) included a lengthy section on mirror recognition in which he did not mention Baldwin. By contrast, his section critically examining Baldwin's developmental theory does not discuss mirror recognition (pp. 133–4).

Lacan's *on le sait depuis Baldwin* suggests that the self-recognition in front of the mirror from the age of six months is a matter of common knowledge. The phrase implies that the 'fact' had been generally known for many years. If he had cited Guillaume, Koffka or Wallon, he would have given the impression that this 'fact' was more recent and therefore possibly contestable and not quite so factual. Instead, Lacan's phrase suggests that the fact is firmly established and that everyone has *known* it for a good number of years.

Lacan's rhetoric conveys both a reliance upon observational data and an impatience with the details of mere observation. The imprecision of the reference – indeed its inaccuracy – conveys this duality. Lacan's readers are not being encouraged to check up on the facts of infant recognition. Instead, readers and listeners are to accept the fact as described by Lacan as the point of departure for the interpretation. Because of this, Lacan sees no need to offer details from the sort of examples that Preyer and Darwin gave of their children in front of a mirror.

In Book 1 of the Seminar series, Lacan gave an example of his simultaneous acceptance of psychologists' observations and his disdain for their failures to appreciate what they are observing. At one point, Lacan mentions having shown during the previous year a film by Arnold Gesell, the American educational psychologist. The film, according to Lacan, depicts 'the infant's jubilation in front of the mirror throughout the whole of this period'. Lacan comments that Gesell had 'never so much heard of my mirror stage, and has never asked himself any question of an analytic nature, believe you me' (1988, p. 168). Gesell provides 'facts' whose importance has to be understood by going beyond psychology. Believe you me (*je vous prie de le croire*), Lacan tells his audience, without citing any of Gesell's many books (Lacan, 1970, p. 182). The reference to Baldwin fits the same basic pattern – readers/listeners have to take the reference on trust.

Referring to Bühler

The third psychologist to be cited by Lacan was Charlotte Bühler (1893–1974), who was principally known for her work in developmental psychology. After studying at the universities of Freiburg and Munich, she went to Dresden to work with Karl Bühler, whom she was to marry. Together the Bühlers conducted pioneering psychological research at the Vienna Institute, using the techniques of observation and experimentation. Charlotte Bühler directed a series of research studies that observed the development of child behaviour (e.g. Bühler, 1935, 1940). Like Köhler, each of the Bühlers fled Nazism, first separately to Norway and then ultimately they settled together in the United States. In later life,

Charlotte Bühler's interests turned to humanistic psychology and issues such as personal fulfilment and self-actualisation.

The reference to Charlotte Bühler comes later in the mirror-stage article, when Lacan is elaborating upon the importance of the event before the mirror. He is suggesting that the mirror stage inaugurates a drama that is comparable to the primordial jealousy that is so well recognised 'by the school of Charlotte Bühler in the facts of infantile transitivism' (1966, p. 98). Lacan uses the term 'facts' as if the behavioural data of psychology were not in doubt. He does not specify what these facts are, nor does he reference where information about them might be found.

Lacan also cites Charlotte Bühler in his essay 'Aggressiveness' to exemplify in part what he means by infantile transitivism. Again, his citation employs a curious rhetoric. Lacan writes that one can catch sight of the different stages of the child by simple observation (*la simple observation*). The phrase suggests that psychological observation is a straightforward, incontestable, but limited matter. With regard to simple observation, 'a Charlotte Bühler, an Elsa Köhler and the Chicago school after them have shown us several plans of significant manifestations but to which only analytic experience can give their exact value in making it possible to reintegrate the subjective relation with them' (1966, pp. 111–12).

The phrasing is cumbersome, but the basic meaning is just about apparent: simple observation provides important evidence that must be interpreted psycho-analytically if we are to understand its subjective significance. One sort of significant manifestation, which is revealed by simple observation, is 'infantile transitivism'. This occurs during the mirror stage, between six months and two years. A child will hit another child but then will act as if it is they who have been hit. Similarly, a child who sees another child fall will cry as if it were the one who had fallen. This can be observed, and has been, by psychologists, but psycho-analysts alone can grasp how such behaviour is related to the development of the sense of self. Again, Lacan does not offer an example to be considered in its detail.

It is strange that the reference to Bühler is accompanied by a reference to Elsa Köhler. Whereas Charlotte Bühler along with Wolfgang Köhler and J. M. Baldwin are generally accepted to be significant figures in the history of psychology, Elsa Köhler is not. She was one of the researchers working under the Bühlers at the Vienna Institute and was not related to her illustrious namesake, Wolfgang. She published a monograph in 1926 on the characteristics of three-year-old children; her book appeared in a series edited by Karl Bühler (Köhler, 1926) and is hardly ever cited today. Had Lacan wanted to cite major figures who were observing child behaviour, he could have cited significant francophone psychologists, such as Jean Piaget, Paul Guillaume or Henri Wallon.

The second point to note is Lacan's phrasing: it is '*une* Charlotte Bühler, *une* Elsa Köhler' (1966, p. 111, emphasis added). This is a style that Lacan uses a number of times, especially when referring to more mainstream academics. In the mirror stage article he refers to the French sociologist and anthropologist Roger Caillois as '*un* Roger Caillois' (p. 96). Bruce Fink normalises such phrasing by omitting the indefinite article, rendering 'une Charlotte Bühler', 'une Elsa Köhler' and 'un Roger Caillois' simply as 'Charlotte Bühler', 'Elsa Köhler' and 'Roger Caillois'.

Lacan does not put the indefinite article, which in French is also the numeral 'one', before Sigmund Freud nor generally before those psycho-analytic theorists whom he respects. However, Lacan is not consistent in his distribution of indefinite articles before proper names. In *Écrits* he does refer to 'un Lévi-Strauss' (p. 285) and to 'un Jean-Paul Sartre' (p. 120); he even once refers to 'un Hegel' (p. 121). On the other hand, in *La causalité psychique*, he refers to Charlotte Bühler and her work on transitivism without using the indefinite article. In a footnote he provides full bibliographic reference to Bühler, adding the conventional scholarly 'see also' (*voir aussi*) Elsa Köhler's book (1966, p. 180).

Often the addition of the indefinite article or single numeral before a proper name can be used to downgrade the importance of the person or to suggest their comparative lack of renown. There was an example in Chapter 3 when an early nineteenth-century English scholar referred to the author of *The Light of Nature Pursued* as 'a Mr Tucker'. But *un Hegel* does not fit this pattern. On the other hand, it is possible to use the indefinite article to indicate that a named individual is being included as one member of a more general category rather than being treated as individual and unique. If the category is commendatory, then the indefinite article/single numeral can be used to indicate commendation. In the third paragraph of this chapter, I laid a little linguistic trap: I referred to 'a Freud' and 'a James' with the context making it clear that I was expressing my admiration for both.

It is the context in which the indefinite article appears before a name that can give the phrase its meaning. The reference to 'a Bühler' in 'Aggressiveness' conveys that her work does not depend upon the particular individual, for the individual belongs to a class of similar people who are able to do the work of simple observation. In this sort of context, 'un Freud' is impossible because only one person could have created Freudian theory. But anyone could have performed the tasks of simple observation. It could have been a Charlotte Bühler or an Elsa Köhler or someone else. One simple observer is substitutable for another. Significantly, when referring to Bühler in *La causalité psychique*, Lacan adds the phrase 'to cite only her', implying that other researchers have found the same findings and also that he is familiar with their work.

Maybe it is understandable that Fink in his English translation should omit the indefinite article before names, as if it carries no specific meaning in the original French – as if it were only one of Lacan's verbal tics. As always when considering the meaning of Lacan's turns of phrases, even his verbal tics, we should return to the oral performance. What does it look like to see a speaker referring to 'a Charlotte Bühler' or 'a Hegel'? Is this not a polymath who can move others, whether big or small, around the intellectual chessboard? We can watch him sweep a bishop, *un Hegel*, across the board, and then advance a pawn, *une Elsa Köhler*, by a single square. This is *le maître* in play.

Evidential Basis

The child's behaviour in front of the mirror is, for Lacan, the evidential basis for the mirror stage. He claims that the child sees the Gestalt of its own body as a coordinated whole. From this Lacan makes a series of speculations. The Gestalt that the child perceives in the mirror contrasts with the child's previous feelings of bodily 'incoordination'. The specular image of the whole body becomes the ideal image of the self. This accounts for the fascination and pleasure that children take in the mirrored reflection of themselves. However, this image is mirrored and reversed, and thereby inaccurate. It is a trap that ensnares the child. Moreover, it is external to the self, and it prefigures a disturbing split within the ego. This prepares the way for the further splitting that occurs when the child enters the symbolic world of language and learns to use the conventional first person singular to describe himself or herself. One can see why film theorists should be attracted to Lacanian theory for it places the visual image right at the heart of matters.

Malcolm Bowie (1991), who clearly admires Lacan's imaginative speculation about the mirror stage, recognises that his theory is built upon a 'very limited fund of empirical data' (p. 22). The question is whether even this limited fund holds up satisfactorily to scrutiny. In the classic paper, Lacan provides no psycho-analytic evidence to support his ideas about the relations between the perceived mirror image and the splitting of the ego. There is no detailed example to show how individual children can be so captivated by their reflected image. Oddly, Lacan does not even cite the section in 'Beyond the pleasure principle' where Freud tells a story about the behaviour of his eighteen-month-old grandson in front of a mirror.[6]

A basic question should be asked: whether the phenomena on which Lacan bases his theoretical speculations are evidentially sound. His descriptions of the child before the mirror make a number of assumptions. First, there is the implication that the child displays jubilation as a result of recognising itself. However, what seems a simple observation – the child showing pleasure at its own image in the mirror – might not be quite so straightforward. Even when describing Gesell's images, Lacan is doing more than providing a simple description: he implies that the jubilant scene caught on film by Gesell occurs throughout the mirror stage but does not precede it. He implies that such jubilation does not occur in the behaviour of a child who observes an image in the mirror but cannot yet recognise the image as its own reflection.

The evidence that was available to Lacan would suggest that pleasure in mirror images can precede the child recognising itself. Darwin (1877) describes his son at four and a half months smiling at seeing his own image and that of his father, while mistaking these images for real objects. Preyer held his son up to the mirror from eleven weeks onwards. Initially the little boy was indifferent to his mirror image, but by his seventeenth week, he was beginning to laugh at the image. This laughter was not accompanied by recognition. Preyer notes that by the thirty-fifth week, 'the child gaily and with interest grasps at his image in the glass, and is surprised when his hand comes against the smooth surface' (1889, p. 198). For several more weeks the image is 'greeted with a laugh' while the child grasps the mirror and feels for the object behind it. Such grasping indicates that the boy has not recognised that the image is just an image and that he himself is the subject of the image.

In his book *Imitation in Children*, Paul Guillaume reported children showing delight in mirror images before they are able to recognise themselves (1926/1971, pp. 150–51). Guillaume's interpretation is connected

---

[6] Freud recounts that his grandson, little Ernst, was in the habit of playing a game that Freud called the *fort* (gone)/*da* (there) game. The child would make objects, such as toys and other things, disappear, saying a childish version of *fort*; and then with great pleasure and, often after great effort, he would find them again, saying *da*. According to Freud, by repeatedly playing this *fort/da* game, Ernst was trying to gain control over the trauma of separation from his mother. One day, when his mother went out, he played the game with his image in the mirror, crouching below the mirror to make the image disappear and then bringing it back by standing up (Freud, 1920/1991, pp. 283–5; see Benveniste, 2014, for details of Freud's relationship with little Ernst). Lacan does discuss Freud's *fort/da* in other places in *Écrits*, but without mentioning the mirror version of the game (1966, pp. 101, 205 and 223). In fact, Lacan claims that the objects that the child makes to disappear and then reappear in the *fort/da* game were insignificant (*insignifiant*) (p. 223). The child's image in the mirror was insignificant? Curious.

with his general theory that imitation is crucial in the development of the child. He considered that the delight before the mirror was similar to the delight shown by the child's imitation of another, or when another person, such as a parent, imitates the child's movements. The mirror image seems to imitate the child, and when the child, in turn, imitates the image, then the image, as it were, is responding with further imitation. Thus imitative playfulness, together with the accompaniment of pleasure as a response to the mirror image, does not depend on self-recognition, but, as Guillaume suggested, it may be a necessary step towards self-recognition.[7]

The implications are important with respect to Lacan's description of the child's behaviour. According to Lacan, the sense of recognition is immediate – hence his use of the Gestaltist terminology to indicate the sudden 'aha' leap of problem-solving. The solution depends on the perception of the whole bodily Gestalt, which provides the visual basis for the ideal image of the self. Thus, recognition of the self, according to Lacan's account, is not slowly built up over time, bit by bodily bit. However, Lacan also says that recognition of the image results in the child making a series of gestures by which the child playfully tests (*il éprouve ludiquement*) the relations between its movements and the reflected image (1966, p. 93).

By contrast, Guillaume's analysis suggested that the testing is part of a lengthy process of self-recognition. According to Guillaume, the key element is not the recognition of a visual Gestalt, but the imitation of bodily movements. He writes, 'One must not exaggerate the precision of the visual image of the body itself which results from this mirror perception' (1926/1971, pp. 152–3). As so often happens, an example can be particularly revealing. Guillaume describes an episode that throws doubt on an account that gives priority to the visual image when describing how the child comes to recognise itself in the mirror. The example concerns his daughter when she was two years and eight months and had been able to recognise her mirror image for a while. Guillaume took a photograph of her in a group of children but, when he showed her the photograph, she was able to recognise all the others except herself. Guillaume pressed her on the point and asked who this girl was. She could only reply that it was a little girl whom she did not know. This episode demonstrates, according

---

[7] Freud obviously believed that little Ernst recognised his own image in the mirror, but the evidence that he presents is by no means conclusive. When the mother returned, little Ernst told her in babyish language, 'Baby gone'. Freud thought that he was talking about himself, because he had made his mirror image disappear. Equally, Ernst might have thought the image was another baby whom he had made to disappear and reappear (1920/1991, p. 284n). We do not know if Ernst at this period was in the habit of referring to himself as 'Baby'.

to Guillaume, 'how very tenuous is the precise notion of one's own visual form, in spite of what the child learns from looking in the mirror' (1926/ 1971, p. 153). Lacan does not mention Guillaume's work, and certainly not this episode, which conflicts with his own version of mirror recognition.

Guillaume, who taught at the Sorbonne, was a notable figure in French psychology. Not only was he known for his work on child development but he was directly influenced by Wolfgang Köhler. In fact, he translated Köhler's *Mentality of Apes* into French. During the 1930s Guillaume wrote a series of articles in *Journal de Psychologie* examining how chimpanzees use instruments, and he published a book on the subject in 1943. At that time, he was recognised as the most important exponent of Gestalt psychology in France. That means that when Lacan was writing about chimpanzee self-recognition, the mirror Gestalt and the child's recognition of its own visual image, he did not refer to the most eminent French authority on these topics – an authority whose 'simple observations' did not match the Lacanian view.

In evaluating the strength of Lacan's ideas today, one should ask whether his accounts have been supported by subsequent studies. There is evidence that points to mirror self-recognition being the result of piecemeal kinaesthetic-visual matching, as described by Guillaume, rather than being a result of perceiving an overall visual Gestalt (Asendorpf, Warkentin and Baudonnière, 1996; Vyt, 2001; but see also Gallup, Anderson and Shillito, 2002; Keenan, Gallup and Falk, 2003). In developing the work of Guillaume, Mitchell (1997) argued that mirror self-recognition is a lengthy process of self-imitation; there is, accordingly, no decisive 'aha' moment. Some psychologists are now claiming that 'mirror neurons' provide a physiological basis for imitation (e.g. Gallese and Goldman, 1998; Stamenov and Gallese, 2002; Rizzolatti and Craighero, 2004). These neurons have been found in the frontal lobes of some primates as well as in humans. As with the case of mirror recognition, which was once thought to be confined to primates, there is now evidence that other species also possess the neurological basis for empathy (Panksepp and Panksepp, 2013).

The so-called mirror neurons fire when the organism performs a particular action and also when it sees another member of its species performing the same action. It is said that those species possessing such mirror neurons are neurologically primed to imitate the actions and gestures of others. That would explain why certain species can recognise themselves in mirrors: they will 'imitate' their own mirrored actions, and this imitation is the vital step in achieving self-recognition. Other species which lack such neurological capacities may be perfectly capable of perceiving whole visual Gestalts but not of engaging in the action of self-imitation that is the key to recognising the self in mirror images.

If mirror neurons turn out to have great psychological significance for understanding child development, then there might be a case for revising the meaning of the mirror trope that has become so important in cultural analysis, principally thanks to Lacanian theory. What is comparatively unimportant in the mirror image is the child's perception of its own body as a fixed visual Gestalt. Of greater significance would be the ability of the child to use its body to mirror, or imitate, its own reflected actions, just as it mirrors the actions of others. The theoretical emphasis, then, would be turned from the purely visual towards the active aspects of children's behaviour.

It must be emphasised again that Lacan cannot be criticised for failing to anticipate research, including research into 'mirror neurons'. On the other hand, his pattern of citing those sources that were available to him is puzzling. Elsa Köhler is cited, but not Paul Guillaume, whose systematic observations of the child before the mirror could easily have been consulted by Lacan's French-speaking followers. Wolfgang Köhler is cited as if he had written the opposite of what he did about the reactions of chimpanzees to their reflected images. Something is going on beyond the use of so-called simple observation to provide the basis for psychoanalytic interpretation.

Omitting Wallon

The most worrying omission in Lacan's psychological citations about the mirror stage is not Paul Guillaume – large though that omission is – but his failure to mention Henri Wallon, a Marxist French psychologist, professor at the Collège de France and a major figure in French psychology between the wars. In ignoring Guillaume, Lacan was ignoring someone with very different views than his own. In the case of Wallon, he was ignoring someone with very similar views to his own. The problem was that Wallon outlined his views about children and mirrors a few years before Lacan. So striking are the coincidences between Lacan's views and Wallon's that Roudinesco (1990, 1997, 2003), despite her admiration for Lacan, suggests that he plagiarised Wallon. So does Jalley (1998), who points out that Lacan almost certainly knew Wallon personally, having met him at psychiatric congresses from 1930 onwards. The charge of plagiarism is serious, so it is important to look closely at Wallon's views about children and mirrors and also at Lacan's non-citation of those views.

In his book *Les Origines du Caractère chez l'Enfant*, first published in 1934, Wallon discussed at great length children's reactions in front of a mirror. He also included a section about animal behaviour. These discussions had originally formed the basis of an article in *Journal de Psychologie* in 1931. Wallon's book also discussed the issue of transitivism, and he drew extensively upon the work of Charlotte Bühler and Elsa Köhler (Wallon, 1934/1949, pp. 212ff.). To illustrate transitivism, Wallon used Elsa Köhler's example of a young girl aged two years and nine months who hits another child and then claims to have been hit by that child (p. 217). Lacan alludes to this example in 'Aggressiveness', but without giving the details and bibliographic reference that Wallon provides. One might wonder why Lacan should have mentioned Elsa Köhler but not the much more readily available discussion of her work in Wallon's book, which Lacan does not even accord a brief *voir aussi*. There is a further point. Jalley (1998) comments that when Lacan refers to Bühler's and Köhler's work on transitivism, he mentions nothing that he could not have derived second-hand from Wallon. Jalley is of the view that Lacan did not read the original sources for himself but took from Wallon without acknowledging him.

Wallon's descriptions of mirror behaviour are particularly interesting. Wallon cites previous authorities, including Preyer, Darwin and Guillaume. In common with Guillaume, Wallon stressed the importance of imitation both as a general part of intellectual and social development, and also in relation to behaviour in front of the mirror. What is striking is the extent to which Wallon outlined themes and used phrases that Lacan was to take up in his discussion of the mirror stage, especially when Wallon discussed the importance of the 'specular image' in the development of the infant's sense of self and sense of others.

Wallon used a developmental psychology of stages and pointed to the importance of the mirror image. He did not call the period in which the child recognises its mirror image the 'mirror stage', but he locates it within a developmental stage that he calls 'the stage of juxtaposition' (*le stade de juxtaposition*) (1934/1949, pp. 168ff.). Wallon emphasised the importance of children's recognition of themselves in the mirror for their development of a sense of self. He stressed, as Lacan would do later, that the mirror image provides the only complete image of the child's body, which previously the child has only seen in fragments (Wallon, 1934/1949, p. 172; see Jalley, 1998, for an appreciation of Wallon's originality).

According to Wallon, recognising the self in the mirror is part of a process that fixes the traits of identity and finally permits the child to understand itself 'as a body amongst bodies, as a being among other beings' (p. 173). Unlike Lacan, but in common with Guillaume, Wallon suggests that self-recognition in the mirror occurs gradually as the child combines visual images and internal proprioceptive feelings. However, Wallon also quoted Darwin's account of his son who recognised his image with a 'ha!' (Darwin, 1877, p. 293). Interestingly, Wolfgang Köhler did not use 'aha', and certainly not *Aha-Erlebnis*, in relation to chimpanzees' self-recognition in the mirror.

Wallon presents further arguments that later appear in Lacan's work. For example, Wallon claims that recognising the mirror image is a necessary intermediate step before entering the symbolic world and that this step undermines the infant's sense of reality. Recognising the mirror image involves what Wallon called a 'double necessity'. The child must recognise that images only have the appearance of reality: the reflected image is an image, not a real person. Yet, the child must also admit the reality of these images for they are not fantasies. According to Wallon, 'the dilemma is posed in these terms: perceptual images, but unreal; real images but subtracted from sensory knowledge' (1934/1949, p. 175).

Lacan would express the same idea in his seminars. He claimed that the mirror relation illustrates that 'in so far as one part of reality is imagined, the other is real and inversely, in so far as one part is reality, the other becomes imaginary' (1988, p. 82). Lacan used this description when he was criticising Melanie Klein for lacking theories of the imaginary and of the ego. He writes that 'it is up to us to introduce these notions' (p. 82). He does not suggest that in introducing such notions, he might be introducing notions that Wallon had earlier introduced.

More than any previous investigator, Wallon pointed to the importance of the mirror experience for the development of symbolic understanding. Wallon's view was that the child enters the world of representations by understanding the mirror reflection. After experiencing the mirror, the child's world is no longer a simple perceptual one. Roudinesco writes, 'In Wallon, the mirror experience specified the dialectical transition from the specular to the imaginary, then from the imaginary to the symbolic' (1990, p. 143). The experience of the mirror is, according to Wallon, 'the prelude of symbolic activity' by which the mind comes to transform generally the givens of perception' (Wallon, 1934/1949, p. 175).

Wallon expressed clearly why, in his view, the mirror image is related to the development of the imaginary. Wallon's descriptions also contain a sense of splitting that is also to be found in Lacan. The world of the child is no longer complete or safe: the real has become unreal and vice versa. Certainly Lacan's mirror stage article does not state exactly why the experience in front of the mirror should involve *méconnaissance* or misrecognition (1966, p. 99). Had Lacan wanted to explain why the apprehension of the Gestalt – or the mirrored specular image – should be so tied to *méconnaissance*, almost certainly he would have reverted to something similar to Wallon's formulation of the double necessity. As we have seen, when Lacan referred to 'my mirror stage' (1988, p. 168), he was not referring to the distant event when Mme Lacan held little Jacques up to the mirror, but he was using the possessive pronoun to indicate that the adult Jacques was the owner of the idea. More accurately, he was the owner of the new label that he was attaching to Wallon's idea.

Citing and Not Citing Wallon

Écrits contains a short article 'De nos antécédents' in which Lacan describes his intellectual forebears. Lacan briefly mentions the 1936 conference at Marienbad where 'we' produced the mirror stage (1966, p. 67). In discussing his antecedents, Lacan mentions Clérambault as 'our sole master in psychiatry' (p. 65). He does not mention Wallon, just as he did not mention him in the mirror stage article. However, Wallon is not completely absent from *Écrits*, for two articles mention his name, but in neither case does Lacan mention Wallon's ideas about the role of mirror recognition in the development of the child's sense of self.

In Chapter 3, when discussing the way that English philosopher Shadworth Hodgson cited Abraham Tucker, I referred to his pattern of selective citation. Hodgson tended to cite Tucker when he disagreed with him but did not mention him when he was repeating some of Tucker's ideas. Lacan's citations of Wallon are analogously selective. In *La causalité psychique*, Lacan mentions Wallon but not Wallon's work. Lacan was discussing 'my construction called "the mirror stage"' (*ma construction dite 'du stade du miroir'*; 1966, p. 184) and then he outlines the origins of his idea. Here he tells his story of talking at Marienbad and being interrupted by Jones. Right after the story, which I discussed earlier in this chapter, Lacan states that 'you would be able to find the essence of it [the mirror stage talk] in several lines in my article on the family that appeared in 1938 in the *Encyclopédie française*' (p. 185). Lacan then adds a footnote giving the full bibliographic reference of his *Encyclopédie* article, including the information that the article appeared in the section of the encyclopaedia on 'mental life' which was edited by Henri Wallon.

Lacan goes on to comment further on the history of the idea of the mirror stage, saying that after his 1936 talk and his 1938 article, the idea has subsequently made its way (*l'idée a fait son chemin*; 1966, p. 185). In making its way, his idea met the ideas of other researchers (*autres chercheurs*). At this point, Lacan becomes unusually precise. He mention one of these other researchers: Lhermitte, whose book *L'Image du Corps propre* (The image of one's own body) Lacan identifies as having appeared in

1939. Why all this precision with dates? More usually, Lacan is wayward in his handling of bibliographic detail.

The answer is simple: Lacan is establishing his priority to the idea of the mirror stage. He is saying that he talked about the idea in 1936 and published several lines in 1938. This is before Lhermitte's book on the same theme appeared in 1939. Significantly, Lacan mentions Wallon as the editor, who published Lacan's encyclopaedia article, but not as another *chercheur* who might have contributed to the ideas of the mirror stage. Certainly Wallon is not presented as someone whose ideas pre-date those of Lacan. Thus, by his careful pattern of inclusion, exclusion and precise dating, Lacan avoids the suggestion that his mirror stage might have owed anything to the man whose name he mentions in the footnote, safely attached to Lacan's own self-citation which is being used to establish his ownership of the mirror stage.

The second reference to Wallon comes in the 'Aggressiveness' article. Lacan is discussing the development of the sense of self and its relations to aggressivity. He mentions that there is bodily and emotional coordination. The subordination of the functions of tonic postures and vegetative tension to social relativity is something 'whose prevalence in the expressive constitution of human emotions a Wallon [*un Wallon*] has remarkably underlined' (1966, p. 112). The use of technical terms is typically heavy, and so is their lack of clarity. Lacan also characteristically uses an indefinite article, and he provides no bibliographic detail for what Wallon remarkably underlined.

The implication of substitutability that appears in 'une Charlotte Bühler' and 'une Elsa Köhler' fits uneasily with the rest of the statement that pays tribute to Wallon for having done some remarkable work. Sheridan's English translation, which keeps the indefinite pronoun in the references to Bühler and Köhler, omits it here, as does Fink in his translation. Straight after the reference to 'un Wallon', Lacan begins describing the mirror stage and the perception of the mirrored Gestalt. He specifically uses the first person singular, writing that this is what 'I have called the mirror stage' (*ce que j'ai appelé le stade du miroir*; 1966, p. 113). Of course, he does not say that what he calls the 'mirror stage' is something that Wallon described in very similar terms but which he claimed to be part of the stage of juxtaposition.

The two references to Wallon in *Écrits* share two common characteristics. First, they are 'safe' references – they do not refer to Wallon's ideas about children's responses in front of the mirror and the importance of these responses in splitting the child's sense of reality. In one case, Lacan explicitly praises Wallon for his remarkable work – and this is not his work on mirror recognition. In the other instance, Wallon is only mentioned as part of Lacan's bibliographic reference to his own publication about mirror recognition.

Second, both references appear in close proximity, not just to Lacan's descriptions of the mirror stage but to Lacan's proprietary claims for the stage. It is *my* construction that *I* have named. Lacan even gives the precise dates of his talk and publication to bolster his claim, while at the same time omitting any mention of Wallon's relevant, prior publications. Rhetorically, the conjunction of 'safe' references to Wallon and the proprietary claim to the mirror stage serve to make Wallon's mirror ideas invisible. Rhetorically, in this context, Wallon's ideas have become Lacan's. Roudinesco has written that Lacan, having neglected to cite Wallon's name when borrowing his ideas and terminology, subsequently 'always suppressed Wallon's name' (2014, p. 19).

Therefore, both Lacan's citations of Wallon in *Écrits* are highly selective. They are too precisely constructed and too carefully positioned to be considered merely coincidental. If one accepts psycho-analytic assumptions, then one should seek underlying motives for atypical, curious behaviour. Lacan's claim to have discovered the mirror stage just when he fails to mention the contribution of Wallon is certainly curious – especially since he knows Wallon's work and probably the man himself. It does not take a trained psycho-analyst to suspect a motive of self-interest.

Scholarly Practices

Why bother with the tiny details of the way that Lacan cited others? It hardly seems to be a topic worthy of interest. Surely it would have been more edifying to have considered Lacan's work more widely rather than focus on a single, six-page publication and its unobtrusive turns of phrase. This is really dragging down the work of someone who has been much praised as a major, creative thinker. Only a pedant could consider the apparatus of pedantry as being remotely interesting, as if all that matters are an ordered reference list and the correct way to quote a text – such is pedantry's small-mindedness.

There are, nevertheless, wider issues at stake. Amongst his admirers, Lacan has the reputation as a polymath, possessing knowledge of linguistics, mathematics, physics and many other fields besides. No attempt here has been made to assess his knowledge of these widely disparate fields, only something very specific: his knowledge of psychology as displayed in his mirror stage paper. Here it is possible to say that Lacan presents his knowledge of psychology with greater confidence than accuracy; nor is this knowledge based on being familiar with the original sources. Also it has been useful to look at matters that are so small that they can easily escape attention, especially the attention of those who prefer to focus on big theory. We can see how Lacan can reveal himself in his small words. When he does, then we can appreciate why the apparatus of scholarship might have value.

A number of commentators besides Émile Jalley and Élisabeth Roudinesco have mentioned the similarities between Lacan's ideas about the mirror stage and Wallon's ideas (e.g. Homer, 2005; Nobus, 2017b; Stavrakakis, 1999; Zwart, 2014).[8] Lacan's mythology as a lone, creative polymath is compromised if he is seen to have borrowed key ideas, such as the mirror stage, from others. If he hides his intellectual debts, then the borrowing becomes theft. That is why some followers who recognise the similarity between Lacan's ideas and those of Wallon sometimes claim that Lacan added extra elements not found in Wallon. Dany Nobus (2017b), for example, suggests that although Wallon described the child's pleasure in seeing its own mirror image, Lacan 'magnified and centralised this detail, making it a key component of the child's experience'; Nobus also suggests that Lacan added the element of the *Aha-Erlebnis* (p. 107). The major issue, of course, is not whether Lacan made pleasure the key component of the child's experience but whether the evidence suggests that he was right to do so – and also whether there is a sudden aha moment.

The problem is that both the elements which, according to Nobus, Lacan added to Wallon's ideas are almost certainly unsatisfactory as a description of the child's experience. As has been argued, the pleasure that the child feels in front of the mirror seems not to be specifically derived from the child recognising its image, as Lacan suggests; rather it appears to stem from the child enjoying the way that the mirror appears to 'imitate' its own movements. Similarly, the recognition of the self does not seem to occur in a single aha moment in the way Lacan implied, but it develops much more slowly through imitation.

---

[8] Emphasising the importance of the scholarly apparatus does not mean that one always succeeds in avoiding bibliographic or other errors. Sadly mistakes are always possible. Stavrakakis (2007), writing in response to an earlier and shorter journal article (Billig, 2006b), noted that I had wrongly implied that he had not mentioned Wallon in his book *Lacan and the Political* (Stavrakakis, 1999). He also suggested that I underestimated the extent to which Lacanians recognise Wallon's work. I am pleased here to correct any such error or misleading impression. I do not think that these corrections affect the main arguments of this chapter and I have been able to present these arguments here in much greater detail than was possible in the limited space of the journal article. One of the advantages of the shared culture of scholarship is that fellow academics can point out mistakes, which an author can then recognise and seek to rectify. That is not possible when thinkers put themselves above the mundane disciplines of bibliographic referencing and make general statements about how things occur without citing evidence.

The theory of the mirror stage might sound good. However, when it spins free from evidence and especially free from convincing examples, then it becomes, to use the phrase of Abraham Tucker, a mere abstraction. There are, to be sure, times when pure theories have a role. This is especially true when theories are not presented as descriptions of the present but as a means to keep alive as yet unrealised hopes for humanity's future. For instance, we might entertain a theory that imagines a common inclusive sense of humanity as being one day possible. But this would be different from a theory that routinely, unthinkingly excludes blind girls and boys from the supposedly decisive moment of human development.

***

The practice of selective citation might be trivial in itself; if it were to be eradicated, no wars would be avoided or diseases cured. Yet, the fact that large numbers of academics can regularly excuse, overlook or dismiss such faults should not be trivial. An objection might be expected from Lacan's followers. They are likely to argue that too much attention is being given here to standard scholarly practices of citation. These, so it might be objected, are matters of form, not content. If Lacan did not cite others in the normal ways, then this was because he was deliberately subverting the standard practices of scholarship, so as to set free a way of thinking that was far riskier and far more intellectually creative than ordinary academic thinking. It would be a mistake, therefore, to try to rein back Lacan, because he was so unlike the rest of us academic time servers, who have difficulty seeing beyond a world of careful citation.

There is a problem with such a defence. The way that writers treat their readers is part of the world of social relations, and as such, it is part of the wider, moral world. Academic conventions may be pernickety, but at their best, they can serve egalitarian and sceptical functions. We, the lumpen pedants, can ask our betters – the so-called academic superstars – for their evidence and for their illustrative examples. With proper bibliographic references, we can then read and assess the evidence for ourselves. We do not have to take the masters at their word, especially when that word is so difficult to understand but all too tempting to follow.

We can ask, What does Lacan reveal about himself when he dispenses with the conventions for citation? His pattern of self-revelation is not random. He does not free himself from scholarly convention in order to mock himself with self-effacing humour, as Tucker and Shaftesbury did. Freeing himself from scholarly restrictions, Lacan was not as equally likely to hide his own achievements as he was to display himself proudly before his audience. The balance always seems to tip the same way.

Through his own words, Lacan revealed his unstoppable ego, as he commanded attention, praised himself and reacted angrily to perceived slights. Week after week he stood before his followers, a magnificent, mystifying presence. His spoken words have been solidified into books, which are now assigned as compulsory reading for students, and his fame has spread far beyond the specialists. Lacan was returning to Freud as a colonialist might return to a captured territory.

Towards the end of his life, Freud, in his *New Introductory Lectures*, declared his hope for the future: 'Where id was, there ego shall be' (1932/1991, p. 112). But surely not every ego represents a hope for the future. Lacan demonstrated by his own example that in one respect, Freud was wrong: yes, there can be too much ego – especially an ego that is largely unreasonable and unreasonably large.

6   Lewin
Is There Nothing as Practical as a Good Example?

Kurt Lewin has become a semi-mythological figure. In a tribute published in *Psychological Review* following Lewin's death in 1947, the learning theorist Edward Tolman put Lewin alongside Freud in terms of his achievements and contributions to psychology. Tolman predicted that out of all the psychologists from his own lifetime, only Freud and Lewin would 'always be remembered' because 'their contrasting but complementary insights' made psychology a science which was applicable to real individuals and real society (1948, p. 4). It has not quite worked out that way. Freud, to be sure, remains a household name, although more cited beyond psychology than within it, where he is seldom recognised as a scientific creator. Lewin's general fame never reached that of Freud, but most certainly he has not been forgotten in the academic world. Within two areas of study, Lewin remains cherished as a founding figure.

The textbooks of social psychology frequently declare Lewin to be the father of modern social psychology (Billig, 2015b; Delouvée, Kalampalikis and Pétard, 2011). Robert Levine, when introducing a collection of essays written by some of the most senior social psychologists of his generation, described Lewin to be 'our founding father' (2008, p. ix). If that is not sufficient, then in management sciences Lewin is 'widely considered' to be 'the founding father of change management' (Cummings, Bridgman and Brown, 2016, p. 34; see also Burnes and Bargal, 2017). To be heralded as the founding father of two sub-disciplines is a rare achievement.

In addition to describing Lewin as their founding father, the textbooks of social psychology often cite Lewin's motto that 'There is nothing as practical as a good theory'. Levine quoted this motto, claiming that Lewin's own work fulfilled his dictum (2008, p. xi). It is as if Lewin not only founded social psychology but bequeathed an enduring profundity which, according to one of his former pupils, has become part of the 'folklore of social psychology' (Cartwright, 1978, p. 169). Today's textbooks tend to assume that Lewin created the motto, and so did many of his American pupils who personally heard him utter the phrase so often

(Marrow, 1969). However, in Lewin's native Germany, the motto has had a much longer history, going back possibly to the time of Kant.[1]

It is not the history of the motto that concerns me here but the relations between theory and practice that the motto treats as being unproblematic. There is a case for saying that there was nothing as impractical as Lewin's own type of supposedly good theory. Exploring these issues will involve looking closely at Lewin's theory, his methodological practice and his commitment to using psychology to improve the state of the world. Lewin was a genuinely creative intellectual, and his major methodological innovation is especially relevant here, for, in effect, he devised a new type of example.

Lewin's examples went far beyond the examples which Abraham Tucker used and which enduringly humanised William James' discussion of mental processes. Literary innovation in the style of James should not be expected from Lewin, whose many talents, in truth, did not include those of being writerly with words. Lewin's methodological innovation produced the richness of detail to be found in Freud's case histories, but with one major difference. Freud had to wait for his examples to occur. That was even true when he was analysing himself. In Chapter 4 I looked at the example of his forgetting the name of Signorelli in a chance conversation. Freud could not have planned to have forgotten the name in advance – that would have defeated the object of the whole exercise.

Lewin transformed the relationship between psychological example and happenstance. An impatient man, he and his co-workers did not passively wait for their examples to crop up in real life. They carefully planned how to create social examples in practice, and then they observed how events unfolded over time. Once the unfolding had started, the researchers were unable to control matters quite as they might have hoped. As an example, I will use Lewin's famous study of democratic and autocratic leadership; and as an example of Lewin's writing, I will examine how he and his co-workers reported their study in the *Journal of Social Psychology*.

There should be two advance words of caution. First, I am crediting Lewin with inventing the sort of real-life experiment that he advocated. Perhaps a specialist in the history of social psychology might find cause to dispute this. Since Lewin's claim to his famous phrase can be questioned, and since his 'good' theory will be criticised later, I hope to redress the balance a little: I will treat him as if he were the inventor of his

---

[1] Lewin was not even the first psychologist to use the motto. The American psychologist G. Stanley Hall, who met William James at Harvard and who invited Freud to America, had used the saying in his book *Youth* (1906, p. 331) and then later in his autobiography (Hall, 1923, p. 447; see Billig, 2015b).

methodological practice. A touch of academic generosity to a remarkable man is not exactly a dangerous risk.

The second word of caution is perhaps more important. Lewin's social experiments were not the sort of tightly controlled experiments that have come to predominate within social psychology and that the textbooks assume Lewin to have fathered. The familiar modern experiment constructs brief and highly artificial moments for which participants are tightly locked into group samples so that none can ever escape to become a telling example. As will be seen, Lewin dismissed this type of controlled experiment as being unscientific. Kurt Danziger has written that modern social psychologists ignore their academic father's methods, which to this day remain 'something of a buried treasure' (1994a, p. 178; see also Ash, 1998; Colucci and Colombo, 2018).

Social psychologists have also tended to overlook Lewin's views on 'good' theories, which are not so much buried treasure as forgotten embarrassment. If we are to understand the relations between Lewin's theory and his practice, then it will be necessary to recall this embarrassment. This will entail taking his philosophical background seriously. Although experimental social psychologists today want to claim Lewin as one of their own, he was always much more than an orthodox social psychologist. Lewin's second wife, Gertrud, was to tell her husband's biographer that Kurt 'never abandoned philosophy' (Marrow, 1969, p. 17). The problem, it will be suggested, was not that Lewin retained too much philosophy but that he abandoned too much of the philosophy that his teacher Ernst Cassirer had taught.

Lewin: a Life of Theory and Practice

An essential element of Lewin's psychology was that a person cannot be studied in isolation because each individual belongs to a wider social world and to a network of relationships. Thus, all individuals – their ideas and their actions – must be examined in relation to their total situation or lifeworld. So it is with Lewin himself. His ideas about the lifeworlds of others came from his own situation.

Lewin was born in 1890 in the small town of Mogilno, which was then part of Germany but is now in central Poland. His family were Jewish middle class, but not the wealthy middle class or professional bourgeoisie: his father owned a small general store and a farm. There were only about thirty-five Jewish families in Mogilno, and as Lewin was later to recall, the Christians of the area, whether rich or poor, held anti-Semitic views whose truth they took for granted (Lewin, 1998). The family moved to Berlin when Kurt was about fifteen, and his parents encouraged him to attend university, which his father, who had left school at sixteen, never did. Initially Kurt enrolled at Freiburg University to study medicine and then switched to Munich to study biology (Burnes and Bargal, 2017; Smith, 2001). Finally, in 1910, he enrolled to study philosophy and psychology at Berlin University, where he was to remain and take his doctorate. He showed a particular interest in the philosophy of science, and he attended Cassirer's lectures on the subject (Marrow, 1969).

At Berlin University, Lewin came into contact with a remarkable group of Gestalt psychologists, including Max Wertheimer, Kurt Koffka and Wolfgang Köhler, who worked in the university's Psychological Institute. Throughout his career as a psychologist, Lewin was to remain committed to the fundamental premises of Gestaltism – namely that the whole is more than the sum of its parts and that insights do not come from breaking down psychological phenomena into their smallest parts, as the associationists assumed. Lewin's particular insight was to see that individuals are influenced by their whole life situation, and this included the groups to which they belonged – and these groups themselves lived within a group lifeworld. In terms of the conflict between atomists and holists, discussed in Chapter 2, Lewin and the Gestaltists were firmly on the side of the holists. Lewin proposed that the behaviour (B) of any person (P) is a function (f) of that person and their total environment (E). He expressed this idea in terms of an equation: $B = f(PE)$ (Lewin, 1936, p. 32). Textbooks of social psychology still cite this formula.

From 1921 until 1932 Lewin worked as a lecturer at Berlin's Psychological Institute, and he published a series of highly original papers. Most of Lewin's papers from his Berlin days concerned psychological research into issues such as needs, tensions and motives. He also maintained an interest in the philosophy of science. He sought to apply Cassirer's views on the philosophy of science to the sort of work that psychologists should be producing if they were to turn psychology into a genuinely modern science. The most important of Lewin's theoretical papers was one in which he distinguished between Aristotelian and Galilean modes of science (Lewin, 1931/1999). This paper will be discussed later, for it crystallised Lewin's views about what constitutes a 'good' theory. Lewin's Berlin papers tended not to reflect his interests in practical psychology or what would become known as 'action research'. His early paper on the psychology of industrial production was published a year before he obtained his Berlin lectureship (1920/1999).

While Lewin was working in Berlin, the political situation in Germany was deteriorating especially for Jews. In 1932, Lewin was invited to spend six months at Stanford University in California. The timing was fortunate, because Hitler would take power the following year. In the States,

Lewin was able to make academic contacts, who would arrange for him to return the following year as a refugee from Nazism. He was first appointed to Cornell University, and after two years there, he moved to the Child Welfare Research Station at Iowa University, where he stayed for twelve years, reproducing in the American Midwest the sort of co-operative research atmosphere that he had enjoyed in Berlin (Ash, 1992). In 1945, Lewin moved to MIT to establish the Research Centre for Group Dynamics. Lewin made it clear that his new centre would not be training people to brainwash or manipulate others; rather, there he would explore how human potential could be freed and how prejudices could be overcome (Marrow, 1969).

Lewin hoped that he had left behind the racism and anti-Semitism of Germany, but he was disappointed by the prejudices he encountered in the States (Marrow, 1969). Nevertheless, he eagerly embraced the American culture, contrasting its open, democratic ways with the autocratic, hierarchical norms of Germany. Marrow's biography of Lewin contains a photograph of Lewin eating a hamburger at the 1939 World's Fair in New York. Lewin is standing, looking directly at the camera as he bites into his food. He seems somewhat awkward, as if afraid that at any moment the package of food might fall apart in his hands. Lewin's lack of practice with the eating of hamburgers is not the point; his eagerness to eat in the classless American style is. One cannot imagine many German professors, especially those from the previous generation, being photographed eating, let alone standing in public and eating with their hands. One might guess that when Wilhelm Wundt ate, he would sit at a dining table with plates, cutlery and a servant in attendance.[2]

It was in the States that Lewin developed his practical research, looking at questions such as how to create harmonious group dynamics, or how Jewish immigrants could adjust to their new environment, or how to persuade people to eat more frugally during wartime shortages. He threw himself into 'action research' without abandoning his interest in philosophy. By the force of his personality, his unwavering optimism and the originality of his intellect, Lewin was able to attract a group of talented young researchers first to Iowa and then to Massachusetts. They enjoyed the democratic atmosphere that Lewin encouraged in his research teams. Many of these researchers would go on to become leading figures in the

---

[2] This paragraph might have exaggerated gap between Lewin's informality and that of German academics of his own generation, who might not have shared the conservative formality of Wundt's generation. Julia Boyd (2017) includes an account of a young pro-Nazi academic in the 1930s who was informal in the company of his (pro-Nazi) students and enjoyed taking open-air ice creams with them.

next generation of social psychologists – the largely American-born generation that established experimental social psychology as a major subdiscipline of American psychology and that Robert Levine was to speak for when describing Lewin as the founding father of social psychology.

Lewin's time at Iowa is notable for another reason, for he conducted his experiment comparing authoritarian and autocratic atmospheres there. This experiment pioneered the methodology by which the researcher could create and monitor an example of social life. The connection of the study with Lewin's own lifeworld is obvious. He was comparing the autocratic atmosphere of Germany with the democratic atmosphere of the country that literally saved his life.

Two Great Influences

Lewin might have been influenced by his contact with Gestalt psychologists at Berlin, but there were two highly original thinkers outside of psychology who deeply affected his thoughts about science, practice and 'good' theories. He came into contact with both during his time as an undergraduate in Berlin. They were his teacher of philosophy, Ernst Cassirer, and his longtime friend, the Marxist writer and politician Karl Korsch. Each symbolically represented one side of Lewin's dual theoretical and practical interests. Despite Lewin's reputation as an empirical psychologist, his continuing admiration for Cassirer testifies to his philosophical interests. His friendship with Korsch marks Lewin out as being a man of the Left, committed to finding ways of improving the world in practice.

Ernst Cassirer was sixteen years older than Lewin and was, in the words of Lewin's daughter Miriam, part peer and part mentor (Lewin, 1998). Cassirer was one of the most intellectual and scholarly philosophers of the twentieth century. He was not a worldly or practical man. His learning was famed, as was his productivity: throughout his academic life he wrote book after book on all manner of philosophical topics. Cassirer possessed an encyclopaedic knowledge of philosophers, not just the obvious big names – the Kants, the Leibnitzes, the Descartes, etc. – but also the little known, minor ones. In Chapter 2, I quoted him on Shaftesbury and the English Platonists, about whom, of course, he wrote a book (Cassirer, 1932/1953).

Cassirer had a vast knowledge beyond philosophy. He believed that if philosophers sought to understand the bases of human knowledge, then they must familiarise themselves with the varieties of human knowledge and not merely pronounce upon science or art from the grand heights of philosophy. So, Cassirer read and wrote about physicists, biologists, mathematicians, psychologists, anthropologists, linguists, historians and many others. This was his 'anthropological philosophy'. Cassirer's aim was to explore the similarities and differences between the various strands of human culture, including science, social science, poetry and myth. His was, in essence, an intellectual task without direct practical consequences. The library, rather than the factory, parliament or street, was the natural habitat of this gentle, short-sighted scholar who could remember by heart whole pages from the books he read.

In his grand project, Cassirer sought to understand the best products of the human mind. Edward Skidelsky (2011), in his superb intellectual biography of Cassirer, called him the last philosopher of culture. Cassirer did not analyse the violent prejudices and irrational bigotries of his own day, even though, as a Jewish professor in Germany, he was a target for some of the worst imaginable creations of the human mind. By contrast, Lewin, who sought to carry out practical analyses, examined some of the less noble products of the human mind. In common with Lewin, Cassirer was able to leave Germany shortly after the Nazis came to power. He worked at Oxford and Gothenberg universities before moving to Columbia University in New York.

After the war Cassirer's admirers planned to publish a volume of essays about his philosophy for a series entitled Library of Living Philosophers. Contributors were recruited, and among them was Lewin, who was known for his belief that Cassirer's work had profound implications for the practice and theory of psychology and other social sciences. However, Cassirer died in 1945 when the book was still in its early stages of preparation. The contributors persuaded the editor that Cassirer's death should not preclude the book from being part of a series on living philosophers because his philosophy continued to live on (Schilpp, 1949). Lewin's chapter was entitled 'Cassirer's philosophy of science and social science', and by the time the volume finally appeared in 1949, Lewin had also died.

The second influence on Lewin was his friend Karl Korsch, whom he met as a student at Berlin University. Korsch's wife, Hedda, was a close friend of Lewin's first wife, Maria (Marrow, 1969; van Elteren, 1992; John et al., 1989). Korsch and Lewin were to maintain their deep friendship, even after they had both fled to the States. Korsch was not Jewish, but he was in as much danger from the Nazi regime as was Lewin by virtue of being an active and known Marxist.

Korsch was very much an unconventional Marxist. In 1919 he had joined the Independent Socialist Party of Germany, which a year later merged with the official (pro-Soviet) Communist Party (KPD) to form the VKPD (Unified Communist Party). Although serving as a member of the Thuringian parliament, Korsch was unable to follow the line of the newly unified party. He was expelled in 1926 for deviationist, ultra-left tendencies. While a member of the VKPD, Korsch wrote his book *Marxism and Philosophy*. After his expulsion, he continued to write about basic issues of Marxist theory. His reputation as an original thinker remained high among post-war Marxist scholars. Perry Anderson (1979) credited Korsch with being one of the three founders of 'Western Marxism', the other two being Antonio Gramsci and Georg Lukács. In Douglas Kellner's view, Korsch was 'one of the most interesting, neglected and most relevant political theorists of the century' (Kellner, 1977, p. 4).

The concept of totality, which was a strong element in Lewin's version of Gestaltism, was central to Korsch's thinking (Jay, 1984). So too was the notion of practice. In *Marxism and Philosophy*, Korsch argued that because Marxist ideas arose from the practical struggles of the working class, Marxism had no need to develop a purely theoretical philosophy. Significantly, when Korsch founded a journal of Marxist thought, he called it *Praktischer Sozialismus* (Practical socialism). For Korsch, there was nothing as practical as the living theory of Marxism.

Before he took up his lectureship at Berlin, Lewin published an article in Korsch's *Praktischer Sozialismus* on the need for a science of production that would be based on workers' interests rather than on the interests of owners (Lewin, 1920/1999). The title of Lewin's piece was 'Die Sozialisierung des Taylor Systems'. In the context, *Sozialisierung* was a politically significant concept. As Korsch made clear in a number of publications, he used the word to refer to the programme of practical socialism (e.g. Korsch, 1975). *Sozialisierung*, literally 'socialisation', referred to the historical process of making humans 'social'; and socialism was the political and ideological movement for achieving this end. It opposed 'individualism' or capitalism's process of turning humans into disconnected individuals. For Korsch, the terms 'socialism' and 'socialisation' were closely linked semantically and politically. He wrote, '*Socialisation is the social revolution* – it is the socialistic concept in flesh and reality developed through practical human-sensuous activity' (Korsch, 1977, p. 125, emphasis in original).

It could be no accident that Lewin was using the term 'socialisation' in Korsch's journal. Nor is it accidental that, when Lewin's article was translated into English many years later, the word *Sozialisierung* in the title lost its connection with socialism. Martin Gold (1999) included a translation in his compilation of Lewin's major papers published by the American Psychological Association. The translated title was 'Socializing the Taylor system'. For psychologists, to whom Gold's compilation was addressed, 'socialising' refers to the incorporation of the child into its social environment. Korsch had used the word to mean virtually the opposite: not the child adapting to the demands of society but adapting society to the needs of its members. The translated title makes no sense, so long as 'socialisation' is understood in its usual psychological sense rather than carrying the very specific and outdated meaning that it had in German left-wing politics a century ago. How can a system of economic production be socialised in the way that a child is now said to be socialised?

Gold was not consistent in translating *Sozialisierung* as 'socialising'. In his article, Lewin discussed whether or not the Taylor system of production was contrary to socialist principles – he concluded that it was. In arguing this point, Lewin quoted from Korsch's 'Was is Sozialisierung?', whose title Gold translates as 'What is socialism?' (Lewin, 1920/1999, p. 307). When Lewin uses *Sozialisierung* in an article's title, he apparently means 'socialising', but when his closest friend uses the same word, he means 'socialism'.

Another publication of the American Psychological Association also politically softened the title of Lewin's *Sozialisierung* article. Lewin's daughter Miriam wrote an article, reflecting on her father, for the multi-volume series *Portraits of Pioneers of Psychology*. She mentioned the *Sozialisierung* article, which is listed in her bibliography with its original German title, together with an English translation: 'The humanization of Taylor systems' (Lewin, 1998, p. 118). America's official psychological society seems concerned not to imply that Lewin wrote an article with the word 'socialism' in its title. They treat the word as if it were a germ that might infect the reputation of such a notable psychologist.

Yet, Lewin was a man of the Left, and his article on the Taylor system argued that socialism needed a scientific psychology of production and consumption. According to Lewin's second wife, Gertrud, although Lewin thought of himself as progressive, he did not think of himself as a Marxist (van Elteren, 1992). Korsch was not Lewin's sole contact with Marxists, for he seems to have had contacts with the unconventional Marxists of the Frankfurt School (Gottfried, 2005, pp. 105–6). Lewin wrote a book review for the first edition of *Zeitschrift für Sozialforschung*, the school's journal, edited by Max Horkheimer. The book that he reviewed was *Experimental Social Psychology* (1931) by Gardner Murphy and Lois Barclay Murphy. Lewin commended the authors for providing an excellent factual summary of research in social psychology. Lewin noted that the authors devoted twenty-two pages to American studies about the effects of race on hiring employees but only one page to the effects of class. European socialists at that time were generally more concerned with class than race.

Lewin ended his review by saying that it was necessary to go beyond the usual definition of problems in order to pose deeper questions (Lewin, 1932, p. 170). That final comment would have gone down well with the editor of *Zeitschrift*. However, Horkheimer's Hegelian and essentially non-practical Marxism, which he shared with other members of the Frankfurt School, in the long run would have alienated Lewin. It would also alienate Korsch, who wrote four book reviews for *Zeitschrift* in its first year. For both Lewin and Korsch, theorising was no substitute for social practice.

After Lewin moved to the States, he devoted much of his attention to practical problems, suggesting a preference for gradual reform over sudden revolutionary change. Hedda Korsch thought that Lewin embraced American culture too readily. Perhaps he was aware that any direct connection with socialism would blight his chances of an academic career as it was certainly blighting Korsch's chances (van Elteren, 1992). Or perhaps the democratic, hamburger-eating culture was genuinely convincing Lewin that there were more ways to equality than class-bound European socialists had imagined. Still Lewin kept his contact with Korsch. It was in America, not in Germany, that they collaborated to write their only joint article: 'Mathematical constructs in psychology and sociology' was due to appear in volume 8 of *Erkenntnis*, the journal that supported the Vienna circle of logical positivists. Because of the war, the journal ceased publication before Lewin and Korsch's article appeared. The journal was revived in 1975, and Lewin and Korsch's article was finally published in 1976.

Dorwin Cartwright, Lewin's former doctoral student and his research worker in both Iowa and Massachusetts, tells an intriguing story (Cartwright, 1978). He recalled that one night in late 1946 or early 1947, Lewin came round to his house in great excitement, saying that he now realised 'Freud was wrong and Marx was right'. He told Cartwright that he would have to revise his previous work, because he had failed to account for the limitations that social and political factors placed on individuals – something that Korsch had long urged him to recognise (van Elteren, 1992).

Cartwright felt that Lewin was on the verge of taking his work in a new direction. Maybe Lewin would openly and fearlessly develop Marx's ideas in an empirical manner. Senator McCarthy had not yet got into his stride of harrying those he suspected of being communists, especially Jewish communists. More importantly, the worst that could be imagined had already happened: Lewin's mother and other members of his family had been murdered in the death camps. We shall never know the new directions that Lewin intended to take. Within weeks of his conversation with Cartwright, Lewin suffered a sudden, fatal heart attack.

Experiments as Examples

From his early days in Berlin as a student of Cassirer to the visit he made to Cartwright's house to talk about his new direction, Lewin never wavered in his belief that psychology should be a science and that it should take physics as its model. In his article with Korsch, Lewin discussed the features that a scientific psychology should possess. Foremost was 'the development of strict experimental procedures' (Lewin and Korsch, 1976, p. 401). That may sound like the typically bland statement that today's textbooks make in their opening chapter: psychology is scientific because it is experimental. The surprise is that Lewin dismissed standard psychological experiments as being insufficiently scientific.

Lewin was advocating a different sort of experiment, one that psychologists rarely conduct. His views on experiments stemmed from the philosophy of science that he attributed to Cassirer. At that time, Cassirer was deeply concerned with the philosophy of physics. In the year that Lewin began his Berlin studies, Cassirer published *Substanzbegriff und Funktionsbegriff*, which would be translated into English as *Substance and Function* (1910/1923). Cassirer was interested in tracing the development of the concepts that modern physicists used, and he noted how Aristotle's idea of substance differed from the concepts that physicists have used since the days of Galileo.

Lewin was to base his critique of the modern psychological experiment on Cassirer's distinction between Aristotelian and Galilean science (Lewin, 1931/1999). In Lewin's view, the modern psychological experiment was not, after all, very modern, because it represented the sort of Aristotelian thinking that physicists had been rejecting for the past 300 years. Lewin was criticising the type of experimental research that Gardner and Lois Murphy had surveyed and that continues to dominate psychological research today.[3] Robert Levine and other experimental social psychologists might claim Lewin to be their founding father, but

---

[3] Gardner and Lois Murphy (1931) had written of the 'amazing' growth of experimental social psychology in the previous five years (p. 31). By the time they came to publish a second edition of their book, just a year before Lewin started his leadership studies, the number of experiments in social psychology had increased exponentially (Murphy, Murphy and Newcomb, 1937). As historians of psychology have noted, social psychology was by then well on its way to becoming principally an experimental discipline (Danziger, 2000; MacMartin and Winston, 2000).

in the main they continue to conduct the sort of experiment that Lewin dismissed as pre-scientific and Aristotelian.

The conventional psychological experiment is conducted in tightly controlled situations, often in laboratories where the participants are removed from their everyday lives. In its most basic form, this type of experiment has two conditions that are identical apart from the presence or absence of the variable whose effects the experimenters are testing. Most modern experiments have more complicated designs but are still based on controlled differences between conditions. The experimenters will ensure that the responses of the participants can be translated into mathematical scores. They will test sufficient numbers of participants in each condition so that the scores for the participants in each condition can be combined and statistically compared. Then, the experimenters will be in a position to say whether the aggregated scores of one condition are, as a whole, 'significantly' different from the aggregated scores of the other condition. If they are, they will claim that the variable, which differentiates the conditions, has caused the groups of respondents to differ.

All students of psychology will be familiar with this basic procedure, which is taught on standard courses of psychology. Students will be told that this methodological procedure is scientific and that is the reason why they need to take courses in statistics, which very few students of psychology would willingly choose to do. It will be disconcerting for most teachers of psychology, but not necessarily for most of their students, to discover that Kurt Lewin, a firm believer in scientific psychology, considered these sorts of experiments to be poor, outmoded ways of doing science.

Lewin (1931/1999) argued that modern physics looked at the characteristics and movements of real objects, not idealised notional objects. Physicists, he suggested, were increasingly concerned to study 'individual cases' and to draw their general laws from 'concrete particular cases' (Lewin, 1931/1999, p. 44, italics in original). Likewise, Lewin and Korsch argued that a truly scientific psychology would analyse 'the individual event ... in its particular setting' (1976, p. 401).

If psychologists followed this suggestion, then they would not collect multiple instances in each experimental condition, so as to make statistical comparisons. Aggregate scores, in Lewin's opinion, did not have the reality of individual cases, and he recommended that 'each trial must be treated as a separate, *concrete* event, i.e. in an essentially non-statistical way' (Lewin 1926/1938, p. 284, italics in original). This argument had clear methodological and theoretical implications. Lewin attacked 'the commanding significance of statistics in psychology', declaring that the 'statistical procedure' is 'the most striking expression' of psychology's Aristotelian thinking (Lewin, 1931/1999, p. 47).

In advocating that psychologists should study specific, concrete events unfolding over time, Lewin was, in effect, advocating a psychology of examples that would be rich in detail, rather like Freud's case histories. Lewin's comments on Freud are revealing. Unlike most experimental psychologists of his day, with notable exceptions such as Edward Tolman and Stanley Hall, Lewin was not instinctively anti-Freudian. On the first page of *Principles of Topological Psychology* (1936), a deeply technical work, Lewin complained that most experimental work was 'too artificial and abstract to give an insight into real practices'. The only deeper approach at present was, in his view, 'the brilliant work of Freud', although Lewin doubted whether general laws of psychology could be based 'entirely on case studies and therapeutical work' (1936, p. 3).

What Lewin did not say about Freud was as significant as what he did say. He did not dismiss Freud because his evidence was soft qualitative data rather than so-called hard, statistically proven data. The real problem was not the qualitative nature of Freud's evidence but Freud's choice of examples to be studied in depth. If Freud wanted to formulate general laws of human motives and actions – and he most certainly wanted to – then, in Lewin's view, he should have explored in equal detail other types of example rather than his case histories (which, of course, Freud did with his collections of jokes, dreams and slips of the tongue).

The standard experiment would have been totally inadequate for Freud's or Lewin's purposes. We might describe the standard methodology as being anti-example because it ignores the individual case. Generally the experimenter is only interested in the statistical differences between aggregated scores, derived from reactions to artificially created situations which are abstracted from lives as actually lived. In consequence, one cannot discover from the standard experiment what exactly specific individuals were doing. What Lewin called the 'statistical procedure' leads to the exaggeration of small differences between group scores and to the concealment of variations in the ways experimental participants behave (Billig, 2013, chapter 8). The statistically analysed experiment, whose success depends on the discovery of significant differences between conditions, encourages what Freud (1921/1985) in a very different context called 'the narcissism of minor differences'. As Lewin argued from his early days in Berlin to his last works in the United States, another type of experiment was required – an experiment of concrete examples.

The Language of Good Theory

To be on a par with physics, psychology would also need, according to Lewin, a different type of theory with different types of concepts. He thought that the psychological theories and concepts of his day were inadequately Aristotelian. Lewin's belief in physics as the model for all sciences was not an individual eccentricity. Many logical positivists, particularly those involved with *Erkenntnis*, the journal to which Lewin and Korsch submitted their paper, believed in the goal of a unified science with physics at its centre. Many of those logical positivists were, like Lewin and Korsch, politically on the Left. The vast majority, of course, were not psychologists.

If physics was the ideal science, then psychologists should try to follow the lead of physicists in building a mathematised discipline. From his time in Berlin, Lewin had been drawn to the possibilities of using mathematics to formulate psychological theories. In 1929, Lewin wrote to his friend, the Gestalt psychologist Max Wertheimer, that he was 'learning mathematics furiously' (King and Wertheimer, 2005, p. 206). It was in the United States that Lewin really developed what he called 'topological psychology'. In numerous books and articles he outlined his commitment to developing theories that would explain psychological phenomena using mathematical formulae together with geometrical or hodological spatial representations of the mind and lifeworlds (Lewin, 1936, 1938, 1951/ 1997). Mathematics was to be the mark of a good theory, but Lewin specifically excluded statistics from the sort of mathematics that he believed psychological theory to need.

Lewin and Korsch outlined this position in their article, and they were optimistic that psychology was already making considerable progress. The conclusion of their article was that 'psychology is well on the way to reaching a scientific level on which its hitherto sporadic derivations will become part of an integrated system of mathematically formulated and experimentally confirmed theorems' (1976, p. 402). Lewin and Korsch did not mention that, in praising the progress of mathematically formulated psychology, they were referring almost exclusively to the work of Lewin and his co-workers. The two authors regretted that they saw no sign of analogous progress in sociology.

Mathematical formulae were not the only markers of post-Galilean science. Drawing on distinctions that Cassirer made in *Substance and Function*, Lewin claimed that Galilean and Aristotelian sciences used very different sorts of concepts. The Galilean concepts, unlike those of Aristotelian science, were non-binary and non-valuative. In his article on Aristotelian and Galilean modes of thought, Lewin suggested that most psychologists were using concepts that were both valuative and binary.

Valuative concepts. Lewin gave the example of clinical psychologists distinguishing between 'normal' and 'pathological'

behaviour. Both concepts were value-laden: 'normal' behaviour is to be preferred over 'pathological' behaviour, which
clinical psychologists attempt to cure (1931/1999, pp. 38–9).
By contrast, the concepts of physics, such as gravitational
force, were essentially non-valuative.

Binary concepts. Lewin suggested that psychologists should move
from binary concepts, such as normal/pathological, that divide
the world into 'paired opposites', and use Galilean concepts that
depict 'continuous gradations'. Galilean concepts, such as forces,
tensions and vectors were unitary concepts and, as will be shown,
Lewin used these sort of concepts when he interpreted findings
from his new sort of experiment (1931/1999, p. 39).

In Lewin's commitment to mathematised theories, which would use
non-binary and non-valuative concepts, we can see what he meant by
a 'good theory'. The trouble is, as I will try to show, that Lewin's good
type of theory conflicted with the good methodology that he was proposing. Also it did not permit realistic and detailed interpretations of human
actions. A little more Cassirer and a little more Marx would be required,
but that would pull psychology from the path which Lewin and Korsch,
students of Cassirer and Marx, respectively, had advocated. This needs to
be shown, not by more theory, but by a practical example – Lewin's
innovatory study of leadership.

The Leadership Studies: an Experimental Experiment

The leadership study, which Lewin conducted with his doctoral students
Ronald Lippitt and Ralph White at the Iowa Child Research Centre, was
perfect example of his new sort of experiment. The topic was a socially
significant one: whether democratic leadership was preferable to autocratic leadership. Lewin, the immigrant to the United States, was surprised by the cultural differences between the country he had left and the
country that was providing him with a new, more secure home. It was not
just that America was a political democracy whereas Germany was being
ruled by a dictator. Democracy involved more than the right to vote –
important though that was. Democracy, for Lewin, was a cultural atmosphere that affects so many levels of social life.

Lewin wrote a note to Lippitt and White, expressing why the study was
needed. Immigrants to the States from fascist European countries want to
believe in democracy, but they are guarded. Because they have been told
again and again in their old countries that democracy is just chaos,
decadence and 'a big bluff', they need to be persuaded of democracy's
value. Therefore, continued Lewin, it is important for science to

'establish the reality of democracy' and to prove its superiority to autocracy 'with facts close to the everyday life of the individual person' (quoted in White and Lippitt, 1960, pp. viii–ix).

This, then, was research with a practical, political purpose: to persuade ordinary people of the value of democracy just when that value was being seriously questioned. Methodologically the researchers sought to use procedures that would avoid Aristotelian thinking. Lewin and Lippitt designed their original experiment to examine concrete actual cases in depth, observing over time whether a group with a democratic leader would behave differently than a group with an autocratic leader. There was to be a second, more methodologically complex experiment, when White joined the team of Lewin and Lippitt. Both experiments represented the sort of study that Lewin hoped would be practical and could contribute to the development of good psychological theory

Subsequent social scientists have recognised the importance of Lewin's experiments, especially in establishing 'leadership' as a topic that could be studied empirically. The experiments have been described as 'the benchmark' study of its time (Ledlow and Coppola, 2011, p. 62). According to Javier Lezaun and Nerea Calvillo, who have written an excellent analysis of how Lewin and his team conducted the experiments, this research represents 'a foundational moment in the history of experimental social psychology'. Its significance, they suggest, stretches far beyond 'its role in inaugurating a scientific discipline' because it was the first time that the superiority of democracy was experimentally tested (2014, p. 435).

Lewin was in no doubt that experiments like these were difficult to conduct. In his tribute to Cassirer, he wrote that if an experiment is to be successful, it has to take into account 'all of the various factors that happen to be important for the case in hand'. Group experimentation was, he wrote, like 'social management', and 'a major omission or misjudgement' will make 'the experiment fail' (Lewin, 1949/1999, p. 31). Furthermore, in the case of the leadership experiments, the very practice of the research involved the topic of the research. The experimental manager, who in this case was Lewin, might be too democratic or too autocratic in managing his research team, but until the experiment had been successfully completed it would be scientifically impossible to tell which would be the more productive style of management. Lewin was betting his money, and the conduct of his experiment, on democratic leadership. He wanted his study to exemplify the benefits of a democratic culture.

The initial leadership study was conducted in 1938 using children, aged between nine and eleven years, mainly boys. The eleven children participating in the experiment were divided into two groups, or clubs, which met after school to participate in the activity of making masks. The groups met regularly once a week over eleven weeks in the attic of a building on Iowa University's campus. Lezaun and Calvillo (2014) have used archival records to reconstruct how the experimenters and children used this attic space.

With one group, Lippitt acted as a 'democratic' leader, while with the other he acted as an 'authoritarian' leader. When he was a democratic leader, Lippitt sought the opinions of the children, encouraged them to discuss their common tasks and involved them in making decisions about their work. As an autocratic leader, Lippitt gave the children orders, seldom offered them encouragement and generally acted in a brisk, formal manner. Trained observers noted how the children behaved in the various sessions. Lewin and Lippitt (1938) reported the initial results of the first experiment, and Lippitt (1940) wrote up the findings in detail.

Ralph White joined Lippitt to help run the second experiment, which Lewin also directed. They used the same basic procedure, but with a more complex design. This time, there were four groups, and all the children were boys. Four graduate students acted as leaders. In addition, there was a third leadership style – the laissez-faire style, where the leader hardly intervened at all. Each group experienced three different leaders, each acting in one of the three leadership styles. Again, trained observers observed the children, but this time there were also filmed recordings of their behaviour (see Lezaun and Calvillo, 2014, for details).

Lewin and his two co-workers published an article in the *Journal of Social Psychology* describing the two experiments and their main results. I will be looking at this article in some detail and will begin by illustrating how Lewin's new sort of experiment was clashing with the assumptions of the type of laboratory experiment that was becoming standard in the journals of social psychology. This was not just a theoretical and methodological clash – it was also a rhetorical one.

This rhetorical clash is reflected in the way that Lewin, Lippitt and White (1939/1999) described, or to be more precise, did not describe, how the third leadership style – the laissez-faire style – came to be studied. The authors followed the conventions of scientific report writing by using the passive voice to describe the method of their second experiment: 'Four new clubs of 10-year-old boys were organized ... the variety of clubs was extended ... To the variable of authoritarian and democratic procedures was added a third, "*laissez-faire*"' (p. 227, italics in original). The passive voice permits researchers to describe their methods without indicating who set up the experimental situation and precisely how they did so (Biber and Conrad, 2009; Billig, 2011, 2013). The passive voice indicates that the procedures matter more than the personnel and that, if anyone were to follow those procedures, they would obtain the same results. That would be the standard scientific assumption for a controlled laboratory experiment in physics or chemistry. The passive voice also allows researchers to be economical with the history of their studies. In this case, by using the passive voice, Lewin, Lippitt and White could state that a new variable was added to the second experiment without describing how and why this decision was made and who made it.

Lewin and his team conveyed, but did not assert, that the order of events followed the structure of the research report: the idea for the design preceded the running of the experiment, which preceded the collection of data, which preceded the analysis of the data. This is not what happened. We are fortunate to have three less formal accounts of the second experiment: the book by White and Lippitt (1960), Miriam Lewin's memoir of her father (Lewin, 1998) and Marrow's (1969) biography of Lewin. There are also the archival records that Lezaun and Cavillo (2014) consulted. Apparently the experimenters initially decided that the second study, like the first, would only compare democratic and authoritarian styles of leadership. They soon became aware that when White acted in the role of democratic leader, the boys were not behaving as expected: the atmosphere of the group 'had become so anarchic, and the leader so generally ignored', that the group was not functioning as 'a well-integrated democracy' (White and Lippitt, 1960, p. 110).

This experience may have lain behind Lewin's comments in his tribute to Cassirer about the difficulties of managing social experiments. Perhaps the newcomer to the team had not been given sufficiently clear instructions about how a democratic leader should behave; or maybe he had failed to follow instructions; or perhaps he lacked the personal characteristics that a successful democratic leader needed in that specific situation. White and Lippitt (1960) considered another possibility: they suggested that the boys in that group might have been awkward, trouble-makers, constantly challenging the leaders; one of the boys was particularly disrespectful, treating the leaders as if they were his equals (see Billig, 2015a, for details).

Whatever the reasons, the experiment seemed on the point of failing to produce evidence for the benefits of democratic leadership. Lewin saved the day. He noted that White was inactive as a leader and was not giving directions to the boys, as the other democratic leaders were doing. Lewin suggested that White was behaving in a laissez-faire manner and that this should henceforth be built into the structure of the study. There would now be other sessions of laissez-faire leadership for all the groups, and the laissez-faire groups would be compared with the democratic and authoritarian ones.

The official published reports of the experiment did not describe how the researchers developed the third style of leadership. What happened transgressed the standard procedures of experimental methodology, where the design of a study should be fixed in advance of the incoming results. However, it did not transgress the principles of Lewin's new experimental form of experiment, which, he believed, should be allowed to develop organically. White's style of democratic leadership could have become a concrete event to be examined in terms of its effects not only on the boys but also on the other experimenters and their need to reclassify his style of democratic leadership. This would have meant examining the interaction between the lifeworlds of the boys and those of the experimenters, with the conduct of the research itself becoming a topic of the research. However, the creation of 'laissez-faire' leadership never became a topic in this way. Lewin did not reveal the origins of this third style of leadership when he published the study in research journals. Instead, he deferred to the rhetorical conventions for reporting experiments.

If the study was clashing methodologically with orthodox experiments, then it was also clashing with Lewin's notions good theory. The study was not derived from non-binary, non-evaluative thinking. It was deeply embedded in binary and evaluative politics. The leadership study was constructed as a study of 'democracy' and 'autocracy' with the practical purpose of providing evidence for the superiority of democracy. The terms, which gave the experiment its meaning, are inherently value laden and binary. 'Democracy' and 'autocracy' were construed as binary opposites rather than gradations on the same scale. If the experiment had been designed by fascists, and, at that time, there were considerable numbers of open supporters of fascism, the terms would still have been value laden, but laden with different values.

The Leadership Experiments: Describing the Results

Lewin might have seen his leadership experiments as a practical reaction against Aristotelian thinking, but the closer we look at them, the more Aristotelian his thinking appears. Lewin did not design the experiments to test a specific, precise hypothesis, derived from a tight, non-Aristotelian scientific theory. Not only was the core meaning of the experiment phrased in politically evaluative concepts but the experiment was intended to provide examples showing the superiority of democracy over autocracy. In this way, the function of the experiments was to provide the basis for what Aristotle in his *Rhetorica* (II, xx, 2–9) called arguments by example.[4]

The moral and political views of the researchers were reflected in the language that they used to present their research. The researchers wrote about the results on a number of occasions. Lippitt (1940) published the results from the first experiment, while Lippitt and White (1958) combined the results from the two studies. In their book *Autocracy and Democracy*, White and Lippitt (1960) wrote in much greater detail and with less formality on the conduct, history and findings of both experiments. Lewin frequently referred to and interpreted the results of the studies in his technical, topological writings (e.g. Lewin, 1946/1997, 1947/1997). He also discussed the results when he was addressing non-specialist audiences (e.g. Lewin, 1948, chapters 3 and 5).

Lewin, Lippitt and White published findings from the two experiments in their *Journal of Social Psychology* article. There, the authors concentrated on aggressive actions, especially those relating to the leadership styles. They used the conventional structure for reporting experiments in social psychology. Following the opening section entitled 'Problems and methods' came the second section, 'Results'. The third section was 'Interpretive comments'. The structure implies that the problems and methods were worked out before the results were collected – and this, as we have seen, was not the case. It also implies that the presentation of results and their interpretation are separate and thus that results can be described without being interpreted. As will be suggested, that is not an appropriate assumption for the analysis of examples.

Although Lewin had criticised psychologists for not examining unique events, the results section in the *Journal of Social Psychology* paper is heavily weighted in favour of presenting aggregate scores, especially scores based on calculating the number of different types of aggressive acts that the children produced in the different leadership conditions. Figure 1 in the report presents the aggregated amount of aggressive scapegoating shown by members of the autocratic group in the first

---

[4] A number of classic experiments in social psychology were not designed to test specific, theory-based hypotheses but to produce dramatic examples. This includes probably the most famous experiment in social psychology's history: the Milgram study of obedience (Milgram, 1974). Recently, Stephen Gibson (2018) has written about the Milgram experiment in words that would equally fit Lewin's study of leadership: 'He did not set out to test specific hypotheses derived from theory, but rather used the experimental method to dramatize and illustrate particular conceptual issues that he saw as being of social importance' (p. 9). Gibson argues that the study was not an example of 'obedience' as Milgram believed (see also Reicher and Haslam, 2011; Kaposi, 2017). In the next chapter, Henri Tajfel's minimal intergroup experiment will be discussed. According to Susan Condor (2003), this experiment also was designed to exemplify a phenomenon rather than test a hypothesis.

experiment. Figures 2, 3 and 4 presented the average amounts of aggression per session produced by the different groups in both experiments. This is not the psychology of the concrete case. The authors might not have conducted any statistical tests on the aggregated scores, but, as they commented, critical ratios could have been computed.

So far, so conventional, but with one exception. The groups with an autocratic leader tended to show either very low or very high levels of aggression. If a mean average were taken of all autocratic groups, then their score would show much less aggression than the mean average of the children with a democratic leader. That was not what the experiment was intended to reveal, and it would serve only to confirm Lewin's suspicions about mean scores. Instead of conceding the superiority of autocracy in certain circumstances, the researchers used value-laden rhetoric to match their results to the moral and political meaning of the study.

Lewin, Lippitt and White (1939/1999) split the autocratic groups into two categories based on their aggregated amounts of aggression. The two sorts of autocratic groups needed to be labelled separately. There were the 'aggressive autocracies' which showed high average levels of aggression (but not as high as the average for the laissez-faire groups). The name that the researchers chose for the low-scoring autocratic group is revealing. They did not contrast the 'aggressive autocracies' with 'non-aggressive autocracies'. Instead, they described the second group as 'apathetic autocracies'.

When justifying the choice of the term 'apathetic', Lewin, Lippitt and White (1939/1999) claimed that these autocratic groups were, according to the observers of the experimental sessions, 'dull' and 'lifeless' with little joking or smiling (p. 238). Beyond these brief descriptions, Lewin and his co-workers did not present the ratings of the observers. In any case, the descriptions may have oversimplified what went on in those non-aggressive, or apathetic groups, with autocratic leaders. Lippitt and White (1958) reported that the children with autocratic leaders produced as much work-related conversation as did the children with democratic and laissez-faire leaders (p. 502). So, the word 'apathy' might not tell the whole story.

In the *Journal of Social Psychology* article, the choice of the term 'apathetic' rather than 'non-aggressive' was clearly value-laden, as well as establishing a binary distinction. When the authors reported that the observers had found these groups 'lifeless' and 'dull', they did not need to explain that these were negative judgements. They were taking for granted that, had the experiment and its results been described without using value-laden terminology, much of the experiment's meaning would have been lost. Still little sign of Galilean thinking.

The Leadership Study: Describing the Examples

The results section of the *Journal of Social Psychology* paper contained more than the aggregate scores for various types of aggression. Had it only listed these scores, it would not have fulfilled Lewin's ambition of producing a new sort of experiment with new sorts of data about concrete, particular incidents. After the aggregate scores came descriptions of various incidents, some of which were very brief. Lewin, Lippitt and White (1939/1999) concentrated on incidents that involved aggressive behaviour. In the results section, none of these examples was analysed according to topological, or field, theory; these analyses came in the section that followed the results. The new sort of experiment was like a fountain continuously spraying potential examples. Every moment was an incident that could potentially be selected to be analysed further, if the researchers so wished

Unlike the aggregated scores, the incidents were not presented to emphasise the differences between the three types of leadership. Lewin, Lippitt and White began with descriptions of two 'wars' which occurred in the second experiment when two groups were meeting at the same time in different parts of the attic. It was intended that curtains would divide the space into separate sections for the groups, but as Lezaun and Calvillo (2014) indicate, it was easy for group members to leave their allotted spaces and make contact with members of the other group. The authors stressed that the 'wars' were primarily playful, more like a game than the expression of genuine hostility. In neither case was an autocratic group involved. The first 'war' was between a democratic and a laissez-faire group and the second between two democratic groups.

Lewin, Lippitt and White (1939/1999) described different types of aggressive incident besides the 'wars'. These included reciprocal aggression between members of the same group, scapegoating individual members, a 'strike', 'rebellious acts' and so on (p. 241). The rebellious acts included carving on the posts in the clubroom, deliberately walking behind the curtains without permission, leaving the club meeting early and pretending not to hear when spoken to by the leader. Did the fact that Lewin, Lippitt and White could list strikes and rebellious acts, including disobeying the leader, as 'aggression' indicate a bias? This is a question to which I will be returning.

The results section ends with two incidents that are described in greater detail. Lewin, Lippitt and White refer to them as 'two very interesting examples of what we have tentatively called "release behaviour through an impersonal hate object"' (p. 242). The two incidents demand attention, while the phrase 'release behaviour' indicates the sort of theory that Lewin, Lippitt and White were using to interpret their data.

The first example occurred in the autocratic group of the first experiment. During the eleventh meeting of the club, the leader had announced that there would be a 'secret ballot' on the issue whether the members would like the club to cease meeting that session or whether they would like to meet again for a twelfth session. The incident occurred just after the leader announced that the group members had voted not to meet again. Lewin and his co-workers quote from the records made by one of the observers who reported that, after the result was announced, 'peculiar actions' followed (p. 242). The peculiar actions included running and jumping on the paper that the leader told them to put on the floor, throwing the masks that they had made, pretending to jump on the masks and two members chasing each other round the room. Lewin, Lippitt and White's comment that 'rather clearly, the work products of this authoritarian atmosphere seemed to be the object of aggressive attack rather than prideful ownership' (p. 242).

The second example came from a group in the second experiment under democratic leadership. The experimenters had planned a deliberate interruption during a moment when the leader had left the room. A graduate student, acting in the role of a janitor, entered to sweep the floor. He made dust fly about, then made the boys stand up and stop what they were doing. The janitor broke a piece of the boys' glasswork before criticising the artwork of the club. When he had left, the boys started complaining 'bitterly and loudly'. They then started to destroy a large wooden sign that they had made with the club's name painted on it. The observer records that they were excited: 'F' is wielding two hammers; 'R' is pulling out nails. The boys appear 'to be getting a great deal of "pure animal pleasure" of the pillage' (p. 242).

In both incidents, the direct object of the aggression was not another person or group but inanimate objects the children themselves had made. Although Lewin, Lippitt and White were tentatively classifying the incidents as 'release behaviour through an impersonal hate object', in the first incident the children were not actually showing aggression against their masks; they were just pretending to, and they were certainly not displaying hate. As the observer of the first incident recorded, it seemed 'peculiar'.

Leadership Study: Interpretive Comments

In the *Journal of Social Psychology* article the presentation of results was followed by the section 'Interpretive Comments'. It is standard practice in many psychology journals to follow the presentation of mean scores, graphs, statistical analyses and so on, with interpretations of those numerically based findings. It is as if it is possible to describe results without interpreting them. Whether such a separation is equally valid with examples is another matter. As we have already seen in previous chapters, descriptions of events include interpretations of what happened. In the case of the so-called hatred of impersonal objects, phrases such 'peculiar actions', 'pure animal pleasure', 'release behaviour' and even the terms 'aggression' and 'hatred' mix description and interpretation.

Basically, the interpretive section translated descriptions of children's actions into the mathematical and geometrical language of Lewin's field theory. With regard to theoretical terminology the authors were concerned to represent the build-up and release of 'tension'. Many of the translations were based on aggregate data rather than specific incidents. For example, some of the interpretations involved geometric diagrams that were intended to depict the supposed lifeworlds of the children in the various different conditions. These diagrams seem to be derived from aggregate data. Figure 7 contains two diagrams depicting the differing pressures on children in terms of the unsolicited directives that autocratic and democratic leaders gave them. It was claimed that differences between the two diagrams illustrated that autocratic leaders exerted six times as many 'directing approaches' as democratic leaders (Lewin, Lippitt and White, 1939/1999, p. 291).

In the diagrams of their Figure 7, 'directing approaches' were labelled by the quasi-algebraic term $(l_{L,Ch})$. The diagrams were not depicting the various 'directing approaches' which a specific leader had actually made or which a specific child had received. Nor did they depict the case of a specific 'directing approach' and its specific effects. In fact, the authors did not give an example of a 'directing approach' to illustrate what they meant by the term, nor an example of how such an act might increase a child's tension. The diagrams with their combinations of algebraic terms and geometric spaces seem removed from actual examples or concrete cases. The authors were providing representations, which translated a complex, mobile and changing action into simplified, static and abstract spaces.

The interpretive comments in the *Journal of Social Psychology* article touched on but did not fully explore a key question: was the low level of aggression in some of the autocratic groups a reflection of tensions and constraints that could yet produce high levels of violence when the situation was favourable to the lifting of constraints? The leader leaving the room was one such situation. Lewin discussed the question in some of his technical, topological writings in which he explored the presumed fields and forces within the apathetic groups (e.g. Lewin, 1946/1997, 1947/

1997). In these discussions, he was translating ordinary language into a highly specialist language, just as the *Journal of Social Psychology* paper had translated unsolicited directives given by a leader, or 'directing approaches', into the term $(l_{L,Ch})$.

Such translations added little, if anything, that was conceptually original. In discussing why some autocratic groups produced low levels of aggression, Lewin (1947/1997) devised some complex topological formulae, which, he claimed, represented the various forces in the situation. The low outward aggression in 'apathetic autocracy' did not indicate less aggression as a force in those groups. Instead, in these groups, it indicated, according to Lewin, greater autocratic control against outward displays of aggression. Lewin expressed the point technically: 'We are inclined to assume that the autocratic leadership form implies an additional force $(f_{Gr,c})$ which corresponds to the higher degree of authoritarian control and which in these situations has the direction against open aggression' (1947/1997, p. 316).

Two points can be noted. The first is that this topological explanation exemplifies the sort of explanation that Gerd Gigerenzer (2010) has criticised for being tautological and that he claims is all too common in psychology. Lewin explains the absence of outward aggression in terms of an underlying force directed against the outward expression of aggression. How do we know there is such a force in apathetic autocracies? Because there is little outward aggression. In short, what is to be explained is explained by the fact that it has occurred. Lewin provides no example of an autocratic leader actually preventing or threatening to punish the open expression of aggression.

The second point is that the explanation depends on the assumption that autocratic leadership implies a high degree of authoritarian control: the autocratic leader can prevent the children from behaving aggressively. At first sight this would appear to be a reasonable assumption. Certainly in the extreme political autocracy from which Lewin had escaped, the leader could exert direct threats, punishments and violence. However, the assumption that autocratic leaders in the leadership experiments exerted control scarcely reflected the reality of the situation. Lippitt (1940) recorded that a couple of children in the autocratic group thought that the leader could have been stricter (p. 130). He reported children yelling hysterically and ignoring the so-called autocratic leader, who displays 'exaggerated patience' and merely stares at the offenders without saying anything (p. 86). Not only would it have been unethical for the leaders to have punished participants but it would have been methodologically counter-productive. As Lewin and Lippitt (1938) recognised, the experiment needed to be conducted in a context 'where group life can proceed freely' (p. 292); the children would not have responded freely had they been punished for behaving in particular ways (Billig, 2015a).[5]

Lewin (1947/1997, p. 316) presented a formula to express the relationship between authoritarian control and outward aggression: $m + n$ $(f_{\mathrm{PAGr},c}) = p > (m + n)$. The symbol $(f_{\mathrm{PAGr},c})$ represents the 'force' of autocratic control against open aggression and m and n the increases and decreases of the force. Although exemplifying Lewin's Galilean ambitions, the formula essentially adds no new explanation: it is a translation from ordinary language, but a translation that loses meaning. Each time such formulae are unpacked, they inevitably are simplifications of what people were doing. The non-mathematical descriptions of what the children were doing in the experiments are richer than the formulae which translate statements about individuals and their actions into abstract quasi-mathematical equations about hypothetical forces and tensions.

We can see this reduction of meaning in the brief interpretive comments that Lewin, Lippitt and White (1939/1999) gave for the two incidents of aggression against impersonal objects. They interpreted the behaviour of the children in terms of tension and its release. In the first sub-section of 'Interpretive comments', the authors claim that tension 'was created' by the janitor, and in the autocratic atmosphere, 'the behaviour of the leader probably annoyed the children considerably' (p. 243). The interpretations are thin, and they possess a tautological quality. The aggression against the inanimate objects is to be explained by a rise in tension. And how do we know that there has been a rise in tension? Because of the aggression shown by the children.

There is an additional point: explanations in terms of tensions and their release do not make sense of what the children's actions may have meant to the children themselves. In the second example, the children were specifically destroying a sign. Lewin, Lippitt and White quoted an observer likening the action to 'pure animal pleasure'. Yet, animals do not get particular pleasure from destroying a sign, especially a sign that they have written. To explore this further, it is necessary to add a bit more Cassirer rather than rely on the bits that Lewin took from *Substance and Function*.

---

[5] The problem is not confined to Lewin's experiments. Other researchers conducting naturally occurring experiments on schoolchildren have faced a similar problem and have been reluctant to discipline so-called bad behaviour. Muzafer and Carolyn Sherif, who were great admirers of Lewin's style of experimentation, ran a boys' summer camp in order to conduct a study that examined the developing relations between two artificially created groups (Sherif and Sherif, 1953; Sherif, 1966). Gina Parry (2014, 2018) has looked at the archival records and interviewed surviving participants of the study. She found that some of the boys thought it odd that the camp authorities did not intervene to prevent or punish 'bad' behaviour.

A Touch of Cassirer

Lewin's tribute to Cassirer contains a significant absence, or, to be more accurate, a series of significant absences. Of all his teacher's many books, the only one that Lewin cites is *Substance and Function*. Lewin ignores Cassirer's later work, but he does know of it. On the first page of the tribute, Lewin wrote that the value of Cassirer's philosophy lay in his analysis of concept-formation in the natural sciences rather than 'in his treatment of specific problems of psychology', adding that Cassirer's contributions on the latter were 'of great interest' (Lewin, 1949/1999, p. 23). 'Of great interest' appear to be polite words. The phrasing is impersonal: Lewin does not say that he personally is greatly interested in these aspects of Cassirer's work. Lewin's actions speak more clearly than his courteous words. Cassirer's psychological and cultural writings are significant by their absence within a piece that ostensibly discusses Cassirer's philosophy of the social sciences.

Cassirer's grand project was quite the opposite of that espoused by Lewin. Rather than putting the concepts of physics at the centre of human knowledge, Cassirer sought to explore the various different ways that humans construct knowledge – whether through myth, language, art or science – and to show how each uses different sorts of concepts or symbolic forms. However much these four forms of knowledge differed from each other, they shared the common function of creating distinct worlds. Cassirer expressed this view in the introduction to the first volume of *Philosophy of Symbolic Forms* (1923/1955). In *Language and Myth* he wrote that as far as myth, language, art and science were concerned, each 'produces and posits a world of its own' and each constructs symbolic forms that are 'organs of reality' (1953, p. 8).

Cassirer was arguing that no form of knowledge produces an ideal model to which the others must concede superiority, as if deferring to an unbending autocratic leader. Cassirer may have admired modern physics but he recognised that it did not even provide a model for all sciences, let alone for art and myth. The mathematicised language of modern physics was not suitable for the human and biological sciences. As always, Cassirer considered matters both historically and philosophically. In the first volume of *Philosophy of Symbolic Forms* he sympathetically quoted Diderot, who argued that human self-understanding could not be based on mathematics because the truths of mathematics were essentially limited (1923/1955, pp. 141ff.; see also Cassirer, 1932/1951, pp. 74ff.). Cassirer specifically linked Diderot's critique of the systematising spirit of mathematics with Shaftesbury, whose arguments against systems had inspired Diderot.

Cassirer was clear that the sciences did not, and should not, all use the same sorts of concepts. In his view, the sort of non-binary concepts that are suitable for physics were unsuited for the biological sciences. Cassirer argued that evolutionary theory is based on division rather than gradation. Members of the same species may differ from one another along various continua, but the evolution of a new species depends upon mutation and non-continuous differences between species. Consequently, the processes of evolution, Cassirer argued, cannot be described without concepts that divide up the biological world into distinctively different entities.[6]

Nowhere is this clearer than in the case of humans and language. In Cassirer's view there was a qualitative difference between humans and all other species because humans are the symbol-creating, symbol-using species (1944/1962). He considered that Darwin had made a mistake in *The Expression of the Emotions in Man and Animals* (1872) when he implied that the natural forms of expressing emotions existed along a continuum. In *Philosophy of Symbolic Forms*, Cassirer stressed that, although humans use language to express emotions, because human language is propositional as well as expressive, it is qualitatively different from the expressive systems of other species. Consequently, there is no continuum of communication linking humans to other species, as Darwin had supposed (Cassirer, 1923/1955, pp. 180–81; 1996, pp. 39–40).

In his *Essay on Man* (1944/1962) Cassirer discussed in detail the psychology of human thinking. He agreed with the Gestaltists that when we see, we do not combine particulars but see the whole perceptual field. However, as Cassirer points out, the Gestalt theory of perception can be, and has been, applied to animals as well as humans. That meant that an understanding of human thinking should not be based on the model of perception, because cognitively there is a sharp line between language-using humans and all other mammals, while no such division exists perceptually.[7] Cassirer writes, 'The difference between *propositional language* and *emotional language* is the real landmark between the human and the animal world' (1944/1962, p. 30, italics in original). This is basically the same point that Cassirer made against Darwin in *Symbolic Forms*, but in his *Essay*, Cassirer clarifies the psychological implications. Animals can see relations between particular objects in the perceptual field, but they are unable to do something that the vast majority of humans regularly do: animals cannot reflect abstractly on what they see.

---

[6] For an excellent discussion of Cassirer's views on biology, see Krois (2004).
[7] In the fourth volume of *Symbolic Forms*, Cassirer argued that intellectual development follows 'the law of mutation' rather than that of gradation: there is simply not 'wave after wave in a uniform flow; rather, here one clear and distinct configuration confronts the next' (1996, p. 40). Cassirer made a similar point in the first volume of *Symbolic Forms* (1923/1955, p. 180).

To say that those boys in the leadership experiment who destroyed their club's sign were reacting with pure animal pleasure would be incorrect: if they were animals, they would not have been capable of reflecting on their behaviour, giving it meaning and justifying their reactions. As Cassirer constantly emphasised in his later work, humans live in symbolic orders. We might say that the pleasures of destruction exist within such orders. Lewin, Lippitt and White reported that after the destructive outburst, the group meeting 'ended with three or four minutes of pleasant conversation' (1939/1999, p. 243). The group's outburst had not been wanton destruction: the property of the University of Iowa had not been attacked, only the sign and its symbols. The authors, however, offered little clue, let alone interpretation, about the symbolic meaning of the aggression that the boys inflicted upon a physical sign.

Description and Interpretation

So far, the touch of Cassirer has suggested that Lewin's philosophy teacher did not share some of the views that Lewin claimed to have derived from him. Cassirer did not see the concepts of physics as providing the key to all knowledge; the non-binary concepts of physics were not suitable for all sciences, especially not for biological sciences. Nor would they help us to understand how humans use symbols. Cassirer stressed that there were other routes to knowledge besides physics and its mathematised explanations. There is still a bit more to be taken from Cassirer if we want to begin to understand what might have occurred when the children in Lewin's study attacked inanimate objects.

In *Essay on Man*, Cassirer discussed the works of notable psychologists such as Köhler, Wertheimer, Thorndike, Yerkes and Münsterberg, but he never added a qualifying comment to the effect that 'we should be cautious about this work, because it is not properly scientific as it uses binary concepts and lacks mathematical theorising'. In the fourth volume of *Philosophy of Symbolic Forms* Cassirer repeated Karl Bühler's view that there was a crisis in psychology. This had not arisen from a lack of good theory but because psychologists failed to describe the complex ways that people use language, and as a result, psychologists oversimplify 'fundamental elements of mental life' (Cassirer, 1996, p. 153; Bühler, 1934/2011; see also Halawa, 2009).[8]

---

[8] Wittgenstein, in his later philosophy, is well known for taking a descriptive approach to language. Instead of formulating an overall philosophy of language, he described how we use particular words and phrases, especially 'psychological words'. What is less well known is that, in this matter, Wittgenstein may have been following the lead of Karl

Cassirer compared scientific explanations with the sorts of insight that art and myths can provide. In *Essay on Man* he wrote that 'science means abstraction and abstraction is always an impoverishment of reality' (Cassirer, 1944/1962, p. 143). In contrast to science, art can achieve 'an intensification of reality' (p. 143). The artist is able expand a moment of experience, thereby giving it depth rather than impoverishing that moment. Cassirer's comment that science impoverishes reality is similar to the remark of William James, cited in Chapter 3, that theory mutilates reality. As befits their respective personalities, Cassirer used a gentler metaphor than James to express a similar thought.

Certainly, the formulae that Lewin used as theoretical explanations of the children's behaviour in the leadership studies simplified what happened. The so-called force ($f_{Gr,c}$) exerted by an authoritarian leader neither explains nor describes what the leaders actually did: inevitably, it reduces the complex realities of the situation to an abstracted simplification. However, the issue of impoverishing or intensifying moments may not rest upon a contrast between science and art. Social scientists can produce abstract theories that simplify social reality, but, like James and Freud, they can also intensify experiences. With recording devices, social scientists have their microscopes for exploring the details of concrete examples. Social scientists, like novelists or poets, can observe and intensify the complexity of the moment.

If social scientists like Lewin wish to examine a concrete, particular incident, then they need to describe it in all its particularity, rather than convert it into an abstraction. Interestingly, the psychologist who probably most influenced Cassirer was his cousin, the unorthodox neuropsychologist Kurt Goldstein, who studied the links between brain damage and aphasia.[9] Goldstein argued that, even when treating patients with identifiable brain disorders, doctors should pay attention to the whole person because every illness takes its own, individual course (Goldstein, 1940; see Ludwig, 2012).

According to Goldstein, doctors should listen carefully to what aphasic patients say, for, rather than displaying a broad inability to talk coherently, such patients often are only able to talk about specific matters in specific contexts. This is because they have lost the capacity to think abstractly and hypothetically (Goldstein, 1948). In explicating his psychological ideas, Goldstein drew upon his cousin's ideas about symbolic thinking (Goldstein, 1940, pp. 216–17), whilst Cassirer, in return, cited

Bühler, who had argued that speakers use language to perform complex, everyday actions (Brock, 1994; Mulligan, 1997).

[9] For an example of the links between Goldstein and Cassirer, see Cassirer (1925/1999), and for a discussion of such links, see Carini (1973).

Goldstein's findings and case histories (1944/1962, pp. 57–8). Both claimed that the deficits of aphasia showed how frequently adult humans without brain damage use abstract thinking in their everyday lives. Abstract thinking, thus, is not the exclusive property of scientists and philosophers.

Goldstein's conclusion, rather like James' use of the concept of 'ideo-motor action', stemmed from closely observing and describing concrete individual cases. Conventionally scientists often assume that there is a distinction between describing and explaining. The rhetorical format which Lewin, Lippitt and White (1939/1999) used separates results from interpretations: first the 'facts' are described, and then, in a separate section, these facts are explained. In *Substance and Function*, the book that inspired Lewin, Cassirer suggested that this distinction might be misplaced, as good descriptions provide ways of understanding what happens.

In one passage, Cassirer quotes Robert Mayer, the nineteenth-century founder of thermodynamics, who stated that 'the most important, not to say the only, rule for the true investigation of nature is this: to remain persuaded that it is our task to learn to know the phenomena before we seek explanations or ask about higher causes'. Mayer went on to suggest that once a fact 'is known on all sides, it is thereby explained and the work of science is ended'. Some might claim that this is a trivial assertion, Mayer wrote, but this rule has often been neglected, and 'all speculative attempts, even of the most brilliant intellects, to raise themselves above facts instead of taking possession of them, have up till now borne only barren fruit' (quoted Cassirer, 1910/1923, p. 139).

After quoting Mayer, Cassirer comments that this is precisely the language that Kepler and Galileo used against the metaphysicians of their day. Mayer's point was that a full description of the facts involves explaining them. Once we have described something in sufficient detail – once the fact is known on all sides – we have explained it. There is no need for a further speculative theory, for, in the words of Mayer, the work of science is ended.

Mayer was, of course, in favour of using mathematics to describe the facts of thermodynamics. However, his argument can be extended to cover people's actions, such as those of the children in the leadership experiments. If we want to understand such actions, then we must describe them in language rather than in mathematical formulae. If someone objected that language-based descriptions are not explanations – and that psychologists should aspire to explaining rather than merely describing – then *Substance and Function* contains another relevant quotation.

This time it is from Cassirer's great hero, Goethe: 'all that is factual is already theory' (Cassirer, 1910/1923, p. 243).[10]

A Touch of Marx

We are nearly ready to return to the examples of children attacking inanimate objects – or rather to the first example in which the children were throwing the masks that they had made. Cassirer's point about descriptions as interpretations means that we should look for longer descriptions of the episodes than Lewin, Lippitt and White provided in their *Journal of Social Psychology* article. Lippitt (1940) gave more information about the first example, particularly about what happened just before the outburst of so-called aggression (pp. 99–100). The published sources do not contain longer descriptions of the second episode.

From the longer description in Lippitt (1940), it is possible to produce what Clifford Geertz (1973) would call a thicker description of the incident – one that makes the children's so-called peculiar actions appear not quite so peculiar. As Cassirer would suggest, we should not try to translate those descriptions into the abstract language of forces for that would inevitably lead towards a thinning of the event. Before that, however, we need to add a touch of Marx. We might not know what Lewin had in mind when he excitedly told Dorwin Cartwright that Marx had been right; and we can only guess how Lewin might have incorporated into his own work ideas from Marx, which he might possibly have gained via his old friend Karl Korsch. At the minimum, Marx directed attention to the operations of power and politics in social life, and to follow the spirit of Lewin, so should we.

Politics and power were present in the lives of the children participating in the clubs. The children would not have been in control of their own lives: at school they had teachers exerting power over them and at home parents exercising their authority. In the clubs, adult leaders had taken over the role of teachers, although they lacked the power to punish. Even the democratic leaders had not been democratically chosen by the children but had been imposed on them. Like the autocratic leaders, the democratic leaders gave orders; although they might have phrased their orders with less brusqueness, they were, nevertheless, expecting the children to comply (for details, see Billig, 2015a).

Power might be comparatively easy to observe in the conduct of the experiments, but one might ask, 'Where are the politics?' In the case of the

[10] The same quotation is also to be found in the fourth volume of *Philosophy of Symbolic Forms* (Cassirer, 1996, p. 243).

first episode, the politics are plainly visible, although they become less visible when Lewin, Lippitt and White suggest that the children's behaviour followed a build-up of tension. We have to ask why the incident of the children throwing masks occurred when it did. Why in the eleventh meeting of the group? And why precisely then, and not earlier or later, in that meeting? To answer that question, we have to know whether something extraordinary occurred just before the outbreak of the peculiar behaviour.

Lippitt (1940) reports what happened just before the incident. After about fifteen minutes of the eleventh meeting, the autocratic leader announces the ballot of the group members concerning a further meeting. An observer notes that all the children take the voting 'very seriously' and all make 'exaggerated efforts to conceal their voting' (p. 99). One boy leaves his completed card under a book; a girl hands hers to the leader 'with obvious embarrassment' (p. 99). The leader announces the result: the majority of members had voted to end the club that day.

Knowing what happened before the incident puts us in a position to offer an interpretation that makes the actions of the group members not quite so 'peculiar'. The preference for ending the club could not simply be explained in terms of a rise in tension caused by the behaviour of the autocratic leader. It occurs just after the autocratic leader gives a democratic choice to those whom he has been leading for weeks. Also, when the democratic group had their chance to vote on the same issues, there was no majority in favour of continuing. Something else must also have been at work.

If we cannot know the precise cause of the children's votes, we can observe their effects. It is no coincidence that the first of the 'peculiar actions' occurred just after the announcement of the result. Lewin, Lippitt and White depicted the ballot as being secret, but it was not: Lippitt (1940) informs us how each child voted. The embarrassment of the girl and her fellow members is understandable. They were voting against their leader, and they knew that he would know that they had voted against him. But still they exercise their vote.

What happens next is decisive. The leader tells two boys to put paper on the floor – something that they have been routinely told to do when they are about to work on their masks. The boys put down the paper as usual, but then they run and jump on the paper 'in a wild manner' (p. 100). Their action is not random but has symbolic meaning. They are demonstrating to the leader, to their fellows and to themselves that the leader no longer has power over them. They have been given a choice, and despite being under the eyes of the leader, they have chosen freedom. As if to emphasise their liberty from the tasks imposed on them, they then throw their masks around, even pretending to jump on them. They are demonstrating that those masks mean less to them than does the present exercise of freedom.

To describe this as aggression, even hatred, towards inanimate objects simplifies, and thereby distorts, what is happening. The children are celebrating their democratic choice by taking command of the moment. The leader can only stand powerless as they run around, not caring about the objects that he has instructed them to make. They are not actually destroying or jumping on the masks – their acts are playful pretence. No-one is taking a hammer to the masks, unlike the acts in the second example when the boys destroy the sign that they have made.

It does not stretch the meaning of the word 'politics' to see the incident as political. By using the democratic means granted to them, the children have asserted their will and overthrown adult authority. To treat the children's actions merely as a release inner tensions is to overlook the politics. In fact, this type of interpretation is itself political because, by what it ignores, it reflects the view of authority – as does the labelling of 'pretending not to hear when spoken to by the leader' as an act of aggression (Lewin, Lippitt and White, 1939/1999, p. 241). In recent years, we have seen dictators being overthrown by the concerted action of their subjects. Statues of the dictator are often pulled down in moments of collective joy. The dictators and their supporters tend to view such actions as wanton, incomprehensible acts of aggression, as if they cannot understand the joy of the intensely political moment. Nor, apparently, could the leaders of the experiment understand what was happening before their eyes. It is as if the possession and then dispossession of power can disrupt the capacity to notice.

Karl Korsch knew well the famous phrase from the *Communist Manifesto* that 'the ruling ideas of an age have ever been the ideas of its ruling class' (Marx and Engels, 1848/2004, p. 46). In fact, Korsch quoted the phrase in his biography of Marx (1938/2016, p. 25). Both Marx and Korsch had in mind the historical spread of ideas across whole eras and societies, but the phrase can also be applied at a micro-level, even within Lewin's experiments, which themselves are micro-examples of much larger processes.

In the experiment, there are incidents when the ideas of the leaders become metaphorically and literally leading ideas. The ideas of the adults in the situation – that children need to be led and that rebellion is irrational aggression – are reflected theoretically in the publications about the situation. That is unsurprising when the democratically rejected leader is also one of the authors of the official academic interpretation of what happened.

Within small, restricted parts of the academic world, it is possible to detect links between ruling ideas and the exercise of power. The sub-discipline of social psychology is no exception. Its leaders – those who have the powers to appoint academics, to decide on policies of publication and to award funding for research – commonly promote ideas which are contrary to Lewin's theoretical and methodological ideas. Yet, at the same time, they claim Lewin to be their inspirational father. As Korsch would have recognised, leaders, rulers and ruling classes do not look too directly at the ways they exercise their powers. In consequence, ruling ideas tend to distort the social reality over which they rule.

A Balance Sheet

It is time to draw up some sort of balance sheet. Perhaps the previous sections have dwelt too long on the weaknesses of Lewin's theory, rather than on the strength of his methodological innovations. In arguing for a mathematised psychology, based on the model of physics, Lewin occasionally exaggerated the extent to which the discipline of psychology was turning towards his view. He was always optimistic, believing that the scientific perspective would inevitably prevail, whether in psychology or in the world at large. But it was not to be. In 1954, seven years after Lewin's death, the first *Handbook of Social Psychology* was published (Lindzey, 1954). Out of its thirty chapters, only one was devoted to field theory, written by Lewin's former student Morton Deutsch (1954). Even Deutsch would soon cease using field theory (e.g. Deutsch, 1973). The next generation of social psychologists would neither use Lewin's theory nor follow his methodological practice. In their research they would employ the sorts of laboratory experiments and statistical analyses that he rejected.

So it has continued to the present. Lewin's has been a curious type of leadership – one that was not studied in his experiments. Even those who know little of his writings can claim Lewin as their 'father' (Cummings, Bridgman and Brown 2016). There are also admirers who wish to re-invigorate Lewin's work by dropping the mathematical bits and developing a non-mathematised field theory (Burnes, 2004; Burnes and Cooke, 2013; Burnes and Bargal, 2017; Gerard, 2017). It is as if Lewin's mathematised theory were just wrapping paper that can be torn off and thrown away when the parcel is opened. What would be left, however, would be a theory that explains human behaviour in terms of forces, vectors and other concepts derived from physics. As has been suggested here, a 'good' Galilean theory would impoverish the concrete analysis of humans living in the symbolic world.

Lewin's own case illustrates the weakness of his motto: his mathematised, good theory was anything but useful. His motto, however, does not specify for whom the good theory will be useful. Perhaps modern society, in which academic work has become a commercialised commodity, is not the environment for uniting theory and practice in the ways that Lewin and Korsch would have wished. In present conditions, his motto can be used as a 'soothing mantra', offering reassurance, especially to theorists (Weik, 2003, p. 459). There is a case for saying that it is second-rate theories, rather than good ones, that are now useful, for they can be most easily sold to grant awarders, sponsors and commercial interests (Slaughter and Rhoades, 2004; Billig, 2015a). As for mathematics, a crude theorem can have its commercially persuasive uses, such as positive psychology's theorem for happiness: $H = S + C + V$ (Seligman, 2003, pp. 45–6). Barbara Ehrenreich (2009) has written an amusing but precise evisceration of this profitably successful formula.[11]

Maybe this misses the main point: Lewin as an academic and as a person set an example, and that possibly matters most. His obsession was not to build a discipline or to promote himself as a success but to produce a union of theory and practice that would replace prejudice with science. If he exaggerated when predicting the success of his vision, then this is no more than might be expected of someone who genuinely – or more precisely, innocently – believed in the utility of his ideas. It is not the greatest fault for academics to hope that their work will add to the betterment of human life.

By devoting himself to practical and theoretical inquiries, while conducting methodologically difficult studies and showing loyal concern for his students, Lewin wore himself out. Still he continued. Despite everything – his experiences as a Jew in Germany, his feelings as an outsider in the States without a permanent academic position, his continual worries and later his grief about those he left behind in the homeland that had ceased to be a home – he retained the political optimism of his youth.[12] Science, study and commitment mattered. The world should be a better

[11] Barbara Ehrenreich makes play with the arbitrariness of Seligman's formula, where H stands for happiness, S the 'set range', C the life circumstances and V the factors under voluntary control. She asks, Why are its factors added together, rather than multiplied, or combined in more complex ways? The formula's function, Ehrenreich suggests, is to appear to be scientific rather than actually to be scientific (see also Billig, 2018a). Lewin's formulae are very different, for he was genuinely attempting to be scientific.

[12] As Tolman (1948) indicated in his tribute, before the war, Lewin did not generally discuss his worries about family and friends left behind in Germany; after the war, he only talked with his closest intimates about the great losses that he, and they, had suffered.

place. Even at the end, when he stood on his former student's doorstep, Lewin's eagerness to learn, to understand and to share with others overcame the exhaustion that was weakening his body.

Here is an example that should not be forgotten. It is not an example of a theory or a methodology. Nor is it an example to fit Lewin's own motto, whose glib interpretation fits the commercialism of today's academic world. Those of us who have lived in untroubled times by comparison with Lewin, but who are now witnessing the re-emergence of aggressively nationalist movements, may need the guidance of an example. If we keep in our minds the example of Lewin, his hopes and his humane vision, then, as we turn towards the future, we might declare of him that 'there is nothing as practical as a good example'.

7   Tajfel and Bernstein
The Limits of Theory

It is entirely appropriate to follow a chapter on Kurt Lewin with one about Henri Tajfel. Both were intellectually creative figures who sought to transform the nature of social psychology. Both burst through the disciplinary confines of conventional psychology. As we have seen, Lewin never lost his interest in philosophy, and his vision of psychological theory was shaped by physics and mathematics. Unlike Lewin, Tajfel sought inspiration from history, sociology and anthropology; he believed that social psychology should be take its place in the social, rather than natural, sciences. Despite these differences, Lewin and Tajfel shared the aim of creating a genuinely social form psychology – one which would recognise that people are shaped by their social backgrounds. Both knew this from their own experiences.

As European Jews living through the worst years of the twentieth century, Lewin and Tajfel shared a common social background. In the preface to her book *Men in Dark Times*, Hannah Arendt wrote that even in the darkest of times, 'we have the right to expect some illumination'; this may well come less from 'concepts and theories' than from an 'uncertain, flickering and often weak light' (1970, p. ix). We can see this in the cases of Lewin and Tajfel. Their concepts and theories contained definite limitations. Some of Lewin's limitations were discussed in the previous chapter, and the present chapter will not overlook those of Tajfel. However, their flickering insights contained a depth well beyond the brittle certainty of mere concepts and theories.

Lewin developed many of his key ideas in Germany in the years before the Second World War, doing so against a background of rising anti-Semitism, but before the full murderous direction of that hatred had become clear. He died not long after the end of the war. By the end of his life, he must have been aware that however good the pre-war theories of Jewish psychologists like Max Wertheimer or philosophers like Cassirer had been, none were sufficient to avert disaster. 'There is nothing as practical as a good theory' was not an adequate motto for those darkest days. Unsurprisingly, Lewin in the last weeks of his life believed that his thinking needed to move in a new direction.

Tajfel belonged to the next generation of European Jews. He was born in Włocławek, Poland, in 1919, and his intellectual career did not start – indeed, could not start – until the war was over. In 1937, he had gone to France to study science, but after two years war broke out, and the young Tajfel had to abandon his studies. He joined the French army and, as a result, was granted French citizenship, a decision that enabled him to escape the slaughter of Jews in Poland. Anyone wishing to understand the effect of the Holocaust on Tajfel should read the brief, moving account that he gave in the opening pages of his book *Human Groups and Social Categories* (1981). There he compared his current, comfortable academic life with the death of millions 'who formed, in the most concrete sense of the term, my "social background"'. In 1945, he had discovered that 'hardly anyone I knew in 1939 – including my own family – was left alive' (p. 1). Tajfel was saying so much in so few words. He described the work that he did after the war to rehabilitate surviving victims and how this work led him to study psychology. He would often say that his work with young refugees was more important than anything else that he ever did in his life. He knew from his own experience that there were far more practical things than a good theory.

Before the war Lewin may have hoped that reason and scientific evidence would combat the growing irrationality of the time. By the time Tajfel was able to return to academic study, the unimaginable had already occurred. The most sophisticated academic theories could not have predicted, let alone prevented, the deliberate slaughter of European Jews. History could not be reversed – what had occurred could not be undone. Tajfel believed that if we could understand the roots of prejudice, then this knowledge might in the future help us to prevent a repetition of events (Jahoda, 2004).

At this point, and certainly before I start analysing Tajfel's work, I must declare a personal interest. This chapter differs from all the others in this book. In those chapters I write about persons whom I have encountered through their writings. My contact with Tajfel was different. He was my teacher, and I am aware how much I owe to him. Had I had not been fortuitously assigned to his tutorial group halfway through my final year as an undergraduate student at Bristol University, my life would have been very different. Until then, I had found psychology tedious. I would not have contemplated taking up academic study had Tajfel not persuaded me, quite forcefully at times, to undertake a doctorate under his supervision. When I had completed my doctorate, he continued his forceful persuasion, encouraging me to seek an academic post. I experienced at first-hand his intellectual vigour and generous spirit.

I have read that Lewin's students were grateful to their teacher both for the inspiration of his ideas and for the power of his personality (e.g. Cartwright, 1978; Levine, Rodrigues and Zelezny, 2008). I feel exactly the same about

Tajfel. So do others who were fortunate to come to social psychology under his supervision. Several years after Tajfel's death in 1982, an edited volume with contributions from his former students was published (Robinson, 1996). Some of the contributors had already made notable contributions to developing Tajfel's work on social identity and social categorisation. Several of us had struck out academically in other directions. Whether or not we were consciously developing his concepts and theories, we all shared a depth of gratitude for the example that Henri Tajfel had given us.

Selecting a Specific Text as an Example

The previous chapters have examined thinkers by focussing on specific pieces of writing rather than trying to summarise their total oeuvre. In each instance, wider issues were refracted through the chosen piece of writing. That leaves a question for the present chapter: which of Tajfel's many publications should be the object of focus? It would be easy to presume that one, or perhaps two, of his best-known publications should be selected. A quick glance at textbooks of social psychology and non-specialist works would suggest which publications these might be. Tajfel is remembered for his social identity theory, which explains how people develop social identities by comparing their group with other groups (Tajfel and Turner, 1979), and for his 'minimal group experiment', which showed that schoolboy participants discriminated in favour of members of their own group, and against members of an outgroup, despite the groups being meaningless (Tajfel, 1970; Tajfel et al., 1971). So it might be expected that I should choose one of Tajfel's publications that describes his major theory or his major experiment.

It would not be difficult to justify such a choice. Graham Vaughan, writing a biography in *Encyclopaedia Britannica*, states that Tajfel is best known for the concept of social identity and for his social identity theory. Saul McLeod (2007), on the website study guide Simply Psychology, writes that 'Henri Tajfel's greatest contribution to psychology was social identity theory'. McLeod summarises the theory simply: 'In order to increase our self-image we enhance the status of the group to which we belong'. He adds that the results of Tajfel's minimal group experiment can be explained by social identity theory: by discriminating in favour of members of their own group, the participants were 'emphasizing the desirability' of their own group and were 'focusing on distinctions between other "lesser groups"' (McLeod, 2007).[1]

---

[1] The attention given to Tajfel's theory of social identity has led to a tendency to overlook the significance of his earlier work on categorisation (e.g. Tajfel, 1969; Tajfel and Wilkes,

It is worth noting how McLeod describes Tajfel's major contribution to social psychology. He writes that 'we' increase 'our' self-image; 'we' enhance the status of the group to which 'we' belong. It is as if 'we' all do this: all humans regardless of their culture or the historical era in which they live. As such, this sort of psychological language uses a universal rhetoric. The specific schoolboys who took part in the original minimal group experiment stand for humanity as a whole, for they were simply doing what all of 'us' as humans do.

McLeod's language is expressing a familiar psychological trope. Kurt Danziger (2009) has argued that psychologists tend to write in universal ways; they assume that their concepts and theories apply to all humans and also that their experiments reveal basic processes of mind rather than culturally or historically specific phenomena. According to Danziger, this habit is deeply ingrained in psychologists, and it illustrates that 'psychology as a science has always clung to its foundational postulate of universality' (2009, p. 3; see also Danziger, 2006; Brock, 2016a; Moghaddam and Lee, 2006). As will be seen, Tajfel tried to break free from this assumption, although at times he, too, wrote universally.

I could have selected one of Tajfel's major publications, such as his 1970 *Scientific American* article in which he first discussed his minimal group experiments or his first article in a social psychological journal presenting the results of these experiments (Tajfel et al., 1971).[2] It would not be difficult to show that the language Tajfel used was anything but universal. He wrote that the schoolboys in the study were following cultural norms to demonstrate loyalty to whichever groups they belonged. In the conclusion of his *Scientific American* article, Tajfel suggested that the boys had been socialised into 'groupness' and he hoped that the educators 'in our competitive societies', who are so keen on 'teams' and

---

1963). Tajfel demonstrated experimentally that when a range of lines are classed into two different categories on the basis of their length, people tend to accentuate the differences between the lengths of lines from different categories and to minimise the differences between lines within the same category. Tajfel was pointing out how some of the basic effects of perceptual categorisation seem to resemble stereotyped judgements about social groups. For instance, 'we' exaggerate the differences between 'us' and 'them'; and 'we' imagine that all of 'us' are much more similar than 'we' actually are, and conversely that all of 'them' are much more similar to each other than 'they' actually are. Eiser (1996) has argued that this work, linking prejudice to basic cognitive operations, is every bit as important as Tajfel's work on social identity.

[2] I was fortunate to be one of the authors of Tajfel et al. (1971). I had just graduated from Bristol University, and that summer, Tajfel employed me to help design, run and analyse the original minimal group experiment. I am proud to have been involved, and I gained so much from the experience. However, I cannot claim any credit for the thinking that gave rise to the experiments. It took me several years to begin to appreciate the originality and depth of Tajfel's ideas.

'team spirit', would pause to give thought to his experimental results (1970, p. 102).

At first sight Tajfel's phrase 'our competitive societies' would appear similar to McLeod's 'our self-image' in that both use the first person plural. However, there is a breadth of difference between these two uses of the same pronoun. In English, as in most European languages and many non-European languages, 'we' and 'our' are the most ambiguous pronouns, not least because they can be used both inclusively and exclusively (Billig and Marinho, 2017, chapter 4; Mühlhaüsler and Harré, 1990; Pavlidou, 2014). Tajfel's 'our competitive societies' is not inclusive, for he is not including all societies: he is implying that some societies are not competitive and have not socialised their members to behave in this way, but, in the modern Western world, 'our' societies are competitive. McLeod's use of 'we', by contrast, suggests that 'we' all behave in the same way. His use of the first person plural presumes universality – as if it is normal the world over to act in such a way and that it has always been so.

I could have selected other texts from Tajfel's work that resist the conventional universality of much psychological writing. For example, Tajfel (1972) argued that experimentalists do not take sufficiently seriously the obvious point that their laboratories are not culture-free zones. Participants do not discard their norms and cultural beliefs when they walk through the laboratory door, but their behaviour in the laboratory is determined by the fact that they are cultural beings, living in historically specific times. It is only because participants have such cultural beliefs that they can understand how to participate in a laboratory experiment.

Most social psychologists who argue that laboratory results reflect culture and history tend to reject experiments as a way of doing social psychological research (see e.g. the classic article by Gergen, 1973). What made Tajfel's critique so interesting was that he remained an experimentalist and, like Lewin, saw experiments as a means for exploring the cultural aspects of psychological phenomena. In consequence, Tajfel is one of the few experimentalists who has been praised for being a critical psychologist (Colucci and Montali, 2013). In fact, he argued that social psychology was not an 'objective' science that stood above culture but rather reflected the culture in which it was produced. That was why Tajfel was so committed to developing a genuinely European social psychology that would reflect the particular experiences of Europe in the twentieth century. Such a social psychology would, he hoped, differ crucially from the social psychology that was being produced within America.[3]

---

[3] Tajfel devoted considerable time and energy helping to establish the European Association of Experimental Social Psychology. The Association aimed to bring together

Tajfel, however, was not consistent in avoiding universalism. Especially in articles that he published in major American-based psychology journals (e.g. Tajfel and Billig, 1974; Tajfel, 1982a), he would use conventionally universal language. Similarly, he tended to write in universal terms in his early work when he examined the effects of categorising stimuli on perceptual judgements. Here, Tajfel seemed to be identifying basic cognitive processes. If imposing a category on perceptual stimuli induces a basic tendency to judge the stimuli within each category as more similar and between categories as more dissimilar, then 'basic' in this context implies universal. When reporting his experiments on judgement and categories, Tajfel did not suggest that the experimental participants might have been responding to the social norms of competitive societies (see e.g. Tajfel, 1981, chapter 5).

I could have two selected pieces of writing by Tajfel to show his oscillation between writing universally and non-universally. However, this has already been done, and done extremely well, by Susan Condor (2003), who was also a former student of Tajfel. It was almost as if Tajfel were theoretically bi-lingual. However, Condor was not arguing that Tajfel used two different, but equally valuable, ways of writing about social psychological phenomena. Condor's sympathies were with Tajfel's 'sociopsychological' or non-universal way of theorising because, in her view, this approach pointed towards a more original and richer way of understanding social behaviour. Condor also suggested that some of Tajfel's prominent followers tended to treat social identity theory as a universal theory, revolving around the assumption that (all) individuals are motivated to boost their own sense of identity. As will be seen later, in some of his final works Tajfel expressed his concern about the way social identity theory was being developed.

The choice of text for this chapter will probably surprise Tajfel's many admirers, for I have not selected one of his 'big' papers. Instead I have chosen a largely overlooked short piece, in which Tajfel discussed a thinker who has been almost completely overlooked by social psychologists: Peretz (or Fritz) Bernstein. That is why the title of the present chapter title contains two names, because in discussing Tajfel's views on Bernstein, I will also be discussing Bernstein's views.

The significance of Tajfel on Bernstein does not lie in the development of big theories or universally applicable major concepts. Quite the

the diffuse, isolated social psychologists, who were working within Europe in the years following the Second World War. Many of those social psychologists had lived through the war and had experiences that were quite different from those of American social psychologists. The story of the creation of the European Association and Tajfel's significant role in its creation is told by Moscovici and Marková (2006).

contrary, it lies in Tajfel and Bernstein recognising that, when trying to understand the very particular fate of European Jews, universal theories and an overtly 'scientific' approach had become wholly inappropriate. This is why Tajfel's paper on Bernstein directly relates to Arendt's important point about the flickering light that illuminates the darkest of times.

Tajfel's paper is distinctive because it is one of the very few in which he directly wrote about the Holocaust. He did so, of course, in the opening pages of *Human Groups*, but there he was describing in direct, non-theoretical language how the events of those times had brought him into the academic world. He was not retrospectively applying the theoretical concepts that he used and developed in his later work – concepts such as 'social identity', 'social comparison' and 'social distinctiveness' – to make sense of his own journey and, more generally, the fate of other European Jews. In those intense paragraphs, there is an absence of academic language, with the possible exception of the phrase 'social background' – a phrase which in any case has passed into general usage.

The short essay on Bernstein is different. Tajfel discusses, as Bernstein had done, how anti-Semitism should be understood after the Holocaust. Ten years before Hitler came to power, Bernstein had proposed a universal psychological theory of anti-Semitism. As we will see, both Tajfel and Bernstein recognised that such a theory was unsuitable after the war, not because it had been proved wrong but because it suggested that the historically specific fate of European Jews could be explained in terms of universal psychological concepts. As Arendt implied, theories and concepts can be inappropriate in ways that are beyond the simple rubric of proof and disproof. All this can be seen in Tajfel's brief article, as well as in Bernstein's own reflections upon his younger, theorising self – reflections that Tajfel discussed with deep acuity and feeling.

Fritz Bernstein

Fritz Bernstein was born in Germany in 1890, in the same year as Kurt Lewin. His parents were not Orthodox Jews, but they sent the young Fritz to a *cheder*, or religion school, on Sundays, while he attended a regular non-Jewish school during the week (for details of Bernstein's life, see van Praag, 2009; Krah, 2016). Fritz grew up with a strong sense of Jewish identity as well as a modern, secular outlook on the world. He did not go to university, but as a young man, he went to Rotterdam for an apprenticeship. He returned to Germany for his military service and then went back to the Netherlands to work in the coffee trade. He worked for a company owned by a businessman who would become his father-in-law. When Bernstein had acquired sufficient knowledge of the coffee trade, he set up his own trading company.

Although Bernstein did not have a university education, he developed strong academic interests, especially as he sought to understand the perplexing tenacity of anti-Semitism. Why should a modern Jew like himself be the object of such ancient bigotry? He began working on a book about the psychological and sociological roots of the hatred of Jews. Bernstein finished writing his book in 1923, and although he was living in the Netherlands, he wanted to find a German publisher for his book. However, he struggled to find one. As a businessman, he had few contacts with the academic world and he found that most publishers at that time believed that the topic of anti-Semitism would not attract a wide German readership. Eventually, in 1926, the Jewish publishing house Jüdischer Verlag published Bernstein's book under the title *of Der Antisemitismus als eine Grouppenerscheinung* (Anti-Semitism as a group phenomenon). The book bore the subtitle of *Versuch einer Soziologie des Judenhasses* (Exploration of a sociology of Jew-hatred). The title and subtitle indicate that Bernstein was seeking to understand the specificity of Jew-hatred in terms of something more general – as an example of a 'group phenomenon' which could be examined sociologically.

Jüdischer Verlag had been established in 1902, and it published many pro-Zionist books, including those by Theodor Herzl, Chaim Weizmann and the poet Hayim Bialik. More mainstream, non-Jewish publishers had been commercially correct to view Bernstein's manuscript with caution. They had not overlooked a potential best seller, for only about 300 copies of his book were sold in Germany. Bernstein personally bought up the remaining copies to distribute in the Netherlands (van Praag, 2009). The book seemed to fall between potential markets: the title suggested that the work was an academic tome, and so general readers were put off. However, academics were not going to be impressed by a book that had been written by a young coffee trader and that contained no scholarly footnotes nor cited any academic references. Then, as now, academic specialists tend to look down on amateurs who create their own theories. Charles Boasson (1973/1991), a Dutch Jew who knew Bernstein in the Netherlands and later in Israel, cites an instance of a well-known sociologist dismissing Bernstein's book without reading it.

General, non-Jewish readers in Germany who were interested in the topic of anti-Semitism would have wanted something more dramatic, such as a tract 'showing' how Jews, by their actions, weakness of character and plots to take over the world had brought misfortune upon themselves and upon everyone else. Bernstein's aim was completely the opposite. He sought to show that the prejudices against Jews were not based upon anything that the Jews actually did. Whether Jews were rich or poor, religious or secular, socialist or capitalist, the hostility, or Jew-hatred, remained undiminished. Its source was not the actions of Jews but their sociological position living as a minority group amidst majority groups. In this regard, anti-Semitism was, according to Bernstein, a group phenomenon that reflected the insecurities of the majority group – the Jew-haters.

That might have been the end of the story for Bernstein's obscure book, but it was not. Bernstein migrated to Palestine in 1936, changing his first name from the German 'Fritz' to the Hebrew 'Peretz'. By migrating, he was able to escape the Holocaust, unlike most of his family and friends. In Palestine, he worked as a journalist, editing the newspaper *HaBoker* (The Morning), and became prominent in Zionist politics. Whereas many Zionist activists of that time were politically on the Left, Bernstein was on the Right, especially with regard to economic issues (Sofer, 2009). His wing of the pre-independence General Zionists party was to form the basis for the right-wing Liberal Party. In 1948 Bernstein was one of the thirty-six signatories of the new State of Israel's Declaration of Independence, and he became minister of trade in the first provisional government. He died in 1970.

After the war, Bernstein's American friend Rabbi Abba Hillel Silver persuaded him that his old book on anti-Semitism was still important and that it should be translated into English. The New York–based Philosophical Library, which specialised in publishing works by European intellectuals such as Sartre, Einstein and de Beauvoir, agreed to publish an English translation. Bernstein, then deeply preoccupied with the politics and security of the new state, had no time to revise his book for a second edition. He realised, however, that the measured tone which he had adopted when writing in the early 1920s was no longer suitable. Rather than re-writing the book, he agreed to write a short epilogue about the inappropriateness of his book's tone after the war. When the translated edition appeared in 1951, Bernstein's epilogue was published as a prologue. The book was published with the title of *Jew Hate as a Sociological Problem* under the author's Hebrew name – Peretz F. Bernstein. His son, David Saraph, was the translator.

For anyone interested in the relations between social psychological ideas and the passage of history, Bernstein's prologue should be a crucial text. Bernstein reflected not only on the history of his own book but also on the recent history that inevitably made his book appear to belong to earlier, more innocent times. In addition, Bernstein's prologue touched on the more technical aspects of the relations between psychological (or sociological) understanding and historical understanding. In writing on these matters, Bernstein would be laying the groundwork for his book's most significant brush with academic psychology. This would occur almost thirty years later, when Henri Tajfel wrote his short appreciation.

Peretz Bernstein's 1951 Prologue

On the first page of his post-war epilogue/prologue, Bernstein wrote about his original difficulty in finding a German publisher. He was now astonished that he ever managed to find one. At that time, there was more than 'mere general lack of interest' in the issue of anti-Semitism: there was 'an aversion' to looking at the problem (2009, p. 1).[4] Jews certainly discussed anti-Semitism, but only amongst themselves, and then 'with muted voices', for they feared being overheard by non-Jews (p. 2). By publishing with Jüdischer Verlag, Bernstein had, in effect, been talking with fellow Jews, and the smallness of the publisher and the limits of its print run ensured that his voice remained muted in the Germany of 1926.

Bernstein also commented on his book's 'rather awkward' structure, for *Der Antisemitismus* contained two parts (2009, p. 7). In the first part Bernstein presented a general theory of group hatred and in the second part he analysed the specific issue of anti-Semitism in the light of the theory that he had outlined in the first part. As Bernstein explained in his epilogue/prologue, he had not wanted to treat anti-Semitism as if it were unique but he wanted to examine it as an example of the more general phenomenon of group enmity. To do this, he needed to draw upon a suitable sociological or psychological framework for explaining group enmity in general. However, he had been unable to find an appropriate theory, and, as a result, he had needed to invent his own 'group theory' (p. 7).

The German professors of the time might not have appreciated Bernstein's theorising, but today his talent for innovative thinking is much clearer. If hatred of Jews is not the product of Jewish actions, then its source must be sought in other factors, which Bernstein termed 'sociological'. In modern academic terms, we might call these factors 'social psychological', for Bernstein was combining psychological and social factors to account for the irrationality of anti-Semitism. Whether one calls his approach 'sociological' or 'social psychological', one thing was clear: it was not historical.

---

[4] All quotations from Bernstein's book are taken from the 2009 edition, published by Transaction of Rutgers University and containing an excellent introduction by the Dutch economist Bernard van Praag.

Bernstein was not looking for the causes of anti-Semitism in specific historical circumstances. He was not, for example, explaining mediaeval anti-Semitism in terms of old religious beliefs or twentieth-century anti-Semitism in terms of the new insecurities of modern life. Instead, he used universal rhetoric to link anti-Semitism generally to a very basic, and thus universal, condition of human life: the need for humans to live in social groups. This was theoretically significant, as Tajfel was to recognise, because he was not explaining anti-Semitism in terms of the personal characteristics of the anti-Semite, as if it were the projection of personal insecurities onto a group of outsiders. It was a projection, according to Bernstein, but the projection was based on group, rather than individual, insecurities.

In many respects Bernstein's argument was similar to the frustration-aggression theory which was originally proposed by group of psychologists from Yale University just before the Second World War (Dollard et al., 1939) and which was to be revised by Leonard Berkowitz in the 1960s and 1970s (e.g. Berkowitz, 1969, 1974). In *Der Antisemitismus*, Bernstein noted that we are often provoked and feel anger which we cannot freely express against those who have provoked the anger. Bernstein offered the hypothetical example of a merchant who becomes angry after losing a contract to a business rival but who needs to remain on good terms with that rival. It was a situation that Bernstein would have known well as a coffee dealer, for one of his close business rivals was his own father-in-law, with whom he needed to maintain good family relations. Bernstein postulated that if the merchant could not be directly hostile to his rival, his anger would not disappear, but 'must be vented in some way and in some direction'. This is because 'the outbreak of a hostile feeling cannot be totally suppressed' but 'seeks an outlet' (2009, p. 84). The result is that the merchant will find other ways to express his feelings; he might find fault with his employees, even provoking them to make mistakes 'in order to find a pretext for ventilating his anger' (p. 84).

There, in Bernstein's account, written in the early 1920s, is the essence of the frustration-aggression theory (see Boasson, 1973/1991, for a brief discussion of the similarities). The assumption is that frustration produces anger and that, if this anger cannot be directly expressed against the frustrator, then it will not dissipate but will seek another target. The idea can be used as a model of group prejudice. Instead of talking about a merchant and his rival, we could talk about a frustrated group seeking an outlet for their frustrations. Frustration-aggression theorists wrote about situations where members of groups direct their anger at scapegoats who are not the real cause of their frustrations.

There were three main differences between Bernstein's theory and the later ideas of the frustration-aggression theorists. First, the frustration-aggression theorists expressed their ideas in technical, psychological terms; by contrast, Bernstein, apart from using some semi-psycho-analytic terms such as 'projection', basically stuck with non-technical language. Second, the frustration-aggression theorists were experimental psychologists, and they tended to cite experimental studies in support of their hypotheses, whereas Bernstein was not concerned with the results of experimental studies. As someone working outside university circles, he may not have known about the experimental research that was beginning to be conducted by Gestalt and other psychologists. Lewin's major work on frustration, aggression and authority would not be published until the 1940s and so could not have been cited by Bernstein (Lewin et al., 1944).

The third major difference between Bernstein and the frustration-aggression theorists is probably the most important. Bernstein did not reduce the problems of group enmity to personal feelings of hostility, as some of the later frustration-aggression theorists would do. This aspect certainly influenced Tajfel's view of Bernstein, for Tajfel continually stressed that inter-group relations should not be reduced to interpersonal relations or to individual motives. For this reason, Tajfel was critical of frustration-aggression theory; he doubted whether the results of the frustration-aggression experiments, which generally examined the frustrations of individuals, could be applied 'to intergroup behaviour at large' (Tajfel, 1981, p. 20).

Bernstein's hypothetical example of the merchant might have suggested that he was basing his analysis of group enmity on an individual model: the frustrated merchant complained about his ungrateful workers, but this process had been set in motion by the personal accident of his failing to obtain a contract. However, Bernstein argued that group hatred did not originate in the personal vagaries of the hater, for there was something systematic, or sociological, about the phenomenon of group enmity, as compared with the notional example of the coffee merchant's personal feelings. Group enmity was, according to Bernstein, the inevitable consequence of the very existence of groups, and therefore it existed over and beyond any personal jealousies or frustrations.

Life in a group invariably produces tensions, but in order to preserve the group, the members must discipline themselves to suppress feelings of anger against their fellow members. In consequence, enmity which could not be expressed against fellow group members would build up within the group; and eventually this reservoir of enmity would be projected onto those outside the group. It was because Bernstein was linking group enmity to the formation of groups, rather than to the particular psychology of its individual members, that he considered his approach to be 'sociological'. Nowadays, it might be thought that his approach of linking individually experienced feelings of enmity to the social structure of groups might just as well be described as 'social psychological'.

Bernstein was proposing an explanation of group hatred that was universal since he applied it to all societies, regardless of their specific culture or historical epoch. Also he applied it to all forms of group hatred, not just anti-Semitism. Bernstein was suggesting that so long as humans lived in groups, then the displacement of hatred onto other groups was inevitable. Bernstein believed that it was important to understand this universal point if one wanted to understand any historically specific form of group hatred. The structure of *Der Antisemitismus*, as Bernstein wrote in his 1951 prologue, reflected the assumption that anti-Semitism was 'a very small, though specific, aspect of a general phenomenon' (p. 7).

He made this clear in the conclusion of his book, where he argued that it was 'erroneous' to consider anti-Semitism to be unique, for all the characteristics of anti-Semitism 'can be observed in other group enmities' (p. 288). Because Jews had lived for centuries as outsiders, it was inevitable that their more powerful neighbours would direct their enmity against them. Jews, therefore, had been convenient targets for all the built-up enmity, but any other group of outsiders would have sufficed. Jean-Paul Sartre would write something similar in his *Anti-Semite and Jew* (1948) when he had suggested that groups other than Jews could be the target of anti-Semitism.

Nowadays, it has become second nature for social psychologists to explain the particular in terms of the general. Experimentalists will declare their scientific credentials, and for them, that involves more than using scientific methods (such as experiments): it also means using universal concepts in order to explain specific phenomena in terms of universal psychological processes. For example, social psychologists tend not to treat anti-Semitism, or Islamophobia, or hatred of Romanies merely as historically specific phenomena, but they will treat them all as instances of something more general – as 'group prejudice', or what Bernstein in 1926 called 'group enmity'.

Having categorised the specific in terms of the general, social psychologists will then try to formulate general theories, such as theories of prejudice or of inter-group relations which can be applied to the historically specific instances (e.g. Brown, 1995). No matter whether such theories stress the importance of frustration, the effects of identifying with a group or the lack of contact between groups, social psychologists will tend to assume that there are universal processes leading to prejudice. In this regard, the strategy that the young Bernstein pursued has become standard within social psychology. His theory resembles the frustration-aggression theory both in its specific content and in its universalism. Indeed, the authors of the original frustration-aggression theory believed that their theory also applied to some animals. For Tajfel (1972) this was a weakness not a strength of the frustration-aggression theory, and amongst other faults, he criticised it for its universalism.

The power of universalism in psychological thinking can be seen in the fate of the most famous historically specific, social psychological analysis of bigotry: *The Authoritarian Personality* (1951) by Adorno, Frenkel-Brunswik, Levinson and Sanford. Adorno and his colleagues saw themselves as investigating something historically specific, namely psychological roots of fascism. They devised the 'F Scale' (or 'Fascism Scale'), which was intended to detect the susceptibility of individuals to fascist propaganda and was designed to correlate with the A-S scale (anti-Semitism scale). The authors did not assume that 'fascism' was a universal category. The fascist mentality, according to them, had emerged because of a constellation of factors that were particular to the twentieth century.

However, the work of Adorno et al. (1951) has been transformed into something more universal with the politically and historically specific category of 'fascism' being replaced by the more general term 'authoritarianism'. The 'F' scale is now known as a measure of 'authoritarianism', which has come to be treated as if it were a personality characteristic. It is presumed that authoritarians can be found in all eras and societies. Whether in modern democracies or mediaeval autocracies, there will be people who for personal reasons need social hierarchies, are intolerant of ambiguity and become stricter than average parents. The 'F' in scale's name appears to exist as a historical relic rather than an analytic insight.

Bernstein began his prologue/epilogue by mentioning that he had written his book in 1923 and that it had been published in 1926: 'I mention those dates to explain the painstaking suppression of the emotional moment observed throughout the book' (p. 1). It was obvious, he wrote, why a researcher such as himself might suppress his emotions: he was approaching a topic that touched him personally. If he did not detach himself, he might become too emotionally bound up in the topic to be sufficiently scientific. Bernstein stated that, as a Jew researching anti-Semitism in 1923, he had needed to step back from his feelings and to consider his topic in a detached spirit 'somewhat along the lines practised in scientific research of physical and chemical processes' (2009, pp. 9–10). Treating anti-Semitism as an instance of something universal, about which a theory could be formulated, was a means of being scientifically detached.

Writing after the war, Bernstein noted the difference between the present times and the times when he had written his book. During the early 1920s it 'was still possible' for a Jew to eliminate personal feeling when discussing anti-Semitism. After the war, that was impossible. His theory had not necessarily been inaccurate but its tone of detachment had become inappropriate. With the benefit of hindsight, he could now see that his earlier detachment belonged to earlier times. The intervening years had brought 'anti-Jewish persecution and mass slaughter to an unprecedented degree of fierceness', and this now meant that even the most strenuous attempt at 'scientific detachment would have been in vain' (p. 1).

Bernstein's words indicated that the balance between the particular and the general – between the specific example and the universal theory – had fatefully shifted. What had changed this balance was not a new scientific insight or new empirical findings but the events of history, which had been, to use his words, 'unprecedented'. Those events would be diminished if they were treated merely as instances of 'group prejudice' or 'projected enmity'. What was unprecedented would then appear as if it had precedents, and then it would be little more than just another example of something much more common, even universal.

In this way, Bernstein was saying that after the Holocaust it was no longer possible for Jews to contemplate the issue of anti-Semitism as they might have done twenty-five years earlier, when a young Jew like himself was innocently unaware of what was about to happen. If, after the war, one approached those events dispassionately, classifying them under general categories like a botanist classifying plants, then one would be displaying a failure of understanding – historical understanding, scientific understanding and, above all, moral understanding. As Arendt implied, no general category or universal theory could possibly represent the savage particularity of what happened.

A Neglected Masterpiece

If that had been the end of the story, Bernstein's book would have remained little more than a passing curiosity. Just like the sales of the pre-war German edition, the sales of the post-war English language edition were not good. There were a number of reviews, including several from academics, but overall the book had no impact on either sociology or social psychology – or on public opinion generally. American researchers, examining prejudice and anti-Semitism, preferred to cite the work by Adorno et al. (1951) or the work of the frustration-aggression theorists or the growing number of studies examining prejudice in terms of 'social cognition'. Post-war social psychologists felt no need to consult the work of an amateur who a generation earlier had speculated without the methodological benefits of a laboratory or the career benefits of a university position.

This is not a story with a happy ending. Bernstein's book, after many years of neglect, was not finally discovered and hailed by experts from around the world as a forgotten work of genius. This has not happened yet and probably never will. At the time of writing (September 2018), I have looked at Google Scholar and found that the *Der Antisemitismus* has been cited sixty-four times since its first appearance in 1926. Many of these citations are comparatively recent and are to be found in historical works about the study of anti-Semitism in Germany, especially pre-war Germany. These works mention Bernstein's book as a historical object, not as a source for understanding the psychological and sociological roots of hatred (e.g. Krah, 2016; Patterson, 2015; Gloy, 2015). The 1951 English edition, *Jew-Hate as a Sociological Problem*, has only been cited thirteen times. There was a further English language edition in 2009 with yet another title, which curiously did not contain the word 'anti-Semitism': *The Social Roots of Discrimination: the Case of the Jews*. Google Scholar lists this English edition as being cited five times.

Even allowing for the incompleteness of Google Scholar, eighty-two citations in eighty-five years hardly indicates that Bernstein's book has been a stunning success. Actually, due to the vagaries of Google Scholar, six of those eighty-two citations are attributed to an earlier version of the present chapter. Given that Bernstein's original edition made very little impact, his book should not properly speaking be called a forgotten work, for it enjoyed no former heyday which has now slipped from scholarly memory. The book has been consistently neglected. Social psychologists have almost completely ignored the book since 1926. If we ask how many social psychological publications, excluding those written by Henri Tajfel or me, are listed by Google Scholar as having cited Bernstein's book in any of its editions, then the answer is one (Mummendey, Linneweber and Löschper, 1984).

Of course, this would not be surprising if the book had not been worth remembering. Experimental social psychologists might say that Bernstein's failure to cite experiments is sufficient reason to doubt the quality of his work. There is an episode in the history of the book that should give pause for thought. After the English edition had been published in 1951, the Philosophical Library received a letter from one of its other authors, congratulating the publishing house for recognising the value of Bernstein's book and praising it as 'a classical masterwork' (quoted van Praag, 2009, p. xiv). The letter writer was Albert Einstein.

How many other social psychological books have been praised as masterpieces by Einstein but have been neglected by virtually every expert?

More than fifty years after the first edition, Wissenschaftliche Buchgesellschaft, an academic German publishing house based in Darmstadt, decided that it was time to try for another German edition. The publishers thought that a new edition would benefit if it were backed by a notable academic. In May 1977, Rita Orgel wrote to Henri Tajfel on behalf of the publisher, inviting him to write a preface for the new edition.[5] It is hard to know how much the representative from Wissenschaftliche Buchgesellschaft knew about Tajfel's life and work, but her choice was felicitous. Tajfel was one of the few social psychologists of his day who was entirely appropriate for the task and who could personally and intellectually appreciate the significance of what he was being invited to write.

Tajfel immediately accepted Orgel's invitation and asked if she would send him a copy of the 1951 English translation, since it would be easier for him to read that version rather than 're-reading' the original German. Tajfel's words implied that he was acquainted with Bernstein's original German edition, although he was not to mention this again in his correspondence with the publisher or in the foreword that he eventually wrote. Problems soon arose between Tajfel and the publisher. Wissenschaftliche Buchgesellschaft had expected Tajfel to write his preface in German, but Tajfel insisted that he would write it in English and that the publisher should pay for the costs of translation – something that the publisher was reluctant to do. Its budget was small, Orgel wrote, and it was intending to print only around 300 copies – coincidentally, the same number of the first edition that had been sold in Germany. Clearly the new edition was not expected to fare any better in Germany than the original.

The publisher was unable to find a copy of the English translation to send Tajfel, who continued to maintain that he could not start writing his preface until he received one. In February 1978, Wissenschaftliche Buchgesellschaft passed the project on to Jüdische Verlag, who would publish the book under the auspices of the much larger Athenäum publishing company. Once again, only a Jewish publisher could be found to publish *Der Antisemitismus* in Germany. The new publisher also failed to locate an English copy to send Tajfel, and in the end, Athenäum advised him to obtain a copy through his university library. There was to be further wrangling between Tajfel and Athenäum, including arguments

---

[5] Details of Tajfel's correspondence with the German publishers are contained in the Tajfel archives, the Wellcome Library, London, in box PSY/TAJ/1/3/4.

about the small fee that Tajfel had been promised for his preface and that the publisher was hoping he might waive.

In January 1979, Tajfel finally sent the publisher an eight-page manuscript in English, simply entitled 'Foreword'. When the new edition came out in 1980, Tajfel's Foreword actually appeared as an epilogue (*Nachwort*) at the end of the book. The new German edition did not contain Bernstein's 1951 prologue, which, in contrast to Tajfel's foreword, had been written as an epilogue but had been published as a prologue. Despite Tajfel's commendation, the book hardly attracted great interest. Coincidentally, a Hebrew translation of *Der Antisemitismus* also appeared in the same year.

It seems as if the neglect of Bernstein has been contagious. Most of Tajfel's writings, especially those which he published towards the end of his life, have been richly cited (Dumont and Louw, 2009). By contrast, his piece on Bernstein, according to the evidence of Dumont and Louw, seems not to have been cited in any major journal of social psychology, at least in the first eighteen years after its publications. As far as I am aware, none of Tajfel's students or followers aside from myself has quoted his foreword/epilogue. However, I cannot claim any superior virtue. When I examined Tajfel's ideas about the cognitive roots of prejudice and argued that these ideas were limited for understanding extreme bigotry, especially for the bigotry that led to the Holocaust, I failed to cite his piece on Bernstein (Billig, 2002). By the same token, I would never have known about Bernstein or his book had it not been for Tajfel's foreword/epilogue.

The lack of interest which social psychologists have shown in Tajfel's short piece is exemplified by the bibliography of Tajfel's writings which Brown, Schipper and Wandersleben (1996) compiled for the posthumous tribute to Tajfel. They divided Tajfel's publications into three categories: 'Inter-group relations', 'Social perception and related topics' and 'Other publications'. The foreword/epilogue to Bernstein was put into 'Other publications', as if to separate it from his writings on the central themes of his work, including 'inter-group relations', which, of course, was the central theme of Bernstein's theory of anti-Semitism.

Tajfel often told his students that he came into social psychology in order to understand how genocide was possible. However, his technical papers did not directly approach the topic of genocide or the Holocaust in particular (Billig, 2002). But there, virtually unnoticed amidst 'Other publications', was one of the few papers in which Tajfel directly discussed the issue that was central to his whole work.

Henri Tajfel, Social Identity and History

Anyone who only knows Tajfel as the formulator of social identity theory might find his foreword to Bernstein's book a bit perplexing and certainly unexpected. A modern social psychologist commending an old, forgotten book would be likely to praise it for influencing their own thinking or for providing an early, imperfect variety of their own approach. Tajfel, however, did not claim Bernstein to be a social identity theorist *avant la lettre*, and as we shall see, he was not entirely comfortable with the term 'social identity theory'. Instead, Tajfel had much deeper reasons to link himself with Bernstein.

In his foreword, Tajfel noted that Bernstein appeared to draw inferences from individual frustration to understanding wider social prejudice. However, according to Tajfel, Bernstein went much further than the frustration-aggression theorists because he linked frustration with the structural properties of groups, and this was 'something which was never done by the Yale psychologists' (Tajfel, 1980, p. 6).[6] According to Tajfel, Bernstein understood that what needs to be explained 'is the *collective* phenomenon of hostility between groups which share a common and structured social and historical reality' (p. 6, emphasis in original). That, in Tajfel's view, was one of the reasons why Bernstein had been able to write 'a book which ... keeps so much of its value today' (1980, p. 6).

Nevertheless, Tajfel was sceptical of Bernstein's explanation about the origins of group enmity. Bernstein had assumed that love and hate were two basic emotions and that the 'quantities' of the one emotion could be used in the discharge of the other emotion. Tajfel wrote that he 'personally' did not believe that aspect of Bernstein's theory 'will stand the test of further advances in the biological and social sciences', although it was 'no better and no worse' than many other theories that biologists and social scientists were proposing (p. 5). That leaves a question: how could Tajfel commend a book, one of whose basic theoretical premise he thought would not stand the test of time, and which, in many respects, resembled a theory that Tajfel rejected? The very question seems to assume that, when it comes to understanding the social world, sharing theories is more important than sharing a history.

The underlying point of Tajfel's foreword was not to promote his own theoretical position at the expense of Bernstein's but to reflect on how to understand their shared history. Tajfel began by discussing Bernstein's 1951 prologue, which Tajfel describes as an apology phrased as 'a question as deeply felt as it is desperate: how could anyone have foreseen in

---

[6] All quotations and cited page numbers are taken from Tajfel's English manuscript of his foreword/epilogue.

1923 the horror that was to come so soon?' (1980, p. 1). The unimaginable had happened and 'no human endeavour, in art or in science, could
ever hope to reflect, understand or explain the enormity of the suffering
and of the crimes' (p. 1). Tajfel recalled watching Charlie Chaplin's film
The Great Dictator in France at around the time that Bernstein must have
been writing his post-war prologue. Tajfel wrote that he had to leave the
cinema, unable to watch Chaplin's 'restrained account' of Nazism. It was
no good telling himself that when Chaplin made his film before the war,
he had no way of knowing what was to come. Similarly, Bernstein's
dispassionate theorising in 1923 was unbearably inappropriate 'when
set against the enormity of what had really happened' (Tajfel, 1980, p. 1).

Tajfel's point was that one cannot blame the young Bernstein or the
young Chaplin for failing to predict an unimaginable future, but those
with hindsight cannot ignore the past. This means that the exceptional
moments of history cannot be treated as equivalent to the more mundane,
as if all historical events can be slotted into the same general categories.
Although Tajfel took up psychology in order to understand how genocide
occurred, he never used his ideas about social identity to understand the
Holocaust (Billig, 1996, 2002). Nor did he use his earlier works such as
his article 'Cognitive aspects of prejudice' (1969), which was a superbly
original piece aiming to highlight the basic, and thus universal, cognitive
factors underlying prejudice – cognitive factors such as the accentuation
of judgements following categorisation and the assimilation of cultural
stereotypes. By not specifically discussing the prejudices underlying the
Holocaust, Tajfel was implying, but not stating, that those prejudices
should not be treated as if equivalent to all other prejudices.

Principally, Tajfel applied his theoretical writings about social identity
to highlight the strategies open to groups who have been excluded from
power. He discussed groups such as feminists or Black Power activists,
who changed a negative social identity into a positive one in order to
collectively change social reality (e.g. Tajfel, 1975, 1976; see also Reicher,
1996; Reicher, Spears and Haslam, 2010). Tajfel applied his ideas about
social comparison and differentiation to the creation of a new identity
after the war by young Jews in Israel, who rejected 'their elders' passive
acceptance of a wholesale slaughter of a people' (Tajfel, 1981, p. 286).
Tajfel, however, did not apply those same ideas to the identity of those
who created the social movement that perpetrated the wholesale
slaughter.

This was no oversight. It would be inappropriate to 'explain' the
Holocaust, using the same set of terms that might be used for understanding other types of group identification, especially those that can lead
to positive social actions. The cognitive aspects of 'ordinary' prejudices,

the sort which all of 'us' might hold, could not possibly explain the specific ideological prejudice that Bernstein described as leading to unprecedented horror.

Imagine if Tajfel, or anyone else, applied the main concepts of social identity theory to explain the Holocaust. A social identity theorist might speculate: the rise of Nazism occurred because the Germans wished to develop a sense of positive identity after the defeat of the First World War. In consequence, they differentiated themselves from Jews and other non-Aryans, in ways that resemble the ways that participants in a number of laboratory experiments have made their self-identity more positive by stressing their social distinctiveness. Thus, Nazism and the Holocaust were ways of developing a distinctive, positive, new German identity. The statements in a literal sense might be true, but it would be the sort of truth that is so empty of content that it tells us nothing. Actually, it is a truth that is so beside the point in its oversimplified triviality that it constitutes an untruth.

Indeed, the Holocaust is one of several historical events that resist explanation, for to 'explain' the Holocaust would be to risk explaining it away. That, in essence, was what Bernstein was saying in his 1951 prologue, when he reflected how wrong it would have been to continue with his earlier dispassionate, scientific tone and to treat the Holocaust as just another effect of group formation. As Bernstein wrote, anti-Semitism had 'proved to be far more murderous and far more infectious than I thought possible' (1951, p. 19). To understand why that had been the case, one cannot rely on ideas that seem appropriate for understanding lower intensities of group hatred. Even in 1923, Bernstein had been aware of the dangers of explaining the unforgiveable. He wrote that if one tries to enumerate the causal factors behind a crime, one risks diminishing the guilt that should be attached to the criminal for '*tout comprendre c'est tout pardonner*' (Bernstein, 2009, p. 98). After the war, that had become unthinkable.

Universal Psychology and Historical Particularity

As a social psychologist Tajfel was never concerned to produce technically proficient experiments or well-constructed theories for their own sake, and in the years before his death he was becoming deeply uneasy about the direction in which social psychology was moving. In his important paper 'Experiments in a vacuum', Tajfel (1972) argued that social psychology was becoming increasingly trivial; an atmosphere of fun and games was prevailing over serious intellectual inquiry. Many social psychologists, constructing their elaborate experiments, were acting on the assumption that their results represented basic, universal truths about humans. Far from trying to exclude culture and history by vainly trying to create 'pure' environments, social psychologists, according to Tajfel, should be seeking to understand cultural history and how it affects psychological processes.

If social psychologists are to produce meaningful theories, then, according to Tajfel, they should try to study social psychological factors within particular cultural and historical contexts. He gave the example of the art historian E. H. Gombrich, who adapted psychological concepts from the Gestaltists and particularly from the British cognitive psychologist Frederic Bartlett. In his book *Art and Illusion*, Gombrich (1960) had argued that artists used 'stereotypes'; representatives from different artistic schools constructed and employed different visual stereotypes. Tajfel noted that Gombrich could hardly stop there, as if he had solved the problems of art simply by saying that artists used different stereotypes. Historians of art, when studying particular groups of artists, needed to be familiar with what the artists 'intended to communicate, how they wished to communicate it, and why they chose their particular idioms' (Tajfel, 1981, p. 26).

In short, historians, anthropologists or social psychologists must get down to the particularities of the world; otherwise, they will end up with bland generalities. General categories, such as 'stereotypes' or 'attributions' or 'group identity', are only valuable if they enable us to see particular features in new ways. The problem is that social psychologists, in contrast to historians, typically favour the general over the particular (Byford and Tileagă, 2014; Brock, 2016a; Tileagă and Byford, 2014). They treat their universal concepts as primary, and they use the particularities of the world to serve and to 'prove' the categories of their theories. In the hands of most psychologists, general concepts become greedy concepts, devouring the individual, unique features of the social world. The result is less, not greater, theoretical understanding.

Social identity theorists have tended to produce general, universal formulations as they seek to work out the relations between a widening list of universal variables relating to 'social identity', 'social categorisation' and 'social differentiation' (e.g. Abrams and Hogg, 1990; Brewer and Hewstone, 2004; Capozza and Brown, 2000; Ellemers, Spears and Doosje, 1999). To give just one example of the way social identity theorists make universal statements, here is a comment from one of the theory's many advocates: 'SIT [social identity theory] assumes that we show all kinds of "group" behaviour, such as solidarity within our groups and discrimination against out-groups as part of social identity processes, with the aim to achieve positive social self-esteem and self-enhancement'

(Trepte, 2006, p. 256). The statement resembles the quotation from the teaching aid quoted at the start of this chapter. The first person plural is used in its inclusive sense to incorporate all of 'us'. It is as if the complexities of the world – 'all kinds' of group behaviour – are being reduced to the simple and supposedly universal motive of achieving positive social self-esteem.

The universal terminology of some versions of social identity theory can flatten the particularities of the world in ways that are inappropriate when applied to the Holocaust. John Turner, who co-wrote with Tajfel the classic statements of social identity theory (Tajfel and Turner, 1979), made 'depersonalisation' a key component of his theory of self-categorisation. Turner did not use the word 'depersonalisation' in its usual sense to describe the way that some myths and ideologies depict other groups of humans as less than human – even as rats or vermin whose elimination would improve the world. Turner used the concept as something that occurs universally in 'the process of self-stereotyping' when people come to perceive themselves 'more as the interchangeable exemplars of a social category than as unique personalities' (Turner, 1987, p. 50). It is as if all of us depersonalise ourselves when we think of ourselves as members of a group – any group. The concept has lost its specificity that could be used to identify how dangerous ideologies such as Nazism rob others of their humanity, not because they offer an identity to believers but because of the content of the beliefs that they disseminate about others.

Marie Jahoda, whose work will be discussed in the following chapter, claimed that 'the major merit' of Tajfel's position was that he put 'theory in its place' – and its place was not at the top of social psychological tree (1981b, p. 861). In some of his final pieces of writings Tajfel expressed his concern about developments of social identity theory, including tactfully pointing out gaps in John Turner's analyses.[7] In his self-categorisation theory, Turner examined how individuals formed groups through coming to categorise themselves as group members (Turner, 1982, 1987; see also Reicher, Spears and Haslam 2010). Tajfel was concerned with the way that this perspective begins with the subjective views of individuals and thereby

---

[7] Rupert Brown, another of Tajfel's former students, is currently writing a biography of Tajfel. According to Brown (personal communication), the Wellcome archive contains a written manuscript of the Tajfel and Turner (1979) classic statement of social identity theory. The manuscript is entirely written in John Turner's hand, and this suggests that the piece may have been drafted by Turner. If so, it reflects well on Turner that, out of respect for Tajfel's ideas and their influence on his own thinking, he ensured that his former teacher took the first authorship. But it also suggests how Tajfel may have come to have some misgivings about the theoretical perspective of which he was the first named author.

'leaves out a preliminary stage that might perhaps be referred to as the pre-history of group formation' (Tajfel, 1982b, pp. 502–3). This stage of 'pre-history' was, of course, very much part of wider history – the history of economic and political relations, as well as the history of myths and beliefs. Tajfel's point was that the decisions which individuals take about their sense of identity should not be separated from this history.

In this spirit, Tajfel discussed how some social psychologists, including those developing his work, were over-simplifying the history and function of social stereotypes by explaining them in terms of individuals' needs for a positive identity. He wrote that 'the blame must be firmly assigned to an over-extension of what has come to be known as the "social identity" theory' (Tajfel, 1984, p. 699). The use of quotation marks around 'social identity' indicates his unease with the term. He wrote that questions about social identity are 'to some extent represented in the so-called "social identity" perspective, but social identity is not enough', and issues about identity must be considered in relation to the creation and diffusion of social myths (1984, p. 713). Tajfel discussed how social myths can be used in times of conflict to sanction extreme actions. The sort of violence which would be considered criminal if used against individuals then becomes acceptable, even demanded, when it is pursued for the sake of the group against its 'enemies'. He added, 'Examples are unnecessary for anyone who is familiar with even a small part of the history of the present century' (1984, p. 708).

Tajfel was undoubtedly referring to the history which he experienced first-hand and which he described briefly, but with such intensity, in the opening pages of *Human Groups*. To understand the anti-Semitism, which Bernstein described as turning out to be more infectious and murderous than he had imagined in 1923, it is not sufficient merely to say that it was psychologically more intense or that it expressed greater quantities of aggression. Tajfel was saying that we have to look at the myths and cultural beliefs that were being held against Jews. Tajfel's remark certainly distances him from those social psychologists who assume that analysts can only trust events, which have been created in laboratories under controlled conditions. Regarding his statements about individual and collective violence, Tajfel was not saying 'we must conduct an experiment to see whether this is true'. He knew it was true: the evidence from history, especially the history that he had lived through, was more than sufficient, so that further examples were unnecessary.

History and Anti-Semitism

Tajfel's reservations about universal social psychological theories could be applied equally to Bernstein's theory of group enmity. In ascribing the causes of anti-Semitism to group formation, Bernstein had been simultaneously explaining too much and too little. In very general terms Bernstein's theory might seem to explain why anti-Semitism existed in Germany during the 1920s, but that theory could not explain why such anti-Semitism should have increased in intensity over the following years and resulted in a scale of violence beyond imagining.

So, why was Tajfel so keen to commend Bernstein's work? The answer does not lie in the nature of social identity theory. It lies in Tajfel's knowledge about anti-Semitism and his deep fear that history in the late 1970s might be about to repeat itself. If it did repeat itself, the result would not be, as Marx once famously commented, that tragedy would be repeated as comedy.

In his foreword/afterword, Tajfel quoted Bernstein, who in his own prologue had written that back in the 1920s, there had been an aversion to discussing anti-Semitism. Tajfel commented, 'We have now come back to where Bernstein had started from' (1980, p. 2). After the end of the Second World War, there had been a great deal of writing about anti-Semitism, and there had been no way of avoiding the subject. However, according to Tajfel, now in the late 1970s and early 1980s, 'the "aversion" is back with us' (p. 2). Some outward forms of anti-Semitism were changing, with old ideas about Jewish conspiracies now appearing as 'anti-Zionism' and the extreme Right often employing codes to avoid directly mentioning Jews: 'Although it would be preposterous to claim that all anti-"Zionists" are anti-Semitic, there is very little doubt that the new terminology and the Middle East conflict have caused much old wine to be poured into new bottles' (p. 3). Tajfel feared that there was a parallel between the 1920s and the late 1970s, as people were being faced 'with a combination of circumstances very similar to that which Bernstein had to overcome when he tried to publish his book in the early twenties' (1980, p. 3).

For someone who had lived through history as Tajfel had done, anti-Semitism could never be the outcome of just another group formation or an expression of the search for a positive social identity. The Tajfel archives, housed in the Wellcome Trust Library, reveal the depth of Tajfel's concern to combat new forms of fascism and anti-Semitism. He was a signatory member of the left-wing Anti-Nazi League, which advocated direct action against the far Right groups of the time.

Tajfel was aware how the writers of history can reproduce old myths in new forms. The archive reveals his worries about a booklet, entitled *Arab-Israeli Conflict*, which the Schools Council History Project had produced in 1980 to be circulated in British schools.[8] Tajfel wrote to the publisher

---

[8] Wellcome Library, London, box PSY/TAJ/6/50.

to complain that the booklet was biased in that it contained no statement about the scale of the Holocaust and its impact on Jews. He also objected that the booklet ignored the fact that many of the post-war immigrants to Israel had come from Arab countries. Tajfel copied his letter to a number of prominent academics and politicians. The philosopher Isaiah Berlin, a Jewish refugee originally from Russia, wrote back offering his support and commending Tajfel for his fight against bigotry. Tajfel replied to Berlin saying that both the far Left and far Right were producing 'the kind of rumblings that scare me out of my wits' (31 March 1980).

The issue is not whether Tajfel was correct in seeing parallels between the anti-Semitism of the 1920s and that of the late 1970s and early 1980s – or indeed whether there are parallels with the summer of 2018, when anti-Semitism has once again become an issue in mainstream British politics. There are clear differences as well as the similarities that so troubled Tajfel. Nevertheless, we can see why Tajfel sought to understand the present in terms of the past, and to do that, he could not simply put his faith in a universal theory. He understood that no social psychological theory, however much laboratory data its advocates mustered in its support, could replace the need to understand the particularities of the past.

Like Lewin before him, Tajfel was at the time of his death moving towards a new form of social psychological understanding, the details of which must sadly remain unclear. In Tajfel's case, there are clues about his new direction. He was suggesting that it was necessary to examine directly the particular content of myths and how they are transmitted. Moreover, it seems that, after a long period of public silence, he was beginning to feel able to write about the issues that had originally brought him to social psychology. These issues could not be subsumed under universal theories or general categories. As William James had realised in much gentler times, theory by its simplifications mutilates reality. To respect the reality that Tajfel and Bernstein had known, anything more than the flickering of understanding and the particulars of historical detail would risk being a gross mutilation of memory.

In light of the Holocaust the relations between theory and example had shifted. It can be argued, and has been argued in earlier chapters, that theory should not be pure, but specific examples need to be written to illustrate how theory might work in practice. In these conditions, examples can still be used to serve the rhetorical interests of theory. That may be fitting for some issues, but, as Bernstein, Tajfel and Arendt realised, the Holocaust is too significant, too incomprehensible, to be treated as a mere example whose function is to serve wider interests of theory. As the historical particularity of the events overwhelms conventional theoretical concepts, so the importance of theory, especially universal theory, is diminished. We whose lives have been passed in fortunate times should be grateful to the flickering illumination that has come from those who lived in the darkest of historical moments; today their flickering of understanding remains as the flickering of a memorial candle.

8   Jahoda
The Ultimate Example

Having discussed how psychologists have written about the mind and having argued that psychologists should use more examples in their writings, I can expect readers to start asking, 'Well, who are you going to put forward as your example of a writer who does all this? Whose example should we all try to follow?' The questions may be obvious but the answers are not. It is no good my saying that William James or Sigmund Freud were great literary stylists, so they are the ones we should all try to copy. There is little to be gained from setting literary standards unreachably high. Our exemplar should not be a figure who has to be admired from a distance, but it should be someone whose example we might be able to follow if we try hard enough.

The earlier chapters have been leading up to the present appreciation of Marie Jahoda. She, it will be suggested, exemplifies the virtues that have been praised earlier. Her clear style of writing and her use of examples combine to make her a hero within these pages, but within the history of psychology Marie Jahoda is a somewhat secondary figure. She might not be as obscure as Abraham Tucker or Peretz Bernstein, but she certainly is not one of the 'big boys' of twentieth-century psychology.

It would be wrong to imply that Marie Jahoda was totally overlooked during her lifetime. She was a public figure as well as being an academic; she received a number of academic awards; and in Britain she was awarded the national honour of Commander of the British Empire. When she died in 2001 at the age of ninety-four, the disciplinary obituaries quite properly stressed her substantial achievements, but they never said words to the effect that 'for many years Marie Jahoda was the commanding presence in English/British/European/world social psychology'. She never sought to be a commanding presence, whether in the world of social psychology or elsewhere. By contrast, many conventionally successful academic figures who stride commandingly within their disciplinary domains have not received a royal commendation for being a symbolic Commander of a defunct British Empire.

Some readers who have worked their way through the preceding chapters might be puzzled that those chapters have been leading up to Marie

Jahoda. They might consider her to be something of an anti-climax. Why isn't my chosen example one of the big names in psychology? Jahoda hardly troubles the writers of social psychology's major textbooks, but that is precisely the point. If the standard ways of writing psychology are flawed, then a good example is more likely to found on the margins of the discipline than in its central positions.

Today, admirers of Marie Jahoda consider that she has not received the recognition that she deserves. In David Fryer's view, she was 'one of the most distinguished psychologists in the discipline's history and one of the foremost intellectuals of our times' (2002, p. 5). Fryer points out that her academic contribution now tends to be placed under the narrower heading of 'community psychology', rather than 'social psychology'; but even so, according to Fryer, most US histories of community psychology overlook her (Fryer, 2008). In recent years, some feminist psychologists are beginning to see Jahoda as an important voice in the history of women psychologists, and they have complained that she 'has been all but disregarded' (Rutherford, Unger and Cherry, 2011, p. 54; see also Rutherford, 2010, 2011). These feminist psychologists have been attempting to revive Jahoda's intellectual heritage, especially her particular way of doing psychology, which was based on the idea that psychologists should immerse themselves in the lives of those whom they study.[1]

This chapter will not be examining Jahoda's writing as if it can be detached from her wider social, political and humanitarian outlook. Distinctive writings are more than distinctive bundles of words and paragraphs, for they reflect the distinctive stance of their authors. Jahoda's academic values, including her views on academic writing, are an important part of her story. Nearly fifty years ago, she complained about the volume of academic publishing that was being produced. Psychologists, in her opinion, were constantly publishing trivialities that were not worth the paper on which they were printed (Jahoda, 1970). Not just psychologists but academics generally were drowning in a deluge of publications, and Marie Jahoda stood back from the mania to publish ever more and more (Jahoda, 1981a). She had strong moral, political and personal reasons for not publishing some of her own research, and she knew from her experience that there were far more important things in life than having a mega-long list of publications. Jahoda was prescient in her complaints, for in the twenty-first century, the flood levels of publication

---

[1] It is no coincidence that, in the history of psychology which Alexandra Rutherford cowrote with Wade Pickren, Marie Jahoda is for once accorded due recognition for 'her long and remarkable career in social psychology' (Pickren and Rutherford, 2015, p. 190).

continue to rise at even faster rates and with ever more destructive consequences (Billig, 2013).

One reason why Marie Jahoda may have had the confidence to resist the prevailing atmosphere of 'publish or perish' is that as a young academic, she was the author of a classic book in the social sciences. That work, which described an unemployed community near Vienna, showed readers how to look at the sharp points of the social world. It also encapsulates the views that Jahoda continued to hold about the value of examples and the comparative unimportance of theory. We have already encountered the latter view in the previous chapter. There Jahoda was quoted as praising Henri Tajfel for putting theory in its place.

First, however, the outlines of her long life will be presented to show how her early political commitments drew her towards psychology, and then towards a very particular way of doing psychology.

Life of Marie Jahoda

Marie Jahoda was a multiple outsider – by ethnicity, politics, culture, nationality, intellectual values and, of course, gender. David Fryer, in the fascinating interview which he conducted with her when she was in her early eighties, asked her, In which community did she feel 'totally at home'? She replied, 'Oh, I'm just a rootless refugee' (Fryer, 1986, p. 118). Younger than Lewin and twelve years older than Tajfel, Jahoda, like them, was a European Jew who had fled from aggressive anti-Semitism.

Of course, no one is entirely rootless. Marie Jahoda grew up in a liberal-minded, middle-class Jewish family in Vienna. As she told Fryer, her parents strongly believed that daughters should receive as much education as sons. At that time, many middle-class Jewish parents hoped that education would protect their children against the anti-Semitism that was, to quote Jahoda (1983), 'endemic'. The nationalist parties were accusing Jewish citizens of being rootless cosmopolitans who were undermining the integrity of the nation – an accusation whose echoes Jahoda was mocking many years later in her interview with Fryer.

After the First World War, Viennese political life changed direction. The Left came to power, and the young Marie Jahoda became involved in socialist politics even before she went to university. As she told Fryer, politics determined her decision to study psychology at the University of Vienna, for she genuinely believed that one day she would be the country's socialist minister of education. The study of psychology, she said, would provide ideal training for the post, especially as she had already qualified as a schoolteacher. Even if her youthful ambition was never to be fulfilled, it left an enduring impact. Throughout her long career, she believed that psychological inquiry should serve social and political ends. Research for its own sake was never sufficiently practical. In her old age, after many years in academic life, she did not disavow the young, radical Marie.

Studying as a student at the University of Vienna in the newly established Psychological Institute, Marie Jahoda was fortunate in her teacher of psychology. She described Karl Bühler, the Institute's founder, as 'a great man, a great, gentle scholar' (Fryer, 1986, p. 116). Although Karl Bühler lived for many years in the same city as Freud, the two never met (Jahoda, 1969). On the other hand, Marie Jahoda's world overlapped with the psycho-analytic world. She recounted how she was taking tea with her friend Anna Freud when Anna's father dropped by (Fryer, 2002). Between 1930 and 1931 Marie Jahoda underwent psycho-analysis with Heinz Hartmann, who had been personally analysed by Freud and was, according to Ernest Jones (1964), one of 'Freud's favourite pupils' (p. 652). Jahoda deeply admired Hartmann as a thinker, especially his work to connect psycho-analytic ideas with the psychological study of the mind (Jahoda, 1969).[2]

Jahoda was encouraged to study for a doctorate at the Psychological Institute and also to participate in its various research projects. Most of Jahoda's young colleagues at the Institute were socialists like her, supporting the democratic left-wing Austro-Marxism that was being championed by the Social Democratic government of Vienna. Many years later, Jahoda would still write in praise of Austro-Marxism: it was a mass movement 'pervaded by a spirit of hope that, I believe, has no parallel in the twentieth century' (1983, p. 343).

At a summer camp of the socialist youth movement in 1919, Jahoda met the young Paul Lazarsfeld, who also combined an involvement in Austro-Marxism with an interest in psychology. Paul and Marie married in 1927, and they had a daughter, Lotte, who would become a distinguished academic in the United States. Lazarsfeld also worked at the Psychological Institute, primarily as a methodologist, and he was to pioneer a number of quantitative techniques that were suitable for applied social research. At that time Lazarsfeld was torn between pursuing an academic career and devoting himself full-time to radical politics.

---

[2] See Palombo, Bendicsen and Koch (2009, chapter 2) for a biography of Hartmann. According to them, Hartmann was deeply interested in theory and rarely cited case histories in his writings; in fact, Anna Freud found his work overly theoretical. Palombo et al. comment that 'his qualities as a human being were extraordinary' (p. 51).

Academic life would eventually win out.[3] The marriage of Paul and Marie, however, did not last, and the couple divorced in 1934. Paul had already started a new relationship with another of Karl Bühler's young students. For Paul the new relationship would lead to another marriage, and then to another divorce.

While Paul and Marie were still married, they co-operated with Hans Zeisel, a lawyer and childhood friend of Lazarsfeld, on the study of Marienthal, an industrial village twenty miles from Vienna with almost 100 per cent unemployment. The study will be discussed separately below. It was a brilliant, pioneering piece of work which represented for Marie Jahoda the perfect balance between intellectual inquiry and political significance. As will be seen, Paul Lazarsfeld had a rather different, more professionally methodological take on the study.

With growing economic crises within the borders of Austria, and the rise of anti-democratic nationalism across the border in Germany, politics in Vienna was moving fiercely towards the Right. In 1934, the year after Hitler had come to power in Germany, Austria's conservative chancellor, Englebert Dollfuss, suppressed the Social Democrats and initiated the rule of 'Austro-fascism'. Dollfuss was assassinated in the same year, and his successor Kurt Schuschnigg continued to support 'Austro-fascism' until Hitler's invasion and annexation of Austria in 1938, when 'Austro-fascism' merged into full-blooded German Nazism.

The fall of 'Red Vienna' had direct consequences for the members of the Psychological Institute, including those, like Karl Bühler and his wife, Charlotte, who were not radical left-wingers. Karl, who was not Jewish, was arrested and imprisoned. In Jahoda's words, 'this sensitive and gentle scholar was crushed by his experiences in an Austrian prison' (1969, p. 429). When Karl was released, he fled Vienna, finally settling in the United States, where Charlotte was to fare much better academically than him. In part, he was still suffering the after-effects of his imprisonment, but this on its own does not explain how a thinker of Karl's stature – someone whose work on language had influenced Popper, Wittgenstein, Cassirer and Vygotsky – could in the United States have been, to use Jahoda's words, so 'strangely unappreciated' (1977, p. 2). Karl Bühler failed to obtain a university position, let alone a prestigious one (Brock, 1994, 2016b). The fate of Karl Bühler in the States provides yet another

---

[3] Christian Fleck (1998) provides a detailed account of Lazarsfeld's time at the Psychological Institute. Fleck traces the influence of Karl Bühler on Lazarsfeld's thinking, especially in drawing him to appreciate the importance of psychological questions. Bühler appreciated Lazarsfeld's methodological and statistical skills, as well as his ability manage research projects.

example, as if one were needed, that outstanding academic quality does not necessarily guarantee outstanding academic success.

Paul Lazarsfeld was also able to leave Austria for the United States, taking Lotte with him, but Marie remained in Vienna. It was a dangerous time for a Jewish socialist. She used her research position in the Psychological Institute as a cover for secret resistance work against the pro-fascist regime. The subterfuge did not last, and she was arrested in 1936. At the time of her arrest, Jahoda had been working on a project about humour, looking at the differences between jokes about urban Jews and jokes about aristocrats. The police had confiscated her collection of jokes and seemed perplexed by them. What was a radical young Jew doing with such stuff? Many years later, she wrote that the interrogation by the Austrian state police about the jokes was 'one of the most uncannily hilarious episodes of my life' (Jahoda, 1981a, p. 209).

Jahoda was tried in 1937 on the charge of assisting the underground organisation of the banned Social Democrats. Unsurprisingly, she was found guilty and spent eight months in prison, mostly in solitary confinement (Klein, 2009). As her later comments about the interrogation by the Austrian police suggest, she refused to let herself be overcome by the experience. She was released on the condition that she immediately leave the country and renounce her citizenship – which she did. She was never given back her collection of jokes, and she never completed that study.

So began Marie Jahoda's life as a rootless refugee. She initially left for Britain, and she worked on various research projects, including examining whether substitute unpaid work would lessen the psychological effects of unemployment for miners in Wales. She also held a fellowship at Cambridge University and conducted a pioneering fieldwork study of factory life, supervised by the psychologist Frederic Bartlett (Fryer, 2008). During the war Jahoda worked with the British Ministry of Information on a series of opinion surveys, and she also made regular radio broadcasts to Austria (for details of her work at this time, see Cook, 1990).

Marie Jahoda would not be re-united with her daughter until just before the end of the Second World War, when she went to the United States. There she worked as a researcher for the American Jewish Committee, which had commissioned Max Horkheimer to set up a number of projects investigating the social and psychological roots of anti-Semitism. These projects included *The Authoritarian Personality*, amongst whose authors was Theodor Adorno, Horkheimer's colleague from the Marxist influenced Frankfurt Institute. As part of the general project Jahoda was to co-edit an assessment of *The Authoritarian*

Personality with Richard Christie, as well as working on a project investigating the emotional roots of anti-Semitism (Christie and Jahoda, 1954). From 1949 to 1958 she worked at New York University as professor of social psychology (Cook, 1990).

In her interview with David Fryer, Marie Jahoda seems to deny that she ever suffered from gender discrimination in her academic career. However, it is easy to suspect that Horkheimer and Adorno, who were at home in the hyper-Hegelian, very masculine environment of the Frankfurt School, did not find it easy to work with such a confident, politically active woman. According to the documents which Christian Fleck (2011) studied, Marie Jahoda thought that Horkheimer was employing her in the United States at a level that fell well short of her experience and capabilities – a charge that Horkheimer dismissed. Adorno wanted Jahoda to change her introduction to the edited volume about *The Authoritarian Personality* because he feared being expelled from the US on account of the 'charming Mitzi' (Fleck, 2011, p. 250). On the other hand, it was not gender that led some of the members of the old Frankfurt School to describe Paul Lazarsfeld's contribution to the anti-Semitism project as a 'catastrophe' (Jacobs, 2015, p. 82).

Marie Jahoda returned to England in 1958 to marry the Labour Member of Parliament, Austen Albu, whom she had met the previous year. She lived in England for the rest of her life, first working to establish a psychology degree at Brunel College of Advanced Technology, which became a university in 1962. Three years later, in 1965, she became professor of social psychology at the new University of Sussex. *Nature* (5 September 1964, pp. 1014–15) announced her appointment at Sussex and published a short biography which, presumably for reasons of misplaced tact, did not mention that, between her directorship of 'a research institute' in Vienna and the award in 1937 of her Pinsent–Darwin Fellowship at Cambridge University, Marie Jahoda had served a prison sentence.

While Marie Jahoda was at Sussex University, she continued to conduct applied research, including research into the psychological consequences of unemployment. She also published articles in which she criticised the dominant theoretical and methodological trends of social psychology. Unusually for a British academic psychologist of that time, she maintained her interest in psycho-analysis, publishing *Freud and the Dilemmas of Psychology* in 1977. While so much energy in European social psychology was being divided between Henri Tajfel's social identity theory and Serge Moscovici's Paris-based social representation theory, Marie Jahoda appeared somewhat peripheral. For reasons that will become clearer, she was never going to challenge the big two theories with an even bigger one of her own.[4]

Marienthal: the Story of a Classic Publication

The story how the unemployed of Marienthal came to be studied by Marie Jahoda and her colleagues at the Psychological Institute has been told a number of times. Paul Lazarsfeld (1969) has recounted that, as the director of the Institute's new research centre, he wanted a politically motivated project to balance the market research that he had been directing. He went to see Otto Bauer, the leader of the Austrian Socialists, with the idea of conducting a survey to help the recently unemployed make use of their enforced leisure time. Bauer responded in no uncertain terms. According to the statistician and sociologist Paul Neurath (1995), Bauer exploded: Had they all gone out of their minds? Did they really want to study leisure activities when what the unemployed most needed was work? Bauer suggested the researchers examine the consequences of almost total unemployment on the life of a community. He recommended them to look at Marienthal, a strongly Social Democratic village not far from Vienna, where the main employer had closed down the flax mill, leaving most of the households without a wage earner.

The project began in 1930, and in the words of Christian Fleck in his introduction to the latest English edition of *Marienthal*, its 'matching of politics and scholarship has seldom been replicated' (2002, p. xix). The politically committed researchers needed the backing of intellectually committed politicians. Bauer was certainly intellectually minded: he had written a major study on nationalism and was sympathetic to psychoanalysis. His sister Ida Bauer was Freud's famous patient 'Dora', and Otto, after his marriage in 1914, had consulted Freud, who advised him to give up politics and become a university teacher. Freud had warned

---

[4] I should mention an extraordinary coincidence which might help to explain why I often refer to 'Marie Jahoda' rather than using the surname-only, gender-free name 'Jahoda'. Marie was not the only Viennese Jahoda to be employed as a professor of social psychology in Britain at that time. Gustav Jahoda, no relation and thirteen years younger than Marie, had also been raised in a non-religious, middle-class Jewish family and had also managed to escape. Like Marie, Gustav read widely, and his experiences as a refugee made him deeply aware of the influence of culture on psychological processes. He also rejected the dominant ways of doing social psychology and especially the assumptions of universality. As he looked back on his life, Gustav recounted how he refused to follow the standard paths for a successful career in the world of psychology (Jahoda, 2016). Gustav's admirers, like those of Marie – and in the present case, the two categories definitely overlap – felt that his achievements did not receive the full recognition that they deserved (Billig, 2018b; Marková, 2018; Marková and Jesuino, 2018).

Otto about wanting to change the world: 'Don't try to make people happy; people don't want to be happy' (Decker, 1991, p. 160).

If the study of Marienthal originated in specific circumstances, then the report of the research had an unusual history. It was originally published in Germany as a short book in the spring of 1933, just weeks after Hitler had taken power. The publisher, which was based in Leipzig, did not want to draw attention to its latest product. It kept the Jewish-sounding names of the three authors – Jahoda, Lazarsfeld and Zeisel – from the front cover, lest enthusiastic anti-Semites, of which there was no shortage, create trouble. The book was merely described as being edited by the Austrian Research Unit for Economic Psychology. It did not bear an attention-grabbing title. The literal English translation of the German title is *The Unemployed of Marienthal: a Sociographic Essay on the Consequences of Long-Term Unemployment, with an Appendix on the History of Sociography.*

It is unclear whether the Nazis actually burned *Marienthal* in the book-burning spectacles that they staged in university cities throughout Germany. The works of famous Jewish psychologists, most notably those of Freud, were amongst those that were thrown onto the fires. *Marienthal* and its authors were much less famous, and in any case, the book's publisher had taken care to prevent casual readers from coming across the work. Perhaps its caution had ensured that the book did not come to the attention of the authorities, and consequently it may not have taken its place on the heaped pyres.

Political censorship might have initially damaged the fortunes of *Marienthal*, and the book was to remain unpublicised for years. However it was not totally ignored, and it attracted several favourable and some critical reviews (Fleck, 1998); it also had a great influence on Polish sociology (Sułek, 2007). However, it was not the fears of the original German publisher that would ensure that there would be no English translation of *Marienthal* for almost forty years. When it was finally translated, Fleck wrote that the book's history showed that in the social sciences, 'outstanding work can live at the very margins of the scholarly world' (2002, p. xxvii).

The three authors were the principal directors of the project, and it was their responsibility to oversee the collection of the data from the research team.[5] Lazarsfeld, the overall director, wrote the book's short introduction, in which he outlined the methodological and political aims of the research.

---

[5] For details of the research team and other aspects of the project, see the website on Marienthal maintained by the University of Graz: http://agso.uni-graz.at/marienthal/e/pr ojectteam/00.htm. The research team comprised nine women and six men. It included Marie Jahoda's cousin, Clara Jahoda, and also Hedwig Deutsch, who would later marry Marie Jahoda's brother Fritz. For a summary of the various research methods used in the project, see Fleck (1998).

He wrote that the project combined numerical data with information that emerged as the researchers immersed themselves in the life of the community. Lazarsfeld also detailed what the community gained from participating in the research. The research team arranged for free medical consultations, organised gymnastic classes for the young girls and a pattern design course for their mothers and generally the researchers offered guidance and advice to parents. The researchers also rewarded the villagers for their cooperation with second-hand clothes (Lazarsfeld, 1969).

Hans Zeisel wrote the afterword, which, strangely did not reflect back on the research that was reported in the main body of the book. Instead, the afterword provided a history of 'sociographic' research – or research which investigated a particular community in detail. In effect, Zeisel's afterword was a 'literature review', surveying the results and methods of previous research. In research that was designed to make a political impact, a literature review was not the most vital of chapters, so, contrary to conventional academic practice, it was tucked away at the end.

In between Lazarsfeld's introduction and Zeisel's afterword came the main body of the text, which Jahoda wrote. She did not present the findings as if they were testing a theory about the psychological consequences of unemployment. In fact, like Lazarsfeld in the introduction, she did not refer to other research. Many years later, Jahoda (1982a) would describe the study as being radically atheoretical. Today, researchers in the social sciences are taught to present their work in terms of a theoretical approach or a hypothesis (Billig, 2013). The Marienthal authors were doing just what young social scientists are nowadays told not to do.

Jahoda would claim that the lack of theory was a substantial benefit because the researchers could look directly at the world to see what happens when a community is economically destroyed (Jahoda, 1982a). Their task was not to test a hypothesis (as if they needed to test the hypothesis that collective poverty was not a collective benefit); nor was it to test a methodology (as if the most important thing was to use the unemployed to test the strengths and weaknesses of various techniques of measurement). The researchers were engaging in what Jahoda called 'descriptive fieldwork' (1982a, p. 357). Description, not theory, was to be the key as the researchers sought 'to make visible in its complexity what is otherwise invisible'– to show that the people of Marienthal were suffering in ways that outsiders might fail to notice.

Marienthal: the Written Report and Its Examples

If the Marienthal research project was to be descriptive fieldwork, then Jahoda, as the author of the main report, needed to pursue a rhetorical strategy for describing the life of the village. Her strategy can be briefly summed up by two significant absences and one significant presence. Specialist terminology, especially theoretical constructs, and references to academic publications are the absences. Jahoda described the community in terms of official statistics and in terms of what the researchers noticed about its members and their patterns of life. In these descriptions, there is a significant presence: at all times she offered specific examples to bring the general descriptions and the official numbers to life, showing individual families caught in desperate times (for an appreciation of Jahoda's writing, see Müller, 2012).

Concrete examples can be found in all the chapters presenting results, even in chapters that seemingly concentrate on numerical summaries. In chapter 4, Jahoda presented the findings about menus and budgets. She started with a summary of the number of meals eaten by those who participated in the survey. For example, 75 per cent had three meals a day. Just over half the families (54 per cent) had meat once a week. Forty-five per cent had coffee and bread for their evening meal, while 40 per cent ate left-overs from the lunchtime meal in the evening. The average figures are disturbing: this is not a community that is eating well and the health statistics supported this.

However, Jahoda did not leave the average numbers to speak for themselves. She presented the menus of two specific families for a week, as well as giving their average weekly spending on food. There, we can see the pattern of deprivation clearly. On Tuesday, the first family had coffee and bread for breakfast, cabbage and potato for lunch and cabbage for the evening meal. We can see how the mother of the family tried to spice up the monotony of the meals on the Thursday by adding paprika to the potatoes that formed both the family lunch and the evening meal. It is the particulars that bring the averages to life.

One of the most famous findings of the Marienthal research was that unemployment destroyed the structure of the men's days. Most had nothing to do. Now unemployed, many of the men seemed psychologically lost. While their wives were looking after the home, many of the men wandered about aimlessly. With seemingly unlimited time they nevertheless dropped their former leisure pursuits, giving up activities such as football or reading library books. The researchers timed how long it took men and women to walk around the village. The women tended to walk briskly without stopping – they had tasks that needed to be done. The men dawdled, stopping frequently to talk as they filled time. Again, there were specific examples to illustrate the general point. The idea of measuring the speed of walking came from no methodology textbook: it came from the researchers noticing what was happening before their eyes.

The report demonstrated that description was not straightforward. Lazarsfeld, in his introduction, reported that the researchers came away from the village with boxes of material weighing more than sixty-six pounds (Jahoda, Lazarsfeld and Zeisel, 2002, p. 9). Only a tiny fraction of that material could be used as examples in the final report and Jahoda had to select the details to be used. If metonymy represents describing a whole in terms of a part, then metonymic selection is key to the vivid use of examples that enables a particular case to stand for a much greater whole.[6] This rhetorical skill will be overlooked if social scientific research is seen merely as theory plus methodology – as if the describing of social reality is too obvious to require attention.

One particular example shows the importance of metonymic selection. How could the author illustrate the communal spirit of Marienthal and the simultaneous threat that poverty makes to that spirit? No amount of statistics could make the point as forcefully as a detail from the lives of villagers. In the second chapter, Jahoda reported: 'When a cat or a dog disappears, the owner no longer bothers to report the loss; he knows that someone must have eaten the animal, and he does not want to find out who' (Jahoda, Lazarsfeld and Zeisel, 2002, p. 22).

The detail sticks in the mind long after percentage points are forgotten. We can imagine adults not wanting to discover which neighbours might have eaten the family's pet – fearing that they too might soon be reduced to such desperate theft. We can also imagine them being relieved that they no longer have to feed a cat or a dog loved by their children, when they can barely provide more than potatoes and poor quality bread for those children. It takes skill for an author to find the telling detail among sixty-six pounds of documentation. Selecting the detail is only half the task. The detail then has to be described so that it appears to speak for itself without heavy-handed explanation. Small words can be decisive: 'no longer' conveys so much without drawing attention to the changes wrought by unemployment. The skills of description, when exercised precisely, seem to disappear from sight.

The Balance between Quantitative and Qualitative Analysis

From her experience of being involved in the Marienthal research, Marie Jahoda derived three lessons that would last the rest of her long,

---

[6] Actually metonymy involves more complicated part–whole relations than just describing a whole in terms of a part (Littlemore, 2015; Radden and Kövecses, 2007). For the sake of convenience, and to emphasise the role of examples, attention here is limited to the metonymic relation of the part standing for the whole.

productive life: the importance of using qualitative material to understand the lives of individuals within a community; the importance of realising that people do not react to the same circumstances in identical ways; and if research is based on social problems, then there are reasons beyond theory and methodology for deciding whether or not to publish the findings. We will consider each of these lessons in turn. Taken together, all three ensured that Jahoda would later remain outside the dominant trends of social psychology.

Jahoda's views about the balance between qualitative and quantitative methods have to be reconstructed carefully. She was not a naturally polemical or contentious person. Certainly, within the small world of academia, she never picked academic arguments to boost her own visibility. Even when criticising the views of other academics, she did so politely, usually pointing out the strengths of their contributions while making her criticisms. We can see her fairness and delicacy, balancing specific criticism with wider understanding. For example, in her interview with Fryer (1986), she suggested that much of Lewin's approach was over-theoretical, but she did not elaborate this into a specific critique of Lewin's view of social psychology. Elsewhere, Jahoda mentioned that Lewin's 'influence did not transcend academic circles' (1969, p. 444), but characteristically she balanced her criticism with praise. In the same passage she described Lewin as one of Gestalt psychology's 'outstanding representatives', and she said that he did more than anyone to awaken the social conscience of professional colleagues.

In such comments we can see Jahoda's tactful way of presenting differences with other academic figures. She did not conceal differences, but she did not magnify them. Her tact was all the greater when she wrote about the balance between quantitative and qualitative work in relation to Marienthal. On this matter, she was differing from the views of her former husband. It would go against the grain intellectually, morally and personally for her to conduct a public argument with Lazarsfeld.

When Jahoda and Lazarsfeld came to reflect separately on the Marienthal research, and especially on the relations between quantitative and qualitative aspects of the study, the differences between the two would become apparent, although neither would draw attention to this. Lazarsfeld wrote a new introduction for the first English translation, published in 1972, drawing upon parts of a longer article that he had written as a chapter for a book about European intellectuals who fled to the United States – a book to which Jahoda also contributed a chapter (Lazarsfeld, 1969, 2002; Jahoda, 1969). Lazarsfeld's chapter concentrated on his own experiences, while Jahoda wrote about the experiences of others.

In his introduction to the English translation of *Marienthal*, Lazarsfeld commented upon the methodological weaknesses of the original study. Some aspects were, he wrote, 'very naïve', and, he continued, 'certain standards on which my collaborators and I would later insist in our teaching were neglected' (2002, p. xxxv). For instance, the researchers had not detailed their sampling procedures or used attitude scales, about which they knew little at that time. Such faults had made him so uncomfortable that 'for a while I refused any offer to publish a translation' (p. xxxv). It should be noted how, at this point, Lazarsfeld switches from the collective 'my collaborators and I', who had been methodologically naïve, to the first person singular: 'I' refused to allow a translation. Jahoda (1982a), in her 'Reflections on Marienthal', did not indicate that she felt uncomfortable about the methodological naivety of the study. Nor did she mention Lazarsfeld's opposition to a translation.

Lazarsfeld's remarks about the relations between quantitative and qualitative methods in the Marienthal research are interesting, especially if examined closely. In his chapter for *Intellectual Migration*, Lazarsfeld mentions how Karl Bühler had entertained a theoretical and methodological ecumenism within psychology, advocating that psychologists should try to combine different approaches and different methodologies. Regarding the Marienthal research, Lazarsfeld claimed that he had followed the spirit of Bühler, feeling that it had been 'almost a moral duty' to combine insight and quantification (1969, p. 283). For Jahoda, methodology was always a means to a moral end rather than being in itself almost a moral duty.

In both his new introduction and in his *Intellectual Migration* chapter, Lazarsfeld spelled out four methodological rules that underlay the Marienthal research (1969, p. 282; 2002, p. xxxvii; see also Fleck, 1998). These were principally rules for combining qualitative and quantitative material. Lazarsfeld describes his rules in such a way that he gives the edge to quantitative materials. For example, the first rule was that when one examines any phenomenon, 'one should have objective observations as well as introspective reports'. Two points can be noted. The first is the word 'objective': it is used in a way that suggests 'introspective reports' are not objective. Once that distinction is made, the edge is given to 'objective' methods over those that appear, by contrast, to be 'subjective'. The second is the implicit bias of the rule: it is phrased to suggest that introspective reports without 'objective observations' are insufficient. He does not reverse the rule to say that one should have 'introspective reports' as well as 'objective observations', as if the latter on their own might be insufficient.

It is the same with Lazarsfeld's second rule: 'Case studies should be properly combined with statistical information'. The ordering of this rule is not reversed to suggest that statistical information should be properly combined with case studies. This impression is emphasised in Lazarsfeld's new introduction, where he specifically wrote of 'our preference for objective information of trends' (2002, p. xxxix). From the context, it is clear that when Lazarsfeld mentioned 'objective information', he meant quantified data. He wrote that 'mere description is not enough'. Again, this is not reversed: he does not say that mere objective data are not enough. Nor does he say what 'mere description' might be.[7]

Jahoda's reflections on Marienthal are very different (Jahoda, 1982a). She does not lay down clear rules for conducting research, but she does say something clearly that Lazarsfeld does not actually state, namely that statistical information on its own is insufficient. She wrote that because no data source is completely trustworthy, it is desirable to use both quantitative and qualitative materials, as well as psychological and economic information in general. There is no implicit bias towards the quantitative or the so-called objective – a term that she does not use in this context. As she was to write, she learned from Paul Neurath and Paul Lazarsfeld their 'respect for quantification of the quantifiable, but not their love for it' (Jahoda, 1983, p. 345).

In the Marienthal report, it was insufficient merely to report the statistics on family spending or the decreasing number of books borrowed from the library. It was vital also to present case histories of families being fractured by decreasing money. As we will see, Jahoda did not assume that case histories or qualitative analyses were unscientific or merely subjective. On the other hand, she did feel that statistical analyses on their own were insufficient for understanding the psychological reactions of people. In her 'Reflections' article, she wrote that if you want to understand what it is like to suffer unemployment, then some fieldwork is necessary. She complained that in many modern studies of unemployment, 'it is hard to realise that the unemployed are human beings; they are dissolved into variables suitable for entry into regression analyses and ANOVAS' (1982a, p. 385). She added that 'the reintroduction of people' into research reports would remind the researchers how much more they need to explain.

Jahoda's strong sense of moral duty shines through such remarks. Her methodological practices were based on the imperative to recognise the

---

[7] We might note a remark by Abraham Tucker which was quoted in Chapter 2. Two centuries before Lazarsfeld was implying the limitations of description by the phrase 'mere description', Tucker had written of the limitations of theory, using the phrase 'mere abstraction' (1763, p. xxii). Also, Lacan's disdain for 'simple observation', as discussed above in Chapter 5, is a rhetorical equivalent to the phrase 'mere description', but in a very different theoretical context.

humanity of people, especially the humanity of the poor. According to Lazarsfeld, mere description is not enough. The very phrase, or rather the specific word 'mere', downgrades the importance of writing about people. As such, the phrase misunderstands the nature of description and over-blows the importance of self-conscious theorising. In Chapter 6, Ernst Cassirer's linking of theory and description was discussed. Cassirer drew upon the insights of Goethe and of Mayer, the founder of thermody-namics, to suggest that accurate description involves theoretical under-standing. Consequently, good description cannot be 'mere' description, for it must always understand what it is describing.

Jahoda certainly did not downgrade description in favour of either statistical data or abstract theory. She argued that 'descriptive fieldwork' was vital if the social sciences were to be genuinely meaningful. Unless researchers write about people, whom they have got to know and in whose lives they have immersed themselves, their writings will lack humanity. A mere psychology of variables, statistics and theory, and devoid of descriptive accounts of people, is a psychology that has lost both its subject matter and its moral purpose.

Describing Different People

Marienthal perfectly illustrates the type of research that Marie Jahoda always believed to be desirable. It was driven by actual social issues, not theory, and it described moments in the lives of people. As she noted, those who only used quantitative methods to study the psychological effects of unemployment would write reports in which the presence of statistically significant results is matched by the absence of people. It is the same with most studies in experimental social psychology – typically they are example-free. Most experimentalists are searching for significant differences between controlled experimental groups. In this search, they not only fail to give examples of people behaving but they also ignore differences between people, for they concentrate on finding differences between the mean scores of different groups. This was something that greatly concerned Jahoda.

She gave an example from the work of an experimentalist whom she greatly admired. Jahoda's review of Henri Tajfel's *Human Groups and Social Categories* was mentioned in the previous chapter (Jahoda, 1981b). Typically Jahoda set her criticisms amidst praise. She commended Tajfel's rich and diversified contribution to social psychology, saying it was the product of an 'original, productive and civilized mind' (p. 861). In particular she praised his 'brief and moving' account of his experiences as a young Polish Jew surviving the war (1981b, p. 860). There was also criticism of Tajfel's minimal group experiment which he had described in a chapter of *Human Groups*. In that experiment, schoolboys were assigned to one of two groups, neither of which had any social reality. On the basis of merely being told they were a member of one of the groups, the experimental participants discriminated in favour of anonymous members of their own group, the ingroup, and against equally anonymous members of the other group, the outgroup. Jahoda noted that Tajfel and his co-experimenters had presented the experimental result in terms of group means. From the mean scores it was impossible to discern how many of the participants had discriminated in favour of their own group members and how many might have sought to act fairly.

This might seem to be a somewhat obscure, technical criticism of a deliberately artificial experiment, but in Jahoda's hands it was much more than that. She was expressing the humane vision that had lain behind her use of examples in *Marienthal*. In actual life, people are not replaceable, one for each other. They do not act in identical ways, as if they are nothing but a variable awaiting to be pushed in a single direction by another variable. The schoolboys participating in the minimal group experiments were doing tasks that had no significance for them but that is no reason to assume that they had all reacted in precisely the same way or that the differences in their reactions were unimportant. Why had not the experimentalists sought to discover and then describe the variety of their responses in this artificially and deliberately restricted environment?

Even if only a small number had refused to discriminate against the members of the other group, it would have been a finding that would be significant in a non-statistical sense. It would have mitigated the pessimism of the overall finding – that merely being categorised as a member of a group is sufficient to produce discrimination against outgroup members. Jahoda supported her point with a historical example that related to her and Tajfel's lives: 'There were, after all, some Germans who helped Jews to survive though fully aware that Jews had been made into an outgroup' (1981b, p. 481).

Jahoda was making a criticism of experimental social psychology: namely that methodologically and theoretically it was a psychology of the majority. She was claiming that experimentalists, in trying to isolate causal variables, were only interested in how the majority of subjects within an experimental situation behaved and that they treated the minority as 'insubordinate subjects' whose behaviour was a nuisance (Jahoda, 1959). Actually the situation is worse than Jahoda described. Studies with sufficiently large samples can find statistically significant differences between experimental and control conditions, even if only a minority of participants in the experimental group are affected by the experimental variable that is being tested. The problem is that researchers follow customary procedures of analysing and writing about their data and, in following these practices, they routinely ignore parts of their evidence and exaggerate group differences. They do not seek to discover how many participants are affected by the variable in question and they write about a significant variable as if it had determined the behaviour of all the participants in the experimental group even if the variable might have only determined the behaviour of a minority (Billig, 2013).

In experiments such as Tajfel's minimal group study, but not in Lewin's non-statistical experimental case studies (described in Chapter 6), experimenters are uninterested in linking the very brief and etiolated moment that they are studying with the wider life of their participants. They are deliberately separating the participants from their lives and then treating those participants as interchangeable. This, in Jahoda's view, was the mark of an impoverished psychology and explained why, against the intellectual trends of the social psychology, she retained her interest in Freud.

As she wrote in her Freud book, academic psychologists separate the different aspects of the person – they either study memory, or emotion, or cognition, etc. For methodological reasons they are very good at dividing up the person, but this routine practice raises the question 'Where is the person in academic psychology?' (Jahoda, 1977, p. 40). In contrast to most experimental psychologists, who are only interested in the briefest of moments of those that they test, Freud maintained that the person as a whole should be understood over time (Jahoda, 1963, p. 114). In Jahoda's view, Freud fully immersed himself in the lives of his patients, just as the Marienthal researchers had sought to immerse themselves in the lives of the unemployed. In consequence, Freud understood that the various parts of a person were interconnected, such as a person's development, motivation, emotion, cognition and social background – in fact, as Jahoda commented, these are the very sub-disciplines into which 'psychology has come to divide its unwieldy subject matter' (1977, p. 49).

Because people's lives are so complex, they are uniquely different. This is one reason why descriptive examples were so important in *Marienthal*. The unemployed were not an aggregate lump. The same devastation of unemployment may have affected nearly all the families in the village, but it affected them in different ways: some families remained unbroken, some were resigned, some were in despair – and, saddest of all, were apathetic families who seemed to have given up all hope as their lives disintegrated. Jahoda, as the report's writer, needed to bring to life different people and different families. She described how some mothers coped resourcefully, managing their meagre budgets with unselfish skill;

others did not manage. It took a woman researcher to realise just how pivotal was the role of the mother in maintaining families, once the men had lost their economic function.

The general trajectory of the families was to go from being unbroken to becoming increasingly broken. The researchers categorised the families under some general headings, such as 'unbroken' or 'resigned'. These categories may suggest similarities between those falling under the heading. The examples were crucial for understanding what the authors meant by their categories. It was more an exercise in ostensive definition. The writer was pointing to a particular family as if saying 'if you want to know what we're calling "a resigned family" was like, then look how this one was just about managing to survive'. But there were always very different ways for families to be 'unbroken' or 'resigned'. Therefore, there needed to be more than one example so that readers of this short book could note differences between the families that the writer might be placing in the same category. What mattered was always the reality of the families, not the categories.

In her final chapter, entitled appropriately 'Fading Resilience', Jahoda offered a series of examples. We see a family 'in despair'. Their house and clothing were spotlessly clean, and the father is sitting on a low stool holding a hammer with a pile of worn-out children's shoes in front of him. He is trying to mend them with roofing felt. He is wearing a faded shirt; he possesses few other clothes, having converted his jackets, spare trousers and overcoat into clothes for the children. He says that on Sundays it's his job to mend the children's shoes so that they can go to school on Monday: 'I don't have to go out but the children must go to school' (Jahoda, Lazarsfeld and Zeisel, 2002, p. 87).

A great artist could have painted the father on his stool in a way that conveys within one image the suffering, the despair and the unselfish spirit. The single scene would then suggest the whole life, not just of one family but of others too. As Ernst Cassirer argued in his *Essay on Man*, art, in contrast to scientific theories, intensifies rather than simplifies – it takes us deeper into the meaning of the particular instance. Marie Jahoda's description of the man sitting on his stool, telling the researcher what he was doing, depicts the specific scene to illustrate the wider pattern of the family's shared life. She was intensifying the scene in ways that a numerical point on a scale could not.

Each family is unique in Jahoda's descriptions, and it is the detail that conveys the book's sense of humanity. Some villagers have lost all hope for the future and yearn for the imagined stability of the past; but there is also the wife who is pleased that her husband can no longer go out drinking with his friends. Some husbands sit around doing little, while others, such as the father on the stool with his children's shoes, help with the home; some fathers grow vegetables in their allotments to supplement the family's diet, and some grow flowers to brighten the home. There are heroes among the victims.

The last example in the book's final chapter cannot have been chosen by chance. Jahoda describes a woman who had once been happily married. Her husband had been killed in the Great War, and she had worked in various jobs to support her children before returning to Marienthal to work in the mill. She was active in the socialist movement, and unlike many others in the village, she had continued to be active even as times became difficult. Her children were now grown, and her sons gave her some money from time to time. Sometimes they took her to see a movie in Vienna. When asked about the happiest time of her life, she replied that it was the present: she was proud of her children, and they were devoted to her. She still had hopes for the future, personally and politically.

Fewer Theories, More Examples

Marie Jahoda's vision of psychology reverses the customary relation between theory and examples. Normally, theory stands above examples. It is said that psychology is a science and that the aim of scientists is to produce predictive, scientific theories. If examples appear at all in psychological reports, then they are there to serve as illustrations for the theoretical distinctions that the scientifically minded psychologist wishes to make. More usually, examples do not make it to experimental reports. In Jahoda's work, however, as theory is ousted from its position of command, so examples fill the vacated space.

We can see this in a statement that she made about Freud. In her view, Freud was a genuine scientist, devoting great efforts to understanding the mind through observation. She argued that 'this effort is inherent in his repeated emphases on observation and its dominance over theory' (Jahoda, 1977, p. 29). The comment is revealing. It suggests a tension between observation and theory, as if the two are in opposition. Just as Jahoda praised Tajfel for taking theory down a step or two in the world of social psychology, so Freud had given theory less prominence than he gave to the details of his patients' lives. If this seems an unusual view of Freud, whom experimentalists often depict as an unempirical bigot devoted to his own theories, then it matches much of what Freud did. He continued to see patients even as his ideas became famous. His most famous theory was his 'Oedipus theory', and his most famous case history, supporting the theory, was the case of Little Hans. Freud's report barely mentions the word 'Oedipus', while it is packed with details and incidents from the life of Hans and his family (Freud, 1909/1990). The details, which are closely observed, cannot be contained by any theoretical description of the Oedipus complex, for they overspill the simplifications of theory.

The word 'observation', which Jahoda used to describe Freud's emphasis, is perhaps not quite accurate, because it is insufficient for an empirically minded psychologist to observe. Psychologists must organise their observations, interpreting what they have seen. Even this is insufficient. The organised observations must then be written – they cannot remain privately within the psychologist's own mind. When they are written, observations become descriptions. These descriptions are not 'mere' descriptions for they are also interpretations. Jahoda was not 'merely' describing the father on his low stool; she was interpreting what he was doing, as well as reporting his own interpretation, and she was using his specific actions to illustrate and to understand the wider circumstances of his family's life. She needed no special theoretical terminology to do this, for ordinary words, including those which were uttered by the father, were more than adequate.

The origins of the Marienthal study perfectly illustrated why Jahoda believed theory to be over-rated. It was not theory that gave rise to the research: it was politics and morality. Without the researchers' commitment to the Social Democrats and without the party's commitment to doing something to help the unemployed, there would have been no study. The researchers did not design the research to test a theoretical prediction. In fact, as Jahoda (1982a, 1983) stressed, the study was not designed in advance: it 'grew organically', and 'improvisation was a permanent feature of all our work' (1983, p. 348). In the words of Rutherford, Unger and Cherry (2011), the Marienthal research represents an approach that situates 'lived human experience, not abstract theory, as central to the formulation of research questions and methods' (p. 48). Because the study was not pre-planned, the researchers depended on their observations. This is how Hans Zeisel came to notice that the men were walking more slowly than the women.

The lack of theory also explains why the study was written without jargon. It had started with a politician's promptings and continued in conversations with the villagers. When Marie Jahoda wrote the main body of the report, she found no need to add words of theory. What she wrote could be understood by specialist and non-specialist alike. The problems of the unemployed were clear, and so were their various reactions to those problems.

Jahoda remained sceptical for the rest of her life whether theory could help researchers observe better. Indeed, she felt that Marienthal remained a model for research, despite Lazarsfeld's misgivings about its so-called methodological blemishes. Nearly fifty years after the original collection of material, Jahoda wrote that 'exclusively theory-oriented research can sometimes function as a straitjacket for thought and observation' (1989, p. 77). If theoretical ideas determine what you are looking for, then you might not properly observe what is happening in front of you. Marie Jahoda was resisting the state of mind that James had identified as 'the psychologist's fallacy'.

Of course, psychological researchers need to explain what is going on, but they do not need to theorise, or generalise abstractly, when they explain. For example, Jahoda explained what the father on his stool was doing and why he was doing it. Her explanation relied on the father's own explanation, and she did not need to add a theory to make his action comprehensible. Her addition was to treat his specific actions as a metonym for wider suffering and courage.

More generally, Jahoda contrasted abstract theories with more homely explanations which do not predict in advance but explain after the event: 'theories are high-level abstractions; explanations are more down to earth'; 'theories tend to ignore deviants; explanations try to encompass them'; 'theories generalize, explanations specify' (1989, p. 77). She could have added to that last difference between theory and explanation Cassirer's comment that theories impoverish, while art intensifies. However, it is not only artists who intensify. Jahoda, when seeking to capture descriptively the lives of the unemployed, was not writing as an artist but as a social scientist. Nevertheless, like an artist, she was specifying what was happening, and her descriptions included the sorts of details that the grids of theories drain away like so much dirty water.

History and Theory

Because Marienthal was the first study of its type, the researchers had little option but to approach their topic naively. There were no theories or previous bodies of evidence to guide them, but such a state of innocence could not last. In future, anyone researching the psychological effects of unemployment would have to take the Marienthal study into account. For empirically minded investigators, there were statistical findings to replicate or refute. Later researchers, if they had done their reading properly, would know about the father on his stool and the mother whose children took her to the cinema.

Because of this, it might perhaps be argued that Marie Jahoda's remarks about theory as a straitjacket on thinking should not be taken too literally. Later researchers have the duty to formulate theories, building on results that are replicated and discounting those that are not. Nevertheless, the goal of producing a solid, predictive theory about the psychology of unemployment has proved elusive. As Jahoda (1982a) noted, later studies did not build up a consistent pattern of evidence. Sometimes researchers found evidence that the economic consequences of unemployment were graver than the psychological ones; and sometimes their results suggested the reverse.

Jahoda observed that both positions have been 'glorified' by the word 'theory' (1982a, p. 356). However, as she stressed, researchers have not produced genuinely predictive theories but explanations of specific phenomena that have already occurred. According to her, no single theory about the psychological impact of unemployment exists, 'and none is likely to emerge' (1982a, p. 357). In her book *Employment and Unemployment*, she wrote that 'there is no single theory that encompasses the full richness of empirical results' (1982b, p. 5). Despite Jahoda's clear criticisms of the limitations of theories and the casual ways that social scientists use the word 'theory', some researchers are so attached to the idea of theories – their own and those of others – that they ascribe to Jahoda a theory of unemployment: 'the latent deprivation theory' (e.g. Janlert and Hammarström, 2009; Sage, 2018).

As was mentioned in the previous chapter, psychologists have a tendency to assume that universal theories are possible; these are theories that are true for all persons, cultures and epochs. Marie Jahoda was aware that the assumption of universality was unrealistic. Like Henri Tajfel and Kenneth Gergen, she recognised that the findings of social psychologists emerge in particular socio-historic contexts which themselves are in the process of changing. Indeed, she pointed out that some things can change more quickly than others. Writing in 1989, she commented that some so-called timeless results of social psychology, such as those of Asch's study of conformity, can no longer be replicated (1989, p. 75).

Jahoda and her colleagues were well aware that the Marienthal, which they were looking at in 1931, was itself in a state of change with the outcome unclear. All conclusions and predictions for the future had to be provisional. As Jahoda wrote in the final chapter, 'how things will continue, we cannot foresee' (Jahoda, Lazarsfeld and Zeisel, 2002, p. 88). It was possible that as conditions deteriorated, the community might rebel in concerted social action; equally it was possible that the bonds of community that were already weakening would dissolve entirely, leaving 'each individual to scramble' after their own salvation (p. 88).

There was another possibility, which the authors only hinted at. Lazarsfeld in his new introduction wrote that the researchers worried that the Nazi movement might provide renewed focus and activity for the fading community. Men, who seemed to have little to do, might be kept busy with paramilitary training and find false order for their chaotic lives (2002, p. xxxiv). In their original report, the researchers did not detail that worry, but they dropped hints. Jahoda wrote that it was impossible to predict how traditional political allegiances would be affected by the newly established branch of the National Socialists in the village (Jahoda, Lazarsfeld and Zeisel, 2002, p. 41). In a delicate, but unelaborated, remark, she noted the economic timetable of the villagers. On the day when unemployment payments were made, the debt collector – the *Ratenjud* or 'instalment Jew' – would call (p. 17). She did not add that the *Ratenjud* did not actually need to be a Jew to be called as such. Nor did she add that it was possible for the most despairing of people to be energised by forces of anger and blame, whose patterns of direction were already ingrained into a community's casual vocabulary.

Even if many members of a despairing, declining community might turn politically towards the extreme Right with its easy targets and its disciplined communal marching, there would be others who would not. There would still be different individual reactions to the shared circumstances. That was why it was important for Jahoda to point out that Tajfel and his fellow researchers had ignored the participants who did not discriminate against members of the other group in the minimal group situation: not all Germans, including those in Austria after the Nazi annexation of 1938, were swept along by the culture of anti-Semitism. Some resisted the force of history's movement, aware that, in time, that too would change. Perhaps some of them lived in Marienthal.

Against the Arrogance of Theory

In her academic work, Marie Jahoda stood against the arrogance of big theory. She always wrote clearly and concisely. Her books were not heavy volumes. *Marienthal* in its English translation is fewer than 130 pages and can be understood by interested non-specialist readers, although Zeisel's afterword on sociography might not hold their attention for long. *Employment and Unemployment* was barely a hundred pages, and in the introduction she wrote that she had tried to avoid 'both jargon and oversimplification' (1982b, p. 3). Jahoda's Freud book, despite containing significant arguments and deep scholarship, is fewer than 200 pages.

Jahoda might have been a Freudian, but she certainly did not write like a Lacanian. The ego psychology that attracted her was the sort of psychoanalysis that Lacan rejected. In *Écrits* he made dismissive comments about Heinz Hartmann, Jahoda's analyst (Lacan, 1966, pp. 490, 599).

Jahoda (1977) was probably the first English-writing social psychologist to cite Lacan, and predictably, she did not mention him favourably. If Lacan is said to have devised 789 neologisms (Bénabou et al., 2002), then that is probably 789 more than Marie Jahoda did. Her prose – unshowy, very much to-the-point and sparing in its use of technical terminology – is not the sort of writing that is currently fashionable amongst those cultural analysts who turn to psycho-analytic theory.

Nor is Jahoda's style of writing the type that tends to bring the big rewards in today's social sciences (Billig, 2013). Jahoda's articles, even those published in specialist academic journals, are short and written in the same clear tone as her books. Some successful academics are bi-lingual in that they can write with heavy technical terminology when publishing articles in specialist journals but use simpler language when writing for students or general readers. Jahoda, a genuinely bi-lingual writer, never switched voices in that way. She always wrote clearly, pre-ferring ordinary words to technical ones. Calling Jahoda's ideas on unem-ployment 'the latent deprivation theory' does her a double injustice. She never packaged and promoted her views as a named theory that could be marketed in the academic world, nor did she line up words to create technical terminology or to impress readers.

In Jahoda's writing, there is no hint of the view expressed in Lewin's famous motto 'There is nothing as practical as a good theory'. In the context of the Marienthal research, the motto would have seemed to be little more than a self-serving platitude. The researchers came to the village trying to give what practical help they could, offering things like second-hand clothes, guidance or classes. Their own Austro-Marxism was, in the word of Jahoda (1983), 'not so much a theory as a view on life' (p. 343). They knew that no theory, however good the theorist believed it to be, would put food on the plates of the poor or clothes on their children. If, instead of providing practical help in return for cooperation with the project, a theorist had told the villagers that 'the researchers were hoping to construct a good theory of unemployment and the villagers should co-operate because there is nothing as practical as a good theory', then you don't need a good theory to guess how the villagers would have responded.

Marie Jahoda's plain way of writing can stand as an example for us today. The politics of bigotry had ensured that the inhabitants of Marienthal would not have had the opportunity to read the great book that she wrote about them. The book had been prevented from reaching academic circles, let alone somewhere as out of the way as Marienthal. Yet, there was little in the main text that would have been inaccessible to those whom the book describes.

Today, we can still have hopes for the future, just as the young Marie Jahoda and her colleagues did. Because of her vivid descriptions in *Marienthal*, we can imagine the characters whom she wrote about. We can also fantasise, imagining them reading the book and recognising themselves in Jahoda's descriptions. Had this been possible, they might have smiled, finding some hope in those printed descriptions which showed that they had not been completely forgotten. When all seems to be failing in practice, the power of description might be able to offer a little bit more than a theory.

9   Concluding Remarks

In the previous chapters I have been looking backwards, discussing the work and lives of historical figures. To a certain extent, each chapter has been self-contained, and some readers will have dipped in to read about a particular person who interests them. The stories of John Locke or of William James are different from those told about Sigmund Freud or Marie Jahoda. I very much hope that readers have enjoyed reading about these writers from the past. Perhaps they will not have known much about some of the more obscure figures, and maybe they will be motivated to find out a bit more about them.

I have not tried to combine these individual stories to tell an overall story about the development of psychology from its early days to the modern era. Nor will I be attempting to outline such a story here in the final chapter. At the same time, this book does not entirely look backwards; nor has each chapter been fully independent of the other chapters. There have been interconnecting themes, especially about the role of examples in psychological writing and about the tensions between theory and examples. Such themes ensure that the book has not been a history book as such, but it has used historical figures and their writings to suggest that it is important to use examples in psychological writing. This argument cannot be purely historical, for it concerns the present and the future.

In this final chapter, I intend to bring together some of the interconnecting themes, but I must stress that I will not be constructing a theory of examples, or even taking preliminary steps towards such a theory. Having praised writers for valuing examples over theory, I am not going to turn tables on them now by saying that the individual studies of historical figures will only prove to have any value if they enable us to advance towards an overall theory of examples.

Nor will I be finally making it clear exactly what an example is or should be. In the course of the previous chapters, I have not offered a definition of 'example', and one should not be expected here. I have been using the word in various senses: often as a synonym for a concrete individual case;

sometimes as an instance which exemplifies an idea or theoretical point; sometimes as someone who should be followed; and sometimes all three, and possibly more, senses together. I will not be using this concluding chapter to tidy up the various senses into separate semantic slots, as if putting pieces of cutlery into different drawers according to whether they come from silver, electro-plated, bone-handled sets, and then sub-dividing each drawer into sections for tea-spoons, soup-spoons, dessert spoons, serving spoons and so on. The lesson to be learnt from Locke, or rather the lesson that Shaftesbury taught in reaction to Locke, was that a neat language with clear and distinct categories is neither attainable nor desirable. As Kurt Lewin did not say: there is nothing as impractical as using language as a cutlery drawer.

On the other hand, it is not necessary to go to the opposite extreme and to assert, in a burst of anti-theoretical enthusiasm, that every particular instance must be dealt with as an isolated example. There are points that can be made by looking across the various historical examples, noting some patterns of similarity and difference, just as some of the preceding chapters have compared pairs of figures. Accordingly, I will not be sug-gesting that the psychological writers from the previous chapters must be kept in isolation from each other, as if any contact between them risks the danger of theoretical infection.

When in the previous chapters I have discussed the featured writers, I have always been looking at more than those writers' use of examples. Their specific writings were not gutted for examples, which then were ripped from their contexts to be analysed purely as literary tropes. In each case, the pieces of work were set in a wider context that embraced the writer's life, theoretical outlook and the times in which they were living. Again and again, a particular point was made: namely, examples overspill the bounds of theory. Similarly, the writers themselves overspill their use of examples. Freud may have collected more than 200 examples of slips of the tongue and lapses of memory for his book *Psychopathology of Everyday Life*, but the book is much more than just a collection of examples, and so was his *Interpretation of Dreams* more than a collection of dreams. As it is for the works, so it is for their author. Freud was much more than a collector, regardless of how avidly he might have collected antiquities, dreams and devotees.

If, at this stage, I were to refuse to look across the chapters, albeit briefly, then readers might conclude that the examination of particular instances – in this case, individual writers and their use of examples – can only throw light on a narrow topic and has no further benefit. Such a suggestion is often made when psychologists or other social scientists conduct a case study of a particular person, episode or place. They face questions that carry a critical tone: How can you generalise from a single case? How do you know whether your example is representative? Perhaps the questioners do not realise that if you want to study a single case properly, then you cannot just study that case. You always have to study more.

C. L. R. James, the great West Indian philosopher and cricket writer, put the point perfectly. He began his semi-autobiographical book on cricket with the maxim 'What do they know of cricket who only cricket know?' (1964, p. 11). His book showed that if you want to understand cricket, or any sport, for that matter, then you must know about more than the particular game, its technical aspects and its statistics, for streams of history, politics, prejudice and so much else besides flow through the game – and through any game. Even if you only want to understand the technical aspects of a sport, then for a proper understanding, you need to know more than just that sport.

So, if someone were to ask me whether I believe that my small sample of writers is representative of all psychologists, I would reply, 'Of course, it isn't'. That does not mean it is valueless. By studying closely particular individuals, we can see how wider social, cultural and historical trends impact on those individual thinkers. Typically such impact appears more vividly in individual cases than in aggregated evidence from representative samples. If we try to follow the maxim of C. L. R. James, then, when we closely examine a particular writer's way of writing psychology, we should be able to see much more than the literary style of that writer. We should try to notice the social movement of ideas, including their past history and even their future direction, in the way that those ideas are being expressed at a particular moment, in a particular place, by a particular writer. The benefit of examining past writers, living under very different conditions from those of today, is that the movement of ideas can be more apparent, because we can see where the particular moment came from and where it was leading to. As C. L. R. James wrote, what matters is not who you are or what you possess, but 'where you have come from, where you are going and the rate at which you are getting there' (1964, pp. 116–17).

Marie Jahoda, who is championed here as the ultimate example of a psychological writer, illustrates to perfection the way that authors colour their works with their lives and thus overspill their works even as they are writing them. In her writing, including her writings about writing and publishing psychology, we see much more than an academic style. We see the person, the times in which she worked, her social wisdom and her courage.

Jahoda's use of examples was never a mere rhetorical adornment, designed to jazz up the sort of weighty tome that, in fact, she never wrote. In consequence, her life and her writings bear lessons for those who might wish to understand more than the effects of unemployment on a particular small community in pre-war Austria. An example, if it is to be an example, has to be an example of something. Jahoda sets an example for us today, for she is an example of a psychologist who produced the sort of socially relevant, clear insight that is capable of capturing the imagination. She did this, not with a structured, formal theory, but with her descriptions of people and especially, to borrow the early title of Locke's *Essay*, with her humane understanding.

I hope that the preceding chapters have demonstrated that not all examples are equal. There are different uses to which examples can be put. If there are patterns, then remarking on them is not tantamount to formulating a theory of examples. Nor does it mean that the particular always has to serve the general. As Abraham Tucker, one of the early heroes in this story of psychological examples, argued in the eighteenth century, we should build our general statements by closely observing concrete cases. Then, and this is the big point, we should not rest content with our generalisations, but we should always bring them back to earth, testing them against further examples taken from ordinary life.

Such further testing cannot be done in this concluding chapter; otherwise, the book would never end, for there would always be much more to be done. Nevertheless, this chapter can, and will, end with some general recommendations. If we want to ensure the humanity of psychology – and Jahoda sets a fine example, as do James and Freud – then we should always be attempting to turn from theories to concrete cases. It will be readers, not the present author, who might return any general recommendations back to earth. In this, they would be following Tucker's advice to ensure that general statements about the human mind lead back to further examples.

Examples and Theory

Of course, examples can be used to advance theories by providing illustrations of key theoretical concepts, but within psychology, that is by no means the sole purpose of examples. They can also be used to illustrate phenomena that do not owe their origins to theory but are part of ordinary, everyday understanding. In addition, they can be situated in the middle, shuttling between theory and ordinary life, showing how the latter will always overspill the simplifications of the former. When examined closely and then described precisely, examples can be a means of discovery.

John Locke provided an example of a psychological writer using an example very much in the service of theory. In the chapter on the association of ideas, which he added to his *Essay Concerning Human Understanding*, Locke discussed and classified different sorts of association. To illustrate the association of antipathies to particular ideas, he provided a hypothetical example: Locke imagined a man who surfeited on honey and then felt sick. Henceforth, whenever this man saw honey, or even heard someone uttering the word 'honey', once again he felt sick.

Clifford Geertz, the American anthropologist, is famous for distinguishing between thin and thick descriptions (Geertz, 1973).[1] To use Geertz's metaphor, Locke's description of the honey-surfeiter was the thinnest of thin descriptions. The surfeiter has no name, and Locke does not say how or why the initial surfeiting might have occurred. Nevertheless, to qualify as an example, any description must contain theoretically surplus details; otherwise, it will be just a restatement of the theory that it is supposedly illustrating. In Locke's example, it was 'honey' that was consumed to excess. It could have been wine, anchovies or sugared bonbons, but it was not. Locke's hypothetical example, therefore, contained a slither of specificity; but it was tightly under the control of theory. In effect, Locke was saying to his readers, if you come across any surprising antipathies, then search for the association of an idea to an unpleasant feeling, as occurred in my hypothetical case of the honey-surfeiter.

In *Marienthal*, Marie Jahoda used examples very differently. She did not use them in the service of theoretical distinctions but to bring alive the conditions of life that the unemployed were being compelled to lead. Throughout the book she backed statistical data with illustrations from life. For instance, she did not just list the foods that the unemployed in her study could afford to eat and those that they could not. Instead, she described the daily diets of several families, illustrating how unhealthy their diets were, as the meanness of their lives closed in. Her descriptions may have been brief in length, but they were thick with emblematic detail.

Jahoda depicted a man seated on a stool, hammering roofing felt onto small shoes. Those who have always lived comfortable lives may find this a strange sight. Geertz suggested that thick descriptions of distant, unfamiliar cultures make them understandable. The starving, unemployed of Marienthal lived in a very different social world than the affluent middle classes did then and do nowadays. Jahoda quoted the man on the stool,

---

[1] Actually, Geertz (1973), as he fully acknowledged, derived the terms 'thick' and 'thin' descriptions from the philosopher Gilbert Ryle. According to Ryle, when philosophers and others describe actions purely in terms of bodily movements (i.e. winking as the closing of one eye), they are giving 'thin' descriptions. 'Thick' descriptions involve describing actions in terms of their meaning (e.g. winking as closing one eye to convey that one is not being serious).

saying that he was repairing his children's shoes so that they could continue to attend school. The description may be brief, but it makes an unfamiliar act immediately understandable.

This man's act of hammering illustrates so much about his circumstances, those of his family and, indeed, those of the other inhabitants of the village. The action of hammering has to be given meaning, for just to describe the mere yielding of the hammer is insufficient. The man on the stool and the boys in Lewin's experiment, who were destroying the sign that they had made, might have been performing physically similar acts, in terms of holding a hammer and swinging their arms, but there is a chasm of meaning differentiating these cases. In Jahoda's description, the man on the stool becomes a symbol for something very different from the boys with the hammers. Moreover, Jahoda required no theoretical category to make the man's act instantly comprehensible.

Psychological writers are not caught between a binary divide of either using examples to illustrate theoretical categories or using them, when thickly described, to make theoretical categories redundant. As has been seen, there are many relations between theory and examples. A writer can use a thickly described example to criticise or to amplify the sparseness of theory. Abraham Tucker deeply admired Locke's *Essay,* and he saw his *Light of Nature Pursued* as adding some examples to the great theoretical structure that Locke had created. Where Locke considered abstractly how people might be moved by feelings, such as hunger or thirst, Tucker produced detailed examples, taken from his own experiences, about his feelings when coming down to dinner or when taking a glass of wine. In all these cases, Tucker's richly observed and thickly described examples show the weakness of Locke's theorising. Here is a case of examples being derived from theoretical categories and then being used to show how weak those categories were when faced with the details of life, not that Tucker wanted to be disrespectful to Locke.

We find something slightly different in William James' *Principles.* James took seriously the notion of 'ideo-motor action', which the neurophysiologist William Carpenter had proposed. However, James found the concept too unspecific. He used as his example how he rose from his warm bed on a cold, winter's morning. He thought closely about the sequence of events and the feelings that led him to make the decision to leave the bed – except that there was no moment of decision because suddenly James was up. It was his body that finally made the decision. James did not discard the category of 'ideo-motor action' but he used his own account to show how such an action might happen and, thus, what the category might mean. The theoretical category becomes understandable in the light of the thick description, rather than vice versa. Previously, the serious-sounding term had sounded as exotic as a distant tribal ritual.

The key point is that when James categorised his getting up as an 'ideo-motor action', he was not adding anything to his thick description. It was the description, and not the theoretical term, that had exposed the every-day action in its detail and thereby had made it understandable. In this way, James had used his specific example as a means of discovering something more general. By taking ordinary examples seriously, Tucker and James were able to draw attention to things that are so familiar that that can be easily overlooked. Everyday actions can hide in plain sight.

There were other writers displaying other relations between theory and examples. Lewin devised a method for producing examples, but he was not content with using ordinary language to describe his examples of children reacting to authoritarian or democratic leadership. He thought it proper to describe his examples in a mathematical language that sub-tracted from, rather than added to, his examples. Then, there were Henri Tajfel and Peretz Bernstein, who suggested that the Holocaust was so historically specific, and so unprecedented, that it should not be treated just as an example of a general theory of prejudice or group relations. No universal theory could explain such an event that was unique in its ferocity and scale, and that marked the lives of Tajfel and Bernstein so directly.

In Freud's writings the relations between theory and examples were particularly complex. His self-analyses were as complex and difficult as Shaftesbury's conversations with himself had been many years earlier: in both cases, there was the constant temptation of self-deception. Unlike Tucker and James, Freud was claiming to have uncovered deeply hidden motives, but when he examined his own slips in everyday life, he did not always offer explanations that cited deeply hidden motives. In his own case, Freud was aware that there were aspects which he could not recount publicly and also that there would be further slips of which he would be unaware. When he analysed, explained and wrote about his forgetting the name of the Italian artist Signorelli, then the very acts of analysing, explaining and writing may have been taking his mind off recent matters that were disturbing to remember.

With Lacan's theory of the mirror stage, which he seemingly proposed to usurp Freud's Oedipus complex as the key childhood event, we see theory triumphing over example. In Lacan's famous paper introducing the idea of a mirror stage, theory appears to stride confidently onwards, as if the theorist feels no obligation to slow down the pace in order to provide supporting examples. The psychological evidence that Lacan airily cites disappears when it is traced back to its sources, but it is not rhetorically replaced by psycho-analytic examples.

As Tucker realised in the eighteenth century, there appears to be tension between examples and theory, as if in adding weight to the one, we lighten the other. We should not assume that there is a universal solution to this tension or even that a solution, which might seem appropriate in one era, would be equally appropriate in another. What might work in the eighteenth century, before the creation of psychology as a discipline, would not necessarily work in the era of James, when psychology and other disciplines were being established; or that either solution would be recognised as appropriate for the twenty-first century when psychology is not just an established discipline, but is a multi-billion-dollar international enterprise.

Today, at least within academic psychology, the balance tilts towards theory rather than examples. Nevertheless, the dominance of theory is not as pronounced as in some other social scientific disciplines. In his book *The Trouble with Theory*, Gavin Kitching (2009) observed that the most promising students in political science are frequently encouraged to take up political theory. Within the discipline of psychology, pure theoreticians are not especially valued, for the leading figures of psychology claim that their discipline is an empirical science. Yet, even in these circumstances, theories can still have the upper hand over examples.

Psychologists often express their preference for theory in a very specific manner. Young psychologists are expected to be empirical scientists and that means that they should seek to test scientific hypotheses empirically. They are taught to present their hypotheses as being derived from psychological theories and their own empirical studies as testing those hypotheses. A 'proper' test involves using samples of respondents and statistically testing aggregated data. Then, 'proper' psychologists should present the results of their test as if they are providing important new evidence that contributes to the further development of theories. The very best of students do not just develop someone else's theory, but they are encouraged to develop their own theories. Gerd Gigerenzer (2010), in his critique of the poor state of theorising in psychology, quotes the remark that psychologists treat theories a bit like toothbrushes: no one likes to use another's.

If writers of research reports test their scientific hypotheses by statistically analysing aggregate scores, as they commonly do, then the rhetorical dominance of theory can be achieved without the appearance of a single example. The rhetorical movement goes from theory to supposedly improved theory via method and group results. Of course, the results of previous experiments will be discussed and presented as if they were examples of the theory, but these examples will typically not contain reports of actual people and concrete incidents, only examples of other example-free experiments and statistical analyses. Over the course of a season with this type of work, theory can defeat examples by many thousands to virtually nil. This is not a competitive league.

Descriptions and Interpretations

If the above argument holds, then any attempt to upgrade examples will involve downgrading theories from their present position. William James' *Principles* finished without a conclusion, but in his *Psychology: Briefer Course*, which was published two years later and which was an abbreviated version of *Principles* intended for students, James added a very short, concluding section – or to be more accurate, a concluding paragraph. In this, he suggested that psychology was not yet a science, but was 'only the hope of a science' (1892, p. 468). If proper sciences should have predictive theories, as James still believed, then nowadays all who enter the discipline of psychology should abandon hope.

Gigerenzer has commented that many theories in psychology amount to little more than tautologies or repetitions of a single term (Gigerenzer, 2008a, 2008b; Gigerenzer and Brighton, 2009). Few such theories have much ability to predict psychological outcomes, and Gigerenzer has demonstrated that laypersons are frequently as good as, if not better than, experts at predicting outcomes. Ordinary people base their predictions on simple factors, while experts, who know about many possible factors, over-complicate their predictions. Where theories fare better, and this includes psychological theories, is in explaining outcomes that have already occurred. Then, the factors, which were relevant to the particular case, may have become apparent to experts. As was discussed in the previous chapter, this was something that Marie Jahoda understood well. She said that most psychological theories did not deserve to be called 'theories' because they were not predictive. They are better seen as 'explanations' because they seek to explain post hoc.

Upgrading the status of examples will entail upgrading descriptions, because examples have to be described. Whether it is Jahoda's man sitting on the stool with his hammer or Tucker rushing down the stairs to his dinner, the action must be put into words. Sometimes in the social sciences, theorists and empirically minded researchers use the phrase 'mere description' as a way of dismissing descriptions. I gave an example of this in the previous chapter, as the empirically minded Paul Lazarsfeld claimed that description was always insufficient for the social sciences. He was suggesting that social scientists need theoretically and empirically determined data rather than 'mere description'. Certainly Kurt Lewin and his followers believed that any description of a psychological action needed to be translated into the language of mathematised theory.

The dismissal of mere descriptions is often based on misunderstanding the nature and value of descriptions. As was suggested in Chapter 6, Lewin favoured mathematical language over description in words, but this involved ignoring an important element in Ernst Cassirer's thinking, which ironically Lewin believed he was following. Cassirer had suggested, using the founder of thermodynamics as his example, that a good description, or what Geertz would call a 'thick description', is also an interpretation. Lewin's description of apathetically passive boys becoming aggressive after their authoritarian leader left the room explains what happened. His mathematically phrased formulae, on the other hand, subtracted details from his descriptions without offering new explanations of what occurred, except to imply that strange 'forces' were producing the observed outcomes. The formulae have little or no value for predicting what might occur the next time a similar episode occurs with a different group of boys.

Jahoda's description of the man on his stool is not just a description of the position of the man's body and the movement of the hammer. As she describes, so she interprets what he is doing. By the same token, when James and Tucker described their own actions, they were simultaneously explaining them, making their behaviour comprehensible, however strange that behaviour might seem when described purely in physical terms. Sometimes by observing closely and using available evidence, as James and Tucker did, it is possible to describe a sequence of events in a way that leads to discovering what the example might possibly be an example of. In these instances, the acts of observing and then describing become means for noticing the previously unnoticed.

In Chapter 4, I looked at Freud's forgetting the name of Signorelli. In his various accounts, Freud was presenting the episode as an example of a lapse of memory and, when the example and its circumstances were described thickly, Freud was able to offer a psycho-analytic explanation for the lapse. In the course of looking at the episode, my focus changed from Freud's forgetting the name to his claims about why he forgot the name. No longer was the episode an example of a lapse of memory, but for me it was becoming an example of how Freud could repress his own troubling, shameful thoughts. In such examples, thickly describing the incidents, and in Freud's case thickly describing the wider context in which the incident occurred, becomes a way of making the incident less mysterious. The resulting descriptions, then, are more than mere descriptions.

As descriptions become thickened, so theoretical explanations can appear comparatively thinned. In the course of the previous chapters,

I have referred on several occasions to Cassirer's view that scientific theories impoverish reality and also to James' comment that theories mutilate reality – and even to Hazlitt's comment that abstraction is a cheat by which half of any subject is ignored. Psychological theories often take episodes, thoughts or actions out of their contexts, strip them of their theoretically superfluous details and then lock them away in a box. The theoretical explanation can lack the depth of understanding that a good description can convey. Lewin and his co-workers seemed unable to comprehend why the children in one of their experiments were behaving in 'peculiar' ways. Lewin's theoretical classification of the incident makes their actions even more 'peculiar', but a longer description of the sequence of events makes the peculiar actions appear not quite so peculiar. James, suddenly finding himself to have risen from his warm bed, was doing more than performing an ideo-motor action. He was getting up to face the day, ceasing to laze about like a good-for-nothing and so on.

If the current balance between theory and examples shifts, then the implications may extend beyond the rhetoric of writing psychology. There may emerge a psychology of examples which currently does not exist. As Gigerenzer (1996) has suggested, when cognitive psychologists produce theories of thinking, they tend to take their own ways of thinking as their model. For example, many cognitive psychologists have modelled thinking on the ways that psychologists make statistical inferences. This may be a particularly pervasive form of psychologist's fallacy. It is also self-praise, as psychologists use a theoretical model that pats themselves collectively on the back for doing what supposedly proper thinkers do. There is a consequence: what psychologists do not do skulks past untheorised, unnoticed and implicitly devalued.

We can see such bias in the way psychologists have studied the use of categories or categorisation. Again, there is a link to the practices of psychologists. Psychological theories need categories which psychologists can apply to their objects of study. In cognitive theories, 'categorisation' is an important concept. Even James, who was often sceptical of the value of theories, applied the notion of 'ideo-motor action' to getting up, thereby locking the particular action inside a more general category. As was mentioned in Chapter 7, Henri Tajfel brilliantly showed the biases of categorisation. A recent study recognises the importance of social categories for understanding the world and for making inductions (or predictions) based on group membership (Liberman, Woodward and Kinzler, 2017). The authors also recognise the problems of uncritically using social categories and seeing people, not as unique individuals, but as members of a social group. This is, of course, just what social psychologists do when they interpret the aggregated responses of their experimental groups and make further predictions.

The problems do not arise from failing to work out whether categorisation is inherently good or bad but from allowing categorisation to stand on its own as a component of thinking. It is as if all that mattered for James was to apply the label 'ideo-motor action' to his experience. What should be acknowledged is how he brilliantly examined the example in its particular detail, rather than just categorising it. When he was examining it, he was, in fact, not categorising it. He was, to use an ugly word that is not greatly used in cognitive psychology, 'particularising' it (Billig, 1987). His real discovery came from this particular, intense scrutiny, not from the application of the general category.

When we describe an event in all its particularity, using it to stand as a unique example for a class of events, we are particularising it. In the previous chapter, I described Marie Jahoda's use of examples as an example of 'metonymic thinking'. The particular person, event or unhealthy diet is not absorbed into the general category but is rescued from it, to be described in its particularity, as it overspills the limitations of the general category. In this respect, particularising is rhetorically the opposite of categorising. Metonymy refers to the practice of letting the particular action stand for a whole class of actions.

We might make a prediction. If describing examples becomes more recognised within psychology, and ceases to be dismissed as 'mere description', then psychologists will begin to create the sort of psychology of examples that is at present lacking. In ordinary life we all engage in exemplifying. For example, we pick out an event and describe that event to a friend when we want to illustrate the strengths or weaknesses of a mutual acquaintance's character. The part is being used to illustrate the whole. When done skilfully, whether in ordinary life, formal rhetoric or in the writings of Tucker, James or Jahoda, this sort of thinking brings insight; it should not be dismissed as concrete thinking, existing on a lower cognitive level than conceptual thinking. When psychologists recognise themselves in their accounts of this type of thinking, then, on the basis of past form, they will put particularising on a footing with categorising. Then we will begin to edge towards a psychology of using examples.

Disadvantages of Theory

The current psychological mind-set is so strongly in favour of theory that it is hard to see how theoretical categories might be a hindrance to understanding, but there are examples to suggest that they can be. Marie Jahoda wrote that the insights of the Marienthal study were possible because the researchers were able to look directly at the social world. They had possessed no prior academic theory, which was telling them what exactly they should be looking for and which was, as it were, standing between them and the villagers. Similarly, James and Tucker could go beyond Locke's theory of mind because, when they examined their own experiences, they were able to rid themselves of theoretical preconceptions, especially those propounded by Locke and his associationist followers. In consequence, they were able to make similar observations about the flow of consciousness that those following the theory of Locke were unable to notice.

Sometimes there are advantages to be gained by looking at the early writings of a thinker before their ideas have become rigid, stiffened or over-systematised. I did not deliberately seek out Freud's *Studies on Hysteria* because it was written before he had fully formulated his psycho-analytic way of thinking. Nevertheless, over the years I have found myself reading and re-reading the book, especially when wanting to find how adults might repress troubling thoughts. Here in the chapter on Freud, when I wanted examples which might help to see how Freud might have pushed an adult memory from his mind, I found them in *Studies on Hysteria*.

Back in the early eighteenth century, Shaftesbury believed that a system was an ingenious way of making you stupid. In the modern era, a theory can also play that role. When James wrote about the psychologist's fallacy, he was warning against the dangers of theory, directing and distorting what psychologists claim to see. Jahoda, too, was arguing for the virtues of researchers freeing themselves from theory – or better still, possessing no theory from which to free themselves. Both saw advantages in observers retaining a sophisticated naivety.[2]

The basic problem is not confined to psychologists. James' contemporary, Thorstein Veblen (1914), using his typically blunt language, warned against 'trained incapacity'. Experts, by virtue of being trained to do one thing expertly, become incapable of doing other things. In another work, Veblen suggested that specialised education widens a student's 'field of ignorance' (1918/1957, p. 163). When scientists become highly

---

[2] The dangers of the psychologist's fallacy persist today, and researchers would do well to heed the warnings of Peter Ashworth (2009). Writing in a journal of qualitative studies, Ashworth suggests that most qualitative researchers, especially those conducting interviews, are prone to the fallacy. When respondents tell them about their experiences, interviewers tend to interpret those experiences in terms of their theories rather than immersing the experiences in the details of the respondents' lives: 'Examples of this can be found in almost any issue of any journal of qualitative research' (Ashworth, 2009, p. 200).

proficient at noticing one set of things, they can fail to see other things. Ludwik Fleck, a bacteriologist with an interest in the philosophy of science, discussed the disadvantages of 'directed perception': scientists can become so over-trained in noticing some details that they cannot observe other phenomena even at a competent level. Fleck gave the example of a surgeon who could spot appendix problems that most other doctors failed to see but who could not, however much he tried, distinguish male from female rats (Fleck, 1935/1986).

Such is the pre-eminence of theory today that is easy to assume that theories give power to a social scientist, and it is just as easy to accept Lewin's maxim that there is nothing so practical as a good theory. However, as James, Tucker and Jahoda in their different ways recognised, there are advantages in undirected perception and untrained capacity. When psychologists, under the influence of theory, lose their intellectual innocence, they can lose much more besides. Like those participating in experiments designed to investigate the effects of prejudice on perception, they sometimes only notice what they expect to see. Looking at social life with a theory can be a bit like observing the world from a television monitor: you only see what the camera team has determined that you see. Reality then becomes, if not a reality show, then at least a theory show.

A Few Recommendations

However interesting the past might be, it is always the next generation that really matters. It is unlikely that psychological ideas and practices in the future will simply reproduce those of today, just as those today have not entirely repeated yesterday's. Therefore, I am ending with a few recommendations that are aimed primarily at post-graduates and young academics, especially those who are hoping to make a career in psychology but who find themselves questioning the prevailing myths and practices of the discipline.

The first recommendation should hardly surprise readers who have worked their way through this book: do not assume that the latest work is necessarily the best work or that it has the most to teach you. Look back at thinkers from psychology's past, but do not look only for the big 'stars'. You might find insights and wisdom in writers who seem to have been forgotten.

If I have concentrated on figures such as Shaftesbury, Tucker and James, do not imagine that they are the main writers worth consulting. They are among my personal favourites, but many, many others from the past deserve to be remembered and re-read, just as there are even more from the present who are best passed over.

And, if you read history, and I would recommend that you do, notice the way that most historians describe and make comprehensible complex events: they generally manage to do this without the clunk-clunk of heavy theory.

Do not be overawed by theory or believe it is necessary to have a theory before you can start researching the world. If anyone senior says to you, 'You must have a theory', just reply, 'Remember Marienthal'. And if anyone says to you, 'There is nothing as practical as a good theory', then ask them for their evidence, or better still, for an example. For good measure, tell them her that there was nothing as impractical as Lewin's own supposedly good theory.

Be conscious of what William James called 'the psychologist's fallacy'. Do not imagine that a methodology will protect you from the dangers and temptations of the psychologist's fallacy. Both quantitative and qualitative researchers can fall foul of the fallacy. Try to aim for a sophisticated naivety.

Make certain to populate your writing, ensuring that you write about people rather than theoretical things or aggregate scores. If you are writing about a general process, then give an extended, thickly described example to show how that process might operate in practice. Students of the mind as diverse as Lewin, Tucker and Freud appreciated that any theoretical description of a process should rest on concrete examples. When examples are examined closely, they can provide a royal route to understanding general processes.

I hope that in your writing, and especially in your choice of examples, you will be doing more than making technical points. May you overspill your examples with your own distinctive character, broad vision and humane understanding!

And finally, to shorten these paragraphs of advice into just five words: *More examples, less theory, please.*

References

Abrams, D. and Hogg, M. A. (1990). *Social Identity Theory*. New York: Springer.

Adorno, T. W., Frenkel-Brunswik, E., Levinson, D. J. and Sanford, R. N. (1951). *The Authoritarian Personality*. New York: Harper.

Ahnert, T. and Manning, S. (eds) (2011). *Character, Self, and Sociability in the Scottish Enlightenment*. New York: Palgrave Macmillan.

Alban, G. M. E. (2017). *The Medusa Gaze in Contemporary Women's Fiction*. Newcastle: Cambridge Scholars.

Alexander, B. K. and Shelton, C. P. (2014). *A History of Psychology in Western Civilization*. Cambridge: Cambridge University Press.

Allen, R. C. (1999). *David Hartley on Human Nature*. Albany: State University of New York Press.

Anderson, P. (1979). *Considerations on Western Marxism*. London: Verso.

Angell, J. R. (1911/1996). William James. In L. Simon (ed), *William James Remembered*. Lincoln: University of Nebraska Press.

Annual Register of the History, Politics and Literature for the Year 1774. (1775). London: J. Dodsley.

Anzieu, D. (1986). *Freud's Self-Analysis*. London: Chatto and Windus.

Appignanesi, L. and Forrester, J. (1993). *Freud's Women*. London: Virago.

Arendt, H. (1958/1998). *The Human Condition*. Chicago: University of Chicago Press.

Arendt, H. (1965/1977). *Eichmann in Jerusalem*. Harmondsworth, UK: Penguin.

Arendt, H. (1970). *Men in Dark Times*. Orlando, FL: Harcourt Brace Jovanovich.

Arendt, H. (1973). Walter Benjamin: 1892–1940. In W. Benjamin (ed), *Illuminations*. London: Fontana/Collins.

Arendt, H. (1978). *The Life of the Mind*. New York: Harcourt.

Aristotle. (1909). *The Rhetoric of Aristotle*. Cambridge: Cambridge University Press.

Asendorpf, J. B., Warkentin, V. and Baudonnière, P. M. (1996). Self-awareness and other-awareness. II. Mirror self-recognition, social contingency awareness, and synchronic imitation. *Developmental Psychology*, 32, 313–21.

Ash, M. G. (1992). Cultural contexts and scientific change in psychology. *American Psychologist*, 47, 198–207.

Ash, M. G. (1998). *Gestalt Psychology in German Culture, 1890–1967*. Cambridge: Cambridge University Press.

Ashworth, P. D. (2009). William James's 'psychologist's fallacy' and contemporary human science research. *International Journal of Qualitative Studies on Health and Well-Being*, 4, 195–206.

Bailey, A. R. (1999). Beyond the fringe: William James on the transitional parts of the stream of consciousness. *Journal of Consciousness Studies*, 6, 141–53.

Baldwin, J. M. (1895). *Mental Development in the Individual and the Race*. London: Macmillan.

Baldwin, J. M. (1897). *Social and Ethical Interpretations in Mental Development: a Study in Social Psychology*. London: Macmillan.

Baldwin, J. M. (1913). *History of Psychology*. London: Watts.

Baldwin, J. M. (1930). Autobiography of James Mark Baldwin. In C. Murchison (ed), *History of Psychology in Autobiography*, vol. 1. Worcester, MA: Clark University Press.

Balibar, E. (2014). Consciousness. In B. Cassin (ed), *Dictionary of Untranslatables*. Princeton, NJ: Princeton University Press.

Bénabou, M., Cornaz, L., de Liège, D. and Pélissier, Y. (2002). *789 Néologismes de Jacques Lacan*. Paris: EPEL.

Benjamin, L. (2007). *A Brief History of Modern Psychology*. Oxford: Blackwell.

Benjamin, W. (1970). *Illuminations*. London: Fontana/Collins.

Benveniste, D. (2014). *The Interwoven Lives of Sigmund, Anna and W. Ernest Freud*. New York: The American Institute for Psychoanalysis.

Berkowitz, L. (1969). The frustration-aggression hypothesis revisited. In L. Berkowitz (ed), *The Roots of Aggression*. New York: Atherton Press.

Berkowitz, L. (1974). Some determinants of impulsive aggression: the role of mediated associations with reinforcements for aggression. *Psychological Review*, 81, 165–76.

Bernstein, F. (1926). *Der Antisemitismus als eine Gruppenerscheinung: Versuch einer Soziologie des Judenhasses*. Berlin: Jüdischer Verlag.

Bernstein, P. F. (1951). *Jew-Hate as a Sociological Problem*. New York: Philosophical Library.

Bernstein, P. F. (1980). *Der Antisemitismus als eine Gruppenerscheinung: Versuch einer Soziologie des Judenhasses*. Königstein: Jüdischer Verlag.

Bernstein, P. F. (2009). *The Social Roots of Discrimination: the Case of the Jews*. Piscataway, NJ: Transaction.

Biber, D. and Conrad, S. (2009). *Register, Genre and Style*. Cambridge: Cambridge University Press.

Biber, D. and Gray, B. (2010). Challenging stereotypes about academic writing: complexity, elaboration, explicitness. *Journal of English for Academic Purposes*, 9, 2–20.

Billig, M. (1987). *Arguing and Thinking*. Cambridge: Cambridge University Press.

Billig, M. (1991). *Ideology and Opinions*. London: Sage.

Billig, M. (1996). Remembering the background of social identity theory. In W. P. Robinson (ed), *Social Groups and Identities*. Oxford: Butterworth Heinemann.

Billig, M. (1999). *Freudian Repression: Conversation Creating the Unconscious*. Cambridge: Cambridge University Press.

Billig, M. (2000). Freud's different versions of forgetting 'Signorelli': rhetoric and repression. *International Journal of Psychoanalysis*, 81, 483–98.

Billig, M. (2002). Henri Tajfel's 'Cognitive aspects of prejudice' and the psychology of bigotry. *British Journal of Social Psychology*, 41, 171–88.

Billig, M. (2005). *Laughter and Ridicule*. London: Sage.

Billig, M. (2006a). A psychoanalytic discursive psychology: from consciousness to unconsciousness. *Discourse Studies*, 8, 17–24.

Billig, M. (2006b). Lacan's misuse of psychology: evidence, rhetoric and the mirror stage. *Theory, Culture & Society*, 23, 1–26.

Billig, M. (2008a). *The Hidden Roots of Critical Psychology*. London: Sage.

Billig, M. (2008b). The language of critical discourse analysis: the case of nominalization. *Discourse & Society*, 19, 783–800.

Billig, M. (2008c). Social representations and repression: examining the first formulations of Freud and Moscovici. *Journal for the Theory of Social Behaviour*, 38, 355–68.

Billig, M. (2011). Writing social psychology: fictional things and unpopulated texts. *British Journal of Social Psychology*, 50, 4–20.

Billig, M. (2013). *Learn to Write Badly: How to Succeed in the Social Sciences*. Cambridge: Cambridge University Press.

Billig, M. (2015a). Kurt Lewin's leadership studies and his legacy to social psychology: Is there nothing as practical as a good theory? *Journal for the Theory of Social Behaviour*, 45, 440–60.

Billig, M. (2015b). The myth of Kurt Lewin and the rhetoric of collective memory in social psychology textbooks. *Theory & Psychology*, 25, 703–18.

Billig, M. (2018a). Positive psychology, humour and the virtues of negative thinking. In F. Maon, A. Lindgreen, J. Vanhamme, R. J. Angell and J. Memery (eds), *Not All Claps and Cheers: Humour in Business and Society Relationships*. Abingdon, UK: Routledge.

Billig, M. (2018b). Those who only know of social psychology know not social psychology: a tribute to Gustav Jahoda's historical approach. *Culture & Psychology*, 24, 282–93.

Billig, M. and Marinho, C. (2017). *The Politics and Rhetoric of Commemoration: How the Portuguese Parliament Celebrates the April Revolution*. London: Bloomsbury.

Bloom, H. (1986). Freud the greatest modern writer. *New York Times Book Review*, March 23, 1, 26–7.

Boag, S. (2010). Repression, suppression and conscious awareness. *Psychoanalytic Psychology*, 27, 164–81.

Boag, S. (2012), *Freudian Repression, the Unconscious and the Dynamics of Repression*, London: Karnac Books.

Boasson, C. (1973/1991). The UNESCO tensions Project, conflict residues and Bernstein's sociology of anti-Semitism. In *In Search of Peace Research*. Basingstoke: Macmillan.

Bond, A. H. and Maciejewski, F. (2007). Did Freud sleep with his wife's sister? An expert interview with Franz Maciejewski, PhD. *Medscape*, May 4. www.medscape.com/viewarticle/555692#vp_1 (Accessed 17 November 2018).

Boring, E. G. (1929). *A History of Experimental Psychology*. New York: D. Appleton Century.

Bowie, M. (1991). *Lacan*. London: Fontana Press.

Boyd, J. (2017). *Travellers in the Third Reich*. London: Elliott and Thompson.

Breger, L. (2000). *Freud: Darkness in the Midst of Vision*. New York: John Wiley.

Breger, L. (2009). *A Dream of Undying Fame: How Freud Betrayed His Mentor and Invented Psycho-analysis*. New York: Basic Books.

Brewer, M. B. and Hewstone, M. (eds) (2004). *Self and Social Identity*. Oxford: Blackwell.

Broad, J. (2006). A woman's influence? John Locke and Damaris Masham on moral accountability. *Journal of the History of Ideas*, 67, 489–510.

Brock, A. C. (1994). Whatever happened to Karl Bühler? *Canadian Psychology*, 35, 319–29.

Brock, A. C. (2006a). Introduction. In A. C. Brock, J. Louw and W. van Hoorn (eds), *Rediscovering the History of Psychology*. New York: Kluwer.

Brock, A. C. (2006b). Rediscovering the history of psychology: interview with Kurt Danziger. *History of Psychology*, 9, 1–16.

Brock, A. C. (2016a). The universal and the particular in psychology and the role of history in explaining both. *Annals of Theoretical Psychology*, 14, 29–46.

Brock, A. C. (2016b). The differing paths of an immigrant couple. *Monitor on Psychology*, 47 (2), 74.

Brock, A. C. (2016c). Introduction: the future of the history of psychology revisited. *History of Psychology*, 19, 175–91.

Bromwich, D. (1999). *Hazlitt: the Mind of a Critic*. New Haven, CT: Yale University Press.

Brown, R. (1995). *Prejudice*. Oxford: Blackwell.

Brown, R., Schipper, A. and Wandersleben, N. (1996). Bibliography of publications of Henri Tajfel. In W. P. Robinson (ed), *Social Groups and Identities*. Oxford: Butterworth Heinemann.

Bühler, C. (1935). *From Birth to Maturity*. London: Routledge and Kegan Paul.

Bühler, C. (1940). *The Child and His Family*. London: Routledge and Kegan Paul.

Bühler, K. (1934/2011). *Theory of Language*. Amsterdam: John Benjamins.

Burke, K. (1974). *The Philosophy of Literary Form*. Berkeley: University of California Press.

Burnes, B. (2004). Kurt Lewin and the planned approach to change: a re-appraisal. *Journal of Management Studies*, 41, 977–1002.

Burnes, B. and Bargal, D. (2017). Kurt Lewin: 70 years on. *Journal of Change Management*, 17, 91–100.

Burnes, B. and Cooke, B. (2013). Kurt Lewin's field theory: a review and re-evaluation. *International Journal of Management Reviews*, 15, 408–25.

Byford, J. and Tileagă, C. (2014). Conclusion: barriers to and promises of inter-disciplinary dialogue between psychology and history. In C. Tileagă and J. Byford (eds), *Psychology and History*. Cambridge: Cambridge University Press.

Capozza, D. and Brown, R. (eds) (2000). *Social Identity Processes*. London: Sage.

Carini, L. (1973). Ernest Cassirer's psychology: II. The nature of thinking. *Journal of the History of the Behavioral Sciences*, 9, 266–9.

Carpenter, W. B. (1879). *Principles of Mental Physiology*. London: C. Kegan Paul.

Carter, D. (2011). *Brief Lives: Sigmund Freud*. London: Hesperus Press.

Cartwright, D. (1978). Theory and practice. *Journal of Social Issues*, 34, 168–80.

Cassirer, E. (1910/1923). *Substance and Function*. Chicago: Open Court.

Cassirer, E. (1923/1955). *The Philosophy of Symbolic Forms: Vol. 1. Language*. New Haven, CT: Yale University Press.

Cassirer, E. (1925/1999). Two letters to Kurt Goldstein. *Science in Context*, 12, 661–7.

Cassirer, E. (1932/1951). *Philosophy of the Enlightenment*. Princeton, NJ: Princeton University Press.

Cassirer, E. (1932/1953). *The Platonic Renaissance in England*. Edinburgh: Thomas Nelson.

Cassirer, E. (1944/1962). *An Essay on Man*. New Haven, CT: Yale University Press.

Cassirer, E. (1953). *Language and Myth*. New York: Dover.

Cassirer, E. (1996). *The Philosophy of Symbolic Forms: Vol. 4. The Metaphysics of Symbolic Forms*. New Haven, CT: Yale University Press.

Christie, R. and Jahoda, M. (eds) (1954). *Studies in the Scope and Method of 'The Authoritarian Personality'*. Glencoe, IL: Free Press.

Colucci, F. P. and Colombo, M. (2018). Dewey and Lewin: a neglected relationship and its current relevance to psychology. *Theory & Psychology*, 28, 20–37.

Colucci, F. P. and Montali, L. (2013). The origins, development and characteristics of critical social psychology in Italy. *Annual Review of Critical Psychology*, 10, 596–621.

Condor (2003). 'The least doubtful promise for the future'? The short history of Tajfel's 'sociopsychological' approach to laboratory experimentation. In J. Lázló and W. Wagner (eds), *Theories and Controversies in Societal Psychology*. Budapest: New Mandate.

Connolly, P. J. (2017). The idea of power and Locke's taxonomy of ideas. *Australasian Journal of Philosophy*, 95, 1–16.

Cook, D. J. (1998). Leibniz on enthusiasm. In A. P. Coudert, R. H. Popkin and G. H. Weiner (eds), *Leibniz, Mysticism and Religion*. Dordrecht, Netherlands: Kluwer.

Cook, S. W. (1990). Marie Jahoda. In A. N. O'Connell and N. F. Russo (eds), *Women in Psychology*. Westport, CT: Greenwood Press.

Crawford, B. V., Kern, A. C. and Needleman, M. H. (2007). *American Literature*. New York: Barnes and Noble.

Crews, F. (1995). *The Memory Wars: Freud's Legacy in Dispute*. New York: New York Review of Books.

Cudworth, R. (1731/1996). *A Treatise Concerning Eternal and Immutable Morality*. Cambridge: Cambridge University Press.

Cummings, S., Bridgman, T. and Brown, K. G. (2016). Unfreezing change as three steps: rethinking Kurt Lewin's legacy for change management. *Human Relations*, 69, 33–60.

Damasio, A. (2006). *Descartes' Error*. London: Vintage.

Danziger, K. (1994a). *Constructing the Subject*. Cambridge: Cambridge University Press.

Danziger, K. (1994b). Does the history of psychology have a future? *Theory & Psychology*, 4, 467–84.

Danziger, K. (1997). *Naming the Mind*. London: Sage.

Danziger, K. (2000). Making social psychology experimental: a conceptual history 1920–1970. *Journal of the History of the Behavioral Sciences*, 36, 329–47.

Danziger, K. (2002). How old is psychology, particularly concepts of memory? *History and Philosophy of Psychology*, 4, 1–12.

Danziger, K. (2003). Prospects of a historical psychology. *History and Philosophy of Psychology Bulletin*, 15 (2), 4–10.

Danziger, K. (2006). Universalism and indigenization in the history of modern psychology. In A. C. Brock (ed), *Internationalizing the History of Psychology*. New York: New York University Press.

Danziger, K. (2009). The holy grail of universality. In T. Teo, P. Stenner and A. Rutherford (eds), *Varieties of Theoretical Psychology*. Ontario: Captus.

Darwall, S. (1995). *The British Moralists and the Internal 'Ought'*. Cambridge: Cambridge University Press.

Darwin, C. (1872). *The Expression of the Emotions in Man and Animals*. London: John Murray.

Darwin, C. (1877). A biographical sketch of an infant. *Mind*, 2, 285–94.

Davidoff, L. (2011). *Thicker than Water: Siblings and Their Relations, 1780–1920*. Oxford: Oxford University Press.

Decker, H. S. (1991). *Freud, Dora and Vienna 1900*. New York: Free Press.

Delfour, F. and Marten, K. (2001). Mirror image processing in three marine mammal species: killer whales (Orcinus orca), false killer whales (Pseudorca crassidens) and California sea lions (Zalophus californianus). *Behavioral Processes*, 53, 181–90.

Delouvée, S., Kalampalikis, N. and Pétard, J.-P. (2011). There is nothing so practical as a good … history: Kurt Lewin's place in the historical chapters of French language social psychology textbooks. *Estudios de Psicologia*, 32, 243–55.

Derry, W. (1966). *Dr Parr: a Portrait of the Whig Dr Johnson*. Oxford: Oxford University Press.

Deutsch, M. (1954). Field theory in social psychology. In G. Lindzey (ed), *Handbook of Social Psychology*. Cambridge, MA: Addison-Wesley.

Deutsch, M. (1973). *The Resolution of Conflict*. New Haven, CT: Yale University Press.

De Veer, M. W., Gallup, G. G., Theall, L. A., van den Bos, R. and Povinelli, D. J. (2003). An 8-year longitudinal study of mirror self-recognition in chimpanzees (Pan troglodytes). *Neuropsychologia*, 41, 229–34.

Dollard, J., Doob, L. W., Miller, N. E., Mowrer, O. H. and Sears, R. R. (1939). *Frustration and Aggression*. New Haven, CT: Yale University Press.

Dumont, K. and Louw, J. (2009). A citation analysis of Henri Tajfel's work on intergroup relations. *International Journal of Psychology*, 44, 46–59.

Edwards, D. and Potter, J. (1992). *Discursive Psychology*. London: Sage.

Ehrenreich, B. (2009). *Smile or Die*. London: Granta.

Eiser, J. R. (1996). Accentuation revisited. In W. P. Robinson (ed), *Social Groups and Identities*. Oxford: Butterworth Heinemann.

Ellemers, N., Spears, R. and Doosje, B. (eds) (1999). *Social Identity*. Oxford: Blackwell.

Erwin, E. (1996). *A Final Accounting: Philosophical and Empirical Issues in Freudian Psychology*. Cambridge, MA: MIT Press.

Evans, D. H. (2015). Unstiffening all our theories: William James and the culture of modernism. In D. H. Evans (ed), *Understanding James, Understanding Modernism*. London: Bloomsbury.

Fleck, C. (1998). The choice between market research and sociography, or: what happened to Lazarsfeld in the United States? In J. Lautman and B.-P. Lécuyer (eds), *Paul Lazarsfeld (1901–1976): la Sociologie de Vienne à New York*. Paris: l'Harmattan.

Fleck, C. (2002). Introduction to the Transaction edition. In M. Jahoda, P. F. Lazarsfeld and H. Zeisel (eds), *Marienthal: the Sociography of an Unemployed Community*. New Brunswick, NJ: Transaction.

Fleck, C. (2011). *A Transatlantic History of the Social Sciences*. London: Bloomsbury.

Fleck, L. (1935/1986). Scientific observation and perception in general. In R. S. Cohen and T. Schnelle (eds), *Cognition and Fact*. Dordrecht, Netherlands: D. S. Reidel.

Forrester, J. (1997). Lacan's debt to Freud: how the Ratman paid off his debt. In T. Dufresne (ed), *Returns of the 'French Freud': Freud, Lacan and Beyond*. New York: Routledge.

Freud, S. (1898/1948). Zum psychischen Mechanismus der Vergesslichkeit. In *Gesammelte Werke*, vol. 1. London: Imago. (Originally published in *Monatsschrift für Psychiatrie und Neurologie*, 1, 436–43).

Freud, S. (1898/1960). The psychical mechanism of forgetfulness. *Standard Edition*, 3.

Freud, S. (1900/1991). *The Interpretation of Dreams*. Harmondsworth, UK: Penguin.

Freud, S. (1901/1948). Zur Psychopathologie des Alltagslebens. In *Gesammelte Werke*, vol. 4. London: Imago.

Freud, S. (1901/1975). *The Psychopathology of Everyday Life*. Harmondsworth, UK: Penguin.

Freud, S. (1905/1991). *Jokes and Their Relation to the Unconscious*. Harmondsworth, UK: Penguin.

Freud, S. (1909/1990). Analysis of a phobia in a five-year-old boy ('Little Hans'). In *Case Histories, I*. Harmondsworth, UK: Penguin.

Freud, S. (1911/1991). From the history of an infantile neurosis (the 'Wolf Man'). In *Case Histories, II*. Harmondsworth, UK: Penguin.

Freud, S. (1913/1993). The claims of psychoanalysis to scientific interest. In *Historical and Expository Works on Psychoanalysis*. Harmondsworth, UK: Penguin.

Freud, S. (1914/1993). On the history of the psychoanalytic movement. In *Historical and Expository Works on Psychoanalysis*. Harmondsworth, UK: Penguin.

Freud, S. (1915/1991). *Introductory Lectures on Psychoanalysis*. Harmondsworth, UK: Penguin.

Freud, S. (1920/1991). Beyond the pleasure principle. In *On Metapsychology*. Harmondsworth, UK: Penguin.

Freud, S. (1921/1985). Group psychology and the analysis of the ego. In *Civilization, Society and Religion*. Harmondswoth, UK: Penguin.

Freud, S. (1925/1993). An autobiographical study. In *Historical and Expository Works on Psychoanalysis*. Harmondsworth, UK: Penguin.

Freud, S. (1926/1993). The question of lay analysis. In *Historical and Expository Works on Psychoanalysis*. Harmondsworth, UK: Penguin.

Freud, S. (1930/1990). The Goethe prize: address delivered in the Goethe House at Frankfurt. In *Art and Literature*. Harmondsworth, UK: Penguin.

Freud, S. (1932/1991). *New Introductory Lectures*. Harmondsworth, UK: Penguin.

Freud, S. (1960). *Letters of Sigmund Freud, 1873–1939*. London: Hogarth Press.

Freud, S. (1985). *The Complete Letters of Sigmund Freud to Wilhelm Fliess, 1887–1904*. Cambridge, MA: Harvard University Press.

Freud, S. and Breuer, J. (1895/1952). *Studien über Hysterie*. In *Gesammelte Werke*, vol. 1. London: Imago.

Freud, S. and Breuer, J. (1895/1991). *Studies on Hysteria*. Harmondsworth, UK: Penguin.

Freud Museum (1998). *20 Maresfield Gardens: a Guide to the Freud Museum*. London: Serpent's Tail.

Frosh, S. (2002). *After Words*. London: Palgrave.

Frosh, S. (2006). *For and Against Psychoanalysis*. London: Routledge.

Fryer, D. (1986). The social psychology of the invisible: an interview with Marie Jahoda. *New Ideas in Psychology*, 4, 107–18.

Fryer, D. (2002). A social scientist for and in the real world: an introduction to the address by Professor Marie Jahoda. In K. Isaksson, C. Hogstedt, C. Eriksson and T. Theorell (eds), *Health Effects of the New Labour Market*. Boston: Springer.

Fryer, D. (2008). Some questions about 'the history of community psychology'. *Journal of Community Psychology*, 36, 572–86.

Gale, B. G. (2016). *Love in Vienna: The Sigmund Freud-Minna Bernays Affair*. Santa Barbara, CA: Praeger.

Gallese, V. and Goldman, A. (1998). Mirror neurons and the simulation theory of mind-reading. *Trends in Cognitive Sciences*, 2, 493–501.

Gallup, G. G. and Suarez, S. D. (1991). Social responding to mirrors in rhesus-monkeys (Macaca-mulatta): effects of temporary mirror removal. *Journal of Comparative Psychology*, 105, 376–9.

Gallup, G. G., Anderson, J. R. and Shillito, D. J. (2002). The mirror test. In M. Bekoff, C. Allen and G. M. Burghardt (eds), *The Cognitive Animal*. Cambridge, MA: MIT Press.

Gallup, G. G., Povinelli, D. J., Suarez, S. D., Anderson, J. R., Lethmate, J. and Menzel, E. W. (1995). Further reflections on self-recognition in primates. *Animal Behaviour*, 50, 1525–32.

Gay, P. (1989). *Freud: a Life for Our Time*. London: Macmillan.

Gay, P. (1990). *Reading Freud*. New Haven, CT: Yale University Press.

Geertz, C. (1973). *The Interpretation of Cultures*. New York: Basic Books.

Gentile, B. F. and Miller, B. O. (eds) (2009). *Foundations of Psychological Thought*. London: Sage.

Gerard, N. (2017). 'Marx was right': lessons from Lewin. *The Industrial-Organizational Psychologist*, 54 (4), 83–6.

Gergen, K. J. (1973). Social psychology as history. *Journal of Personality and Social Psychology*, 26, 309–20.

Gibson, J. J. (1983). *The Senses Considered as Perceptual Systems*. Westport, CT: Greenwood.

Gibson, J. J. (1986). *The Ecological Approach to Visual Perception*. London: Routledge.

Gibson, S. (2018). *Arguing, Obeying and Defying: a Rhetorical Perspective on Stanley Milgram's Obedience Experiments*. Cambridge: Cambridge University Press.

Gigerenzer, G. (1996). From tools to theories: discoveries in cognitive psychology. In C. F. Graumann and K. J. Gergen (eds), *Historical Dimensions of Psychological Discourse*. Cambridge: Cambridge University Press.

Gigerenzer, G. (2008a). *Gut Feelings: Short Cuts to Better Decision Making*. London: Penguin.

Gigerenzer, G. (2008b). Why heuristics work. *Perspectives on Psychological Science*, 3, 20–29.

Gigerenzer, G. (2010). Personal reflections on theory and psychology. *Theory & Psychology*, 20, 733–43.

Gigerenzer, G. and Brighton, H. (2009). Homo heuristicus: why biased minds make better inferences. *Topics in Cognitive Science*, 1, 107–43.

Gitre, E. J. K. (2006). William James on divine intimacy: psychical research, cosmological realism and a circumscribed re-reading of The Varieties of Religious Experience. *History of the Human Sciences*, 19, 1–21.

Glassman, R. B. and Buckingham, H. W. (2007). David Hartley's neural vibrations and psychological associations. In H. Whitaker, C. U. M. Smith and S. Finger (eds), *Brain, Mind and Medicine*. New York: Springer.

Gloy, T. (2015). Fritz Bernsteins Soziologie des Judenshasses. In H. J. Hahn and O. Kistenmacher (eds), *Beschreibungsversuche der Judenfeindschaft: Zur Geschichte der Antisemitismusforschung vor 1944*. Oldenbourg: de Gruyter.

Gold, M. (ed) (1999). *The Complete Social Scientist: a Kurt Lewin Reader*. Washington, DC: American Psychological Association.

Goldstein, K. (1940). *The Organism: a Holistic Approach to Biology*. New York: American Book Co.

Goldstein, K. (1948). *Language and Language Disturbances*. New York: Grune and Stratton.

Gombrich, E. H. (1960). *Art and Illusion*. London: Phaidon.

Goodwin, C. J. (2015). *A History of Modern Psychology*. Hoboken, NJ: John Wiley.

Gottfried, P. E. (2005). *The Strange Death of Marxism*. Columbia: University of Missouri Press.

Granzotto, E. (1974). 'This so-called crisis. It does not exist' – Interview with Jacques Lacan. *Panorama*. www.critical-theory.com/this-so-called-crisis-it-does-not-exist-jacques-lacan-on-psychoanalysis-in-1974/ (Accessed 21 October 2018).

Grayling, A. C. (2000). *The Quarrel of the Age: the Life and Times of William Hazlitt*. London: Phoenix Press.

Grayling, A. C. (2002). Freud's genius as author and ideologue. *Guardian Review*, June 22, 5–7.

Greenwood, J. D. (2015). *A Conceptual History of Psychology*. Cambridge: Cambridge University Press.

Gregory, R. L. (1994). *Even Odder Perceptions*. London: Routledge.

Grünbaum, A. (1984). *The Foundations of Psychoanalysis*. Berkeley: University of California Press.

Guillaume, P. (1926/1971). *Imitation in Children*. Chicago: University of Chicago Press.

Hadot, P. (1995). *Philosophy as a Way of Life*. Oxford: Blackwell.

Halawa, M. A. (2009). Karl Bühler's and Ernst Cassirer's semiotic conceptions of man. *Verbum*, 31, 65–88.

Hall, G. S. (1906). *Youth: Its Education, Regimen and Hygiene*. New York: Appleton.

Hall, G. S. (1923). *Life and Confessions of a Psychologist*. New York: Appleton.

Halliday, M. A. K. (2006). *The Language of Science*. London: Continuum.

Harré, R. and Gillett, G. (1994). *The Discursive Mind*. London: Sage.

Hartley, D. (1749/1834). *Observations on Man, His Frame, His Duty and His Expectations*. London: Thomas Tegg.

Hazlitt, W. (1807). Preface. In W. Hazlitt (ed), *An Abridgement of 'The Light of Nature Pursued' by Abraham Tucker*. London: J. Johnson.

Henderson, G. E. (2017). Dialogism versus monologism: Burke, Bakhtin, and the languages of social change. *Journal of the Kenneth Burke Society*, 13 (1). http://kbjournal.org/henderson-on-burke-and-bakhtin (Accessed 28 January 2019).

Henley, T. B. (2007). Remembering William James. In A. Brook (ed), *The Prehistory of Cognitive Psychology*. London: Palgrave Macmillan.

Herder, J. G. (1765/2008). How philosophy can become more universal and more useful for the benefit of the people. In *Philosophical Writings*. Cambridge: Cambridge University Press.

Hergenhahn, B. R. (2001). *An Introduction to the History of Psychology*. Belmont, CA: Wadsworth Thomson.

Hermans, H. (2018). *A Society in the Self*. Oxford: Oxford University Press.

Hermans H. and Gieser, T. (eds) (2014). *Handbook of Dialogical Self Theory*. Cambridge: Cambridge University Press.

Hermans, H. and Hermans-Konopka, A. (2010). *Dialogical Self Theory*. Cambridge: Cambridge University Press.

Hilgard, E. R. (1987). *Psychology in America*. San Diego, CA: Harcourt Brace Jovanovich.

Hirschmüller, A. (2007). Evidence for a sexual relationship between Sigmund Freud and Minna Bernays? *American Imago*, 64, 125–9.

Hodgson, S. H. (1865). *Time and Space*. London: Longman Green.

Hodgson, S. H. (1870). *The Theory of Practice*. London: Longmans, Green, Reader and Dyer.

Hodgson, S. H. (1878). *The Philosophy of Reflection*. London: Longmans, Green.

Hodgson, S. H. (1898). *The Metaphysic of Experience*. London: Longmans, Green.

Homer, S. (2005). *Jacques Lacan*. Abingdon, UK: Routledge.

Hook, D. (2012). *A Critical Psychology of the Postcolonial*. London: Psychology Press.

Horley, J. (2001). After 'the Baltimore Affair': James Mark Baldwin's life and work, 1908–1934. *History of Psychology*, 4, 24–33.

Hothersall, D. (2004). *History of Psychology*. New York: McGraw-Hill.

Hume, D. (1739/1964). *A Treatise of Human Nature*. London: Dent.

Hux, S. (2017). Freud again. *New English Review*, November. www.newenglishreview
.org/Samuel_Hux/Freud_Again/ (Accessed 28 January 2018).

Hyland, K. (2009). *Academic Discourse*. London: Continuum.

Jacobs, J. (2015). *The Frankfurt School, Jewish Lives and Antisemitism*. Cambridge: Cambridge University Press.

Jacobson, A. J. (2007). Doing it his way: Hume's theory of ideas and contemporary cognitive science. In A. Brook (ed), *The Prehistory of Cognitive Psychology*. Basingstoke, UK: Palgrave Macmillan.

Jahoda, G. (2004). Henri Tajfel. In *Oxford Dictionary of National Biography*. Oxford: Oxford University Press.

Jahoda, G. (2016). Seventy years of social psychology: a cultural and personal critique. *Journal of Social and Political Psychology*, 4, 364–80.

Jahoda, M. (1959). Conformity and independence: a psychological analysis. *Human Relations*, 12, 99–120.

Jahoda, M. (1963). Some notes on the influence of psycho-analytic ideas on American psychology. *Human Relations*, 16, 111–29.

Jahoda, M. (1969). The migration of psychoanalysis: its impact on American psychology. In D. Fleming and B. Bailyn (eds), *The Intellectual Migration: Europe and America, 1930–1960*. Cambridge, MA: Harvard University Press.

Jahoda, M. (1970). A time to speak or a time to keep silent? *International Journal of Psychology*, 5, 145–8.

Jahoda, M. (1977). *Freud and the Dilemmas of Psychology*. London: Hogarth Press.

Jahoda, M. (1981a). To publish or not to publish? *Journal of Social Issues*, 37, 208–20.

Jahoda, M. (1981b). Review: H. Tajfel. Human Groups and Social Categories. *Psychological Medicine*, 11, 860–61.

Jahoda, M. (1982a). Reflections on Marienthal and after. *Journal of Occupational and Organizational Psychology*, 65, 355–8.

Jahoda, M. (1982b). *Employment and Unemployment*. Cambridge: Cambridge University Press.

Jahoda, M. (1983). The emergence of social psychology in Vienna: an exercise in long term memory. *British Journal of Social Psychology*, 22, 343–9.

Jahoda, M. (1989). Why a non-reductionist social psychology is almost too difficult to be tackled, but too fascinating to be left alone. *British Journal of Social Psychology*, 28, 71–8.

Jahoda, M., Lazarsfeld, P. F. and Zeisel, H. (2002). *Marienthal: the Sociography of an Unemployed Community*. New Brunswick, NJ: Transaction.

Jalley, É. (1998). *Freud, Wallon, Lacan: l'Enfant au Miroir*. Paris: EPEL.

James, C. L. R. (1964). *Beyond a Boundary*. London: Sportsman's Book Club.

James, H. (ed) (1926). *The Letters of William James*. Boston: Little, Brown.

James, W. (1890). *The Principles of Psychology*. London: Macmillan.

James, W. (1892). *Psychology: Briefer Course*. London: Macmillan.

James, W. (1899). *Talks to Teachers on Psychology*. London: Longmans, Green.

James, W. (1902). *Varieties of Religious Experience*. London: Longmans, Green.

James, W. (1908a). *The Will to Believe*. London: Longmans, Green.

James, W. (1908b). *Pragmatism*. London: Longmans, Green.

James, W. (1911). *Memories and Studies*. London: Longmans, Green.

Janlert, U. and Hammarström, A. (2009). Which theory is best? Explanatory models of the relationship between unemployment and health. *BMC Public Health*, 9, 235.

Janover, M. (2011). Politics and worldliness in the thought of Hannah Arendt. In A. Yeatman, P. Hansen, M. Zolkos and C. Barbour (eds), *Action and Appearance*. London: Bloomsbury.

Jay, D. (1984). *Marxism and Totality*. Oxford: Polity Press.

John, M., Eckardt, G. and Hiebsch, H. (1989). Kurt Lewin's early intentions (dedicated to his 100th birthday). *European Journal of Social Psychology*, 19, 163–9.

Jones, E. (1964). *The Life and Works of Sigmund Freud*. Harmondsworth, UK: Penguin.

Kaposi, D. (2017). The resistance experiments: morality, authority and obedience in Stanley Milgram's account. *Journal for the Theory of Social Behaviour*, 47, 382–401.

Kardas, E. P. (2014). *History of Psychology: the Making of a Science*. Belmont, CA: Wadsworth.

Keenan, J. P., Gallup, G. G. and Falk, D. (2003). *The Face in the Mirror*. New York: Ecco.

Kellner, D. (1977). Korsch's revolutionary Marxism. In D. Kellner (ed), *Karl Korsch: Revolutionary Theory*. Austin: University of Texas Press.

King, D. B. and Wertheimer, M. (2005). *Max Wertheimer and Gestalt Theory*. New Brunswick, NJ: Transaction.

King, D. B. and Woody, W. D. (2016). *A History of Psychology*. New York: Routledge.

Kitching, G. (2009). *The Trouble with Theory*. Sydney, NSW: Allen & Unwin.

Klein, L. (2009). Jahoda, Marie. In *Dictionary of National Biography*. Oxford: Oxford University Press.

Kleist, E. E. (2000). *Judging Appearances*. Dordrecht, Netherlands: Springer.

Knott, M. L. (2015). *Unlearning with Hannah Arendt*. London: Granta Books.

Koffka, K. (1928). *The Growth of the Mind*. New York: Harcourt, Brace.

Köhler, E. (1926). *Die Persönlichkeit des dreijährigen Kindes*. Leipzig: S. Hirzel.

Köhler, W. (1925/1973). *The Mentality of Apes*. London: Routledge and Kegan Paul.

Köhler, W. (1929). *Gestalt Psychology*. New York: Horace Liveright.

Korsch, K. (1938/2016). *Karl Marx*. Leiden: Brill.

Korsch, K. (1975). What is socialization? A programme of practical socialism. *New German Critique*, 6, 60–81.

Korsch, K. (1977). Fundamentals of socialization. In D. Kellner (ed), *Karl Korsch: Revolutionary Theory*. Austin: University of Texas Press.

Korsch, K. (2013). *Marxism and Philosophy*. London: Verso.

Krah, F. (2016). *Ein Ungeheuer, das wenigstens theoretisch besiegt sein muss: Pioniere der Antisemitismusforschung in Deutschland*. Frankfurt: Campus.

Krohn, W. O. (1895). *Practical Lessons in Psychology*. Chicago: Werner.

Krois, J. M. (2004). Ernst Cassirer's philosophy of biology. *Sign Systems Studies*, 32, 277–95.

Lacan, J. (1948). L'agressivité en psychanalyse. *Revue Française de Psychanalyse*, 12, 367–88.

Lacan, J. (1949). Le stade du miroir comme formateur de la fonction du je, telle qu'elle nous est révélée, dans l'expérience psychanalytique. *Revue Française de Psychanalyse*, 13, 449–55.

Lacan, J. (1966). *Écrits*. Paris: Seuil.

Lacan, J. (1970). *Le Séminaire, Livre I: les Écrits techniques de Freud*. Paris: Seuil.

Lacan, J. (1977). *Écrits: a Selection*, trans. A. Sheridan. London: Tavistock.

Lacan, J. (1980). *Television*, trans. D. Hollier, R. Krauss and A. Michelson. New York: W. W. Norton.

Lacan, J. (1988). *The Seminar of Jacques Lacan. Book 1, Freud's Papers on Technique 1953–1954*, trans. J.-A. Miller. New York: W. W. Norton.

Lacan, J. (1991). *The Four Fundamental Concepts of Psycho-Analysis*, trans. A. Sheridan. Harmondsworth, UK: Penguin.

Lacan, J. (1993). *The Seminar of Jacques Lacan. Book III, The Psychoses*, trans. R. Grigg. London: Routledge.

Lacan, J. (2002). *Écrits: a Selection*, trans. B. Fink. New York: W. W. Norton.

Lacan, J. (2007). *Écrits: the First Complete Edition in English*, trans. B. Fink. New York: W. W. Norton.

Lähteenmäki, V. (2014). Locke and active perception. In J. F. Silva and M. Yrjönsuuri (eds), *Active Perception in the History of Philosophy*. New York: Springer.

Laplanche, J. and Pontalis, J.-B. (1983). *The Language of Psycho-Analysis*. London: Hogarth Press.

Lazarsfeld, P. F. (1969). An episode in the history of social research: a memoir. In D. Fleming and B. Bailyn (eds), *The Intellectual Migration: Europe and America, 1930–1960*. Cambridge, MA: Harvard University Press.

Lazarsfeld, P. F. (2002). Foreword to the American edition: forty years later. In M. Jahoda, P. F. Lazarsfeld and H. Zeisel (eds), *Marienthal: the Sociography of an Unemployed Community*. New Brunswick, NJ: Transaction.

Leahey, T. H. (2017). *A History of Psychology from Antiquity to Modernity*. Abingdon, UK: Routledge.

Leary, D. E. (1990). William James on the self and personality: clearing the ground for subsequent theorists, researchers and practitioners. In M. G. Johnson and T. B. Henley (eds), *Reflections on 'The Principles of Psychology'*. Hillsdale, NJ: Lawrence Erlbaum.

Leary, D. E. (2007). Instead of Erklären and Verstehen: William James on human understanding. In U. Feest (ed), *Historical Perspectives on Erklären and Verstehen*. Berlin: Max Plank.

Leary, D. E. (2013). A moralist in an age of scientific analysis and scepticism: habit in the life and work of William James. In T. Sparrow and A. Hutchinson (eds), *A History of Habit*, Lanham, MD: Lexington Books.

Leary, D. E. (2018). *The Routledge Guidebook to James's 'Principles of Psychology'*. Abingdon, UK: Routledge.

Ledlow, G. R. and Coppola, M. N. (2011). *Leadership for Health Professionals*. London: Jones and Bartlett Learning.

Leventhal, R. S. (1990). Critique of subjectivity: Herder's foundation of the human sciences. In K. Mueller-Vollmer (ed), *Herder Today*. Berlin: Walter de Gruyter.

Levine, R. (2008). Introduction. In R. Levine, A. Rodrigues and L. Zelezny (eds), *Journeys in Social Psychology*. Hove, UK: Psychology Press.

Levine, R., Rodrigues, A. and Zelezny, L. (eds) (2008). *Journeys in Social Psychology*. Hove, UK: Psychology Press.

Lewin, G. and Lewin, K. (1941/1999). Democracy and the school. In M. Gold (ed), *The Complete Social Scientist: a Kurt Lewin Reader*. Washington, DC: American Psychological Association.

Lewin, K. (1920/1999). Socializing the Taylor system. In M. Gold (ed), *The Complete Social Scientist: a Kurt Lewin Reader*. Washington, DC: American Psychological Association.

Lewin, K. (1926/1938). Will and needs. In W. D. Ellis (ed), *A Source Book of Gestalt Psychology*. London: Kegan Paul, French, Trubner.

Lewin, K. (1931/1999). The conflict between Aristotelian and Galileian modes of thought in contemporary psychology. In M. Gold (ed), *The Complete Social Scientist: a Kurt Lewin Reader*. Washington, DC: American Psychological Association.

Lewin, K. (1932). Book review: Murphy, Gardner, and Louis Barclay Murphy, Experimental Social Psychology. *Zeitschrift für Sozialforschung*, 1, 169–70.

Lewin, K. (1936). *Principles of Topological Psychology*. New York: McGraw-Hill.

Lewin, K. (1938). *The Conceptual Representation and the Measurement of Psychological Forces*. Durham, NC: Duke University Press.

Lewin, K. (1946/1997). Behaviour and development as a function of the total situation. In *Resolving Social Conflicts and Field Theory in Social Science*. Washington, DC: American Psychological Association.

Lewin, K. (1947/1997). Frontiers in group dynamics. In *Resolving Social Conflicts and Field Theory in Social Science*. Washington, DC: American Psychological Association.

Lewin, K. (1948). *Resolving Social Conflicts*. New York: Harper and Brothers.

Lewin, K. (1949/1999). Cassirer's philosophy of science and the social sciences. In M. Gold (ed), *The Complete Social Scientist: a Kurt Lewin Reader*. Washington, DC: American Psychological Association.

Lewin, K. (1951/1997). *Field Theory in Social Science*. Washington, DC: American Psychological Association.

Lewin, K. and Korsch, K. (1976). Mathematical constructs in psychology and sociology. *The Journal of Unified Science (Erkenntnis)*, 8, 397–403.

Lewin, K. and Lippitt, R. (1938). An experimental approach to the study of autocracy and democracy: a preliminary note. *Sociometry*, 1, 292–300.

Lewin, K., Lippitt, R. and White, R. K. (1939/1999). Patterns of aggressive behaviour in experimentally created 'social climates'. In M. Gold (ed), *The Complete Social Scientist: a Kurt Lewin Reader*. Washington, DC: American Psychological Association. (Originally published in *Journal of Social Psychology*, 10, 271–99).

Lewin, K., Meyers, C. E., Kalhorn, J., Farber, M. L. and French, J. R. P. (1944). *Authority and Frustration*. University of Iowa Studies in Child Welfare 20. Iowa City: University of Iowa Press.

Lewin, M. A. (1977). Kurt Lewin's view of social psychology: the crisis of 1977 and the crisis of 1927. *Personality and Social Psychology Bulletin*, 3, 159–72.

Lewin, M. A. (1998). Kurt Lewin: his psychology and a daughter's recollections. In G. A. Kimble and M. Wertheimer (eds), *Portraits of Pioneers of Psychology*, vol. III. Washington, DC: American Psychological Association.

Lezaun, J. and Calvillo, N. (2014). In the political laboratory: Kurt Lewin's atmospheres. *Journal of Cultural Economy*, 7, 434–57.

Liberman, Z., Woodward, A. L. and Kinzler, K. D. (2017). The origins of social categorization. *Trends in Cognitive Sciences*, 21, 556–68.

Lindzey, G. (ed) (1954). *Handbook of Social Psychology*. Cambridge MA: Addison-Wesley.

Lippitt, R. (1940). An experimental study of the effect of democratic and authoritarian group atmospheres. *University of Iowa Studies in Child Welfare*, 16, 43–195.

Lippitt, R. and White, R. K. (1958). An experimental study of leadership and group life. In E. E. Maccoby, T. M. Newcomb and E. L. Hartley (eds), *Readings in Social Psychology*. New York: Holt, Rinehart and Winston.

Lippman, R. (2008). Freud's failure to recall the name of Luca Signorelli. *International Psychoanalysis*. http://internationalpsychoanalysis-net.ipbooks.net/20 08/07/17/freud%E2%80%99s-failure-to-recall-the-name-of-luca-signorelli-by-robert-lippman/ (Accessed 25 November 2018).

Littlemore, J. (2015). *Metonymy*. Cambridge: Cambridge University Press.

Locke, J. (1690). *An Essay Concerning Human Understanding*. London: Thomas Basset.

Locke, J. (1694). *An Essay Concerning Human Understanding*. 3nd edn. London: Awnsham and John Churchil.

Locke, J. (1700). *An Essay Concerning Human Understanding*. 4th edn. London: Awnsham and John Churchil.

Locke, J. (1706). *An Essay Concerning Human Understanding*. 5th edn. London: Awnsham and John Churchil.

Locke, J. (1824/2002). *Collected Works of John Locke*. Carmel: Liberty Fund. https://oll.libertyfund.org/titles/locke-the-works-of-john-locke-in-nine-volumes (Accessed 25 November 2018).

Lothane, Z. (2007). Sigmund Freud and Minna Bernays: primal curiosity, primal scenes, primal fantasies: and prevarication. *Psychoanalytic Psychology*, 24, 487–95.

Lothane, Z. (2009). Sigmund Freud and Minna Bernays: primal curiosity, primal scenes, primal fantasies: and prevarication. *Forum*, 53, 17–19.

Ludwig, D. (2012). Language and human nature: Kurt Goldstein's neurolinguistic foundation of a holistic philosophy. *Journal of the History of the Behavioral Sciences*, 48, 40–54.

MacCannell, J. F. (1986). *Figuring Lacan*. London: Croom Helm.

Maciejewski, F. (2007). Freud, his wife and his 'wife'. *American Imago*, 63, 497–506.

Maciejewski, F. (2008). Minna Bernays as 'Mrs. Freud': what sort of relationship did Sigmund Freud have with his sister-in-law? *American Imago*, 65, 1–21.

MacKinnon, K. (2001). Curiously, fetishism can be fun. *Film-Philosophy*, 5 (4), 59–61.

MacMartin, C. and Winston, A. C. (2000). The rhetoric of experimental social psychology, 1930–1960: from caution to enthusiasm. *Journal of the History of the Behavioral Sciences*, 36, 349–64.

Mahony, P. J. (1987). *Psychoanalysis and Discourse*. London: Tavistock.

Mandler, G. (2007). *A History of Modern Experimental Psychology: from James and Wundt to Cognitive Science*. Cambridge, MA: MIT Press.

Marková, I. (2016). *The Dialogical Mind*. Cambridge: Cambridge University Press.

Marková, I. (ed) (2018). Across culture, mind and history [special issue]. *Culture & Psychology*, 24 (3).

Marková, I. and Jesuino, J. C. (2018). Social psychology as a developmental discipline in the dynamics of practical life: Gustav Jahoda's pioneering studies on children's social thinking. *Culture & Psychology*, 24, 343–57.

Marrow, A. J. (1969). *The Practical Theorist: the Life and Work of Kurt Lewin*. New York: Basic Books.

Marten, K. and Psarakos, S. (1995). Using self-view television to distinguish between self-examination and social behaviour in the bottlenose dolphin (Tursiops Truncatus). *Consciousness and Cognition*, 4, 205–24.

Martin, R. and Barresi, J. (2000). *Naturalization of the Soul*. London: Routledge.

Marx, K. and Engels, F. (1848/2004). Communist manifesto. In *Karl Marx (with Friedrich Engels)*. London: Collectors' Library of Essential Thinkers.

Mayer, A. (2001–2). Introspective hypnotism and Freud's self-analysis: procedures of self-observation in clinical practice. *Revue d'Histoire des Sciences Humaines*, 5, 171–96.

McLeod, S. (2007). Social psychology. *Simply Psychology*, www.simplypsychology.org/social-psychology.html (Accessed 4 September 2018).

Mercier, H. and Sperber, D. (2011). Why do humans reason? Arguments for an argumentative theory. *Behavioral and Brain Sciences*, 34, 57–111.

Mildmay, H. P. St. J. (1831). Some account of the life of Abraham Tucker, Esq. In A. Tucker, *The Light of Nature Pursued*, vol. 1. Cambridge: Hilliard and Brown.

Milgram, S. (1974). *Obedience to Authority*. London: Tavistock.

Mitchell, R. W. (1997). Kinesthetic-visual matching and the self-concept as explanations of mirror-self-recognition. *Journal for the Theory of Social Behaviour*, 27, 17–39.

Moghaddam, F. M. and Lee, N. (2006). Double reification: the process of universalizing psychology in the three worlds. In A. C. Brock (ed), *Internationalizing the History of Psychology*. New York: New York University Press.

Morrison, R. and Reiss, D. (2018). Precocious development of self-awareness in dolphins. *Plos One*, 13 (1), e0189813.

Moscovici, S. and Marková, I. (2006). *The Making of Modern Social Psychology*. Cambridge: Polity.

Mühlhäusler, P. and Harré, R. (1990). *Pronouns and People*. Oxford: Basil Blackwell.

Müller, R. (2012). The Marienthal study. University of Graz. http://agso.uni-graz.at/marienthal/e/study/00.htm (Accessed 28 September 2018).

Mulligan, K. (1997). The essence of language: Wittgenstein's builders and Bühler's bricks. *Revue de Métaphysique et de Morale*, 2, 193–216.

Mulvey, L. (1975). Visual pleasure and narrative cinema. *Screen*, 16, 6–18.

Mummendey, A., Linneweber, W. and Löschper, G. (1984). Aggression: from act to interaction. In A. Mummendey (ed), *Social Psychology of Aggression*. Berlin: Springer.

Munger, M. P. (2003). *The History of Psychology*. Oxford: Oxford University Press.

Münsterberg, H. (1907/1996). Professor James as a psychologist. In L. Simon (ed), *William James Remembered*. Lincoln: University of Nebraska Press.

Murphy, G. and Murphy, L. B. (1931). *Experimental Social Psychology*. New York: Harper and Brothers.

Murphy, G., Murphy, L. B. and Newcomb, T. M. (1937). *Experimental Social Psychology*. 2nd edn. New York: Harper and Brothers

Myers, G. E. (1997). Pragmatism and introspective psychology. In R. A. Putnam (ed), *The Cambridge Companion to William James*. Cambridge: Cambridge University Press.

Neurath, P. (1995). Sixty years since 'Marienthal'. *Canadian Journal of Sociology*, 20, 91–105.

Nobus, D. (2016). Psychoanalysis as *gai saber*: toward a new episteme of laughter. In P. Gherovici and M. Steinkoler (eds), *Lacan, Psychoanalysis and Comedy*. New York: Cambridge University Press.

Nobus, D. (2017a). Preface. In D. Nobus (cd), *Key Concepts of Lacanian Psychoanalysis*. London: Karnac.

Nobus, D. (2017b). Life and death in the glass: a new look at the mirror stage. In D. Nobus (ed), *Key Concepts of Lacanian Psychoanalysis*. London: Karnac.

Nolan, S. (2009). *Film, Lacan and the Subject of Religion*. London: Continuum.

O'Brien, E (2017). Jacques Lacan. In E. O'Brien (ed), *Oxford Bibliographies in Literary and Critical Theory*. New York: Oxford University Press.

O'Brien, M. T. (1991). Freud's affair with Minna Bernays: his letter of June 4, 1896. *The American Journal of Psychoanalysis*, 51, 173–84.

Owens, M. E. (2004). Forgetting Signorelli: monstrous visions of the resurrection of the dead. *American Imago*, 61, 7–33.

Paley, W. (1791). *The Principles of Moral and Political Philosophy*. London: R. Fauldner.

Palombo, J, Bendicsen, H. K. and Koch, B. J. (2009). *Guide to Psychoanalytic Developmental Theories*. Dordrecht, Netherlands: Springer.

Panksepp, J. and Panksepp, J. A. (2013). Toward a cross-species understanding of empathy. *Trends in Neurosciences*, 36, 489–96.

Parker, I. (2003). Jacques Lacan, barred psychologist. *Theory & Psychology*, 13, 95–115.

Parker, I. (2005). Lacanian discourse analysis in psychology: seven theoretical elements. *Theory & Psychology*, 15, 163–82.

Parker, I. (2011). *Lacanian Psychoanalysis*. Hove, UK: Routledge.

Parr, S. (ed) (1837). *Metaphysical Tracts by English Philosophers of the Eighteenth Century*. London: E. Lumley.

Patterson, D. (2015). *Anti-Semitism and Its Metaphysical Origins*. Cambridge: Cambridge University Press.

Pavlidou, T. S. (2014). Constructing collectivity with 'we': an introduction. In T. S. Pavlidou (ed), *Constructing Collectivity: 'We' across Languages and Contexts*. Amsterdam: John Benjamins.

Pavlov, I. P. (1955). *Selected Works*. Moscow: Foreign Language Publishing.

Perelman, C. (1979). *The New Rhetoric and the Humanities*. Dordrecht, Netherlands: D. Reidel.

Perry, G. (2014). The view from the boys. *The Psychologist*, 27, 834–7.

Perry, G. (2018). *The Lost Boys: Inside Muzafer Sherif's Robbers Cave Experiment*. London: Scribe Books.

Pickren, W. E. and Rutherford, A. (2010). *A History of Modern Psychology in Context*. Hoboken, NJ: John Wiley.

Pierrakos, M. (2006). *Transcribing Lacan's Seminars: Memoirs of a Disgruntled Keybasher Turned Psychoanalyst*. London: Free Association Books.

Plotnik, J. M., de Waal, F. B. M. and Reiss. D. (2006). Self-recognition in an Asian elephant. *Proceedings of the National Academy of Sciences*, 103, 17053–7.

Pons, A. (2014). Genius. In B. Cassin (ed), *Dictionary of Untranslatables*. Princeton, NJ: Princeton University Press.

Poole, B. (2002). Bakhtin and Cassirer: the philosophical origins of Bakhtin's carnival. In M. E. Gardiner (ed), *Mikhail Bakhtin*, vol. 1. London: Sage.

Povinelli, D. J., Gallup, G. G., Eddy, T. J., Bierschwale, D. T., Engstrom, M. C., Perilloux, H. K. and Toxopeus, I. B. (1997). Chimpanzees recognize themselves in mirrors. *Animal Behaviour*, 53, 1083–8.

Preyer, W. (1889). *The Mind of the Child, Part II: the Development of the Intellect*. New York: D. Appleton.

Prince, M. B. (2004). Editing Shaftesbury's Characteristicks. *Essays in Criticism*, 54, 38–59.

Prior, H., Schwarz, A. and Güntürkün, O. (2008). Mirror-induced behaviour in the magpie (Pica pica): evidence of self-recognition. *PLoS Biology*, 6, E202.

Rabaté, J.-M. (2003a). Lacan's turn to Freud. In J.-M. Rabaté (ed), *Cambridge Companion to Lacan*. Cambridge: Cambridge University Press.

Rabaté, J.-M. (2003b). Preface. In J.-M. Rabaté (ed), *Cambridge Companion to Lacan*. Cambridge: Cambridge University Press.

Radden, G. and Kövecses, Z. (2007). Towards a theory of metonymy. In V. Evans, B. Bergen and J. Zinken (eds), *The Cognitive Linguistics Reader*. London: Equinox.

Reicher, S. D. (1996). Social identity and social change: rethinking the context of social psychology. In W. P. Robinson (ed), *Social Groups and Identities*. Oxford: Butterworth Heinemann.

Reicher, S. D. and Haslam, S. A. (2011). After shock? Towards a social identity explanation of the Milgram 'obedience' studies. *British Journal of Social Psychology*, 50, 163–9.

Reicher, S. D., Spears, R. and Haslam, S. A. (2010). The social identity approach in social psychology. In M. Wetherell and C. T. Mohanty (eds), *Sage Handbook of Identities*. London: Sage.

Reik, T. (1956). *The Search Within*. New York: Farrar, Straus and Cudahay.

Reiss, D. and Marino, L. (2001). Mirror self-recognition in the bottlenose dolphin: a case of cognitive convergence. *PNAS*, 98, 5937–42.

Ribot, T. (1870). *La Psychologie Anglaise Contemporaine*. Paris: Ladrange.

Richards, G. (1992). *Mental Machinery*. London: Athlone Press.

Richards, G. (2002). *Putting Psychology in Its Place*. London: Routledge.

Richardson, R. D. (2007). *William James: in the Maelstrom of American Modernism*. Boston: Mariner.

Ricoeur, P. (1970). *Freud and Philosophy*. New Haven, CT: Yale University Press.

Rizzolatti, G. and Craighero, L. (2004). The mirror-neuron system. *Annual Review of Neuroscience*, 27, 167–92.

Roazen, P. (1979). *Freud and His Followers*. Harmondsworth, UK: Penguin.

Roazen, P. (1997). Nietzsche, Freud and the history of psychoanalysis. In T. Dufresne (ed), *Returns of the 'French Freud'*. New York: Routledge.

Robinson, W. P. (ed) (1996). *Social Groups and Identities: Developing the Legacy of Henri Tajfel*. Oxford: Butterworth Heinemann.

Rose, N. (1985). *The Psychological Complex*. London: Routledge and Kegan Paul.

Rösing, L. M. (2016). *Pixar with Lacan: the Hysteric's Guide to Animation*. London: Bloomsbury.

Roudinesco, É. (1990). *Jacques Lacan and Co*. Chicago: University of Chicago Press.

Roudinesco, É. (1997). *Jacques Lacan*. Cambridge: Polity Press.

Roudinesco, É. (2003). The mirror stage: an obliterated archive. In J.-M. Rabaté (ed), *Cambridge Companion to Lacan*. Cambridge: Cambridge University Press.

Roudinesco, É. (2014). *Lacan: in Spite of Everything*. London: Verso.

Rutherford, A. (2010). Profile of Marie Jahoda. In A. Rutherford (ed), *Psychology's Feminist Voices Multimedia Digital Archive*. www.feministvoices.com/marie-jahoda/ (Accessed 6 November 2018).

Rutherford, A. (2011). The life and politics of an early woman leader: Marie Jahoda (1907–2001). *The Feminist Psychologist, Newsletter for the Society of the Psychology of Women (Division 35, APA)*, 38, 10–11.

Rutherford, A., Unger, R. and Cherry, F. (2011). Reclaiming SPSSI's sociological past: Marie Jahoda and the immersion tradition in social psychology. *Journal of Social Issues*, 67, 42–58.

Sage, D. (2018). Reversing the negative experience of unemployment: a mediating role for social policies? *Social Policy and Administration*, 52, 1043–59.

Santayana, G. (1933). *Some Turns of Thought in Modern Philosophy*. Cambridge: Cambridge University Press.

Sartre, J.-P. (1948). *Anti-Semite and Jew*. New York: Schocken Books.

Schafer, R. (1976). *A New Language for Psychoanalysis*. New Haven, CT: Yale University Press.

Scheff, T. J. (1990). *Microsociology*. Chicago: Chicago University Press.

Scheff, T. J. (2006). *Goffman Unbound! A New Paradigm for Social Science*. Boulder, CO: Paradigm.

Scheff, T. J. (2010). Instances and general ideas: parts and wholes. *New English Review*. www.newenglishreview.org/custpage.cfm/frm/60404/sec_id/60404 (Accessed 16 November 2018).

Schiller, F. C. S. (1930/1996). William James. In L. Simon (ed), *William James Remembered*. Lincoln: University of Nebraska Press.

Schilpp, P. A. (1949). Preface. In P. A. Schilpp (ed), *The Philosophy of Ernst Cassirer*. New York: Tudor.

Schools Council History Project. (1977). *Arab-Israeli Conflict*. Edinburgh: Holmes McDougall.

Schultz, D. P. and Schultz, S. E. (2016). *A History of Modern Psychology*. Boston: Cengage Learning.

Scubla, L. (2011). Lévi-Strauss, Lacan, and the symbolic order. *Revue de Mauss*, 25, 253–67.

Seligman, M. E. P. (2003). *Authentic Happiness*. London: Nicholas Brealey.

Sellars, J. (2016). Shaftesbury, stoicism, and philosophy as a way of life. *Sophia*, 55, 395–408.

Shaftesbury, third Earl of. (1711). *Characteristics of Men, Manners, Opinions, Times*. N.p.

Shaftesbury, third Earl of. (1714/2001). *Characteristics of Men, Manners, Opinions, Times*. Cambridge: Cambridge University Press.

Shaftesbury, third Earl of. (1900). *The Life, Unpublished Letters and Philosophical Regime*, ed. B. Rand. London: Swan Sonnenschein.

Sheehan, S. (2012). *Žižek: a Guide for the Perplexed*. London: Continuum.

Sherif, M. (1966). *Group Conflict and Co-operation*. London: Routledge and Kegan Paul.

Sherif, M. and Sherif, C. W. (1953). *Groups in Harmony and Tension*. New York: Harper.

Shillito, D. J., Gallup, G. G. and Beck, B. B. (1999). Factors affecting mirror behaviour in Western Lowland gorillas, Gorilla Gorilla. *Animal Behaviour*, 57, 999–1004.

Shotter, J. (2003). *Cultural Politics of Everyday Life*. Buckingham, UK: Open University.

Shotter, J. (2005a). Moving on by backing away. In G. Yancy and S. Hadley (eds), *Narrative Identities*. London: Jessica Kingsley.

Shotter, J. (2005b). Goethe and the refiguring of intellectual inquiry: from 'aboutness'-thinking to 'withness'-thinking in everyday life. *Janus Head*, 8, 132–61.

Silverstein, B. (2007). What happens in Maloja stays in Maloja: inference and evidence in the 'Minna wars'. *American Imago*, 64, 283–9.

Simmons, L. (2006). *Freud's Italian Journey*. Amsterdam: Rodopi.

Simons, H. W. (2007). The rhetorical legacy of Kenneth Burke. In W. Jost and W. Olmstead (eds), *A Companion to Rhetoric and Rhetorical Criticism*. New York: John Wiley.

Skidelsky, E. (2011). *Ernst Cassirer: the Last Philosopher of Culture*. Princeton, NJ: Princeton University Press.

Slaughter, S. and Rhoades, G. (2004). *Academic Capitalism and the New Economy*. Baltimore: Johns Hopkins University Press.

Smith, A. (1983). *Lectures on Rhetoric and Belles Lettres*. Oxford: Oxford University Press.

Smith, M. K. (2001). Kurt Lewin, groups, experiential learning and action research. *Encyclopedia of Informal Education*. www.infed.org/thinkers/et-lewin.htm (Accessed 30 December 2018).

Smith, R. (1988). Does the history of psychology have a subject? *History of the Human Sciences*, 1, 147–77.

Smith, R. (2010). Looking back: seeking history. *The Psychologist*, 23, 167–8.

Sofer, S. (2009). *Zionism and the Foundations of Israeli Diplomacy*. Cambridge: Cambridge University Press.

Spence, D. P. (1994). *The Rhetorical Voice of Psychoanalysis*. Cambridge, MA: Harvard University Press.

Stamenov, M. I. and Gallese, V. (eds) (2002). *Mirror Neurons and the Evolution of Brain and Language*. Amsterdam: John Benjamins.

Stavrakakis, Y. (1999). *Lacan and the Political*. London: Routledge.

Stavrakakis, Y. (2007). Wallon, Lacan and the Lacanians: citation practices and repression. *Theory, Culture & Society*, 24, 131–8.

Stephen, L. (1876). *History of English Thought in the Eighteenth Century*, vol. II. London: Smith Elder.

Stroud, S. R. (2012). William James and the impetus of Stoic rhetoric. *Philosophy and Rhetoric*, 45, 246–68.

Sułek, A. (2007). The Marienthal 1931/1932 study and contemporary studies on unemployment in Poland. *Polish Sociological Review*, 157, 3–25.

Sully, J. (1895). *Studies of Childhood*. London: Longmans, Green.

Swales, J. M. (2006). *Research Genres*. Cambridge: Cambridge University Press.

Swales, P. (1982). Freud, Minna Bernays and the conquest of Rome. *New American Review*, 1, 1–23.

Swales, P. (2003). Freud, death and sexual pleasures: on the psychical mechanism of Dr. Sigm. Freud. *Arc de Cercle*, 1, 4–74.

Tajfel, H. (1969). Cognitive aspects of prejudice. *Journal of Social Issues*, 25, 79–97.

Tajfel, H. (1970). Experiments in intergroup discrimination. *Scientific American*, 233, 96–102.

Tajfel, H. (1972). Experiments in a vacuum. In J. Israel and H. Tajfel (eds), *The Context of Social Psychology*. London: Academic Press.

Tajfel, H. (1975). The exit of social mobility and the voice of social change: notes on the social psychology of intergroup relations. *Social Science Information*, 14, 101–18.

Tajfel, H. (1976). Exit, voice and intergroup relations. In L. Strickland, F. Aboud and K. Gergen (eds), *Social Psychology in Transition*. New York: Plenum Press.

Tajfel, H. (1980). Foreword. Published as 'Nachwort zur Neuauflage' in F. P. Bernstein, *Der Antisemitismus als eine Gruppenerscheinung: Versuch einer Soziologie des Judenhasses*. Königstein: Jüdischer Verlag.

Tajfel, H. (1981). *Human Groups and Social Categories*. Cambridge: Cambridge University Press.

Tajfel, H. (1982a). Social psychology of intergroup relations. *Annual Review of Psychology*, 33, 1–39.

Tajfel, H. (1982b). Instrumentality, identity and social comparisons. In H. Tajfel (ed), *Social Identity and Intergroup Relations*. Cambridge: Cambridge University Press.

Tajfel, H. (1984). Intergroup relations, social myths and social justice in social psychology. In H. Tajfel (ed), *The Social Dimension*, vol. 2. Cambridge: Cambridge University Press.

Tajfel, H. and Billig, M. (1974). Familiarity and categorization in intergroup behaviour. *Journal of Experimental Social Psychology*, 10, 159–70.

Tajfel, H., Billig, M., Bundy, R. P. and Flament, C. (1971). Social categorization and intergroup behaviour. *European Journal of Social Psychology*, 1, 149–78.

Tajfel, H. and Turner, J. C. (1979). An integrative theory of intergroup conflict. In W. G. Austin and S. Worchel (eds), *The Social Psychology of Intergroup Relations*. Monterey, CA: Brooks/Cole.

Tajfel, H. and Wilkes, A. L. (1963). Classification and quantitative judgment. *British Journal of Psychology*, 54, 101–14.

Taylor, C. (2002). *Varieties of Religion Today: William James Revisited*. London: Harvard University Press.

Tileagă, C. and Byford, J. (2014). Social psychology, history and the study of the Holocaust: the perils of interdisciplinary 'borrowing'. *Journal of Peace Psychology*, 20, 349–64.

Tolman, E. C. (1948). Kurt Lewin: 1890–1947. *Psychological Review*, 55, 1–4.

Trepte, S. (2006). Social identity theory. In J. Bryant and P. Vorderer (eds), *Psychology of Entertainment*. Mahwah, NJ: Lawrence Erlbaum.

Tucker, A. (Anon.) (1755). *The Country Gentleman's Advice to His Son*. London: W. Owen.

Tucker, A. (Search, E.) (1763). *Freewill, Foreknowledge and Fate: a Fragment*. London: R. and J. Dodsley.

Tucker, A. (1763/1837). Man in quest of himself. In S. Parr (ed), *Metaphysical Tracts by English Philosophers of the Eighteenth Century*. London: E. Lumley.

Tucker, A. (Search, E.) (1768). *The Light of Nature Pursued*, vols. I and II. London: T. Payne.

Tucker, A. (Search, E.). (1773). *Vocal Sounds*. London: T. Payne.

Tucker, A. (1777). *The Light of Nature Pursued by Edward Search: Vol. III. The Posthumous Work of Abraham Tucker*. London: T. Payne and Son.

Tucker, A. (1807). *An Abridgement of 'The light of Nature Pursued' by Abraham Tucker*, ed. W. Hazlitt. London: J. Johnson.

Tucker, A. (1848). *The Light of Nature Pursued*, vol. 2. London: Henry Bohn.

Turner, J. C. (1982). Towards a cognitive redefinition of the social group. In H. Tajfel (ed), *Social Identity and Intergroup Relations*. Cambridge: Cambridge University Press.

Turner, J. C. (1987). A self-categorization theory. In *Rediscovering the Social Group*. Oxford: Blackwell.

Ulmer, W. A. (2006). The alienation of the elect in Coleridge's Unitarian prophecies. *Review of English Studies*, 57, 526–44.

van Elteren, M. (1992). Karl Korsch and Lewinian social psychology: failure of a project. *History of the Human Sciences*, 5, 33–61.

van Praag, B. M. S. (2009). Introduction to the Transaction edition. In P. F. Bernstein, *The Social Roots of Discrimination: the Case of the Jews*. Piscataway, NJ: Transaction.

Vaughan, G. M. (2018). Henri Tajfel: Polish-born British social psychologist. *Encyclopaedia Britannica*. www.britannica.com/biography/Henri-Tajfel (Accessed 12 September 2018).

Veblen, T. (1914). *The Instinct of Workmanship and the State of the Industrial Arts*. New York: B. W. Huebsch.

Veblen, T. (1918/1957). *The Higher Learning in America*. New York: Sagamore Press.

Voitle, R. (1984). *The Third Earl of Shaftesbury*. Baton Rouge: Louisiana State University Press.

Vyt, A. (2001). Processes of visual self-recognition in infants: experimental induction of 'mirror' experience via video self-image presentation. *Infant and Child Development*, 10, 173–87.

Wade, N. J. (2005). The persisting vision of David Hartley. *Perception*, 34, 1–6.

Wagemans, J., Elder, J. H., Kubovy, M., Palmer, S. E., Peterson, M. A., Singh, M. and von der Heydt, R. (2012). A century of Gestalt psychology in visual perception I. Perceptual grouping and figure-ground organization. *Psychological Bulletin*, 138, 1172–217.

Walkerdine, V. (1988). *The Mastery of Reason*. London: Routledge.

Wallon, H. (1934/1949). *Les Origines du Caractère chez l'Enfant*. Paris: Presses Universitaires de France.

Walsh, R. T. G., Teo, T. and Baydala, A. (2014). *A Critical History and Philosophy of Psychology*. Cambridge: Cambridge University Press.

Weber, N. F. (2017). *Freud's Trip to Orvieto*. New York: Bellevue.

Weick, K. E. (2003). Theory and practice in the real world. In H. Tsoukas and C. Knudsen (eds), *The Oxford Handbook of Organization Theory: Metatheoretical Perspectives*. Oxford: Oxford University Press.

Wertheimer, M. (1987). *A Brief History of Psychology*. Fort Worth, TX: Harcourt Brace Jovanovich.

Wesbster, R. (1996). *Why Freud Was Wrong*. London: HarperCollins.

West, R. (1916). *Henry James*. New York: Henry Holt.

Wettersten, J. (1988). Kulpe, Bühler, Popper. In A. Eschbach (ed), *Karl Bühler's Theory of Language*. Amsterdam: John Benjamins.

White, R. K. and Lippitt, R. (1960). *Autocracy and Democracy*. New York: Harper.

Wittgenstein, L. (1968). *Philosophical Investigations*. Oxford: Blackwell.

Wittgenstein, L. (1980). *Culture and Value*. Oxford: Blackwell.

Wolters, E. (2013). Noam Chomsky calls Jacques Lacan a 'charlatan'. *Critical Theory*, February 28. www.critical-theory.com/noam-chomsky-calls-jacques-lacan-a-charlatan/ (Accessed 21 October 2018).

Wozniak, R. H. (1999). *Classics in Psychology, 1855–1914*. Bristol: Thoemmes Press.

Yaffe, G. (2002). Earl of Shaftesbury. In S. Nadler (ed), *A Companion to Early Modern Philosophy*. Oxford: Blackwell

Young, B. W. (2004). Tucker, Abraham (1705–1774). In *Oxford Dictionary of National Biography*. Oxford: Oxford University Press.

Young, R. M. (1973). The role of psychology in the nineteenth century evolutionary debate. In M. Henle, J. Jaynes and J. L. Sullivan (eds), *Historical Conceptions of Psychology*. New York: Springer.

Young-Bruehl, E. (1988). *Anna Freud*. London: Macmillan.

Žižek, S. (2001). *Enjoy Your Symptom! Jacques Lacan in Hollywood and Out*. London: Routledge.

Zwart, H. (2014). The elephant, the mirror and the Ark: rereading Lacan's animal philosophy in an era of ontological violence and mass extinction. *Journal of Critical Animal Studies*, 12, 1–32.

Zweig, S. (2009). *The Post Office Girl*. London: Sort of Books.

Zweig, S. (2012). *Freud by Zweig*. Lexington, MA: Plunkett Lake Press.

Index